A Study of Svātantrika

A Study of Svātantrika

Donald S. Lopez, Jr.

Snow Lion Publications
Ithaca, New York USA

Snow Lion Publications
P.O. Box 6483
Ithaca, New York 14851
USA

Printed in USA

Library of Congress Catalogue Number 86-14636

Library of Congress Cataloging-in-Publication Data

Lopez, Donald S., 1952—
A study of Svātantrika.

Bibliography: p.
Includes index.
1. Svatantrika. I. Title.
BQ7478.L67 1987 294.3'92 86-14636
ISBN 0-937938-20-3
ISBN 0-937938-19-X (pbk.)

Table of Contents

Dedicated
to
William Stone Weedon
1908-1984

Acknowledgements

My study of Svātantrika began in 1977 when I began reading Den-dar-hla-ram-ba's (*bsTan-dar-lha-ram-pa*, born 1759) *Presentation of the Lack of Being One or Many* (*gCig du bral gyi rnam gzhag*). Finding it difficult to take full advantage of this text without a broader understanding of the Svātantrika school, I turned my attention to the Svātantrika chapter of Jam-yang-shay-ba's (*'Jam-dbyangs-bzhad-pa*, 1648-1721) *Great Exposition of Tenets* (*Grub mtha' chen mo*). Intending to include this chapter as the translation section of my dissertation, I set out for India under the Fulbright-Hays Doctoral Dissertation Abroad Program. With the kind cooperation of my advisor, Dr. K. K. Mittal of Delhi University, and the assistance of C. S. Ramakrishnan, Director of the United States Educational Foundation in India, I soon left for Dharmsala and the Library of Tibetan Works and Archives, where I completed a rough translation of the Svātantrika chapter of the *Great Exposition of Tenets*, along with Nga-wang-bel-den's (*Ngag-dbang-dpal-ldan*, born 1797) invaluable *Annotations* (*mChan 'grel*). While in Dharmsala, I had the opportunity to study the root text of the Mādhyamika chapter of the *Great Exposition of Tenets* with Go-mang (*sGo-mang*) Geshe (*dGe-bshes*) Den-ba Gyel-tsen (*bsTan-pa-rgyal-mtshan*), later scholar-in-residence at Toyo Bunkyo in Japan. Upon returning to Delhi, I began classes with Geshe Bel-den Drak-ba (*dPal-ldan-grags-pa*), Librarian of Tibet House, who read with me the entire Svātantrika chapter of Jam-yang-shay-ba's *Great Exposition of Tenets*. His skillful exposition kept me in Delhi longer than I had planned.

On a trip to Sarnath, I visited the Central Institute for Higher Tibetan Studies, where I was able to put the questions that were beginning to accumulate to two senior instructors of the Institute, Lo-sel-ling (*bLo-gsal-gling*) Geshe Ye-shay Tap-kay (*Ye-shes-thaps-mkhas*) and Go-mang Geshe Tsul-trim Gya-tso (*Tshul-khrims-rgya-mtsho*).

In January 1979, I made the first of two trips to the Ge-luk monasteries of Gan-den (*dGa'-ldan*) and Dre-bung (*'Bras-spungs*) in Karnataka State. There I was able to study the *Great Exposition of Tenets* with the abbot of Go-mang College, Nga-wang Nyi-ma (*Ngag-dbang-nyi-ma*). Realizing that at some point I should also read the Svātantrika chapter of Jang-gya's (*lCang-skya-rol-pa'i-rdo-rje*, 1717-1786) *Presentation of Tenets* (*Grub pa'i mtha'i rnam par bzhag pa*), I asked the former abbot of Lo-sel-ling College, Yeshe Thupten (*Ye-shes-thub-brten*), to read the text with me. His commentary proved captivating, and I soon decided that Jang-gya's chapter should form the translation section of my thesis. After returning to Dharmsala in April to attend public lectures by the Dalai Lama, I came once again to Dre-bung, where I began to translate Jang-gya. During this second visit I also studied the Yogācāra and Svātantrika chapters of Tsong-kha-pa's *Essence of the Good Explanations* (*Legs bshad snying po*) with Yeshe Thupten. I returned to the United States in August 1980. In 1981, I reviewed Bhāvaviveka's refutation of Yogācāra in Jang-gya's chapter with the former abbot of the Tantric College of Lower Lhasa and present holder of the throne of Gan-den (*dGa' ldan khri pa*), Jam-bel Shen-pen (*'Jam-dpal-gzhan-phan*).

I wish to express my appreciation to all of the scholars mentioned above. Their insights into the world of Buddhist philosophy are the reward to those who learn to speak Tibetan. In addition, I offer my deep thanks to His Holiness the Dalai Lama, who offered penetrating answers to my most difficult questions in audiences in Dharmsala, Montreal, and at Harvard University. Finally, I wish to thank my thesis advisor and mentor, Professor Jeffrey Hopkins, for all of his help and encouragement during my research, both in India and the United States. It is often the case that after studying with one person for an extended period of time we sadly reach the end of his or her learning. This has not been my experience with Professor Hopkins.

Technical Note

The transliteration systems for Tibetan words is that devised by Turrell Wylie[1]; it has been modified slightly in that the first pronounced letter in the names of persons and texts is capitalized. The transliteration of Tibetan words appears in parenthetical citations, notes, glossary, and bibliography. Since it is impossible for non-Tibetan speakers to pronounce Tibetan words correctly using a transliteration system because of the number of unpronounced letters in Tibetan, a revised version of the phonetic transcription system devised by Jeffrey Hopkins[2] is used. This adaptation of the Hopkins system facilitates accurate pronounciation of the Lhasan dialect and is used throughout the text wherever Tibetan names occur. Tonal markers above consonants that are used in the Hopkins system have been omitted in the body of this text.

The conversion table from transliteration to "phonetics" is as follows, with the transliterated form on the left of each column and the phonetic form on the right. Lines above letters indicate that the tone is high, with a sharp and short pronunciation:

ka: ḡa	kha: ka	ga: ga	nga: nga
ca: j̄a	cha: cha	ja: ja	nya: nya
ta: d̄a	tha: ta	da: da	na: na
pa: b̄a	pha: pa	ba: ba	ma: ma
tsa: d̄za	tsha: tsa	dza: dza	wa: wa
zha: sha	za: sa	'a: a	ya: ya

ra: ra	la: la	sha: s̄ha	sa: s̄a
ha: ha	a: a		

The phonetic system is derived by using the phonetic columns above and substituting *k* and *p* for *g* and *b* in the suffix position; prefixes, extra suffixes, and unpronounced superscriptions, subscriptions, and suffixes do not appear in the phonetic form of the word. For vowels, "a" indicates the vowel sound of "opt"; "i" indicates the sound of "it" (with the phonetic suffixes *k*, *n*, *p*, and *m*) or "eat" (with the phonetic suffixes *ng*, *r*, and *l* and with the unpronounced transliterated suffixes *d*, *'a*, and *s*); "u" indicates the vowel sound of "soon"; "ay" indicates the vowel sound of "bake"; "o" indicates the vowel sound of "boat"; and "ö" is pronounced as in German. The hyphens between syllables are retained in the phonetic form so that the beginning and end of the syllables can be easily distinguished.

The names of Tibetan and Mongolians who live in or have published in the West are spelled as they spell them. Aside from these, Tibetan names have been rendered in the system given above in order to bring their pronunciation in accord with the actual spoken Tibetan in the Lhasan dialect, with two exceptions: In deference to common usage, Tsong-kha-pa, actually pronounced D̄zong-ka-b̄a, is retained in its transliterated form. Also, the title "Geshe" (*dGe-bshes*), which in this system would appear as Ge-s̄hay, has not been changed. The transliterated form of each name is given in parentheses after the first occurrence.

Sanskrit equivalents to Tibetan terms are given wherever possible; an asterisk before an entry indicates a reconstruction of the Sanskrit.

With the first occurrence of each Indian title, the Sanskrit is given, if available. The full Sanskrit and Tibetan titles are found in the bibliography, which is arranged alphabetically according to the English titles of sutras and according to the phonetic transcription of authors of Tibetan works. Authors' dates, when available, appear in the bibliography. Throughout the text, the titles of all Sanskrit and Tibetan works have been translated into English. This does not imply that the work itself has been translated into English.

Introduction

The Buddha achieved enlightenment at the age of thirty-five under the Bodhi tree near the town of Gaya. It is said that he remained there for seven weeks before setting out for the Deer Park in Sarnath, where he first turned the wheel of doctrine (*dharmacakra, chos kyi khor lo*). From that time until he passed away at the age of eighty, he traveled through the Gangetic plain of northern India teaching doctrines appropriate to the interests and capacities of his listeners. Thus, unlike Jesus, whose ministry lasted for perhaps three years, the Buddha taught for forty-five, leaving a large body of teachings. As a result of disagreements that arose in the Buddhist community, shortly after his death, as to how the teachings were to be interpreted, the various schools of Buddhist tenets (*siddhānta, grub mtha'*) were established.

With the rise of the Mahāyāna some four hundred years after the death of the Buddha, a large corpus of literature known as the Perfection of Wisdom Sutras (*prajñāpāramitāsūtra, shes rab kyi pha rol tu phyin pa'i mdo*) was gradually introduced into the canon. These texts were not accepted as the word of the Buddha by the Hīnayāna schools, for the most part, but were studied and explicated by philosophers such as Nāgārjuna and Asaṅga, giving rise to the Mahāyāna schools of Mādhyamika and Yogācāra.

Based on the idea that the Buddha taught different things to different people in accordance with their capacities, it is the Mahāyāna position that the Buddha set forth the basic positions of all the various schools of tenets. Later, these positions were expanded into fully developed philosophical systems by the thinkers who have come to be known as the founders of those systems. Thus, it is held that the Buddha taught the doctrine of emptiness (*śūnyatā, stong pa nyid*) in the Perfection of Wisdom Sutras. His teachings were then elaborated upon and developed into the Mādhyamika system by Nāgārjuna, who is considered its founder. The Tibetan word for "founder" in this context is *shing-da-sol-jay* (*shing rta srol 'byed*), which means "opener of the chariotway." The Buddha's initial teaching of the doctrines of the various schools is likened to someone's clearing a new path or blazing a trail. The founders of the individual schools systematized those teachings as someone would expand the path into a roadway, smooth and wide enough for a chariot to traverse.[1]

The Svātantrika School

In the sixth century a fork developed in the Mādhyamika chariotway constructed by Nāgārjuna, foreshadowing the formation of two subschools within Mādhyamika — Svātantrika and Prāsaṅgika. The documentary evidence for this split is found in the commentaries to Nāgārjuna's most famous work, the *Fundamental Treatise on the Middle Way Called "Wisdom"* (*Prajñānāmamūlamadhyamakakārikā*). There were eight Indian commentaries to the *Treatise on the Middle Way*, four of which are not preserved in Tibetan translation, those of Devaśarman, Guṇamati, Guṇaśrī, and Sthiramati. The four commentaries available from the Tibetan are that by Buddhapālita, known simply as the *Buddhapālita Commentary* (*Buddhapālitavṛtti*), Bhāvaviveka's *Lamp for (Nāgārjuna's) Wisdom* (*Prajñāpradīpa*), Candrakīrti's *Clear Words* (*Prasannapadā*), and a commentary called *Akutobhayā*. This last work is traditionally ascribed to Nāgārjuna but is generally considered not to be his work because it is not quoted by any of the other commentators and because it cites one of Nāgārjuna's disciples, Āryadeva.[2] In his commentary to the *Treatise on the Middle Way*, Buddhapālita presented many of his arguments in terms of consequences (*prasaṅga, thal 'gyur*), logical statements put in terms of the opponent's assertions in order to reveal to the opponent the fallacy of his position. In the *Lamp for (Nāgārjuna's) "Wisdom"*, Bhāvaviveka criticized Buddhapālita's use of consequences, insisting that the Mādhyamika's own position must finally be stated in the form of an autonomous syllogism (*svatantraprayoga, rang rgyud kyi sbyor ba*). Subsequently, Candrakīrti came to Buddhapālita's defense in his *Clear Words*, arguing that the faults ascribed by Bhāvaviveka were not entailed by Buddhapālita and that the use of autonomous syllogisms is unsuitable for Mādhyamikas, thereby rejecting Bhāvaviveka's position. The philosophical implications of the use of syllogisms and consequences is analyzed in chapter 2 of this work.

Although Buddhapālita was the first to use consequences in explaining the meaning of Nāgārjuna's text, he is not considered to be the founder of the Prāsaṅgika (Consequentialist) branch of Mādhyamika. In order to be considered the founder of a system, one must consciously prove the validity of the approach of that system and distinguish it from that of rival systems. For this reason, Candrakīrti is held to be the founder of the Prāsaṅgika school. Similarly, Bhāvaviveka is considered to be the founder of the Svātantrika (Autonomy) school, even though he was preceded by Devaśarman, who presented the Svātantrika position in his commentary to the *Treatise on the Middle Way*.[3]

In the eighth century, the great scholar Śāntarakṣita founded a school that supported the general Svātantrika position but disagreed with Bhāvaviveka on a number of important points. Because Śāntarakṣita's school incorporated certain doctrines of the Yogācāra system, it is known as Yogācāra-Svātantrika-Mādhyamika, whereas Bhāvaviveka's school is known as Sautrāntika-Svātantrika-Mādhyamika. During the reign of King Tri-song-day-dzen (*Khri-srong-lde-btsan*, 740-c. 798), Śāntarakṣita was invited to Tibet, where he was instrumental in the establishment of the first monastery in Tibet at Sam-ye (*bSam-yas*) and the ordination of the first Tibetan monks in 767.[4] After the death of Śāntarakṣita, his foremost student, Kamalaśīla, was invited to Tibet to defend the Mādhyamika approach to the path against the arguments of a Northern Ch'an monk known as Ho-shang Mo-ho-yen. Kamalaśīla presented his position in three texts, each entitled the *Stages of Meditation* (*Bhāvanākrama*), and was declared the victor in the controversy that has come to be known as the Council of Lhasa (792-94).[5]

As Mādhyamikas, the Svātantrikas propound a middle way free from the extremes of true existence and utter non-existence. They assert that phenomena do not truly exist or ultimately exist but that they exist conventionally, with impermanent phenomena arising in dependence on causes and conditions and capable of performing functions. The unique meaning of the middle way in the Mādhyamika school is discussed in chapter 1.

That which distinguishes the Svātantrikas from the other branch of Mādhyamika, the Prāsaṅgikas, is their assertion that phenomena exist in and of themselves conventionally. For the Svātantrikas, if things did not exist by way of their own character (*svalakṣaṇa, rang mtshan*) conventionally, they would not exist at all; the Svātantrikas insist on the objective autonomy of phenomena on the conventional level although they refute that phenomena exist by way of their own character ultimately. Things appear to our senses to exist from their own side, and the Svātantrikas assert that such is their conventional mode of being. The Prāsaṅgikas, on the other hand, take a more radical position, holding that things do not exist by way of their own character even conventionally, but rather that phenomena are merely designated by terminology and thought. The fundamental question dividing the Svātantrikas and Prāsaṅgikas is where to draw the line between the hypostatization of phenomena and nihilism. How tenuous can the existence of phenomena be without their disappearing into nothingness? What degree of objective status is required for phenomena to exist?

The Svātantrikas contend that phenomena exist from their own side but that that mode of existence must be posited by the consciousness to which it appears. If phenomena lacked this objective mode of subsistence, this existence by way of their own character, functionality would be impossible and they would cease to exist. They assert that phenomena do not ultimately exist and thereby avoid the extreme of permanence (*śaśvatānta, rtag mtha'*). They assert that phenomena are established from their own side conventionally and thereby avoid the extreme of annihilation (*ucchedānta, chad mtha'*).

The Prāsaṅgikas say that the Svātantrikas go too far, superimposing a false nature on phenomena. They agree with the Svātantrikas that things appear to exist inherently but, unlike the Svātantrikas, they argue that this is a false appearance. Whereas the Svātantrikas hold that the objective existence of phenomena is gained through appearing to consciousnesses, the Prāsaṅgikas contend that such an objective mode of being does not exist even conventionally; phenomena are merely designated by terms and thought consciousnesses. The Prāsaṅgikas are able to reject the inherent existence asserted by the Svātantrikas while maintaining the viability of conventions. For the Prāsaṅgikas, the conventional nature of phenomena is more conditional, more designated, more provisional, than that propounded by the Svātantrikas. The sources and implications of the Svātantrika and Prāsaṅgika views are explored in chapter 2.

It is essential to bear in mind that the Svātantrika and Prāsaṅgika schools are, above all, religious systems and that their assertions on the nature of phenomena, therefore, have religious implications in terms of practice of the path to enlightenment, a state beyond all suffering. Here, Frederick Streng's definition of religion as "a means of ultimate transformation" is appropriate.[6] All of the refutations and proofs put forth by the Mādhyamikas have as their final purpose the identification of the exact nature of the misconception which is the cause of all suffering and the subsequent destruction of that misconception. The Svātantrikas hold that the conception of true existence is the root cause of the cycle of rebirth (*saṃsāra, 'khor ba*) but that one may gain liberation from rebirth by realizing the coarser selflessness of the person (*pudgalanairātmya, gang zag gi bdag med*), without having understood the emptiness of true existence (**satyasat, bden par yod pa*) of phenomena. Bhāvaviveka thus differentiates between the root of cyclic existence and the final root of cyclic existence, the former being the conception of a self of persons and the latter being the conception of true existence.

The Prāsaṅgikas argue that the selflessness of persons and phenomena as identified by the Svātantrikas are superficial and that understanding of them does not result in liberation. Rather, one must understand the more subtle emptiness of inherent existence (*svabhāva, rang bzhin*) of persons and phenomena as presented only in the Prāsaṅgika system in order to destroy the ignorance that is the cause of all suffering, the ignorance that conceives of persons and phenomena to exist inherently. The meaning of self and selflessness in Svātantrika and Prāsaṅgika is pursued in chapter 3.

In order for the ignorance that is the root cause of suffering to be destroyed, it must first be identified and the object of that ignorance delineated. Bhāvaviveka and Kamalaśīla go to some length to identify how phenomena are conceived to exist by the ignorant mind. They identify the meaning of ultimate existence (*paramārthasat, don dam par yod pa*) and true existence (**satyasat, bden par yod pa*), the objects of negation in the Svātantrika system. The structure of their arguments, with special reference to the metaphor of the magician's illusion, is analyzed in chapter 4.

For the Mādhyamikas, the mere absence of what they identify as the object of negation is the final nature of reality. For the Svātantrikas, this reality is the emptiness of true existence and must be understood by all those who seek the ultimate transformation called Buddhahood. Emptiness is the sacred, the realization of which bestows the supreme good. It can, with qualification, be compared to Otto's category of "the holy." For Otto, however, reasoning has no part in the experience of the holy, where, he says, "coercion by proof and demonstration and the mistaken application of logical and juridicial processes should be excluded."[7] The non-conceptual, non-rational numinous cannot be approached with conceptuality and reason for "mysticism has nothing to do with 'reason' and 'rationality.' "[8] In the Mādhyamika system, emptiness is a hidden phenomenon (*parokṣa, lkog gyur*) which means that it cannot be known without first relying on inference and reason. Reasoning thus becomes the fundamental conduit to the holy, the initial passageway to the experience of the sacred. It is not surprising, then, that the Svātantrikas lay great emphasis on the process of reasoning, proving with great care and precision that phenomena do not ultimately exist. It is their position that the rational human mind, properly directed, has the capacity to destroy all misconception, thereby making all suffering impossible. The reasonings employed by the Svātantrikas are explored in chapter 5.

The Mādhyamikas divide all objects of knowledge into two categories, ultimate truths (*paramārthasatya, don dam bden pa*) and conventional truths (*saṃvṛtisatya, kun rdzob bden pa*). Ultimate truths are emptiness; conventional truths are everything else that exists. Ultimate truths are ultimate in the sense that they are objects of the highest consciousness, the wisdom directly realizing emptiness, and truths because they exist as they appear. Conventional truths, literally "truths for a concealer," are true only for an ignorant consciousness that obscures or conceals the nature of reality. This is not to imply that the division of objects of knowledge into ultimate and conventional truths is a classification of the objects of experience into the sacred and profane. If by the sacred one means those objects of religious practice that are worthy of respect or veneration, then many conventional truths, such as the Buddha, his doctrine, and the wisdom consciousness that knows emptiness are to be classed as the sacred. The various divisions of the two truths are considered in chapter 6.

The tenets described above are shared by both branches of the Svātantrika school, Sautrāntika-Svātantrika and Yogācāra-Svātantrika. However, the two subschools disagree on several significant issues, most of which arise out of their encounter with the doctrine of mind-only taught in the Yogācāra school. The Yogācārins assert that objects and the consciousnesses apprending them are the same substantial entity (*dravya, rdzas*); in other words, they assert that external objects do not exist. The school founded by Bhāvaviveka is called Sautrāntika-Svātantrika because it asserts, like the Sautrāntika school, that the objects apprehended by sense consciousnesses are external objects that are composed of minute particles. However, unlike the Sautrāntikas, they do not assert that external objects are truly existent and are ultimate truths. Bhāvaviveka emphatically rejects the Yogācārin assertion that external objects do not exist, devoting the fifth chapter of his *Blaze of Reasoning* (*Tarkajvālā*) to a lengthy refutation of that position.[9] He argues that the assertion that objects are of the nature of consciousness is both logically untenable and contradicts the word of the Buddha. He does not even concede the existence of statements in the canon that ostensibly support the Yogācārin position, explaining that passages such as the statement in the *Sutra on the Ten Grounds* (*Daśabhūmikasūtra*) that, "these three realms are mind only" were made not to indicate that external objects do not exist but that there is no agent other than the mind.[10] The Prāsaṅgikas assert that the Buddha taught the doctrine of mind-only in other passages to those disciples who were temporarily unable to understand the Mādhyamika view, but Bhāvaviveka takes the more extreme position that the Buddha never taught that objects are of the nature of consciousness and that all of the statements which seem to suggest that can be explained to mean something else.[11]

Śāntarakṣita's Yogācāra-Svātantrika school takes a far more accommodating view of the Yogācārin doctrine of the non-existence of external objects. His school is so named because it asserts, like the Yogācārins, that the objects of the senses are of the nature of consciousness. However, unlike the Yogācārins, they do not assert that consciousnesses truly exist. Śāntarakṣita thus integrates the teaching of mind-only into the Mādhyamika system, creating a confluence of the two main streams of Mahāyāna philosophy. The resulting Yogācāra-Svātantrika school represents the final major development of Buddhist philosophy in India. He writes in his *Orna-*

ment for the Middle Way (Madhyamakālaṃkāra):

> The non-existence of external objects should be known
> Through relying on mind-only.
> [Then] relying on this [Mādhyamika] mode, it should be known
> That this [mind] too is completely selfless.[12]

Śāntarakṣita sees the penetration of reality as a process that must proceed in definite stages. One first realizes that the person lacks substantial existence (*dravyasat, rdzas yod*) in the sense of self-sufficiency (*rang rkya thub pa*), that is, one understands the selflessness of the person as set forth in the Hīnayāna systems. One then turns one's attention to the objects of sense experience and comes to realize that these objects that appear to be distant and cut off from the consciousnesses apprehending them are in fact of the nature of consciousness, like the objects in a dream. This, for Śāntarakṣita, is the selflessness understood by the Yogācārins. It is at this point that one analyzes the mode of being of the consciousness of which sense objects are the same nature, employing Mādhyamika reasoning to discover that even consciousness does not ultimately exist.[13] Although Śāntarakṣita is considered the founder of Yogācāra-Svātantrika, the view of the school described above seems to have been current at the time of Bhāvaviveka. This is suggested by a statement by Bhāvaviveka, who, with characteristic polemic, states that accepting the Yogācāra view and then using Mādhyamika reasoning to reject the true existence of the mind is like a fool's intentionally wallowing in mud to get dirty so that he can then wash himself and become clean; it would have been better had he never gotten dirty in the first place.[14]

The Literature

The Svātantrika school has received little attention from Western Buddhologists. Writing in 1962, Edward Conze noted that, "We still have no clear idea of Bhāvaviveka's Svātantrika system. ... Likewise we continue to be puzzled by the teachings and affiliations of the Yogācāra-Mādhyamikas."[15] David Seyfort Ruegg noted in 1967,

> The other schools of Madhyamaka have so far been somewhat neglected. Thus the Svātantrikas — who, unlike the Prāsaṅgikas, employ an independent 'inference' (*svatantra-*

> *anumāna*) or syllogism (*prayoga*) to establish the statements of the Madhyamaka — are only beginning to receive the systematic attention they deserve.[16]

Perhaps the most easily identifiable reason for the neglect of the Svātantrikas is that the greater portion of their works is not preserved in Sanskrit. The primary texts delineating the Sautrāntika-Svātantrika school are Bhāvaviveka's *Essence of the Middle Way* (*Madhyamakahṛdaya*) and its autocommentary, the *Blaze of Reasoning* (*Tarkajvālā*). These texts not only provide a detailed presentation of Bhāvaviveka's own system but also include expositions and critiques of the major Buddhist and non-Buddhist philosophical schools of India in Bhāvaviveka's day. It is as an encyclopedia of other systems rather than as an exposition of Bhāvaviveka's own Sautrāntika-Svātantrika school that the *Essence of the Middlle Way* and the *Blaze of Reasoning* have been valued by modern scholars. Bhāvaviveka's terse commentary to Nāgārjuna's *Treatise on the Middle Way* and the voluminous subcommentary by Avalokitavrata are also important sources for the understanding of Svātantrika, especially when studied with the Prāsaṅgika commentaries of Buddhapālita and Candrakīrti. The other text of central importance attributed to the Sautrāntika-Svātantrika[17] is Jñānagarbha's *Differentiation of the Two Truths* (*Satyadvayavibhaṅga*), renowned as one of "the three [texts] illuminating Svātantrika" (*rang rgyud shar gsum*). With the exception of a portion of the *Essence of the Middle Way*, all of these texts have been lost in the original Sanskrit, and only one chapter of Bhāvaviveka's commentary to the *Treatise on the Middle Way* and fractions of four chapters of the *Essence of the Middle Way* and *Blaze of Reasoning* (discussed below) have been rendered into a Western language from the Tibetan translations.

The Yogācāra-Svātantrika traditionally is said to be set forth in *Śāntarakṣita's *Ornament for the Middle Way* (*Madhyamakālaṃkāra*) and Kamalaśīla's *Illumination of the Middle Way* (*Madhyamakāloka*), the other two texts illuminating Svātantrika. Neither Śāntarakṣita's autocommentary to the *Ornament for the Middle Way* nor Kamalaśīla's *Illumination of the Middle Way* has been translated. Śāntarakṣita's massive encyclopedia of Indian philosophy, the *Compendium of Principles* (*Tattvasaṃgraha*) is a critical survey of Buddhist and non-Buddhist schools and does not explicitly elucidate Śāntarakṣita's own system. Thus, its translation by Ganganatha Jha[18] does not contribute directly to our understanding of Svātantrika.

By far the most extensive study of the Svātantrika school took place in Tibet. The two chief figures of the Yogācāra-Svātantrika subschool, Śāntarakṣita and Kamalaśīla, played a central role in the first dissemination of Buddhism in Tibet in the eighth century. During this early period, many Tibetan scholars adopted the Svātantrika view, whose influence seems to have carried over into the period of the second dissemination during the eleventh century, for it is reported that Atīśa, himself a Prāsaṅgika, lectured on Bhāvaviveka's *Blaze of Reasoning* on numerous occasions.[19] However, with the translation of the works of Candrakīrti by Ba-tsap-nyi-ma-drak (*Pa-tshab-nyi-ma-grags*, 1055-1158?) and Jayānanda, the Prāsaṅgika view began to spread. From this time on, the Prāsaṅgika view continued to gain currency, with the works of Candrakīrti being highly valued by some of the most illustrious scholars of the most creative period in Tibetan thought (1100-1500), including Mar-ba (*Mar-pa*, 1012-1096), Sa-gya (*Sa-skya*) Paṇḍita (1182-1251), Bu-dön (*Bu-ston*, 1290-1364), Ren-da-wa (*Red-mda'-ba*, 1349-1412), and Tsong-kha-pa (1357-1419).

The primacy of the Prāsaṅgika view was firmly established for the Tibetan tradition by Tsong-kha-pa, the founder of the Ge-luk (*dGe-lugs*) order, in works such as the *Great Exposition of the Stages of the Path* (*Lam rim chen mo*), the *Essence of the Good Explanations* (*Legs bshad snying po*), and the *Great Commentary on* (*Candrakīrti's*) *"Supplement"* (*'Jug dik chen mo*). In these works he presents both the central issues and most intricate points of the Prāsaṅgika school with a precision and style unmatched in Buddhist literature. Thus, it can be said that from the time of Tsong-kha-pa, if not before, the Prāsaṅgika school was the dominant philosophical system in Tibet. It is not the case, as A. K. Warder claims, that Śāntarakṣita's "philosophy has formed the basic theoretical outlook of the Buddhist in that country [Tibet]" since the eighth century.[20]

One of the great contributions made by the Tibetans to the study of Buddhist philosophy has been their tenets (*siddhānta, grub mtha'*) texts, surveys of the Indian philosophical systems. Some of the early attempts to present an overview of Buddhist philosophy in a single work are the Ga-dam (*bKa' gdams*) scholar Ü-ba-lo-sel's (*dBus-pa-blo-gsal*) *Treasury Explaining Tenets* (*Grub pa'i mtha' rnam par bshad pa'i mdzod*), the first Dalai Lama, Gen-dun-drup's (*dGe-'den-grub*, 1391-1475) *Ship Entering the Ocean of Tenets* (*Grub mtha' rgya mtshor 'jug pa'i gru rdzings*), the Nying-ma (*rNying-ma*) scholar Long-chen-rap-jam's (*kLong-chen-rab-'byams*, 1308-1363) *Treasury of Tenets* (*Grub mtha' mdzod*), and the Sa-gya (*Sa-skya*) translator Dak-tsang's (*sTag-tshang*, born 1405) *Freedom from Extremes Through Understanding All Tenets* (*Grub mtha' kun shes nas mtha' bral grub pa*). However, the best known of the doxographies are those of two later Ge-luk scholars, Jam-yang-shay-ba's (*'Jam-dbyangs-bzhad-pa*, 1648-1721) *Great Exposition of Tenets* (*Grub mtha' chen mo*) and Jang-gya's (*lCang-skya-rol-pa'i-rdo-rje*, 1717-1786) *Presentation of Tenets* (*Grub pa'i mtha'i rnam par bzhag pa*). These two works seek to present an accurate overview of the schools of Indian philosophy, both Buddhist and non-Buddhist. With extensive citation of Indian texts, they survey the central issues of each system. Beyond this, they attempt to situate the schools in a hierarchical order from bottom to top, beginning among the Buddhist schools with the Vaibhāṣikas and then proceeding to the Sautrāntikas, Cittamātrins (Yogācārins), Svātantrikas, and Prāsaṅgikas. They rely heavily on the perspective of Tsong-kha-pa, often appealing to his statement on a particular point as the final word. At other times, they lift lengthy sections from his writings without citation

In the dominant Ge-luk order, these tenet texts provide an important medium for the study of the Svātantrika school. Traditionally, the most advanced study of Buddhist philosophy took place in one of six colleges in the three great monasteries located in the vicinity of Lhasa — Dre-bung (*'Bras-spungs*), Gan-den (*dGa'-ldan*), and Se-ra (*Se-ra*). Each college, both in Tibet and in the Ge-luk monasteries relocated in India since 1959, has its own curriculum that includes a survey of tenets. Jam-yang-shay-ba and Jang-gya's expositions of tenets are the most extensive and sophisticated of all such surveys and thus have been studied by scholars of all six colleges, although they are formally associated with Go-mang (*sGo-mang*) College of Dre-bung monastery. For most Ge-luk scholars, knowledge of Svātantrika would come, thus, through literature of this genre, in conjunction with the study of textbooks on the structure of the path to enlightenment based on the Yogācāra-Svātantrika Haribhadra's commentaries to Maitreya's *Ornament for Clear Realization* (*Abhisamayālaṃkāra*); it would be a rare scholar who had devoted extensive effort to the study of the original Svātantrika texts in Tibetan translation.

The chief educational technique in the Ge-luk monastic universities is a stylized form of logical debate in which the student is expected to be able to defend the positions of the various Buddhist and non-Buddhist philosophical systems. Thus, although Prāsaṅgika rather than Svātantrika is regarded as the highest system of philosophy, with the result that all Ge-luk-bas consider themselves to be Prāsaṅgikas, a monk's scholarship and intellectual acumen is judged in part by his ability to present the Svātantrika position accurately and defend it against criticisms that might be leveled by a Prāsaṅgika. Therefore, both in the context of writing texts, such as Jang-gya's *Presentation of Tenets*, and in the debating courtyard, the ability to present accurately a view that is not one's own is valued highly. Thus, although Svātantrika is seen as only the penultimate system, a Ge-luk-ba must be able to present it clearly and defend it in debate.

Because of the unique perspective (to be discussed below) provided by the Tibetan tenet genre, the Svātantrika chapter of Jang-gya's *Presentation of Tenets* has been translated in its entirety and forms the second part of this study. Jang-gya's exposition of the Svātantrika school is, in part, a compilation of Tsong-kha-pa's statements concerning the school, drawn from a number of different works. Tsong-kha-pa never wrote a systematic presentation of the Svātantrika school; his only work devoted solely to the Svātantrika view is his *Notes on (Śāntarakṣita's) "Ornament for the Middle Way"* (*dbU ma rgyan zin bris*). However, he devoted important sections of his major works, such as his commentaries to Nāgārjuna's *Treatise on the Middle Way* and Candrakīrti's *Supplement to the Middle Way* (*Madhyamakāvatāra*), the *Essence of the Good Explanations*, and the *Great Exposition of the Stages of the Path*, to discussions of the Svātantrika positions and the differences between Svātantrika and Prāsaṅgika. These are Jam-yang-shay-ba and Jang-gya's main sources. However, their studies are not merely paraphrases of Tsong-kha-pa. For example, Jang-gya's extensive sections on Bhāvaviveka's refutation of Yogācāra and on the reasoning of the lack of being one or many are original studies displaying considerable research in the Indian sources. Jang-gya's fundamental concern with the pivotal issues in the Svātantrika school makes this chapter of his *Presentation of Tenets* the most valuable study of Svātantrika in Tibetan literature.

Purpose and Scope

In order to assess the place of this study, it is worthwhile to survey earlier treatments of Svātantrika in the West. Because Candrakīrti's *Clear Words* is presented in Sanskrit, it is the best known of the commentaries to Nāgārjuna's *Treatise on the Middle Way*. In the first chapter of that text Candrakīrti defends Buddhapālita and attacks Bhāvaviveka. This chapter has until recently been the major source for the Svātantrika position, albeit presented in the words of its most strident critic. The dispute between Candrakīrti and Bhāvaviveka on the question of consequences (*prasaṅga*) and syllogisms (*prayoga*) has been brought to light in the West through the work of Stcherbatsky,[21] Kajiyama,[22] Hopkins,[23], and Thurman.[24]

In 1932, Louis de La Vallée Poussin translated a text attributed to Bhāvaviveka that is not preserved in Tibetan, the *Jewel in Hand* (*Chang-chung-lun*).[25] N. A. Sastri restored the text into Sanskrit and wrote a summary of its contents.[26] Sastri also translated a short work by Bhāvaviveka, the *Condensed Meaning of the Middle Way* (*Madhyamakārthasaṃgraha*).[27] With the discovery of a partial Sanskrit manuscript in 1936, Bhāvaviveka's *Essence of the Middle Way* became available to Sanskritists and a number of chapters have been translated, most of them dealing with non-Buddhist schools.[28]

In view of the wide range of original Tibetan literature on Svātantrika, it is interesting that one brief exposition of the school, drawn from the *Precious Garland of Tenets* (*Grub mtha' rin chen 'phreng pa*) by the eighteenth-century Ge-luk scholar Gon-chok-jik-may-wang-bo (*dKon-mchog-'jigs-med-dbang-po*, 1728-1791) has been translated into English three times.[29]

It is clear, therefore, that previous research on Svātantrika in the West has been limited to selected studies of isolated topics.[30] The one Tibetan exposition of the school that has been translated is so brief as to form merely a sketch. The purpose of the present study is thus first to provide a more comprehensive and detailed presentation of the Svātantrika school as a whole, dwelling at length on a number of central issues. This purpose is fulfilled in part by the translation of the Svātantrika chapter of Jang-gya's *Presentation of Tenets*. From the time that Candrakīrti sought to distinguish the view of Buddhapālita and himself from that of Bhāvaviveka, the difference between Prāsaṅgika and Svātantrika has been an important one for the history of Buddhist thought. Therefore, this study seeks to establish what the two schools have in common as Mādhyamikas and to identify the fundamental questions on which they part company. These are the topics of the first three chapters.

As a school of Buddhism, the Svātantrikas assert that ignorance is the source of all suffering; a basic misconception about the way things exist is the root cause of all desire, pride, hatred, and jealousy. They also hold that through the use of reason and introspection, this misconception can be destroyed, making suffering impossible. Hence, the identification of this misconception and the implementation of the means of destroying it are of primary importance. The Svātantrikas offer a unique interpretation of the fundamental misconception, and this is described in chapter 4. Chapter 5 is the first extensive treatment of one of the reasonings that the Svātantrikas found most effective in destroying the conception of true existence, the reasoning of the lack of being one or many.[31]

This study is thus intended to fill a gap in our understanding not only of Svātantrika and its relationship to Prāsaṅgika but also of the fundamental issues of one of the most creative periods in Indian thought. The Svātantrika school is important not only because Bhāvaviveka's criticism of Buddhapālita provided Candrakīrti with the occasion to delineate the Prāsaṅgika position. The nature and cause of suffering, the identification of the final nature of phenomena, the status of external objects, and the means by which the truth can be known are perennial problems in the history of philosophy and religion, and all of these problems are major ones for the Svātantrika-Mādhyamikas. Their unique way of posing these problems and the solutions they put forth bear our consideration.

First, however, it is essential to identify a conundrum that faces the researcher of Svātantrika: To what extent may we accurately speak of a Svātantrika "system" or "school"? Because the Tibetan terms *rang rgyud pa* and *thal 'gyur ba* have for so long been Sanskritized in Western literature as *Svātantrika* and *Prāsaṅgika*, the conclusion is sometimes drawn that these terms appear in Indian literature as the names of branches of Mādhyamika. They do not. The terms translated as *Svātantrika* and *Prāsaṅgika* were coined by Tibetan scholars, probably in the late eleventh or early twelfth century, following the translation into Tibetan of Candrakīrti's works by Ba-tsap-nyi-ma-drak and the Kashmiri *paṇḍita* Jayānanda. In his *Essence of the Good Explanations*, Tsong-kha-pa notes that none of the great Svātantrika masters — Jñānagarbha, Śāntarakṣita, Kamalaśīla — found any difference between the selflessness (*nairātmya*, *bdag med*) of their own system and that of the system of Buddhapālita and Candrakīrti;[32] that is, the difference between Svātantrika and Prāsaṅgika that Tsong-kha-pa and his followers go to such lengths to unfold was by no means evident to such people as Bhāvaviveka, Avalokitavrata, Jñānagarbha, Śāntarakṣita, and Kamalaśīla. This should give us pause. If the protagonists in the development of Mādhyamika thought in India saw themselves as simply Mādhyamikas, the question must be raised of the efficacy of the retrospective designation *Svātantrika* to what may not have been a self-conscious "system." Were individual subschools of Mādhyamika that were not present in name nonetheless present in fact?

The most detailed and "systematic" presentations of Svātantrika appear in the doxographies by the two Ge-luk scholars already mentioned, Jam-yang-shay-ba and Jang-gya. In these works, they have assumed the formidable task of identifying the shared assertions of those Indian thinkers whom we have come to refer to as Svātantrikas. In studies replete with quotations from the Indian sources, they have sought to assemble the views of the "Svātantrikas" on the central issues of Buddhist thought: the nature of the world, the two truths, the status of external objects, the causes of suffering, the structure of the path to liberation, and the nature of enlightenment. The value of their work for the student of Buddhist thought cannot be overestimated. As David Seyfort Ruegg has noted in reference to the Tibetan Mādhyamikas:

> They thus combine close adherence to the traditions and lines of thought established by their predecessors in India with the production of very valuable contributions of their own in the area of textual exegesis and philosophical hermeneutics as well as in the domain of philosophical and meditative theory and practice.[33]

Despite this importance, however, the question arises whether the works of Jam-yang-shay-ba and Jang-gya are accurate portrayals of what they refer to as the Svātantrika system (*lugs*). To approach it, it is essential to identify their purposes and perspectives. In order to accomplish this, it is perhaps useful to adopt two terms employed by the anthropologist.

In his prodigious study *Language in Relation to a Unified Theory of the Structure of Human Behavior*,[34] Kenneth Pike identifies two standpoints for the description of human behavior, which he labels the emic and etic viewpoints.

> The etic viewpoint studies behavior as from the outside of a particular system, and as an essential initial approach to an alien system. The emic viewpoint results from studying behavior as from inside the system.[35]

Pike goes on to provide a list of differences between the two approaches, two of which are of interest here. The first difference is that etic analyses employ criteria alien to the system under consideration, whereas an emic analyses provide an internal or "insider's" view, making use of criteria obtained from the system under consideration. Theoretically, then, the etic approach should be valid for the analysis and description of several cultures; the emic approach, on the other hand, should be valid only for the culture from which it arose. A second difference noted by Pike concerns the problem of non-integration versus integration:

> The etic view does not require that every unit be viewed as part of a larger setting. The emic view, however, insists that every unit be seen as somehow distributed and functioning within a larger structural unit and setting, in a hierarchy of units and hierarchy of settings as units.[36]

Which approach was taken by Tibetan scholars such as Jam-yang-shay-ba and Jang-gya in their description of Indian Buddhism? Their approach can easily be judged as etic, since they were separated by significant distances in language, culture, place, and time; Jam-yang-shay-ba and Jang-gya wrote a millennium after the authors whose views they sought to represent. It is important to note, however, that Pike defines the etic viewpoint as studying behavior "*as* from outside of a particular system," and the emic as resulting "from studying behavior *as* from inside the system" (emphasis added). Jam-yang-shay-ba and Jang-gya clearly saw themselves as writing from within the system and, despite being removed by the factors just mentioned, they indeed stood within the Mādhyamika tradition, a continuum of study and practice that flowed unbroken from India to the snowy land of Tibet. Ruegg notes that:

> there is no evidence to indicate that they have understood their task to be to set themselves off from their Mādhyamika

> predecessors in India. On the contrary, they have very clearly striven to penetrate, explain, and put into practice the understanding of Buddhism achieved by Nāgārjuna and his disciples up to Abhayākāragupta and Sakya Paṇḍita; to their interpretations they regularly refer, and also defer in a not uncritical manner.[37]

The Ge-luk doxographers did not see themselves as imposing an artificial division on Mādhyamika that was utterly absent in India. There was a precedent in India for identifying trends within Mādhyamika and for ranking one thinker's works above another's.[38] Atīśa says in his *Introduction to the Two Truths* (*Satya-dvayāvatāra*, 14-16ab):

> The wise master Bhavya [Bhāvaviveka] said
> That it is clearly stated in scripture
> That [emptiness] is not understood
> By either a conceptual or non-conceptual consciousness.
>
> Through whom, then, should one realize emptiness?
> Candrakīrti, student of Nāgārjuna,
> Prophesied by the Tathāgatha,
> And who saw the true reality.
> One should realize the true reality
> Through instructions transmitted from him.[39]

Jam-yang-shay-ba and Jang-gya thus felt themselves to be fully consonant with the Indian tradition while at the same time seeking to affirm the interpretations of Tsong-kha-pa, for although Tsong-kha-pa did not himself compose a chronicle of tenets, his works provide much of the basis of the great Ge-luk doxographies. One of Tsong-kha-pa's great contributions to Buddhist thought was his systematization of the Indian materials he had before him, in the arenas of theory and praxis, of sutra and trantra. Nevertheless, the heavy reliance of his great work on the practice of the path, *The Great Exposition of the Stages of the Path to Enlightenment* (*Byang chub lam rim chen mo*), on two late Indian works, Atīśa's *Lamp for the Path to Enlightenment* (*Bodhipathapradīpa*) with its autocommentary (*Bodhi-mārgapradīpapañjikā*) and Kamalaśīla's three *Stages of Meditation* (*Bhāvanākrama*), again suggests the strong sense of tradition that characterizes his work and that of his followers. Yet this is not to imply that Tsong-kha-pa was not, in many respects, an innovator, or that these innovations are discernible only from our etic perspective. Tsong-kha-pa was both praised and criticized for his innovations by Tibetan scholars of his age.[40]

The Ge-luk approach, then, must be judged as essentially emic, and, as such, it displays the characteristics suggested by Pike. The emic approach provides a view from inside the system; in this case, the system is not the Svātantrika but rather, that of Indo-Tibetan thought in general. The Ge-luk authors Jam-yang-shay-ba and Jang-gya continue in the tradition of Bhāvaviveka's *Blaze of Reasoning* and Śāntarakṣita's *Compendium of Principles* in composing texts that seek to bring together summaries of the doctrines of the major schools of Indian philosophy. A crucial difference is that Bhāvaviveka and Śāntarakṣita were, for the most part, writing about their contemporaries, whereas Jam-yang-shay-ba and Jang-gya were writing a thousand years after the demise in India of most of the schools they discuss. Their task, then, is of a fundamentally different character from that of their Indian precursors; Jam-yang-shay-ba and Jang-gya, especially in their work on Svātantrika, were forced to construct a Svātantrika system from the sources before them and, hence, the view of Svātantrika that they present is synthetic.

Because the criteria employed by Jam-yang-shay-ba and Jang-gya to describe and analyze the writings of the Svātantrika masters are emic, their concerns are those of the Buddhist; more accurately, they are those of the Ge-luk scholar-monk. They consequently deal almost exclusively with points of doctrine, paying little attention to historical factors that may have contributed to the development of that doctrine. Their perspective can be viewed as both diachronic and synchronic — diachronic in the sense that they were able to look back from their Himalayan vantage point over the development of Buddhist thought in India. However, although they were aware of much of the chronology of Indian Buddhism and of the various lineages of teaching, their primary sources were the translated *śāstras* of the Indian masters. Hence, their view was also synchronic because all they had to work from were the texts, texts which, for the Tibetan scholar-monk, assume something of a timeless quality. To expect Jam-yang-shay-ba and Jang-gya to provide the type of analysis and to ask the questions of the modern scholar is to misunderstand their perspective.

The purpose of the Tibetan doxographers also diverges from that of the modern student of Buddhist thought. Pike has noted that a second difference between the emic and the etic is that the emic requires that every element under consideration be integrated into and function within a larger whole, whereas the etic does not. This distinction is especially clear in the case of the Ge-luk curriculum in which the study of Buddhist tenets is much more than an academic enterprise. The Ge-luk doxographers rank the schools of Indian Buddhism in a hierarchy and study them from bottom to top, beginning with Vaibhāṣika and ending with Mādhyamika, dealing first with Svātantrika and finally with what they consider to be the final system, Prāsaṅgika. As will be discussed in chapter 4, the study of tenets in this manner has a strong pedagogic and even soteriological value, with the assertions of one school serving as a propaedeutic for the next. The doctrines of Svātantrika are thus seen as an integral part of a larger whole, surpassing Vaibhāṣika, Sautrāntika, and Yogācāra in sophistication and subtlety and, hypothetically, able to defeat them all, while being outshone by Prāsaṅgika. This approach contributes further to a synthetic portrayal of the various schools because the assertions that receive the greatest attention are those which are important within this hierarchical rubric; issues that do not fall under one of the doxographical categories are not emphasized.

To fully understand a given language or culture, Pike argues, both the emic and the etic approaches must be employed; the use of one approach to the exclusion of the other results in a flat, rather than three dimensional image of the subject. And so it is with the study of Svātantrika. To conclude that the image of Svātantrika created by the Ge-luk doxographers is complete, obviating the independent study of their Indian sources, would be a serious error. On the other hand, to ignore the insights provided by authors such as Jam-yang-shay-ba and Jang-gya would be to overlook a most valuable resource. As Ruegg has noted, "with a view to both translation and exegesis Tibetan scholars developed remarkable philological and interpretative methods that could well justify us in regarding them as Indologists avant la lettre."[41] The Tibetan layout of Svātantrika provides a starting point for the study of the Indian masters. Rather than attempting to construct a view of Svātantrika out of nothing, we would probably do better to use the Ge-luk presentation as a grid to be laid across the Indian texts, facilitating the discovery of points of congruence and deviation. This grid should be employed, however, with full recognition that it is itself a construct, developed a millennium after the fact. With this caveat, the Ge-luk doxographers can be used to full advantage, providing a spotlight on arenas of Buddhist thought that otherwise would remain obscured in darkness.

It is safe to say that what we call the Svātantrika school was not as coherent, self-conscious, or monolithic as the Ge-luk authors suggest. It must be recalled that we are considering a period of several centuries of Indian thought populated by philosophers who thought of themselves as Mādhyamikas or simply Buddhists, responding to developments and innovations in a fluid intellectual environment. There were indeed different lines of teaching that were internally consistent, but to infer from this the existence of a Svātantrika creed to which allegiance was sworn is to misunderstand the intention of the Tibetan doxographers. The presentations of the Svātantrika schools developed by the Ge-luk-bas represent a development of Mādhyamika thought. For our understanding of Svātantrika they should be regarded as more than simply heuristic, less than strictly apodictic. They are the reconstruction of a school long dead.

The Svātantrika school described by Jam-yang-shay-ba and Jang-gya is a representation, not that of an eyewitness photographer but that of a portrait painter of a later age, perhaps impressionistic, painted in broad strokes here and intricate detail there, the pentimento of Indian Svātantrika lying below the Tibetan pigments, vaguely visible. The historical accuracy of the Tibetan portrait remains to be discerned; that the portrait is a masterpiece is not in question.

My purpose in undertaking this study is to present a tradition of intepretation — specifically, the Ge-luk interpretation of some of the central issues addressed by the Svātantrika-Mādhyamika school, issues such as the nature of ignorance, the role of reasoning in overcoming that ignorance, the meaning of emptiness, and the two truths — the ultimate and conventional. Because Ge-luk literature — beginning with Tsong-kha-pa and continuing through Jam-yang-shay-ba, Jang-gya, and beyond — provides the most detailed analysis of the difference between Svātantrika and Prāsaṅgika, their positions will be treated at some length. The Ge-luk order has its own development over several centuries and is itself not monolithic; controversies sometimes occurred on important points of Mādhyamika doctrine. These will be noted.

There are many topics with which this study deals only briefly, or not at all. The Svātantrika response to the doctrine of mind-only and the Yogācāra school — Bhāvaviveka's strident critique and Śāntarakṣita's appropriation, the structure of the path to enlightenment as presented by Haribhadra, and the hermeneutics of Svātantrika are touched upon in the translation section. Other studies essential to our understanding of Svātantrika, including the translation and careful exegesis of the first three chapters of Bhāvaviveka's *Blaze of Reasoning*, of Śāntarakṣita's *Ornament for the Middle Way* with its commentaries, and of Kamalaśīla's *Illumination of the Middle Way*, remain desiderata.

In my comments on the preceding pages, I have attempted to indicate the value of the *siddhānta* literature of Jam-yang-shay-ba and Jang-gya while, at the same time, suggesting how their approach differs from our own. The Ge-luk presentation of Svātantrika is a valuable starting point for the study of the Indian school, and my purpose in writing this book is to provide that starting point to the Western student of Buddhism. What I will attempt to present here are some of the major concerns of the Svātantrika school *as understood by the Ge-luk doxographers*. When I say in the following chapters that the "Svātantrika position" is this or that, all of the qualifications and caveats expressed above should be kept in mind. This study, then, should not be viewed as comprehensive, nor as the final word on Svātantrika, but as a preliminary study, an attempt to outline the Ge-luk tradition of interpretation of Svātantrika, a grid through which the works of the Indian masters may usefully be viewed.

Sources and Methods

In the study of the Svātantrika school, eight strata of source material are available to the researcher. In chronological order, the first level is that of the statements attributed to the Buddha, appearing for the most part in the Perfection of Wisdom Sūtras, that provide the canonical basis for the Mādhyamika school. Those statements were interpreted by Nāgārjuna, the founder of Mādhyamika, whose works constitute the second level. Third are the writings of the systematizers of Nāgārjuna's Mādhyamika, the central figures of Prāsaṅgika and Svātantrika — Buddhapālita, Candrakīrti, Bhāvaviveka, Śāntarakṣita, and Jñānagarbha. On the fourth level are the Indian commentators on those authors' works; their explanations are often invaluable for unpacking terse pronouncements of the root texts. In this category are writers such as Avalokitavrata, Kamalaśīla, and Jayānanda. The first four levels occur in Indian literature, lost for the most part in the original Sanskrit but preserved in Tibetan translations.

The next four strata have their origin in Tibet. The first is the writings of Tsong-kha-pa. For the Ge-luk-bas, this is also the most important of the Tibetan levels; just as the Indian writers cite a statement by the Buddha or, among the Mādhyamikas, by Nāgārjuna, as scriptural support for their arguments, so the Ge-luk writers appeal to the works of Tsong-kha-pa. It was his careful scrutiny of the writings of all the authors mentioned above that resulted in the detailed presentation of Mādhyamika that is the hallmark of the Ge-luk curriculum.

The sixth level is that of the tenet literature, represented most notably by the works of Jam-yang-shay-ba and Jang-gya, texts that offer a systematic presentation of the schools of Buddhist philosophy. The seventh level is comprised of Tibetan works that are devoted to a more specific and extensive study of a particular topic. In his category fall such works as Den-dar-hla-ram-ba's (*bsTan-dar-lha-ram-pa*, born 1759) *Presentation of the Lack of Being One or Many* (*gCig du bral gyi rnam gzhag*) and Nga-wang-bel-den's (*Ngag-dbang-dpal-ldan*, born 1797) *Explanation of the Meaning of "Conventional" and "Ultimate" in the Four Tenet Systems* (*Grub mtha' gzhi'i lugs kyi kun rdzob dang don dam pa'i don rnam par bshad pa*).

The eighth and final level of potential sources is traditionally not committed to paper. This is the oral commentary of the Tibetan scholar. None of the Tibetan texts described above is intended to be complete in and of itself; in the traditional Tibetan curriculum these texts serve as lecture notes for the teacher, who expands on and raises questions about points in the text. The texts are often written in such a terse style that certain passages would be incomprehensible without the benefit of a skilled scholar's explanation. In addition to unravelling seemingly intractable problems, the best Tibetan scholars have the ability to bring together problems that are ostensibly unrelated to reveal illuminating conjunctions.

In the preparation of this study, all eight strata were excavated, to varying depths. Using the sixth and eight levels as a basis, I went on to examine the works of Tsong-kha-pa, the writings of the Svātantrika masters and Nāgārjuna, and occasionally their sutra sources. Den-dar-hla-ram-ba's exposition of the reasoning of the lack of being one or many proved to be a most valuable source for unfolding the intricacies of that proof. However, I found myself in moments of difficulty returning again and again to Tsong-kha-pa, especially to his *Essence of the Good Explanations* and *Great Exposition of the Stages of the Path*, for both concise and incisive answers to the most difficult problems. His works became the pivot, providing an explanation of the Indian texts and the source for the Tibetan studies.

1 The Middle Way

> Abandoning the two extremes, the Tathāgata realized the middle path, producing vision, producing knowledge, leading to clairvoyance, enlightenment, and nirvana.
>
> *Saṃyutta Nikāya*

In his first sermon after his enlightenment, the Buddha spoke of a middle way free from the two extremes. Here, the two extremes referred to were the life of self-indulgence he experienced as a prince and the self-mortification he practiced as an ascetic. In his first sermon, he went on to say that the middle way is the eightfold path, beginning with right view (*samyakdṛṣṭi, yang dag pa'i lta ba*). In the centuries following the Buddha's nirvana, schools of Buddhist tenets (*siddhānta, grub mtha'*) arose, each with its own position as to what constitutes the right view, the philosophical middle free from extremes. Although all Buddhist schools consider themselves to be proponents of the middle way, it is only the school founded by Nāgārjuna that overtly calls itself Mādhyamika.

A Mādhyamika is defined by Jang-gya as a person who propounds the correctness of a middle way which is free from the extreme of permanence (*śaśvatānta, rtag mtha'*) — that phenomena ultimately exist (*paramārthasat, don dam par yod pa*) — and the extreme of annihilation (*ucchedānta, chad mtha'*) that phenomena do not exist even conventionally (*vyavahārasat, tha snyad du yod pa*).[1] The extreme of permanence, also known as the extreme of existence (*astyanta, yod mtha'*) and the extreme of superimposition (*āropānta, sgro 'dogs kyi mtha'*) is the true existence (*satyasat, bden par yod pa*), ultimate existence (*paramārthasat, don dam par yod pa*), or real existence (*samyaksat, yang dag par yod pa*) of persons and other phenomena. The extreme of annihilation, also referred to as the extreme of non-existence (*nāstyanta, med mtha'*) and the extreme of denial (*abhyākhyānānta, skur 'debs kyi mtha'*), is the utter non-existence of persons and other phenomena.[2]

Conceiving or actively asserting that things truly exist or that they do not exist even conventionally is a case of falling to an extreme. The extremes are dangerous places, compared to the abyss beneath a rocky precipice[3] and holding one of the extremes is likened to falling off a cliff. There are specific dangers associated with each of the extremes. Through holding the view of utter non-existence, one is reborn in one of the bad realms (*gati, 'gro ba*) as an animal, hungry ghost, or hell being.[4] Presumably, such a nihilistic view would inspire non-virtuous actions, such as murder, which would then serve as the cause of a painful rebirth. Through conceiving phenomena to be truly existent, that is, by falling to the extreme of permanence, one could not be liberated from cyclic existence (*saṃsāra, 'khor ba*).[5] Thus, one might engage in virtuous activities which cause rebirth as a god, demigod, or human, but so long as the conception of true existence underlaid those deeds, one could not cut the final root of cyclic existence.

Jang-gya distinguishes between an extreme and holding to an extreme. An extreme is, for example, the non-existence of cause and effect. Holding to an extreme would, in this case, be the conception of the non-existence of cause and effect. Therefore, as Jang-gya points out, an extreme necessarily does not exist whereas holding to an extreme, that is, the consciousness conceiving of an extreme, does exist.[6]

Tsong-kha-pa clarifies the meaning of the extremes in the first chapter of his commentary to Nāgārjuna's *Treatise on the Middle Way* (*Madhyamakaśāstra*). He emphasizes that the mere presence of the terms "existence" and "non-existence" does not constitute extremes of existence and non-existence. For example, the non-existence of faults in a Buddha is not an extreme of non-existence, nor is the existence of wisdom and mercy in a Buddha an extreme of existence.[7]

More important, the fact that phenomena do not exist ultimately is not an extreme of non-existence. To say that something does not ultimately exist does not mean that it is utterly non-existent. The Mādhyamikas hold that since ultimate/real/true existence does not exist conventionally, non-ultimate/non-real/non-true existence must exist conventionally. Ultimate existence and non-ultimate existence are mutually exclusive, the presence of one precluding the presence of the other. They are also a dichotomy, for when ultimate existence is refuted, its negative — non-ultimate existence — is established as an object of awareness.[8] Therefore, when ultimate existence — the extreme of permanence — is negated, non-ultimate existence is implied; thus, non-ultimate existence is not an extreme of non-existence. Since ultimate existence does not conventionally exist, its opposite, non-ultimate existence, must conventionally exist.[9]

Mādhyamikas are so-called because they abide in the middle free from all extremes. They are able to do this because of their understanding of the relationship between emptiness (*śūnyatā, stong pa nyid*) and dependent arising (*pratītyasamutpāda, rten 'byung*). An emptiness is a phenomenon's lack of true existence. Each phenomenon is empty of true existence and that mere absence of true existence is the final nature of that phenomenon. Dependent arising is, loosely speaking, the positive implication of the absence of true existence. All phenomena are dependent arisings in the sense that they either arise in dependence on causes and conditions, are designated in dependence on their basis of imputation, or are imputed in dependence on a designating term or thought. This third type of dependent arising is the most subtle and is asserted only by the Prāsaṅgikas.[10]

Only the Mādhyamikas assert that all phenomena are empty of true existence and that all phenomena are dependent arisings. Nāgārjuna says in his *Seventy Stanzas on Emptiness* (*Śūnyatāsaptati*):

> The peerless Tathāgata taught
> That because all things
> Are empty of inherent existence,
> Things are dependent arisings.[11]

The other schools of Buddhist tenets assert the true existence of at least some phenomena and limit the category of dependent arisings to impermanent things, taking the term "arising" (*samutpāda, 'byung ba*) in "dependent arising" to mean arising in dependence on causes and conditions. Since whatever is a caused phenomenon is necessarily impermanent (*anitya, mi rtag pa*) according to the Sautrāntikas, Yogācārins, and Mādhyamikas, dependent arisings must be impermanent. The Mādhyamikas, however, take the term *samutpāda* also to mean "established" and assert that all phenomena, caused and uncaused, impermanent and permanent, are dependently established.[12]

Jang-gya notes that dependent arising means being empty of true existence and being empty of true existence means dependent arising.[13] This compatibility of emptiness and dependent arising is a hallmark of Mādhyamika philosophy. Something that lacks ultimate existence cannot be independently established, it must be dependently established, a dependent arising. Something that is a dependent arising cannot be ultimately existent, it must lack ultimate existence, be empty of ultimate existence. This is what is meant by the synonymity of emptiness and dependent arising.

The emptiness of a phenomenon such as a sprout and the sprout's dependent arising are synonymous because if the sprout were truly established it would not be a dependent arising and if it were not a dependent arising, it would be truly established.[14] Technically, however, emptiness and dependent arising are not synonymous because, in that case, whatever was a dependent arising would have to be an emptiness. Although whatever is an emptiness is necessarily a dependent arising, the converse is not true because an emptiness is necessarily a permanent (*nitya, rtag pa*), non-affirming negative (*prasajyapratiṣedha, med 'gag*) phenomenon, whereas dependent arisings include all phenomena, permanent and impermanent. Nonetheless, it is accurate to say that whatever is empty of true existence is a dependent arising and whatever is a dependent arising is empty of true existence.[15]

Dependent arising is called the king of reasonings because it allows the Mādhyamikas to refute both extremes simultaneously. The Yogācārins, for example, need two separate reasons to abandon the two extremes as they define them. They claim that they abandon the extreme of annihilation because they assert that impermanent phenomena truly exist as the same entity as the consciousness perceiving them. They abandon the extreme of permanence by asserting that impermanent phenomena do not have a nature separate from that of consciousness.[16] The Mādhyamikas refute both extremes merely by asserting that all phenomena in the universe are dependent arisings. Specifically, the fact that they are "dependent" refutes the extreme of permanence. Whatever is dependent cannot be truly existent. The fact that they are "arisings" or "established" refutes the extreme of annihilation because whatever is arisen or established cannot be utterly non-existent.[17]

A formal statement of the reasoning of dependent arising in syllogistic form would be "All phenomena do not truly exist because of being dependent arisings." By ascertaining the property of the subject (*pakṣadharma*, *phyogs chos*) — that all phenomena are dependent arisings — the extreme of annihilation is refuted because if something is dependently arisen, it must exist. The extreme of permanence is also refuted because whatever is dependently arisen cannot be independently or ultimately established. Having ascertained the pervasion (*vyāpti*, *khyab pa*), that "whatever is a dependent arising does not truly exist" and having ascertained the property of the subject, that all phenomena are dependent arisings, one ascertains the thesis (*pratijñā*, *dam bca'*), that all phenomena do not truly exist. The thesis further refutes the two extremes because the fact that phenomena do not truly exist avoids the extreme of permanence (that phenomena truly exist) and the extreme of annihilation in that only true existence, not conventional existence, is negated.[18]

That Nāgārjuna found dependent arising to be the most praiseworthy of Buddha's teaching is evident from the expressions of worship of his major works. His *Treatise on the Middle Way* begins:

> Obeisance to the perfect Buddha
> The best of proponents [who teaches]
> That what dependently arises
> Has no cessation, no production,
> No annihilation, no permanence,
> No coming, no going,
> No difference, no sameness,
> Pacified of elaborations, at peace.[19]

Dependent arisings lack truly existent cessation, production, annihilation, permanence, coming, going, sameness, and difference.

His *Sixty Stanzas of Reasoning* (*Yuktiṣaṣṭikākārikā*) beings:

> Obeisance to the King of Subduers (*Munīndra*)
> Who set forth dependent arising,
> This mode by which production and
> Disintegration are abandoned.[20]

Because of being dependent arisings, phenomena lack truly existent production and disintegration.[21]

His *Refutation of Objections* (*Vigrahavyāvartinīkārikā*) begins:

> Obeisance to the perfect Buddha
> Who made the supreme, unique statement
> That emptiness and dependent arising
> Are synonymous with the middle way.[22]

Dependent arising, the middle path free from the two extremes, and the emptiness of true existence are synonyms.[23]

His *Praise of the Inconceivable* (*Acintyastava*) begins:

> Obeisance to the one with incomparable,
> Inconceivable, unparalleled wisdom
> Who taught that dependently arisen things
> Are just without entityness.[24]

Because phenomena are dependent arisings, they lack a truly established entity.[25]

Finally, his *Friendly Letter* (*Suhṛllekha*) says:

> This dependent arising is the most precious and profound
> Of the treasures of the Conqueror's speech.
> Those who see it correctly see the supreme aspect
> Of [the teaching of] the Buddha, the knower of suchness.[26]

Dependent arising is thus praised by Nāgārjuna as the most valuable of all the Buddha's teachings.

Dependent arising and its compatibility with emptiness are seen as a unique tenet of Mādhyamika by the Ge-luk-ba doxographers, distinguishing it from and raising it above the other Buddhist tenet systems. All schools of Buddhist tenets purport to follow the middle way and offer their own interpretation of the extremes. The Vaibhāṣikas and Sautrāntikas assert that all impermanent phenomena are dependent arisings in the sense that they arise in dependence on causes and conditions. They refute the extreme of permanence, which for them is the existence of an unchanging agent such as the principal (*pradhāna, gtso bo*) asserted by the Sāṃkyas. They avoid the extreme of annihilation by upholding the doctrine of the cause and effect of actions, which is rejected by the Cārvākas.[27]

The Yogācārins assert that the extreme of permanence is the true existence of imaginary natures (*parikalpitasvabhāva, kun btags rang bzhin*). Specifically, they identify as cases of holding the extreme of permanence the belief that objects exist as separate entities from the consciousnesses perceiving them and the conception that objects truly exist as the bases of their names. They abandon this extreme because they hold that dependent phenomena (*paratantra, gzhan dbang*) lack this imaginary nature. They identify the extreme of annihilation as the utter non-existence of dependent natures — impermanent phenomena — and consummate natures (*pariniṣpannasvabhāva, yongs grub rang bzhin*) — the emptiness of subject and object existing as separate entities. They avoid this extreme by asserting that these two natures ultimately exist, that is, that objects truly exist as the nature of consciousness, that consciousnesses truly exist, and that the emptiness of the duality of subject and object truly exists.[28]

From the Mādhyamika perspective, the extremes identified by the other tenet systems are *trifling* (*nyi tshe pa*) in the sense that they do not apply to all phenomena and *fabricated* (*blos byas pa*) in the sense that they are inaccurate. The Hīnayāna assertion that impermanent phenomena are free of the extreme of permanence because they arise in dependence on causes and conditions is not rejected by the Mādhyamikas, but it does not apply equally to all phenomena, specifically to permanent phenomena, and is therefore trifling.[29] The Yogācārin middle way is also considered to be trifling. The fact that dependent phenomena and consummate phenomena exist by way of their own character (*svalakṣana, rang gi mtshan nyid*) avoids the extreme of annihilation and the fact that imaginary natures do not exist by way of their own character avoids the extreme of permanence. But because the Yogācārins are incapable of positing one mode of being by which *all* phenomena are free of *both* extremes (as the Mādhyamikas do with dependent arising), the extremes as they understand them are considered to be trifling by the Mādhyamikas.[30]

Furthermore, according to the Mādhyamikas, not only is the Yogācārins middle way trifling, it is wrong. Because the Mādhyamikas (with the exception of the Yogācāra-Svātantrikas) assert that objects conventionally exist as separate entities from the perceiving consciousness, they reject the Yogācārin assertion that the duality of subject and object is an extreme of permanence. Because the Mādhyamikas also assert that all phenomena are empty of true existence, they do not identify the lack of ultimate existence of dependent phenomena as an extreme of annihilation. The Yogācārins come to this view because they assert, in contrast to the Mādhyamikas, that if dependent natures and consummate natures did not ultimately exist, they would not exist at all.[31]

Furthermore, besides contending that the other systems misidentify the extremes, the Mādhyamikas assert that all non-Mādhyamika systems fall to the extremes. The Vaibhāṣikas assert that partless particles are ultimate truths and truly exist.[32] The Sautrāntikas assert that impermanent phenomena are ultimately able to perform functions and truly exist.[33] The Yogācārins assert that dependent and consummate natures truly exist. Thus, although the Vaibhāṣikas, Sautrāntikas, and Yogācārins respectively assert that partless particles, functioning things, and dependent natures are impermanent, from the Mādhyamika perspective they have fallen to the extreme of permanence by asserting true existence.[34] Once they assert true existence, they also implicitly fall to the extreme of annihilation, according to Candrakīrti. In his *Clear Words*, he quotes the *Treatise on the Middle Way* and comments on it:

> Whatever exists inherently is permanent
> Since it does not become non-existent.
> If one says that what arose before is now non-existent,
> Then it follows that this is [an extreme] of annihilation.
>
> Since inherent existence is not overcome, that which is said to exist inherently never becomes non-existent. In that case if follows that through asserting it to be just inherently existent, one has a view of permanence. Because one asserts that things inherently exist at an earlier time and then asserts that now, later, they are destroyed and thus do not exist, it follows that one has a view of annihilation.[35]

If a phenomenon is truly existent, it must be unchanging in nature; thus, for it to cease, it must become utterly non-existent. Since the Vaibhāṣikas, Sautrāntikas, and Yogācārins assert that these impermanent phenomena, which they hold to be truly existent, disintegrate every moment, they thereby come to hold the extreme of annihilation. The Yogācārins explicitly fall to the extreme of annihilation by asserting that sense objects do not exist even conventionally as entities separate from a perceiving consciousness.[36]

The fact that the non-Mādhyamika systems fall to the two extremes does not negate their heuristic value. The Mahāyāna tenet systems believe that Buddha telepathically knew the minds and capacities of his listeners and through his skillful means (*upāyakauśala, thabs shes*) taught what was most appropriate for each. To those who could not accept or understand the view that the self does not exist, he taught that a self does exist. In that way he was able to inspire faith in his teaching and eventually lead these disciples to the more subtle view.[37] Nāgārjuna describes Buddha's approach in his *Precious Garland* (*Ratnāvalī*):

> Just as grammarians
> Begin with reading the alphabet
> So the Buddha teaches doctrines
> That students can bear.
>
> To some, he teaches doctrines
> For reversal of sins.
> To some, for the sake of achieving merit;
> To some, doctrines based on duality;
>
> To some, [he teaches doctrines] based on non-duality.
> To some, the profound, frightening to the fearful,
> Having an essence of emptiness and compassion,
> The means of achieving highest enlightenment.[38]

The first stanza indicates that just as a grammar teacher begins by teaching children the individual letters of the alphabet before teaching them how the letters are put together to form words, the Buddha teaches doctrines which are suitable to the level of awareness of his followers.[39]

The first three lines of the second stanza identify the doctrine of the cause and effect of actions whereby non-virtues may be abandoned and virtuous actions practiced, resulting in the accumulation of merit that will bring rebirth in a good realm. The last line of the second stanza refers to the doctrine taught to followers of the Vaibhāṣika and Sautrāntika lineages to whom the Buddha teaches that a self of persons (*pudgalātman, gang zag gi bdag*) does not exist but that objects and subjects do truly exist as separate entities.

The first line of the third stanza identifies the doctrines taught to those Mahāyānists who are temporarily incapable of understanding the Mādhyamika view and therefore are taught the existence of an emptiness of duality of subject and object. The last three lines refer to the teachings of non-true existence and compassion that the Buddha gives to Mahāyāna disciples of greatest awareness; the teaching of emptiness would frighten those who believe strongly in true existence because they would mistake it for utter non-existence.[40]

This idea of a progression of doctrines, culminating in the Mādhyamika view is also reflected in Āryadeva's *Four Hundred* (*Catuḥśataka*):

> In the beginning non-merit is overcome.
> In the middle self is overcome.
> In the end all [bad] views are overcome.
> Those who understand this are wise.[41]

Initially the Buddha teaches the existence of a substantially existent (*dravyasat*, *rdzas yod*) self which is the accumulator of actions and experiencer of effects in order that his followers may turn away from non-virtues which are causes of rebirth in the lower realms. He then refutes the existence of a substantially existent self in order to make them suitable vessels for the practice of the path. Finally, they are liberated through his teaching of the subtle emptiness of true existence which overcomes all elaborations (*prapañca*, *spros pa*) of bad views.[42]

Thus, as long as the teaching of non-true existence was not compatible with the viability of all phenomena for a student, the Buddha made distinctions, with some phenomena truly existent and some not; students were led gradually, being taught a portion of selflessness in the belief that it is not suitable to set forth even a coarse form of emptiness if there is the possibility that it will undercut the validity of cause and effect. Therefore, for some, the Buddha refuted the true existence of the person but, for the most part, did not refute that of the aggregates (*skandha*, *phung po*). For those of the Yogācārin lineage, he refuted a difference of entity of subject and object but did not refute the true existence of the emptiness of duality of subject and object. When his followers of sharp faculties were able to realize that dependent arising is the meaning of emptiness, there was no purpose in making the distinctions he had made before because it was possible to uphold the viability of all presentations of phenomena in terms of the basis of refutation of true existence.[43] That is, because of the compatability of emptiness and dependent arising, the Mādhyamikas are able to assert that there does not exist, has never existed, and never will exist a single atom which is truly established, while at the same time being able to make accurate presentations of cyclic existence and nirvana, of all the varieties of phenomena in the universe. The very phenomena that are empty of true existence — the bases with respect to which true existence is refuted — are themselves dependently established and validly existent.[44]

This compatibility of dependent arising and emptiness is difficult to maintain. Tsong-kha-pa notes that among those having the Mahāyāna lineage, there are many who are in little danger of falling to the view of annihilation but who refute a coarse form of true existence and do not refute the subtle form. There are also many, he says, who refute the subtle object of negation but thereby are rendered incapable of maintaining validly established phenomena.[45] There has been a greater proclivity to this latter imbalance among Tibetan scholars as well as in the study of Mādhyamika in the West. Due to misunderstanding a number of statements in the Mādhyamika literature, they draw the conclusion that the Mādhyamikas merely refute the views of others and have no system of their own. Let us examine the statements that they put forth as support for their idea that Mādhyamika has no system. Nāgārjuna's *Refutation of Objections* (*Vigrahavyāvartinī*) says:

> If I had any thesis
> Then I would have that fault.
> Because I have no thesis
> I am only faultless.[46]

He says in his *Sixty Stanzas of Reasoning* (*Yuktiṣaṣṭikā*):

> Those of great nature have
> No position and no dispute.
> How could those with no position
> Have another position?[47]

Āryadeva says in his *Four Hundred* (*Catuḥśataka*):

> It is impossible to blame
> Even after a long time
> Someone who does not have a position that [things]
> Exist, do not exist, or [both] exist and not exist.[48]

Based on such statements, a number of Western interpreters of

Mādhyamika have been led to believe that Mādhyamikas only refute the assertions of others and have no position of their own. T.R.V. Murti writes, "The Mādhyamika is a prāsaṅgika or vaitaṇḍika, a dialectician or free-lance debater. The Mādhyamika *disproves* the opponent's thesis, and does *not* prove any thesis of his own."[49] Conze quotes this statement by Murti when he describes the Mādhyamika dialectic in his *Buddhist Thought in India*.[50]

Similar views are expressed by the earlier generation of Indologists. Surendrenath Dasgupta describes the final Mādhyamika view in his *History of Indian Philosophy*, explaining that:

> the nihilistic doctrine is engaged in destroying the misplaced confidence of the people that things are true. Those who are really wise do not find anything either false or true, for to them clearly they do not exist at all and they do not trouble themselves with the question of truth or falsehood. For him who knows thus there are neither works nor cycles of births (*saṃsāra*) and also he does not trouble himself about the existence or non-existence of any of the appearances.[51]

Thus, for Dasgupta, if phenomena are empty, they are necessarily utterly non-existent and causation becomes impossible.

Louis de la Vallée Poussin, in an article entitled "Nihilism (Buddhist)" in the *Encyclopedia of Religion and Ethics* states that, "there is no doubt that the absolute truth (*paramārthasatya*) of the extreme Buddhist and of the extreme Vedāntist is an unqualified negation of the world of appearance, a negation of existence (*saṁsāra*)."[52] Finally, A.B. Keith describes Nāgārjuna's method in his *Buddhist Philosophy in India and Ceylon*:

> Nāgārjuna denies consistently that he has any thesis of his own, for to uphold one would be wholly erroneous; the truth is silence, which is neither affirmation nor negation, for negation in itself is essentially positive in implying a reality. He confines himself to reducing every positive assertion to absurdity, thus showing that the intellect condemns itself as inadequate just as it finds hopeless antimonies in the world of experience.[53]

This leads Keith to conclude that:

> If we accept the strict doctrine of Nāgārjuna, as interpreted

> by Buddhapālita and Candrakīrti, and accepted by Cāntideva, we must admit that the phenomenal world has not merely no existence in absolute truth, but has no phenomenal existence, difficult as this conception is, and numerous as are the failures of its holders to exactly express it.[54]

Opinions similar to those above were held by contemporaries of Tsong-kha-pa, whose positions he reports in his *Great Exposition of Special Insight* (*lHag mthong chen mo*). Tsong-kha-pa refutes the contention that Mādhyamika has no system of its own. His arguments bear consideration because they speak directly against the positions of Murti, Conze, Dasgupta, La Vallée Poussin, and Keith.

Tsong-kha-pa explains the meaning of the passages cited from Nāgāruna and Āryadeva above. With regard to the passage from the *Refutation of Objections* which says, "Because I have no thesis/I am only faultless," Tsong-kha-pa admits that there are explanations of no position and no thesis such as the stanzas cited, but it is also stated many times that one must present one's assertions. Therefore, it is impossible to prove that the Mādhyamikas have no thesis merely by citing that stanza. He then elucidates the context of Nāgārjuna's statement. A Mādhyamika has said, "Things do not inherently exist" to which a Proponent of True Existence (*bhāvavādin*, *dngos smra ba*) responds, "Thus, if the words of that thesis inherently exist, then it is not correct that all things lack inherent existence. If the words of the thesis do not inherently exist, they are incapable of refuting inherent existence." Thus, the context of the passage from the *Refutation of Objections* about having or not having a thesis is not a dispute about the possession of a thesis in general; it is a debate about whether the words of the thesis, "All things lack inherent existence" inherently exist or not. When Nāgārjuna replies:

> If I had any thesis
> Then I would have that fault.
> Because I have no thesis
> I am only faultless.

what he means, Tsong-kha-pa argues, is that, "If I asserted that the words of such a thesis inherently existed, then I would incur the fault of contradicting the thesis that all things lack inherent existence. However, since I do not assert such, I do not have that fault." Thus, for Tsong-kha-pa, this passage from the *Refutation of Objec-*

tions is not suitable as a proof that Mādhyamikas have no thesis. Nāgārjuna is saying that he has no inherently existent thesis and that for the Mādhyamikas there is a very great difference between non-inherent existence and non-existence.[55] The Mādhyamikas uphold the conventional existence of phenomena while denying their true existence. This distinction was not clear to Keith, for example, when he wrote that the Mādhyamikas contend that the world has no phenomenal existence.

The passage cited above from Nagarjuna's *Sixty Stanzas of Reasoning* also makes use of the term "no position," saying that "Those of great nature have/No position and no dispute." Candrakīrti's commentary to this stanza says:

> When the positions of [a truly existent] self and other do not occur because things do not exist in that way, the afflictions of those [yogis] who see such definitely cease.[56]

Here, the non-existence of things (*bhāva*, *dngos po*) is stated as a reason for not having a position. Tsong-kha-pa identifies the term "thing" as referring to existence by way of the object's own character (*svalakṣaṇa*, *rang mtshan*) or inherent existence (*svabhāva*, *rang bzhin*). If it were taken to mean the ability to perform a function, which is its primary meaning, it would be contradictory to say that through seeing the non-existence of functionality the afflictive emotions (*kleśa*, *nyon mongs*) cease. Therefore, in this passage from the *Sixty Stanzas on Reasoning*, having no position refers to having no position which is an assertion of inherent existence.

That "thing" refers to existence by way of its own character is evident from another passage in Candrakīrti's commentary to the *Sixty Stanzas*, where he says:

> If those who have not penetrated this reality of dependent arising and who thoroughly conceive of the existence of things by way of their own character assert [that] things [exist inherently], then it is only certain that:
>
> Disputation will arise
> From holding the unbearable and unsuitable view
> [Which is the basis] of the arising of desire and hatred.[57]

Here, the superimposition of an existence by way of the object's own character onto things is referred to as asserting things. Therefore, according to Tsong-kha-pa the stanza from the *Sixty Stanzas of Reasoning* is not a source proving that the Mādhyamikas have no position.[58]

In commenting on Āryadeva's statement that:

> It is impossible to blame
> Even after a long time
> Someone who does not have a position that [things]
> Exist, do not exist, or [both] exist and not exist.

Candrakīrti says, "This indicates that it is impossible to refute, even after a long time, a proponent of emptiness."[59] Existence and non-existence thus refer to true existence and utter non-existence. Thus, Āryadeva's statement indicates that the Mādhyamikas, who assert that phenomena are imputedly existent (*prajñaptisat*, *btags yod*) and who refute substantial existence (*dravyasat*, *rdzas yod*) (which means to be established by way of the object's own entity), are not refuted by those who propound that things "exist"; that is, that they are established by way of their own entity. Nor are they refuted by those who propound that things "do not exist," who negate all functionality of things such as forms. From this, Tsong-kha-pa concludes that:

> It is exceedingly clear that [Āryadeva's stanza] is not suitable as a source [proving] that [the Mādhyamikas] have no system of their own; the positions of existence, non-existence, etc. are like the positions of the proponents of the two [extremes of permanence and annihilation].[60]

From the foregoing discussion it is clear that the statements by Nāgārjuna and Āryadeva that they have no position cannot be taken at face value but must be understood in the context of the specific argument being put forth at the point at which those statements occur. When Nāgārjuna says that he has no position, he means, according to Tsong-kha-pa, that he has no inherently existent position. When Āryadeva says that he does not have a position that things exist nor that they do not exist, he means that he does not hold that things inherently exist nor that they do not exist even conventionally. By taking these statements literally, the Western scholars cited above have been led to the conclusion that the Mādhyamikas have no position of their own, that they refute all philosophical views while upholding none. From this point it is a short jump to the charge that the Mādhyamikas are nihilists.

In his *Clear Words*, Candrakīrti answers this charge directly:

> [An opponent] says: "If you posit things as without inherent existence in this way, then you would thereby refute all those statements of the Supramundane Victor (*Bhagavan*)[61] like, 'One will experience the fruition of the actions one performs,' and would deny cause and effect. Therefore, you are the chief of Nihilists."
>
> Answer: "We are not Nihilists; we refute the proponents of the two [extremes] of existence and non-existence and illuminate the path free of those two [extremes], leading to the city of nirvana. We also do not say, 'Actions, agents, effects, and so forth do not exist.' What do we propound? We say, 'These do not inherently exist.' If you think, 'That is fallacious because actions and agents are impossible within non-inherent existence,' there is no [such fault] because activities are unobserved only among things which have inherent existence; activities are observed only among things that lack inherent existence.[62]

He makes the same point in his *Commentary to (Ārydeva's) Four Hundred* (*Catuḥśatakaṭīkā*):

> I do not propound that things do not exist because I propound dependent arising. If you ask, "Are you a proponent of true existence?" I am not because of just being a proponent of dependent arising. If you ask, "What do you propound?", I propound dependent arising. If you ask, "What is the meaning of dependent arising?", it has the meaning of non-inherent existence, that is, it has the meaning of non-inherent production, it has the meaning of the arising of effects which have a nature similar to that of magicians' illusions, mirages, reflections, cities of *gandharvas*, emanations, and dreams, and it has the meaning of emptiness and selflessness.[63]

The root of the confusion of both Candrakīrti's opponent and the modern interpreters cited above lies in a misunderstanding of the meaning of the two extremes. The Mādhyamikas refute one form of existence but uphold the other, refute one form of non-existence but uphold the other. The two forms of existence are that all phenomena ultimately exist and that all phenomena conventionally exist. The two forms of non-existence are that no phenomena ultimately exist and that no phenomena conventionally exist. The Mādhyamikas reject the view that all phenomena ultimately exist and label it the extreme of permanence. They reject the view that no phenomena conventionally exist and label it the extreme of annihilation. They uphold the two remaining views, that all phenomena conventionally exist and no phenomena ultimately exist, the former referring to dependent arising, the latter to emptiness. They further contend that the two are in all ways compatible, that the emptiness of true existence does not contradict but makes possible conventional existence and vice versa. This is what they identify as the middle way free from extremes.[64]

Thus, the Mādhyamikas refute the two extremes of ultimate existence and utter non-existence and assert emptiness and dependent arising. Not understanding that the Mādhyamikas assert the compatibility of emptiness and dependent arising, Edward Conze describes Bhāvaviveka as having "upheld the well-nigh incredible thesis that in Mādhyamika logic valid positive statements can be made."[65] Yet in the Mādhyamika texts, positive assertions are easily found. Nāgārjuna's *Refutation of Objections* says:

> We do not put forth the explanation
> That conventionalities are not asserted.[66]

His *Sixty Stanzas of Reasoning* says:

> Those who assert that dependent phenomena
> Are like [reflections] of moons in water,
> Not real and not unreal,
> Are not captivated by views.[67]

His *Praise of the Supramundane* (*Lokātītastava*) says:

> You [Buddha] taught that
> Agent and actions are conventionalities
> You asserted well
> That they are established as mutually dependent.[68]

Also, Candrakīrti writes in his *Supplement to (Nāgārjuna's Treatise on) the Middle Way* (*Madhyamakāvatāra*),[69] "The wise should consider this position to be faultless and beneficial and should indubitably assert it." He also says:

> Therefore, because dependent imputation is asserted in the same way as dependent arising, as mere conditionality, it does not follow that for our position all conventionalities are annihilated. It is suitable that the opponent assert this as well.[70]

In addition to these statements, there are numerous Mādhyamika texts devoted to instructions and advice on the practice of virtue and the path to enlightenment, such as Nāgārjuna's *Compendium of Sutra* (*Sūtrasamuccaya*), *Precious Garland* (*Ratnāvalī*), and *Friendly Letter* (*Suhṛllekha*), and Śāntideva's *Engaging in the Bodhisattva Deeds* (*Bodhi[sattva] caryāvatāra*).[71]

For Tsong-kha-pa, what sets the Mādhyamika school above all others is its ability to refute the ultimate existence of all phenomena, holding that there is not a single particle in the universe which is ultimately established, while at the same time asserting that conventionally all phenomena are validly established. Nāgārjuna says in his *Treatise on the Middle Way* (XXIV. 14):

> For whom emptiness is possible,
> All is possible;
> For whom emptiness is not possible,
> Nothing is possible.

By upholding the compatability of emptiness and appearance in this way, they abandon the two extremes and abide in the middle.

2 *Svātantrika and Prāsaṅgika*

Nāgārjuna is traditionally credited with retrieving several Perfection of Wisdom Sutras, upon which the Mādhyamika system is based, from the land of the *nāgas*. He wrote numerous treatises, such as the Five Collections of Reasoning,[1] commenting on and explaining the meaning of the Perfection of Wisdom Sutras. For these reasons, he is revered as the founder of Mādhyamika. His works and those of his student, Āryadeva, served as models and foundations for all subsequent Mādhyamika authors, such as Buddhapālita, Bhāvaviveka, Candrakīrti, Śāntarakṣita, Kamalaśīla, Śāntideva, and Atīśa. Nāgārjuna and Āryadeva were therefore labelled "Mādhyamikas of the Model Texts" (*gZhung phyi mo'i dbu ma pa*) by early Tibetan scholars. Later Mādhyamikas who disagreed on how the meaning of Nāgārjuna's writings should be interpreted and took positions distinguishing themselves from each other were labelled "Partisan Mādhyamikas" (*Phyogs 'dzin pa'i dbu ma pa*, literally "Mādhyamikas who hold positions").

When one seeks to discover among the Partisan Mādhyamikas exactly what positions were held and by whom, difficulties are encountered. In his *Great Exposition of Special Insight*, Tsong-kha-pa says, "I will delineate how the system of the great Mādhyamikas follows the master Nāgārjuna." He then adds rhetorically, "Who could explain the minor ones?"[2] He reports that some early Tibetan scholars classified the Indian Mādhyamikas according to their position concerning ultimates. Those who asserted that a composite of emptiness and appearance is an ultimate truth were called Establishers of Illusion through Reasoning (*sgyu ma rigs grub pa*, *māyopamādvayavādin*). Those who held that a mere elimination of superimpositions with respect to appearance is an ultimate truth were called Proponents of Thorough Non-Abiding (*rab tu mi gnas par smra ba*, *apratiṣṭhānavādin*). Tsong-kha-pa concurs with the assessment of the translator Lo-den-shay-rap (*bLo ldan shes rab*), who said in his *Drop of Ambrosia* (*bDud rtsi' thigs pa*) that it is deluded to divide Mādhyamika from the point of view of assertions on the ultimate.[3]

Tsong-kha-pa explains that other early Tibetans classified the Indian Mādhyamikas in terms of their position on the conventional status of external objects. Those who asserted that external objects exist as entities separate from consciousness were labelled Sautrāntika-Mādhyamikas because their assertion accorded with that of the Sautrāntika school on that point. Those who asserted that external objects do not exist in that way were labelled Yogācāra-Mādhyamikas because they accorded with the Yogācārins on that point. This system of classifying the Mādhyamika schools was current during the eighth century for we find that the translator Ye-shay-day (*Ye-shes-sde*, c. 800), who was a student of both Padmasambhava and Śāntarakṣita, explains in his *Difference Between the Views* (*lTa ba khyad par*) that:

> In the Mādhyamika treatises composed by the master, the Superior [Nāgārjuna], and his spiritual son [Āryadeva], the mode of existence or non-existence of external objects is not clarified.[4] After that, the master Bhāvaviveka refuted the system of the Vijñāptikas [Yogācārins] and posited a system of the conventional existence of external objects. Then the master Śāntarakṣita, relying on Yogācāra texts, constructed a different type of Mādhyamika [system] which taught that external objects do not exist conventionally and that the mind lacks inherent existence ultimately. Thus, the Mādhyamikas arose as two types, the former called the Sautrāntika-Mādhyamikas and the latter, the Yogācāra-Mādhyamikas.[5]

Such a classification provides an accurate chronology[6] and accounts for the assertions of Bhāvaviveka and Śāntarakṣita, and their followers, but does not provide a category for Candrakīrti because, although he upheld the conventional existence of external objects, his position on the nature of those objects does not accord with those of the Vaibhāṣikas, Sautrāntikas, or Yogācārins[7] (see pp. 72-73).

It is only with the second dissemination of Buddhism to Tibet (marked by the translations of Rin-chen-sang-bo [*Rin-chen-bzang-po*, 958-1055] and the arrival of Atīśa in 1042) that the division of Mādhyamika which is considered standard today gained prevalence. Tsong-kha-pa reports that at the time of the second dissemination Tibetan scholars coined the terms Prāsaṅgika and Svātantrika, dividing Mādhyamika in terms of how the understanding of emptiness is to be produced in the mind of an opponent. This distinction was based on statements made by Candrakīrti in his *Clear Words* (*Prasannapadā*).[8] It was during this period that Ba-tsap Nyi-ma-drak (*Pa-tshab Nyi-ma-grags*, died 1158) collaborated with the Kashmiri scholar Jayānanda to translate the major works of Candrakīrti including the *Clear Words*, the *Supplement to the Middle Way* (*Madhyamakāvatāra*), and his commentary to Nāgārjuna's *Sixty Stanzas of Reasoning* (*Yuktiṣaṣṭikāvṛtti*).[9]

Thus, it is significant to note that the designations "Svātantrika" and "Prāsaṅgika" did not gain currency in India but in Tibet, and not until the eleventh century, not long before the eclipse of Buddhism in India. Although Bhāvaviveka is credited with founding the Svātantrika school, nowhere in his writings do we find him saying, "I am a Svātantrika." Although Candrakīrti uses the adjective *svatantra* four times in his *Clear Words*,[10] he never accuses Bhāvaviveka of being a "Svātantrika" or defends Buddhapālita as a "Prāsaṅgika."

Furthermore, not only were the names unknown to the principals, the implications of those names seem to have escaped all but one, Candrakīrti. Tsong-kha-pa writes in his *Essence of the Good Explanations* (*Legs bshad snying po*) that although Bhāvaviveka found many faults with Buddhapālita's commentary to Nāgārjuna's *Treatise on the Middle Way*, he did not disagree with him on the selflessness of persons and phenomena.[11] Bhāvaviveka's commentator, Avalokitavrata, also finds no disagreement between Buddhapālita and Bhāvaviveka concerning the conventional and ultimate nature of phenomena. He writes:

> The knowledge that external and internal dependent arisings conventionally exist as mere illusions capable of performing functions and that ultimately they are without entityness[12] is the mode of the perfection of wisdom taught

by the proponents of the middle path — the Superior [Nāgārjuna] and his spiritual son [Āryadeva], Bhāvaviveka, Buddhapālita, and so forth.[13]

Tsong-kha-pa goes on to note that none of the great Svātantrikas — Jñānagarbha, Śāntarakṣita, Kamalaśīla — found any difference between the selflessness of their own system and that of the system of Buddhapālita and Candrakīrti.[14]

Candrakīrti did not assert that there was any difference between himself and Buddhapālita concerning the ultimate and conventional. However he, and he alone among the great Mādhyamikas, distinguishes the system that he shares with Buddhapālita from that of the other Mādhyamikas. He writes in the autocommentary to his *Supplement to the Middle Way (Madhyamakāvatāra)*:

> I implore the wise to ascertain that just as, except for [Nāgārjuna's] *Treatise on the Middle Way*, other treatises do not express this doctrine called "emptiness" without perversion, so other systems do not have anything like the doctrine of emptiness that appears in this system in which we state challenges and responses.[15]

Candrakīrti thus contends that his understanding of the doctrine of emptiness is unique and is not shared by others, such as Bhāvaviveka. Exactly how Candrakīrti and Bhāvaviveka differ on the meaning of emptiness will be considered later (see pp. 148-153). The important conclusion to be drawn here is that the difference between Prāsaṅgika and Svātantrika was by no means evident to the Svātantrika masters Bhāvaviveka, Avalokitavrata, Jñānagarbha, Śāntarakṣita, and Kamalaśīla. This is most surprising in the cases of Avalokitavrata, Jñānagarbha, Śāntarakṣita, and Kamalaśīla in that they postdated Candrakīrti[16] and would have had access to his *Clear Words* and *Supplement to the Middle Way* in which Candrakīrti criticizes what came to be known as the Svātantrika position, at times mentioning Bhāvaviveka by name.[17]

It is noteworthy that the significance of the division of Mādhyamika into Svātantrika and Prāsaṅgika has proved confounding to Western Buddhologists. In the early part of this century, La Vallée Poussin wrote:

> There are two branches of Mādhyamika, but the difference between them has not been studied, and seems to consist in

a mere divergence in the method of demonstration.[18]

The implications of this "divergence in the method of demonstration" will be considered later in this chapter. In 1962 Edward Conze noted:

> We still have no clear idea of Bhāvaviveka's Svātantrika system, which can only be studied in Tibetan translations. ... Likewise we continue to be puzzled by the teachings and affiliations of the Yogācāra-Mādhyamikas who were responsible for the final synthesis of the Mahāyāna in India.[19]

More recently, K. Venkata Ramanan has written in his *Nāgārjuna's Philosophy* that, "Buddhapālita and Bhāvaviveka belong to two different traditions (the Prāsaṅgika and Svātantrika) of the Mādhyamika School, although the difference between them is still far from clear."[20]

If the Indian masters of the Svātantrika school did not perceive themselves as different from Buddhapālita and Candrakīrti, on what grounds did the eleventh century Tibetan scholars make the distinction between Svātantrika and Prāsaṅgika? From their vantage point, what essential differences were evident in the literature between Buddhapālita and Candrakīrti on the one hand and Bhāvaviveka, Śāntarakṣita, et al. on the other that would cause them to perform an *ex post facto* bifurcation of Mādhyamika? Is the distinction between Svātantrika and Prāsaṅgika innately evident from the Indian sources or was it an artificial distinction imposed from hindsight? The most articulate elaboration of the distinction between the two Mādhyamikas derives from Tsong-kha-pa and his Ge-luk followers, the most important of whom for our purposes are the tenet chroniclers Jam-yang-shay-ba and Jang-gya. Let us examine their arguments in an effort to determine the efficacy of the Svātantrika-Prāsaṅgika division.

Jang-gya's ostensibly intimidating definition of Svātantrika provides a suitable starting point. The definition will be dissected and examined piece by piece and then reconstructed in an effort to gain a clear perception of the meaning and implications of the term "Svātantrika":

> Autonomous (*svatantra, rang rgyud*) means that an inferential consciousness (*anumāna, rjes dpag*) realizing the thesis (*sādhya, bsgrub bya*) is generated without taking the lead

> merely from the opponent's assertions, but by his having ascertained the establishment of the modes (*rūpa, tshul*) of the sign (*liṅga, rtags*) with respect to a subject that is established as appearing commonly to non-mistaken valid cognizers (*pramāṇa, tshad ma*) of both parties in the debate through the force of an objective mode of subsistence from the side of the basis of designation. Mādhyamikas who assert the correctness of the necessity for such are Svātantrika-Mādhyamikas.[21]

The *Instructions on Name and Gender* (*Nāmaliṅgānuśāsana*) better known as the *Amarakośa*) by the sixth-century Buddhist lexicographer Amarasiṃha[22] lists *svatantra* (own continuum) and *svairi* (own power) as synonyms.[23] The ninth-century Sanskrit-Tibetan encyclopedia, the *Mahāvyutpatti*, glosses the Sanskrit term *svatantra* with the Tibetan *rang dbang* ("independent" or "own-powered").[24] Jam-yang-shay-ba states that the *tantra* of *svatantra* means "establish" (*grub*) or "prove" (*sgrub*) and concludes that:

> Here, taking it as "establish," *svatantra* (autonomous, own continuum) and *svairi* (own-powered) mean established from its own side, established from the side of its mode of subsistence, and established under its own power.[25]

Therefore, Jam-yang-shay-ba and Jang-gya, following Tsong-kha-pa, explain that the term *svatantra* means own-powered or autonomous. What are the philosophical implications of *svatantra's* meaning autonomous, and do these implications apply to Bhāvaviveka and his followers, that is, in what sense are they "Svātantrikas"?

Jang-gya's definition refers to an "inferential consciousness (*anumāna, rjes dpag*) realizing the thesis (*sādhya, bsgrub bya*)" and to "the modes (*rūpa, tshul*) of the sign (*liṅga, rtags*)," thereby indicating that *svatantra* has a special significance in the context of Buddhist logic. In order to elucidate that significance, it is necessary to digress for the moment to a consideration of proof statements (*sādhanavakya, sgrub ngag*).

Dharmakīrti's *Commentary on (Dignāga's) "Compendium of Valid Cognition"* (*Pramāṇavarttika*) says, "Because there are two objects of comprehension (*prameya, gzhal bya*), there are two valid cognizers (*pramāṇa, tshad ma*)."[26] Buddhists hold that there are two valid types of awareness — valid cognizers — because there are two types of objects to be comprehended, manifest phenomena (*abhimukhī, mngon gyur*) and hidden phenomena (*parokṣa, lkog gyur*), which are known by direct perception (*pratyakṣa, mngon sum*) and inference (*anumāna, rje dpag*) respectively.

The definition of a hidden phenomenon is a phenomenon that the short-sighted must necessarily realize initially through relying on a sign.[27] A short-sighted person (literally, "one who looks nearby") is a common being (*pṛthagjana, so so skye bo*), a person who has not achieved the path of seeing (*darśanamārga, mthong lam*). A hidden phenomenon is one which cannot be perceived directly by persons who are not Superiors (*ārya, 'phags pa*), but which must be known through the use of a sign or reason. To cite a favorite example of the Buddhist logicians, although a person looking at a smoky mountain pass from a distance cannot see fire, the presence of fire there can be inferred from the presence of the sign, smoke, which is the effect of fire. Many of the most important phenomena in Buddhist philosophy fall into the category of hidden phenomena, such as subtle impermanence, the existence of former and later lifetimes, liberation from cyclic existence, the existence of a Buddha's omniscient consciousness, and emptiness. The definition states that such phenomena must *initially* be realized in dependence on a sign. This refers to the important tenet that phenomena which are ordinarily inaccessible to direct perception can eventually be directly perceived by gradually transforming the imagistic perception by thought into yogic direct perception (*yogipratyakṣa, rnal 'byor mngon sum*).[28] It is this yogic direct perception which, in the Mādhyamika school, directly realizes emptiness, a hidden phenomenon, and destroys the seeds for rebirth.

A manifest phenomenon is a phenomenon that the short-sighted do not necessarily realize through relying on a sign.[29] Objects ordinarily within the purview of sense perception, such as colors, shapes, sounds, odors, tastes, and objects of touch, are manifest phenomena. Such phenomena may be realized by direct perception without resorting to inference. Direct perception is defined by the non-Prāsaṅgika schools as a non-mistaken knower which is free from conceptuality.[30] Thought consciousnesses are, therefore, necessarily not direct perceivers because they are conceptual. Thought is also eliminated by the qualification "non-mistaken" in that thought is mistaken with respect to its appearing object (**pratibhāsaviṣaya, snang yul*), mistaking the image of the object that appears to it — a meaning-generality (*arthasāmānya, don spyi*) — for the object which it is comprehending (*prameya, gzhal bya*). Direct perception, on the other hand, perceives the object directly, without the medium of a generic image.

The other form of valid cognition, inference, is defined as a determinative knower which, depending on its basis, a correct sign, is incontrovertible with regard to its object of comprehension, a hidden phenomenon.[31] A determinative knower is one which explicitly identifies its object. It is incontrovertible in that it comprehends an object with respect to which superimpositions or misconceptions have been removed.[32]

A correct sign (*samyakliṅga, rtags yang dag*) is a correct reason (*samyaknimitta, rgyu mtshan yang dag*) or a correct proof (*samyaksādhana, sgrub byed yang dag*) and is the basis upon which an inferential valid cognizer is created. A sign is one component of a syllogism (*prayoga, sbyor ba*), the other being the probandum (*sādhya, bsgrub bya*) or that which one is seeking to prove. The probandum in turn is composed of two parts, the subject (*dharmin, chos can*) about which something is sought to be known (also known as the basis of debate) and the predicate of the probandum (*sādhyadharma, bsgrub bya'i chos*). An example of a syllogism is, "The subject, sound, is impermanent, because of being a product." The probandum, also referred to as the thesis (*pratijñā, dam bca'*) or position (*pakṣa, phyogs*), is that sound is an impermanent phenomenon. Sound is the subject and impermanent phenomenon is the predicate of the probandum. Product is the sign or reason.

In order for the syllogism to be correct, thereby yielding an inferential valid cognizer, the sign must be correct. A correct sign in a particular proof must be the three modes (*trirūpa, tshul gsum*) of that proof, in fact, a correct sign is defined as "that which is the three modes."[33] The three modes are three relationships of the sign to other elements of the syllogism.

The first mode is the property of the subject (*pakṣadharma, phyogs chos*), which refers to the presence of the reason in the subject; in order to be a correct reason, that reason must be a property of the subject. In the Sanskrit term *pakṣadharma*, *pakṣa* refers only to the subject and not to the entire probandum. This is one of the four meanings of *pakṣa* according to Dharmakīrti.[34] In the syllogism, "The subject, sound, is impermanent because of being a product," the sign is a property of the subject because product is a property of sound, that is, sound is a product.

The second of the three modes is the forward pervasion (*anvayavyāpti*, *rjes khyab*) which is defined as that ascertained by valid cognition as existing only in the similar class in accordance with the mode of statement.[35] The similar class (*sapakṣa*, *mthun phyogs*) is that class of phenomena of which the sign must be a member in order for the sign to be correct. In the proof that sound is impermanent because of being a product, all phenomena that are impermanent constitute the similar class. In order for product to be a correct sign, it must be ascertained as existent in only the similar class. To exist *only* in the similar class means that the sign must be pervaded by the predicate, that is, it must be coextensive with the similar class or a subclass of the similar class; whatever is the sign A must necessarily be the predicate B. Product exists in the similar class of impermanent phenomena because product and impermanent phenomenon are synonyms (*ekārtha*, *don gcig*).[36] "Object of knowledge", (*jñeya*, *shes bya*) would not serve as a correct sign in the proof that sound is impermanent because, although "object of knowledge" exists in the similar class of impermanent phenomena, it does not exist *only* in the similar class; there are objects of knowledge, such as nirvana, which are not impermanent.

The third of the three modes is the counterpervasion (*vyatireka-vyāpti*, *ldog khyab*) which is that ascertained as only non-existent in the dissimilar class in accordance with the mode of statement.[37] The dissimilar class (*vipakṣa*, *mi mthun phyogs*) is that class of which the negative of the sign must be a member in order for the sign to be correct. In other words, it is that class of which the sign must not be a member. That the sign is only non-existent in the dissimilar class means that the negative of the predicate is pervaded by the negative of the sign, that is, whatever is not the predicate A must necessarily not be the sign B. In the proof that sound is impermanent because of being a product, the dissimilar class is the not impermanent, or permanent phenomena. Since product and impermanent phenomenon are synonyms, product is only non-existent in the dissimilar class of permanent phenomena, and whatever is a permanent phenomenon is necessarily a non-product.[38]

Based on a syllogism of which the sign has the three modes, an incontrovertible inferential valid cognizer realizing the thesis of that syllogism is produced. Syllogisms may be used to generate an inferential consciousness realizing the thesis in oneself or in others. In distinguishing Svātantrika from Prāsaṅgika, the use of the syllogism in generating a correctly inferring consciousness in an opponent is of primary importance. For example, the syllogism, "The subject, sound, is impermanent because of being a product," might be stated to an opponent who believes that sound is permanent. According to the logical system of Dignāga and Dharmakīrti, the stater of the syllogism must accept the three modes of the sign.[39]

This is not the case with the other form of logical statement used by Buddhists in debate, the consequence (*prāsaṅga, thal 'gyur*). A consequence, like a syllogism, is used to bring about an inferential understanding in the opponent in a debate, but unlike the syllogism, it does so by using the opponent's own assertions against him so that the opponent is unable to respond. A correct consequence is stated in such a way that the opponent cannot give a factually concordant answer without contradicting his own assertions.[40] For example, to an opponent who holds that a sound is permanent, that sound is also a product, and that whatever is a product is impermanent, the following consequence might be stated, "It follows that the subject, sound, is not a product, because of being permanent." In this case, the Buddhist stating the consequence does not accept all three modes of the sign; he accepts the forward pervasion and the counterpervasion, that whatever is permanent is necessarily a non-product and that whatever is not a non-product is necessarily not permanent, but he does not accept the property of the subject, that sound is permanent. The opponent, on the other hand, does accept the three modes. He accepts that the sign is a property of the subject — that sound is permanent — as well as the forward and counterpervasions. He is thus unable to make any response to the Buddhist. He cannot respond that the reason is not established (*asiddha, ma sgrub pa*) as a property of the subject because he accepts that it is. He cannot respond that there is no pervasion because he accepts that whatever is permanent is necessarily not a product. He cannot even accept the thesis that sound is not a product because that contradicts his own assertions. He is left logically speechless. Such a consequence is called a consequence implying a proof, which is defined as a consequential statement capable of implying the three modes.[41]

The three modes implied by a consequence implying a proof are those of the syllogism of the correct position. That is, the consequence, "It follows that the subject, sound, is not a product, because of being permanent," stated to an opponent who believes that sound is a product, sound is permanent, and whatever is a product is impermanent, should cause the person to reassess his position so that he may escape the unwanted consequence that sound is not a product. He thus arrives at the implied proof, "The subject, sound, is impermanent, because of being a product," the three modes of which were implied by the consequence.

From this perspective, T.R.V. Murti is clearly wrong when he says in *The Central Philosophy of Buddhism:*

> *Prasaṅga* is not to be understood as an apagogic proof in which we *prove* an assertion *indirectly* by disproving the opposite. *Prasaṅga* is disproof simply, without the least intent to prove any thesis.[42]

Murti here seems to be confusing the Mādhyamikas' mode of proof with what they are proving. When a Mādhyamika states the consequence, "It follows that the subject, a pot, is not a dependent arising because of being truly existent," to a Proponent of True Existence (**bhāvavādin, dngos smra ba*), the Mādhyamika is implying that and wishes the opponent to understand that, "The subject, a pot, does not truly exist because of being a dependent arising." The Mādhyamika thus employs consequences with the full intention of proving a thesis. The thesis that he wishes to prove in this case is that a pot does not truly exist. The non-true existence or emptiness of true existence of the pot is a non-affirming negative (*prasajyaprati ṣedha, med 'gag*), implying no positive phenomenon in its place. The emptiness of the pot is the mere vacuity of the true existence of the pot.[43] Thus, in proofs of emptiness, the Mādhyamika uses consequences to imply a syllogism, but the thesis of that syllogism is a non-affirming negative and implies nothing positive about the subject.

In a consequence that implies a proof, the reason must be accepted by the opponent but must not be validly established; the opponent accepts that sound is permanent, but that is not correct. The opposite of the sign of the consequence will become the predicate of the implied proof. The forward pervasion of the consequence must be validly established. It becomes the counterpervasion of the implied proof. The thesis of the consequence must be refutable by valid cognition; the opposite of the predicate of the consequence becomes the reason of the implied proof, thereby establishing the property of the subject of the syllogism.[44]

Both Svātantrikas and Prāsaṅgikas use syllogisms and consequences. Consequences are used by both schools to break down the opponent's adherence to this wrong view. However, a disagreement that rises out of the commentaries to Nāgārjuna's *Treatise on the Middle Way* is Bhāvaviveka's insistence on the ultimate necessity of explicitly stating the implied syllogism. Candrakīrti objects, saying that the statement of the consequence is sufficient and that the further statement of the syllogism is redundant for an intelligent opponent; the consequence alone is capable of producing an understanding of the implied syllogism.[45]

Thus, Prāsaṅgikas (Consequentialists) are so-called because they assert that an inferential consciousness that understands non-true existence is produced through using a sign the three modes of which are renowned to the opponent.[46] The Svātantrikas hold that this alone is not enough, that the implied syllogism, the three modes of which are accepted by the Svātantrika himself, must eventually be stated to the opponent. This is one difference between Svātantrika and Prāsaṅgika. However, this difference is not merely formal, it is not confined merely to techniques of logical disputation. If this were the case, the Svātantrikas should be called the *Prāyogikas*, the Syllogists. Instead, they are called Svātantrikas because they use *autonomous* syllogisms (*svatantraprayoga, rang rgyud kyi sbyor ba*). The meaning of autonomous in this context and its implications become evident in examining the meaning of valid cognition (*pramāṇa, tshad ma*) in Svātantrika and Prāsaṅgika.

For the Svātantrikas, a direct perceiver is a consciousness that is free from conceptualization and is non-mistaken. Non-mistaken refers to apprehending the object's own character just as it is. Since all five sense direct perceivers apprehend this "own-character" (*svalakṣaṇa, rang mtshan*), their objects' own character is the object comprehended by direct perceivers. Therefore, the Svātantrikas assert that sense direct perceivers are valid cognizers in terms of the existence by way of the own character of their respective objects.[47]

Candrakīrti, however, argues that establishment by way of the object's own character or by way of the object's own entity does not exist even conventionally; therefore, he does not hold, as do the Svātantrikas, that sense consciousnesses are valid cognizers in terms of their perception of own-character. He does not deny that sense consciousnesses perceive objects as existing by way of their own character, but since he holds that that own-character does not exist, he rejects the Svātantrika assertion that the sense consciousnesses are non-mistaken. The Prāsaṅgikas assert that things exist one way but appear in another; specifically, the objects of the sense consciousnesses are not established by way of their own character but appear to be so established. Therefore, the sense consciousnesses cannot be valid with respect to the own-character that they perceive; they are deceived by the false appearance of the inherent existence of the five sense objects.[48]

The Svātantrikas respond that if forms, sounds, and so forth lacked natures that were established by way of their own character, they would lack any capability to perform functions. Therefore, if direct perceivers are not valid in terms of the own-character of the five sense objects, it is impossible for sense direct perceivers to be valid cognizers at all; if these consciousnesses are valid with respect to the five objects, they must be valid in terms of the own-character of the five objects.[49]

For Candrakīrti, if phenomena were established by way of their own character or their own entity, they would be truly established (*satyasiddha, bden par grub pa*). In that case, objects would exist as they appear, and consciousnesses which posit those objects would have to perceive correctly that true existence or existence by way of the object's own character in order to be valid cognizers. However, since the objects are deceptive, appearing one way and existing another, the valid cognizer that posits them need not be valid in terms of own-character. Candrakīrti refutes that sense direct perceivers are valid cognizers with respect to own-character, but in doing so he does not deny that conventional consciousnesses can be valid cognizers in general.[50]

Here, the difference between the Svātantrikas and Prāsaṅgikas rests on two important points: what they understand "non-mistaken" to mean when they define sense direct perceivers as non-mistaken and, secondly, their understanding of the conventional status of phenomena. For the Svātantrikas, a sense consciousness is non-mistaken if it is free from four superficial causes of error:

1 a cause of error existing in the object (*viṣaya, yul*), such as seeing a whirling firebrand as a circle of fire,
2 a cause of error existing in the basis (*āśraya, gzhi*), such as an eye consciousness that perceives a double moon,
3 a cause of error existing in the abode (*sthāna, gnas*), such as seeing

trees move when passing them in a boat, and

4 a cause of error existing in the immediately preceding condition (*samanantarapratyaya, de ma thag rkyen*), such as seeing red due to being angry.[51]

According to the Svātantrikas, if these four superficial causes of error are absent, a sense consciousness perceives the object as it exists. For the Prāsaṅgikas, all sense consciousnesses except those of a Buddha are mistaken because they perceive objects as existing by way of their own character. However, in order not to contradict the world, they uphold the existence of sense direct perceivers which are conventionally non-mistaken. A sense consciousness, due to being affected by ignorance, is mistaken in that objects that do not inherently exist appear to it to inherently exist. However, if that sense consciousness is not polluted by some external or other internal cause of error, it is non-mistaken conventionally.[52] Such a sense direct perceiver is a valid cognizer for the Prāsaṅgikas because, although it is mistaken about the inherent existence of the object, it is valid in terms of the mere existence of the object.

The fundamental difference between the Svātantrikas and Prāsaṅgikas, however, and the reason why they differ on the meaning of valid cognition, is that the Svātantrikas assert that phenomena are established by way of their own character conventionally whereas the Prāsaṅgikas negate the existence of own-character even conventionally. Existence by way of the object's own character is upheld by the Svātantrikas and rejected by the Prāsaṅgikas. This distinction was not made by any of the Indian Svātantrika masters, and it is not accepted by the Sa-gya (*Sa-skya*) order of Tibetan Buddhism.[53] The distinction is made by Tsong-kha-pa and his followers based on careful scrutiny of the writings of Bhāvaviveka, Avalokitavrata, Jñānagarbha, Śāntarakṣita, Kamalaśīla, and Candrakīrti. What evidence does Tsong-kha-pa present to prove that the Svātantrikas assert own-character? How do we know that Bhāvaviveka believed that phenomena inherently exist conventionally?

Tsong-kha-pa says in his *Essence of the Good Explanations:*

> There are many explanations in the Prāsaṅgika texts regarding the conventional existence of its [i.e., the object's own] entityness, its nature, its own character and so forth and there are many [explanations that things] are not established by way of their own entityness, not produced by way of

> their own entityness, not substantially established, and so forth in the texts of this master [Bhāvaviveka]. Thus, it seems difficult to distinguish [Prāsaṅgika and Svātantrika]. However, this explanation of the meaning of the existence and non-existence of the entityness set forth in the *Sutra Unravelling the Thought* (*Saṃdhinirmocana*) is the clearest source [proving that] this master [Bhāvaviveka] asserts that things are established by way of their own character conventionally.[54]

The Perfection of Wisdom Sutras say, "This and that phenomena, from forms to omniscient consciousnesses, lack entityness."[55] The *Sutra Unravelling the Thought* explains this lack of entityness in terms of the three natures (*trisvabhāva, rang bzhin gsum*): the imaginary (*parikalpita, kun btags*), the dependent (*paratantra, gzhan dbang*), and the consummate (*pariniṣpanna, yongs grub*). Imaginaries are said to lack entityness in terms of character, the dependent lack entityness in terms of production, and the consummate are ultimate and lack entityness.

The *Sutra Unravelling the Thought* says, "Since imaginaries do not abide by way of their own character, they lack entityness of character."[56] In the twenty-fifth chapter of his *Lamp for (Nāgārjuna's) "Wisdom"* (*Prajñāpradīpa*), Bhāvaviveka says:

> If you [Yogācārins] say that the entityness of imaginaries, which are mental expressions and verbal expressions, does not exist, then you are deprecating things because of deprecating mental expressions and verbal expressions.[57]

In commenting on this, Avalokitavrata says:

> This [statement by Bhāvaviveka] indicates that, with respect to the Yogācārin statement that imaginary natures lack entityness because of lacking entityness of character, it is unsuitable if they say that the entityness of "form" and specifically the entityness of mental expressions — thought consciousnesses — and verbal imputations — verbal expressions — lack entityness due to lacking an entityness of character because it is a deprecation of things that are conventionally dependent.[58]

The Yogācārins assert that because imaginaries, the imputation of names and attributes, do not have an entity that is established by way of its own character, they lack an entityness of character. Bhāvaviveka refutes this. He takes the category of imaginary phenomena to apply to both imputations and imputers, and regarding imputers, he says that if the Yogācārins assert that names, which are sounds, and thought consciousnesses, which impute entities and qualities, lack an entityness that does not exist by way of its own character conventionally, they are denying dependent phenomena. Therefore, Tsong-kha-pa concludes that it is clear that Bhāvaviveka asserts that dependent phenomena, that is, impermanent phenomena, are entities which are established by way of their own character.[59] Bhāvaviveka apparently upholds this conventional nature but refutes that phenomena exist by way of their character ultimately because he says in his *Lamp for (Nāgārjuna's) "Wisdom"*, "If [the Yogācārins] are refuting things ultimately, they are proponents who follow Mādhyamika."[60]

By including imputers — terms and thought consciousnesses — in the category of the imaginary and saying that if the Yogācārins are holding that these lack an entityness of character, they are denying dependent phenomena, such as terms and thought consciousnesses, Bhāvaviveka implies that terms and thought consciousnesses and, by extension, all impermanent phenomena are established by way of their own character. This seems clear. Whether Bhāvaviveka is correct is suggesting that the Yogācārins classify imputers in the class of imaginaries is another question.

Although Bhāvaviveka rejects the Yogācārin interpretation of the three natures, he does not dismiss the three natures. For him, the factor of true existence that is falsely imputed to phenomena is an imaginary nature because it is superimposed on phenomena and does not accord with their mode of being. In this sense, the imaginary — true existence which is utterly non-existent — can be said to lack entityness of character in Bhāvaviveka's system. Dependent arisings are dependent phenomena and lack entityness of production because they are produced and arise in dependence on another; they ultimately lack inherently existent or own-powered production. Emptinesses of true existence are consummate natures for Bhāvaviveka. Emptiness is an ultimate and a lack of entityness because it is the object of the ultimate consciousness and because it is the absence of the entity of true existence.[61]

Returning to the question of what constitutes valid cognition for

Bhāvaviveka and the implications of his position for the differentiation of Svātantrika and Prāsaṅgika, it is important to scrutinize his understanding of the composition and status of sense objects. In the fifth chapter of the *Blaze of Reasoning* (*Tarkajvālā*), Bhāvaviveka presents his position on the nature of sense objects in response to a Yogācārin attack on those who assert external objects.

According to Bhāvaviveka, the Yogācārin argument is as follows. Individual minute particle (*paramāṇu, rdul phra rab*) of form are not the objects of sense consciousnesses because they are too subtle to be perceived by them. Furthermore, an aggregation (*saṃghāta, 'dus pa*) of minute particles is not the object of a sense consciousness because a mere aggregation, like a double moon, is not a substantial existent (*dravyasat, rdzas yod*). If individual particles are not sense objects and aggregations of many particles are not sense objects, sense perception of external objects composed of minute particles is impossible. Therefore, the Yogācārins conclude that there are no external objects.[62]

Bhāvaviveka responds that the Yogācārins' argument that an individual minute particle is not a sense object is irrelevant because he also asserts that; the Yogācārins are needlessly proving what is already established. To the Yogācārin contention that a composite (*saṃcita, bsags pa*) of minute particles of the same type is not the observed-object-condition (*alambanapratyaya, dmigs rkyen*) producing a sense consciousness because of not being substantially existent, Bhāvaviveka responds that the reason is not established; he disagrees with the Yogācārins, asserting that such a composite is substantially existent. He argues that the entities of the minute particles of one type that aggregate as the entity of the object are connected to each other such that each minute particle contributes to the entity of the object. In that sense, each of the minute particles acts as a part of the entity of the sense object so that an awareness having the aspect of the appearance of an aggregation of subtle particles is produced.[63]

The Yogācārins agree that minute particles are substantially established but hold that they are too subtle to serve as sense objects. However, they also assert that a minute particle is an aggregation of the eight substances: earth, water, fire, wind, form, odor, taste, and tangibility. Bhāvaviveka argues that since it is accepted by the Yogācārins that a minute particle is itself an aggregation while being substantially established, it should be equally true that aggregations such as pots are substantially established.[64]

Tsong-kha-pa concludes that since Bhāvaviveka asserts that each particle in a composite of particles serves as a cause of a sense consciousness and that each of the particles is substantially existent and seems to assert that each particle is final (that is, most subtle), Bhāvaviveka asserts that partless particles are observed-object-conditions (*ālambana-pratyaya*, *dmigs rkyen*) of sense consciousnesses. Bhāvaviveka holds that objects composed of minute particles are established by way of their own character and substantially established and that the sense consciousnesses which perceive those objects are valid cognizers. Therefore, he asserts that a sense consciousness which is not affected by one of the internal or external causes of error is non-mistaken because it perceives an object which is objectively established as a composite of particles.[65] Bhāvaviveka's position on this point accords with that of the Sautrāntikas, except for the fact that the Sautrāntikas assert that sense objects ultimately exist whereas, for Bhāvaviveka, they conventionally exist. This general agreement with the Sautrāntikas on the nature of the observed-object-condition is the basis for calling Bhāvaviveka's branch of Svātantrika the Sautrāntika-Svātantrika-Mādhyamika.[66]

It is important here to distinguish this position from that of Candrakīrti. Bhāvaviveka and Candrakīrti concur in their rejection of the Yogācārins, refutation of external objects. But despite the fact that they agree that external objects exist, they do not agree on the conventional mode of being of those objects. Bhāvaviveka holds that at the conclusion of searching for the object designated among its parts, one finds something which is objectively established.[67]

Candrakīrti asserts that because objects appear falsely to sense consciousnesses, when the object designated is searched for with analysis, it is not found. Therefore, he asserts that minute particles are mere appearances to the awareness designating them and that the objects of sense consciousnesses are imputedly existent phenomena which do not exist from the side of the object.[68] Apparently referring to Bhāvaviveka, Candrakīrti says in his *Supplement to the Middle Way:*

> Some [Mādhyamikas] propound that that which the Sautrāntika system propounds ultimately, the Mādhyamikas assert conventionally. They propound [this] due to completely misunderstanding the suchness [taught] in the *Treatise on the Middle Way.*[69]

Again, in apparent reference to Bhāvaviveka, he says in his *Commentary to (Āryadeva's) "Four Hundred"* (*Catuḥśatakaṭīkā*), "Those of our own school who, like the Vaiśeṣikas, assert that subtle particles are substantially [existent] are not correct."[70]

Thus far, we have examined Tsong-kha-pa's evidence for his assertion that Bhāvaviveka believes that phenomena are established by way of their own character conventionally. There are other statements in Bhāvaviveka's writings that support this claim, and these will be considered in the next chapter in the discussion of the nature of the person and the selflessness of the person. It is necessary at this point to examine the implications of Bhāvaviveka's understanding of the conventional status of objects and the valid cognizers which perceive them in the context of the syllogism. If Bhāvaviveka asserts that phenomena are established by way of their own character (*svalakṣaṇa, rang mtshan, rang gi mtshan nyid*), by way of their own continuum (*svatantra, rang rgyud*), what is the significance of an autonomous syllogism (*svatantraprayoga, rang rgyud kyi sbyor ba*), and how does it differ from a consequence?

That Bhāvaviveka supports the use of autonomous syllogisms is evident to Tsong-kha-pa, at least in part, from a statement Bhāvaviveka makes in his *Lamp for (Nāgārjuna's) "Wisdom"*:

> The thirteenth chapter was composed for the purpose of setting forth the lack of entityness of conditioned phenomena in terms of another aspect, through the force of answers to refutations [by opponents] and own-powered inferences.[71]

Avalokitavrata's commentary says:

> Here, regarding that, the purpose of the chapter is to indicate that conditioned phenomena are just without entityness [through] giving answers to the refutations by opponents and [through] flawless own-powered inferences.[72]

Here, Bhāvaviveka explains that the thirteenth chapter of Nāgārjuna's *Treatise on the Middle Way* teaches emptiness by answering the refutations of opponents and by using autonomous or own-powered inferences. Inference in this context refers not to the consciousness but to the proof statement, a syllogism, intended to produce in the opponent a consciousness inferring the thesis. The fact that Bhāvaviveka refers to such inferences as "own-powered" may indicate that such proof statements are not merely stated in terms of the opponent's position but that they have an autonomous status which is accepted by both parties. This interpretation of the term "own-powered" is strongly supported by two statements from Jñānagarbha's *Differentiation of the Two Truths* (*Satyadvayavibhaṅga*), "Just as what is seen by cowherds and above abides as conventional truths ... " and "No one has any quarrel concerning the factor that appears to the consciousnesses of the two parties [in a debate]."[73] According to Jam-yang-shay-ba's annotator, Nga-wang-bel-den (*Ngag-dbang-dpal-ldan*), the first passage is the clearest source proving that the Svātantrikas assert that phenomena are established from their own side because it says that things exist conventionally in accordance with how they are seen by cowherds and above (those of greater intelligence), and it is undeniable that whatever object appears to ordinary, common beings such as cowherds appears to be established by way of its own character, by way of its own mode of subsistence.[74] It is important to note that Nga-wang-bel-den sees no reason to prove that objects appear to be established by way of their own character; it is something everyone would agree on. The disagreement arises from the fact that the Svātantrikas hold that this appearance is correct, that is, the inherent existence that appears to cowherds conventionally exists, and the Prāsaṅgikas hold that it is false — nothing inherently exists even conventionally.

In the context of debate, this problem manifests itself in the question of a commonly appearing subject (*chos can mthun snang*). A commonly appearing subject refers to a subject that is established within appearing commonly to both parties by a valid cognizer which is non-mistaken with respect to the subject's being established by way of its own character. To be established as commonly appearing means that the subject is established for the challenger by the kind of valid cognizer by which that subject is established for the opponent.[75] That is, the Svātantrikas assert that phenomena are established by way of their own character conventionally; therefore, this type of existence pertains to the components of a syllogism and their relationships, the three modes, as well. Thus, the subject, predicate, and reason exist by way of their own character. The presence of the reason in the subject and the presence of the reason in only the similar class of the predicate exist by way of their own character. Since the Svātantrikas hold that non-conceptual sense consciousnesses which are not defective due to not being polluted by a cause of error are non-mistaken, the objects with respect to which such subjects are non-mistaken must be established by way of their own character because they appear to be.[76] That is, since phenomena appear to be established by way of their own character and also exist that way, according to the Svātantrikas, consciousnesses which correctly perceive that own-character are valid cognizers. Thus, when a phenomena, such as a form, is posited as the subject of a debate, that form appears to exist by way of its own character to the valid cognizers of both parties and they assent to that appearance; it appears commonly.[77]

Therefore, an autonomous syllogism is a syllogism which generates an inference realizing the probandum, without taking the lead from the opponent's assertions, after having ascertained the subject and three modes of the sign with a valid cognizer which is non-mistaken with respect to their existence by way of their own character. Not taking the lead from the assertions of the opponent means that it is not sufficient that the subject and three modes be established by a valid cognizer that is renowned to the opponent alone. Once one uses autonomous syllogisms, one is admitting that the subject appears in the same way to both parties.[78] Jñānagarbha says, "No one has any quarrel concerning the factor which appears to the consciousnesses of the two parties."

There are other statements that can be identified that corroborate the Ge-luk position that the Svātantrikas assert that phenomena exist in the way that they appear, as established by way of their own character. Jñānagarbha says in the autocommentary to his *Differentiation of the Two Truths:* "Real production and so forth do not appear when a thing appears."[79] In other words, when something appears to a sense consciousness, its ultimate production, which is conceived by ignorance, does not appear to the sense consciousness. He says in the root text:

> If you assert that [things]
> As they appear are not [analyzed with] reasoning,
> We agree with that.
> If they were [analyzed with] reasoning, everything would be disturbed.[80]
>
> Because of being entities [which exist] as they appear,
> This [factor] is not analyzed.
> If they were analyzed,

Since they would be other, that would be damaged [by direct perception].[81]

Nga-wang-bel-den glosses these two stanzas as follows:

If the Proponents of True Existence assert that phenomena exist as they appear to an awareness which is not damaged by another valid cognizer and assert that phenomena are not investigated by a reasoning consciousness which analyzes the ultimate, then Jñānagarbha agrees with their assertions. If phenomena as they appear to sense consciousnesses were analyzed with ultimate analysis, all presentations of conventionalities would be confused. Because phenomena are established as they appear to non-defective awareness, ultimate analysis is not applied to this existence by way of the object's own character. If they were investigated with ultimate analysis, they would become other than they are, that is, non-existent. Therefore, that non-existence would be contradicted by direct perception.[82]

Jñānagarbha's position is that ultimate existence is to be analyzed and refuted by reasoning, but existence by way of the object's own character — the way that objects appear to non-defective awarenesses — is not to be analyzed. If it were the object of analysis, since it is a central tenet of Mādhyamika that the object of analysis is not found by the reasoning consciousness investigating the ultimate, the conventional status of phenomena would be negated such that presentations of the world would be impossible. Such things as cause and effect could not be posited for him if objects did not exist in the way that they appear. Such an appearance is certified by direct perception which precludes the possibility of its being scrutinized by ultimate analysis. Thus, for Jñānagarbha, objects must exist in the way that they appear; otherwise, they would not exist at all. He cannot conceive of the possibility of positing conventionalities within the emptiness of inherent existence.

Sāntarakṣita also seems to agree that the unanalyzed perceptions of non-defective awareness exist as they appear when he writes in his *Ornament for the Middle Way*, "From the context of children up to omniscient wisdom, I do not refute the pleasant nature of a single unanalyzed experience."[83]

Thus, although the Svātantrikas assert that phenomena are not truly established (*satyasiddha, bden par grub pa*), ultimately established (*paramārthasiddha, don dam par grub pa*), or established in reality (*samyaksiddha, yang dag par grub pa*), they uphold that phenomena are established by way of their own character (*svalakṣaṇasiddha, rang gi mtshan nyid kyis grub pa*), from their own side (*svarūpasiddha, rang ngos nas grub pa*), and are inherently established (*svabhāvasiddha, rang bzhin gyis grub pa*). For the Prāsaṅgikas, true existence, ultimate existence, existence in reality, existence by way of its own character, existence from the object's own side, and inherent existence are synonyms and are equally utterly non-existent.[84] Therefore, a consciousness that establishes the subject and the three modes of the sign in terms of their existence by way of their own character is not a valid cognizer, it is a wrong consciousness (*viparyayajñāna, log shes*), according to Prāsaṅgika. Therefore, Prāsaṅgikas, who are seeking to prove that phenomena do not exist by way of their own character, reject the use of autonomous syllogisms because an autonomous syllogism requires a commonly appearing subject. Acceptance of a commonly appearing subject implies consent to the appearance of phenomena as being established by way of their own character. The Prāsaṅgikas reject such establishment and, therefore, in the light of their tenets, it is impossible for the subject of the debate to appear in the same way to a Prāsaṅgika and non-Prāsaṅgika.[85] This appears to be Nāgārjuna's point when he says in his *Refutation of Objections* (*Vigrahavyāvartinī*, 30):

> If something were observed,
> Such as an object of direct perception,
> It would be proven or disproven.
> Because it does not exist, I am blameless.[86]

If an object of comprehension which was inherently established and established by way of its own entity were an object observed by a valid cognizer such as a direct perceiver, then it would be suitable that the object observed by such a valid cognizer be either proven or refuted in the opponent's system. However, since in Nāgārjuna's system, such an object of comprehension does not exist even conventionally, Nāgārjuna cannot be blamed for not having an inherently existent thesis.[87] Thus, this passage seems to indicate that inherently existent objects of observation and observers do not exist; it is not suggesting that dependently arisen valid cognizers and objects of comprehension do not exist.[88]

Does this mean that the Prāsaṅgikas are unable to prove the emptiness of non-inherent existence? No, although they are prohibited from using autonomous syllogisms, they use consequences or other-approved syllogisms which do not entail any of the dangers of the autonomous syllogism. If autonomous syllogisms are not asserted, it is sufficient that the subject and three modes be established by a "valid cognizer" of a non-Prāsaṅgika opponent; these do not have to be established as inherently existent for the Prāsaṅgika, in fact, they cannot be.[89]

For the Svātantrikas, when two parties are debating about an attribute of an object such as permanence or true existence, the substratum of that attribute — the subject of the debate — must be established as commonly appearing, it must be demonstrable that the object upon which the attribute is based is objectively established; without an objectively established subject, it is impossible to prove the modes of the sign because the Svātantrikas hold that an attribute which lacks an inherently existent substratum is infeasible. This is the meaning of a commonly appearing subject. For the Prāsaṅgikas, the existence of a subject which is demonstrably established from its own side implies that it is established by way of its own entity which means that it would be ultimately established. Thus, for the Prāsaṅgikas, it is incorrect to assert the existence of a common appearance to both parties when proving qualities in terms of a substratum that exists by way of its own entity.[90]

For the Prāsaṅgika, since existence by way of the object's own entity does not exist, such a commonly appearing subject does not exist. As long as the opponent has not generated the Prāsaṅgika view in his continuum, he is not able to differentiate existence by way of the object's own entity and mere existence. He is not able to understand the modes of the sign in the Prāsaṅgika's terms. He cannot be shown how phenomena are merely conventionally existent until he realizes the view of emptiness. Until this happens, the Prāsaṅgika is unable effectively to state reasons in his own terms because the opponent will not understand them, continuing to confuse inherent existence and conventional existence. Therefore, the Prāsaṅgikas assert that a mode of existence which is objectively established that appears commonly to both parties is not to be found; they assert that a commonly appearing subject does not exist.

Nonetheless, although the Prāsaṅgikas do not assert autonomous reasons, in order for reasoning to provide means of generating valid understanding, they must assert that the three modes of the sign can be ascertained and that the three modes are validly established. They are able to uphold this by using reasons which are renowned to others, taking the lead from the opponent's own assertions. They state reasons that are renowned to the opponent himself or, from the point of view of the Prāsaṅgika, renowned to others; the terms "renowned to oneself" (*svaprasiddha, rang la grags pa*) and "renowned to others" (*paraprasiddha, gzhan la grags pa*) are synonyms, with "oneself" and "other" both referring to the opponent. The Prāsaṅgika is able to generate the view in his opponent by stating reasons, the three signs of which are established in terms of the opponent's assertions, without the Prāsaṅgika having to assert the subject and the three modes himself.[91]

With all of the foregoing discussion in mind, Jang-gya's definition of Svātantrika may be restated in the hope that its meaning will be clear, or at least clearer than it was upon first reading.

> Autonomous means that an inferential consciousness realizing the thesis is generated, without taking the lead from the opponent's assertions, but by his having ascertained the modes of the sign with respect to a subject that is established as commonly appearing to non-mistaken valid cognizers of both parties in the debate through the force of an objective mode of subsistence from the side of its basis of designation. Mādhyamikas who assert the correctness of the necessity for such are Svātantrika-Mādhyamikas.

If the Svātantrikas and Prāsaṅgikas differ so radically on the meaning of valid cognition, the means of generating the view in an opponent, and the conventional status of phenomena, in what sense may they both be called Mādhyamikas? Why are Svātantrika and Prāsaṅgika divisions of the same school? Candrakīrti remarks in his *Clear Words* that, "If one is a Mādhyamika, it is unsuitable to make use of autonomous inferences because another [inherently existent] position is not asserted."[92] Tsong-kha-pa says in his *Great Exposition of Special Insight:*

> In general [Candrakīrti's opponents] are both the Proponents of True Existence, who assert that things have an ultimate nature, and the Svātantrikas, who assert that they have a nature which is established by way of its own character conventionally. The Svātantrikas are also called Proponents of No Entityness (*niḥsvabhāvavādin, ngo bo nyid*

> *med par smra ba*) but here, for the sake of brevity, the proponents of non-inherent existence should be understood to be the Prāsaṅgikas, and the proponents of inherent existence should be understood to be both the Proponents of True Existence and the Svātantrikas.[93]

The twentieth century Tibetan scholar Sha-mar-gen-dun-den-dzin-gya-tso (*Zhwa-dmar-dge-'dun-bstan-'dzin-rgya-mtsho*) raises the argument that the Svatantrikas are not Madhyamikas because they assert that emptiness — the mere, absence of true existence — exists by way of its own character and that all phenomena are established by way of their own character, thereby falling to both extremes.[94]

Despite these statements suggesting the contrary, the Svātantrikas are considered to be members of the Mādhyamika school. Tsong-kha-pa explains Candrakīrti's comment that it is unsuitable for Mādhyamikas to use autonomous syllogisms, contending that it is indeed unsuitable for Mādhyamikas to assert that phenomena exist by way of their own character but it does not follow from that that anyone who asserts that phenomena so exist is not a Mādhyamika, that is, there may be Mādhyamikas who assert inherent existence. For example, he says that although it is unsuitable for a monk to break vows of their formulated code of conduct, there are monks who go against that code but who are nonetheless monks.[95]

Still, just as there must be a certain level of conformance with the code of conduct for a person to be considered a monk, there must also be certain assertions which classify the Svātantrikas as Mādhyamikas. Jang-gya explains what they are. He concedes that the Svātantrikas assert that phenomena exist by way of their own character conventionally and that they hold that the object designated is findable among its bases of designation. However, they assert that all phenomena in the universe are empty of true existence, which they define as being established by way of a mode of subsistence which does not depend on appearing to a non-defective awareness. (This will be explained in chapter 4). This emptiness is accepted by the Prāsaṅgikas (although they would say that it is a coarse emptiness); it is not false as is the Yogācārin emptiness of subject and object being different substantial entities. It is also not a trifling emptiness in that it applies to all phenomena equally; everything lacks true existence. It is compatible with dependent arising, allowing the Svātantrikas to abandon the extremes of existence and non-existence and to establish the viability of conventionalities such as cause and effect within emptiness.[96] Tsong-kha-pa notes that, "These scholars also refute the tenet of the true existence of phenomena through many doors of reasoning and assert non-true existence well. Hence, they are Mādhyamikas."[97] Finally, Nga-wang-bel-den says in his *Annotations* (*mChan 'grel*) to Jam-yang-shay-ba's *Great Exposition of Tenets:*

> Because they propound a middle way free from the extreme of permanence — that phenomena ultimately exist — and the extreme of annihilation — [that phenomena] do not exist conventionally, and because they assert that an entityness which is truly established does not exist, they are called Mādhyamikas and Proponents of No Entityness. The divisions are two, Prāsaṅgika and Svātantrika; those who claim to be Mādhyamikas, other than those two, are merely designated as Mādhyamikas; it is unsuitable that they be Mādhyamikas in fact. Because they are similar in refuting the extreme of non-existence — [that phenomena] do not exist even conventionally — and the extreme of permanence — that things truly exist — and assert a middle which is a non-affirming negative, the mere elimination of true establishment in dependently arisen phenomena, both the Prāsaṅgikas and Svātantrikas are Mādhyamikas. However, that [school] which is free from all subtle extremes of permanence, such as [phenomena] being established from their own side, and extremes of annihilation, such as forms not being established as external objects, is the system of the Prāsaṅgikas.[98]

3 The Root of Cyclic Existence

Another fundamental distinction between the Svātantrikas and Prāsaṅgikas lies in the question of whether the selflessness of phenomena (*dharmanairātmya*, *chos kyi bdag med*) is taught in the Hīnayāna sutras. The positions of the two schools on this point entail further differences concerning the object of the Hīnayāna wisdom, the distinguishing feature of the Mahāyāna, and the root cause of suffering.

Bhāvaviveka argues that the selflessness of phenomena is not taught in the Hearer scriptural collection (*śrāvakapiṭaka*, *nyan thos kyi sde snod*) because the exposition of the selflessness of phenomena is the distinguishing feature which sets the Mahāyāna apart from Hīnayāna. According to Bhāvaviveka, that which obstructs liberation from cyclic existence is the conception of a self of persons (*pudgalātman*, *gang zag gi bdag*). That which obstructs the attainment of Buddhahood is the conception of true existence. If the selflessness of phenomena were set forth in the Hīnayāna scriptures, Hearers[1] (*śrāvaka*, *nyan thos*) and Solitary Realizers[2] (*pratyekabuddha*, *rang rgyal*, *rang sangs rgyas*) — who merely seek liberation from rebirth — would be able to achieve Buddhahood by realizing the selflessness of phenomena taught in their scriptures. In that case, there would be no reason for the Buddha to have taught another vehicle, the Mahāyāna, because the means for achieving Buddhahood, the wisdom of the selflessness of phenomena, is accessible in the Hīnayāna.

In Bhāvaviveka's view, Hīnayānists realize the selflessness of persons in order to overcome the afflictive obstructions (*kleśāvaraṇa*/

nyon sgrib) and thereby gain liberation. It is unnecessary for them to realize the more subtle selflessness of phenomena, the object of Bodhisattvas' wisdom. Thus, Bhāvaviveka admits that it is possible to be liberated from cyclic existence without penetrating the final nature of reality — the selflessness of phenomena.

The Prāsaṅgikas, in the persons of Buddhapālita and Candrakīrti, hold that the selflessness of phenomena is taught in the Hearer scriptural collection and that Hīnayanists realize the subtle selflessness. They assert that there is no difference in subtlety between the selflessness of persons and the selflessness of phenomena and that in order to achieve the enlightenment of the Hīnayāna or Mahāyāna path, both selflessnesses must be realized. Therefore, unlike Bhāvaviveka, the Prāsaṅgikas see no difference between Hīnayāna and Mahāyāna in terms of the subtlety of the object of their wisdom; Foe Destroyers[3] (*arhan*, *dgra bcom pa*) and Buddhas realize the same subtle emptiness of inherent existence. For the Prāsaṅgikas, the Mahāyāna is distinguished from the Hīnayāna in terms of method, not wisdom.

As is the case with the debate over syllogisms and consequences, the commentaries to Nāgārjuna's *Treatise on the Middle Way* provide the context for this controversy. In commenting on the seventh stanza of the fourth chapter of the *Treatise*, "Analysis of the Aggregates" (*Skandhaparikṣā*), Buddhapālita cites the following passage from a Hīnayāna sutra:

> Form is like a ball of foam.
> Feeling is like a bubble.
> Discrimination is like a mirage.
> Compositional factors are like a banana tree.
> Consciousness is like an illusion.
> So said the Sun-Friend[4] [Buddha].[5]

Before considering the Prāsaṅgika and Svātantrika positions on whether the selflessness of phenomena is taught in the Hīnayāna sutras, it is worthwhile to digress into a general analysis of the meaning of this stanza in order to provide a background for the discussion to follow.

In this stanza, Buddha describes the insubstantial nature of the five aggregates (*pañcaskandha*, *phung po lnga*). The form aggregate (*rūpaskandha*, *gzugs kyi phung po*) encompasses not only visible forms which are objects of the eye consciousness, but includes also sounds, odors, tastes, and tangible objects. The five sense powers (*indriya, dbang po*) which provide the physical bases for the eye, ear, nose, tongue, and body consciousnesses are also instances of the form aggregate. A final category included within the form aggregate are those forms which are imperceptible by the sense consciousnesses and can only be known by the mental consciousness, such as a single minute particle.

FORM IS LIKE A BALL OF FOAM[6]

Forms are compared to a ball of foam that when seen from a distance appears to be a solid whole but disappears when one tries to separate it into parts. In the same way, a form appears to be a single mass until reasoning is used to analyze the apparent whole, dividing it into its component parts, at which point the subjective apprehension of the form as a solid unit disappears.

The use of analysis to destroy the misconception of objects as single, independent wholes is found throughout Buddhist philosophy. In the Vaibhāṣika school, anything which can be broken down into parts, either physically or analytically such that the thought apprehending that object ceases, is identified as a conventional truth[7] (*saṃvṛtisatya, kun rdzob bden pa*), a truth for ignorance which does not exist in the way that it appears. A clay pot, for example, is a conventional truth because, although it appears to be a solid whole, the thought apprehending that pot ceases when it is smashed with a hammer. The Vaibhāṣikas assert that there exist directionally partless physical particles and temporally partless moments of consciousness which cannot be broken down into component parts. These subtle particles and moments of consciousness are identified as ultimate truths by the Vaibhāṣikas.[8] The existence of partless particles is refuted by the Sautrāntikas Following Reasoning, the Yogācārins, and Mādhyamikas.[9]

In the Mādhyamika school, the assertion that all phenomena, permanent and impermanent, have parts provides the foundation for the reasoning of the lack of being either one or many which proves that all phenomena are empty of true existence (see pp. 167-191).

FEELING IS LIKE A BUBBLE

The second of the five aggregates, feeling (*vedanā, tshor ba*), is one of the five omnipresent (*sarvatraga, kun 'gro*) mental factors (*caitta, sems byung*), which accompany every moment of an eye consciousness, ear consciousness, nose consciousness, tongue consciousness, body consciousness, or mental consciousness. The other four omnipresent mental factors are discrimination (*saṃjñā*, *'du shes*), intention (*cetanā*, *sems pa*), contact (*sparśa*, *reg pa*) and mental engagement (*manaskāra*, *yid la byed pa*).[10]

In Asaṅga's *Compendium of Knowledge* (*Abhidharmasamuccaya*), feeling is defined as "that which has the character of experience, that is, the entity of experience which experiences individually the fruitions that are the effects of virtuous and non-virtuous actions."[11] Feelings are of three types — those of pleasure (*sukhā*, *bde ba*), of pain (*duḥkha*, *sdug bsngal*), and of neutrality (*aduḥkhasukhā*, *sdug bsngal yang ma yin bde ba yang ma yin*), pleasure being that which one wishes to meet with again when it ceases, pain being that which one wishes to separate from when it arises, and neutral feeling, that which one wishes neither to meet with nor separate from when it arises.[12] All feelings of pleasure and pain, all happiness and suffering, are the effects of past actions, the fruitions of potencies established on the mind by virtuous and non-virtuous activities of body, speech, and mind performed in the past. A clear understanding of the cause and effect of actions is seen as an essential prerequisite for the practice of the path because with the understanding that one's happiness and suffering is a direct result of one's own action, virtue is adopted and non-virtue discarded. Tsong-kha-pa writes in his *Great Exposition of the Stages of the Path*:

> Nāgārjuna's *Precious Garland* (*Ratnāvalī*) [Stanza 21] says:
>
> From non-virtues come all sufferings
> As do all bad migrations.
> From virtues come all good migrations
> As do the pleasures of all births.
>
> Therefore, one determines that pleasures and suffering do not arise causelessly, nor do they arise from a dissimilar cause, such as the principal (*pradhāna*, *gtso bo*) or Īśvara, [and one recognizes] the definite, incontrovertible [relationship] of action and effect in which general pleasure and suffering arise respectively from general virtue and non-virtue, and the variety of specific pleasures and sufferings [arise respectively] from the variety of specific [cases]

> of the two actions without the slightest disorder. This is called the correct view of all Buddhists and is praised as the foundation of all pure qualities.[13]

The Buddhists reject the assertions of the non-Buddhist schools, such as the Nihilists (*carvāka, ayata, rgyang 'phen pa*) who assert that happiness and suffering arise causelessly, of the non-theistic Sāṃkhyas who assert that all manifest objects, including happiness and suffering, are transformations of the general principal (*pradhāna, gtso bo*), and the theistic Sāṃkhyas who hold that pleasure and pain are creations of the god Īśvara.[14] It is the Buddhist position that all experiences of pleasure and pain — the general, such as rebirth in a happy or bad realm, and the specific, such as the individual feelings of pleasure and pain in a given lifetime — are the definite results of actions performed in the past and that this relationship of cause and effect is unconfused in the sense that happiness always arises from virtue and suffering always arises from non-virtue. Furthermore, a person never experiences the effect of an action that he did not perform.[15]

Thus, the happiness of cyclic existence is achieved through the practice of virtue, which brings pleasurable feelings, and the manifest sufferings of cyclic existence are avoided by abandoning non-virtuous activities, which fructify in feelings of pain. However, this identification of the means for gaining pleasant feelings and avoiding unpleasant feelings is not the final position; the Buddha indicates the unsatisfactory nature of all feelings when he states that, "Feeling is like a bubble."

Feeling is compared to a bubble for two reasons, the first being that just as a water bubble is destroyed as soon as it appears, so feeling disintegrates in the moment following its production and becomes non-existent. This metaphor points to the impermanent nature of all feelings, whether they be pleasurable, painful, or neutral. The Sautrāntikas, Yogācārins, and Mādhyamikas assert that all conditioned phenomena (*saṃskṛtadharma, 'dus byas kyi chos*) are produced and cease every moment. Unlike the Vaibhāṣikas, who assert that production (*utpatti, skyed pa*), abiding (*sthiti, gnas pa*), aging (*jarā, rga ba*), and disintegration (*vināśa, 'jig pa*) are four external agents that affect a conditioned phenomenon in succession, the other schools hold production, abiding, aging, and disintegration to be four qualities of the object itself that exist simultaneously.[16] Thus, the object's quality of being the arising of that which did not exist before is its production, its remaining as a type similar to the former moment is its abiding, its being of a different character from the former moment is its aging, and its not staying for a second moment is its disintegration. Rather than being four agents acting on the object in sequence, production, abiding, aging, and disintegration are four different perspectives on one instant, with the object ceasing in the very moment that it is produced. Thus, according to the Sautrāntikas, Yogācārins, and Mādhyamikas, conditioned phenomena are unable to last beyond the moment of their production; momentary disintegration is inherent in everything that is produced from causes and conditions.[17] Feelings, which are conditioned phenomena produced by actions in the past, are produced and disintegrate every instant.

The second reason why feelings are compared to water bubbles is that just as bubbles have a nature of water, so feelings have a nature of suffering. In order to understand the meaning of this statement, it is essential that the three types of suffering — the suffering of pain (*duḥkhaduḥkhatā, sdug bsngal gyi sdug bsngal*) the suffering of change (*vipariṇāmaduḥkhatā, 'gyur ba'i sdug bsngal*), and the suffering of conditioning (*saṃskāraduḥkhatā, 'du byed kyi sdug bsngal*) — be identified.

Sufferings of pain include all feelings of physical or mental pain, discomfort, or dissatisfaction, that is, all feelings ordinarily identified as unpleasant in the world. Such manifest forms of suffering are commonly recognized as having a nature of suffering.

All feelings of pleasure in cyclic existence are sufferings of change, so called because such feelings inevitably turn into suffering. When feelings of pleasure are observed over a long period of time, it is seen that suffering eventually arises, such that what is imagined to be pleasure is in fact merely the period between the gradual cessation of one suffering and the gradual arising of another. For example, if one remains in the shade too long and becomes cold, one moves into the sunlight. If standing in the warmth of the sun was truly pleasurable, then no matter how long one stayed in the sun, pleasure would continue without any feeling of discomfort. Since this is not the case and one must eventually return to the shade to avoid suffering the heat of the sun, the feeling of pleasure that initially arose from moving to the sunlight is a suffering of change. What was experienced as pleasure was the period between the cessation of the feeling of cold and the time at which the feeling of warmth became uncomfortable — a suffering of pain. If one has become exhausted by walking a long distance, sitting down appears to be pleasurable, but this apparent pleasure is the cessation of the suffering of standing. Because the suffering of sitting is increasing gradually, it is not manifest. When the suffering becomes apparent, one must get up and go for a walk. Upon rising the suffering of sitting quickly ceases and the suffering of standing gradually is produced, even though it is not immediately evident.[18]

Tsong-kha-pa writes in his *Great Exposition of the Stages of the Path*:

> Furthermore, present feelings of pleasure that increase attachment are for the most part cases of creating an awareness of pleasure in a lessening of suffering; there is no pleasure that does not depend on the elimination of suffering. For example, when one suffers because of traveling too much, the awareness of pleasure arises through resting. At that time of the rapid cessation of suffering, pleasure appears to be gradually increasing, but it is not pleasurable by nature because again, if one rests too long, suffering is produced as before. If it were naturally a cause of pleasure, then just as due to merely relying on a cause of suffering, suffering continues to increase, so as long as one relies on such things as moving and resting, sleep, food and drink, sunlight, and shade, pleasure should continue to increase for that long. However, [if one relies on these] for too long, it seems that only suffering is produced.[19]

The existence of feelings of pleasure is not being denied. The essential point is that those activities identified as pleasurable are so only in relation to a corresponding decrease of suffering. Further, nothing in cyclic existence has an inherent nature of pleasure such that one could continually eat a certain food or listen to a particular piece of music and constantly derive enjoyment from doing so. Unlike causes of suffering which will continue to bring discomfort indefinitely, these activities commonly identified as sources of pleasure will eventually bring pain. Since feelings of pleasure turn into suffering, they are said to have a nature of suffering and are identified as sufferings of change.

Contaminated feelings of equanimity are identified as pervasive sufferings of conditioning (*vyāptisaṃskāraduḥkhatā*, *khyab pa 'du byed kyi sdug bsngal*), the most subtle and difficult to comprehend of the three types of suffering. Lacking the manifest discomfort of the suffering of pain and the observable tendency to turn into suffering of the suffering of change, feelings of equanimity are identified as suffering because of being under the "other power" of contaminated actions and afflictions. Although a feeling of equanimity is neither pleasurable nor painful, since it is an impermanent phenomenon, suffering can arise in an instant upon the aggregation of suitable causes and conditions. As soon as one has a mind and body under the power of contaminated actions and afflictions, even though manifest suffering may be temporarily absent, suffering is ready to appear immediately. Therefore, the pervasive suffering of conditioning is extended to all five aggregates and is not limited to feelings of equanimity. Tsong-kha-pa's *Great Exposition of the Stages of the Path* says:

> In carrying a great burden, inasmuch as that burden must be carried, there is no pleasure. Similarly, as long as one must bear the burden of the appropriated aggregates (*upādānaskandha*, *nyer len gyi phung po*), so long must one suffer. When the suffering of conditioning exists due to these aggregates having as their basis the assumption of the bad states of suffering and the afflictions, although there occasionally occur times when there are no feelings of suffering temporarily, many sufferings are produced immediately from a myriad of sources. Therefore, the suffering of conditioning pervades all suffering and is the root of the other two types of suffering.[20]

The suffering of conditioning is then called pervasive because it pervades sufferings of pain and sufferings of change; the domination of mind and body by the power of contaminated actions and afflictions, the fact that mind and body are so conditioned so as always to be ready to experience feelings of pleasure and pain make the first two types of suffering possible.

The third type of suffering is called pervasive also because it is a quality of the three realms and nine levels of cyclic existence. Sufferings of pain occur only in the Desire Realm, sufferings of change occur in the Desire Realm and the first three Concentrations of the Form Realm; in the Fourth Concentration and the four levels of the Formless Realm the feeling is only one of equanimity.[21]

The pervasive suffering of conditioning, though serving as the root of the sufferings of pain and change, is difficult to understand and is not identified as a suffering by common beings. As it says in sutra:

> Just as a wisp of wool in the hand is not felt by men
> But when it gets in the eye creates displeasure and pain,
> A fool, like the palm of the hand, does not feel the wisp of
> the suffering of conditioning.
> But, like the eye, the wise one is greatly moved by just
> that.[22]

Worldly beings do not identify the aggregates as sources of suffering and continue to seek pleasure in cyclic existence whereas the wise understand that as long as mind and body are under the power of past actions and the afflictions of desire, hatred, and ignorance, there can be no final happiness and no control over the indiscriminate occurrence of feelings of pain. Worldly beings allow feelings of pain and pleasure to serve as the causes of future suffering by becoming attached to pleasurable feelings and hating feelings of pain, with attachment producing the suffering of future births in cyclic existence and hatred producing sorrow in this life and rebirth in the bad realms in the future. The wise, on the other hand, see feelings of pleasure as suffering and stop desire. Since the aggregates are a collection of causes for suffering, the wise consider feelings of pain as arising from the aggregates and endeavor to stop the hatred of pain. They see feelings of equanimity as impermanent and having a nature of extinction and cessation and thus stop obscuration. In this way the wise do not allow the three feelings, which have a nature of suffering, to become causes of the three poisons — desire, hatred, and obscuration — the sources of future suffering.[23]

The doctrine of the three types of suffering points out that almost all experience is suffering on some level, in the sense of being manifest feelings of pain, feelings of pleasure that are merely designated to periods of non-manifest suffering, or feelings of equanimity that are so conditioned as to be ready to turn into suffering upon the aggregation of appropriate conditions. It is not being said that feelings of pleasure are feelings of pain. When the Buddha said, "Whatever is experienced here is suffering," he did not mean that all feelings are feeling of actual pain. Rather, as he says, "Ānanda, I said that 'Whatever is experienced here is suffering,' referring to the impermanence of conditioned things and the change of conditioned things."[24] Experience is a form of suffering because the three feelings have a nature of impermanence and are produced by contaminated actions and afflictions, and are, therefore, unable to provide any final source of happiness. All those activities that sentient beings perform in hope of gaining final happiness in cyclic existence are thus doomed by their very nature to end in failure, or as the Buddha says in the chapter on impermanence in the *Verses of Uplift* (*Udānavarga*, I. 22):

> The end of all amassing is depletion.
> The end of rising is collapse.
> The end of meeting, separation.
> The end of living is death.[25]

Thus, nothing in cyclic existence can provide a final source of happiness, and specifically, none of the three feelings offers satisfaction. Tsong-kha-pa graphically illustrates the displeasing nature of the three feelings when he compares feelings of pleasure to the relief felt by pouring cool water on a burn, feelings of pain to the added suffering of pouring hot water on a burn, and feelings of equanimity to the sensation just at the moment of being burned before the pain becomes intense.[26] From this analogy it can be gathered that what is perceived as pleasure is merely a brief lessening of pain, what is perceived as pain is an intensification of already present suffering, and feelings of equanimity are capable of yielding feelings of pain in the next moment.

In the verse, feelings are compared to bubbles because just as a bubble is destroyed as soon as it arises, feelings disintegrate in the second moment after their production. This expresses the impermanent nature of feelings, that they disintegrate as soon as they arise, and thus cannot provide a permanent source of happiness. On the contrary, just as a bubble has a nature of water, all contaminated feelings — pleasurable, painful, and neutral — have a nature of suffering, as the presentation of the three types of suffering — of pain, change, and pervasive conditioning — indicates.

DISCRIMINATION IS LIKE A MIRAGE

Discrimination, the third of the five aggregates, is, like feeling, an omnipresent mental factor that accompanies every main mind whether it be a sense or mental direct perceiver or a conceptual thought consciousness. It is that factor which apprehends the uncommon signs of an object. Discrimination involves the distinguishing and identification of objects.[27] The fact that we are able to differentiate one object from another and identify an object as something we have seen before is the result of discrimination.

Discrimination is compared to a mirage in the sense that, just as a mirage appears to be water but is not, discrimination appears to be something owned by a self-sufficient person but is not established as such. An individual's discriminations falsely appear to be self-sufficient possessions of the person due to considering one's own discriminations to be valid and those of others to be invalid.[28]

COMPOSITIONAL FACTORS ARE LIKE A BANANA TREE

In the division of awarenesses into minds and mental factors, the six main minds — the eye, ear, nose, tongue, body, and mental perceivers — constitute the fifth aggregate, consciousnesses. The fifty-one mental factors are divided into six categories: the five omnipresent factors (*sarvatraga, kun 'gro*) [feeling (*vedanā, tshor ba*), discrimination (*samjña, 'du shes*), intention (*cetanā, sems pa*), contact (*sparśa, reg pa*), mental engagement (*manaskāra, yid la byed pa*)], the five determining factors (*viniyata, yul nges*) [aspiration (*chanda, 'dun pa*), belief (*adhimokṣa, mos pa*), mindfulness (*smṛti, dran pa*), stabilization (*samādhiting nge dzin*), knowledge (*prajñā, shes rab*)], the eleven virtuous factors (*kuśala, dge ba*) [faith (*śraddhā, dad pa*), shame (*hrī, ngo tsha shes pa*), embarrassment (*apatrāpya, khrel yod pa*), non-attachment (*alobha, ma chags pa*), non-hatred (*adveṣa, zhe sdang med pa*), non-ignorance (*amoha, gti mug med pa*), effort (*vīrya, brtson 'grus*), pliancy (*prasrabdhi, shin tu sbyangs pa*)), conscientiousness (*apramāda, bag yod pa*), equanimity (*upekṣā, btang snyoms*), non-harmfulness (*avihiṃsā, rnam par mi'tshe ba*)], the six root afflictions (*mūlakleśa, rtsa nyon*) [desire (*rāga, 'dod chags*), anger (*pratigha, khong khro*), pride (*māna, nga rgyal*), ignorance (*avidyā, ma rig pa*), doubt (*vicikitsā, the tshom*), afflicted view (*dṛṣṭi, lta ba nyon mongs can*)], the twenty secondary afflictions (*upakleśa, nye nyon*) [belligerence (*krodha,khro ba*), resentment (*upanāha, 'khon 'dzin*), concealment (*mrakṣa, 'chab pa*), spite (*pradāśa, 'tshig pa*), jealousy (*irṣya, phrag dog*), miserliness (*mātsarya, ser sna*), deceit (*māyā, sgyu*), dissimulation (*śaṭhya, g.yo*), haughtiness (*mada, rgyags pa*), harmfulness (*vihiṃsā, rnam par 'tshe ba*), non-shame (*āhrīkya, ngo tsha med pa*), non-embarrassment (*anapatrāpya, khrel med pa*), lethargy (*styāna, rmugs pa*), excitement (*auddhatya, rgod pa*), non-faith (*āśraddhya, ma dad pa*), laziness (*kausīdya, le lo*), non-conscientiousness (*pramāda, bag med pa*), forgetfulness (*muṣitasmṛtitā, brjed nges pa*), non-introspection (*asaṃprajanya, shes bzhin ma yin pa*), distraction (*vikṣepa, rnam par g.yeng ba*)], and the four changeable factors (*aniyata, gzhan 'gyur*) [sleep (*middha, gnyid*), contrition (*kaukṛtya, 'gyod pa*), investigation (*vitarka, rtog pa*), analysis (*vicāra, dpyod pa*)].[29] From among the five omnipresent factors, two — feeling and discrimination — are distinguished as separate aggregates because they are causes of disputation; discrimination serves as the basis of quarrels among philosophical systems and feeling serves as the basis of quarrels among ordinary people.[30] The other three omnipresent factors — intention (*cetanā, sems pa*), contact (*sparśa, reg pa*), and mental engagement (*manaskāra, yid la byed pa*) — and the remaining forty-six mental factors fall into the category of compositional factors, specifically as compositional factors associated with mind (*cittaprayuktasaṃskāra, sems dang ldan pa'i 'du byed*).

The other components of the compositional factor aggregate are those which are neither form nor consciousness, numbering twenty-four according to the Sautrāntikas, Yogācārins, and Mādhyamikas, fifteen according to the Vaibhāṣikas. These are the non-associated compositional factors (*viprayuktasaṃskāra, ldan min 'du byed*), called non-associated because of not being associated with minds or mental factors. They are called compositional because they allow for the aggregation of the causes and conditions and allow for the production, abiding, and cessation of products.[31]

The twenty-four non-associated compositional factors are: person (*pudgala, gang zag*), acquisition (*prāpti, thob pa*), absorption without discrimination (*asaṃjñisamāpatti, 'du shes med pa'i snyoms 'jug*), absorption of cessation (*nirodhasamāpatti, 'gog pa'i snyoms 'jug*), one having no discrimination (*āsaṃjñika, 'du shes med pa pa*), life faculty (*jīvitendriya, srog gi dbang po*), similarity of type (*nikāyasabhāgata, rigs 'thun pa*), birth (*jāti, skye ba*), aging (*jarā, rga ba*), duration (*sthiti, gnas pa*), impermanence (*anityatā, mi rtag pa*), group of stems (*nāmakāya, ming gi tshogs*), group of words (*padakāya, tshig gi tshogs*), group of letters (*vyañjanakāya, yi ge'i tshogs*), state of an ordinary being (*pṛthagjanatva, so so skye bo nyid*), continuity (*pravṛtti, 'jug pa*), distinction (*pratiniyama, so sor nges pa*), relatedness (*yoga, 'byor 'grel*), rapidity (*jāva, 'gyogs pa*), order (*anukrama, go rim*), time (*kāla, dus*), area (*deśa, yul*), number (*saṃkhyā, grangs*), and collection (*sāmagrī, tshog pa*).[32] Since these are factors which apply to both form and consciousness, they cannot be placed in the form aggregate or in one of the mental aggregates, but are placed in a separate category, the aggregate of compositional factors.

These compositional factors are compared to a banana or plantain tree (*Musa Sapientum*). The Buddha provides the background of the metaphor in the *Kindred Sayings* (*Saṃyuttanikāya III*) where he describes a man who goes into the forest in search of heartwood, the hard, dry core of a tree trunk. He comes upon a tall, strong plantain tree and chops it down. Having cut off the top, he begins to peel away layers of bark to reach the heartwood. But below the first layer, he finds a second; he peels away the layers until there is nothing left, for the plantain tree has no heartwood, no core.[33]

Just as a banana tree is taken apart in many ways but a core does not appear, so compositional factors are analyzed with numerous reasonings, but the essence of something owned by a substantially existent person is not found.

CONSCIOUSNESS IS LIKE AN ILLUSION

The fifth aggregate includes the six minds: the eye consciousness (*cakṣurvijñāna, mig gi rnam par shes pa*), which observes visible forms, the ear consciousness (*śrotravijñāna, rna ba'i rnam par shes pa*) which observes sounds, the nose consciousness (*ghrāṇavijñāna, sna'i rnam par shes pa*) which observes odors, the tongue consciousness (*jihvāvijñāna, lce'i rnam par shes pa*) which observes tastes, the body consciousness (*kāyavijñāna, lus kyi rnam par shes pa*) which observes tangible objects, and the mental consciousness (*manovijñāna, yid kyi rnam par shes pa*) which observes phenomena. No mental factors are included in the consciousness aggregate. The six consciousnesses, like all impermanent phenomena, arise in dependence on causes and conditions with three conditions being necessary for the production of any consciousness: 1) the uncommon empowering condition (*asādhāraṇa-adhipatipratyaya/thun mong ma yin pa'i bdag rkyen*) which for the five sense consciousnesses is clear subtle matter located in the eye, ear, nose, tongue, and throughout the body. These are the physical sense powers (*indriya, dbang po*) which provide the physical ability to perceive objects. For the mental consciousness, the uncommon empowering condition is not physical; any former moment of consciousness can act as the uncommon empowering condition of a mental consciousness. 2) The observed-object-condition (*ālambanapratyaya, dmigs rkyen*) is the object of observation of the consciousness, that is, the visible form, sound, odor, taste, tangible object, or phenomenon apprehended by the particular consciousness. 3) The immediately preceding condition (*samanantarapratyaya, de ma thag rkyen*) is a former moment of any of the six consciousnesses which serves as a cause of similar type of the consciousness produced and accounts for the fact that the continuum of consciousness is never severed; at least one of the six types of consciousness is constantly operating.[34]

The five sense consciousnesses (**indriyajñāna, dbang shes*) are necessarily non-conceptual (*nirvikalpaka, rtog med*) whereas the mental consciousness can be either non-conceptual as in the case of a yogic direct perceiver (*yogipratyakṣa, rnal 'byor mngon sum*) and superknowledge (*abhijñā, mngon shes*) or conceptual, as in the case of thought (*kalpanā, rtog pa*).

The Buddha compares consciousness to an illusion. A magician is able to cause a pebble to appear as a horse to his audience by casting a mantra that affects their eyes. The illusion appears to be a real horse but, in truth, is not. In the same way, consciousness appears to be a self-sufficient person but is not established as such.

When consciousness is spoken of as appearing as a self-sufficient person, it is the mental consciousness that is being referred to more than the five sense consciousnesses. The mental consciousness which thinks thoughts, makes assumptions, draws conclusions, and directs activities of body and speech is wrongly conceived to be a substantially existent person in the sense of being self-sufficient. The nature of this misconception must be explored.

The term substantial existence (*dravyasat, rdzas yod*) occurs in many different contexts in Buddhist literature, in most cases meaning one of the following:

1 substantial existence which is established by reasoning; this is synonymous with being an object of knowledge (*jñeya, shes bya*)
2 substantial existence which is steady and unchanging; this is synonymous with permanent phenomenon (*nitya, rtag pa*)
3 substantial existence which is the ability to perform a function; this is synonymous with impermanent thing (*bhāva, dngos po*)
4 substantial existence in the sense of self-sufficiency (Tib. *rang-rkya-thub-pa*, literally "the ability to support itself").

This last sense of substantial existence is of interest in delineating the manner in which the mental consciousness is misconceived to be a self. All four schools of Buddhist tenets agree that substantial existence in the sense of self-sufficiency refers (hypothetically) to an existence which does not depend on the apprehension of some other phenomenon in order to be identified.[35] Nothing substantially exists in that sense. In the context of the conception of a substantially existent or self-sufficient self, it is the conception of the existence of a self which can be identified independently without recourse to the identification of the aggregates.[36]

When consciousness is said to appear as a substantially existent self, it is difficult to construe consciousness as such a self in the sense of being identified without depending on the aggregates, since consciousness is itself the fifth of the five aggregates. Rather the mental consciousness is wrongly conceived to be a substantially existent self in the sense of being the master or controller of the aggregates, the servants — those controlled. This conception of self does not require that the self be a different entity from the aggregates, be totally independent of them, or have a character completely unlike that of the aggregates.

A magician's illusion appears to be a horse but is not established as such. In the same way, the mental consciousness appears to be a substantially existent person but, in fact, is not. Such a person does not substantially exist because its identification must depend on the appearance of other phenomena.[37] Therefore, the mental consciousness is not a substantially existent self. In the Svātantrika system, the mental consciousness is identified as the imputedly existent (*prajñaptisat*, *btags yod*) person, as will be explained below (pp. 109-114). All four tenet systems refute the existence of a substantially existent person.[38]

Having thus explained the manner in which form is like a ball of foam, feeling is like a bubble, discrimination is like a mirage, compositional factors are like a banana tree, and consciousness is like an illusion, it remains to be seen how this stanza from a Hīnayāna sutra became a point of contention between the Svātantrikas and Prāsaṅgikas.

In commenting on the thirty-fourth stanza of the seventh chapter of Nāgārjuna's *Treatise on the Middle Way* which says:

> Production, abiding, and disintegration
> Are said to be like

A dream, an illusion,
And a city of the *gandharvas*.

Buddhapālita writes:

> In this way, the Supramundane Victor set forth the categories of an illusion, an echo, a reflection, a mirage, a dream, a ball of foam, a water bubble, and a banana tree as examples of the selflessness of conditioned phenomena. There is nothing whatsoever real or non-mistaken in these. It is said that these are elaborations, these are falsities. In the statement, "All phenomena are selfless," selfless means non-entityness because the term "self" is a word for entityness.[39]

The Buddha used the examples of deceptive phenomena such as illusions, mirages, and dreams to indicate that phenomena do not exist in the way that they appear. All phenomena are selfless in the sense that they lack inherent existence and do not exist by way of their own entity. When the Buddha said in Hīnayāna sutras that form is like a ball of foam, feeling is like a water bubble, discrimination is like a mirage, compositional factors are like a banana tree, and consciousness is like an illusion, he was indicating that all conditioned phenomena are selfless, empty of inherent existence. This is Buddhapālita's position.

In commenting on the same verse from Nāgārjuna's *Treatise on the Middle Way* (VII. 34), Bhāvaviveka disagrees with Buddhapālita's assertion that the selflessness of phenomena is taught in Hīnayāna sutras:

> Self and mine are without entityness, but they are perceived in that way. Therefore, as an antidote to the afflictive obstructions, the Supramundane Victor taught in the [scriptures of the] Hearer vehicle:
>
> The Seer of Reality [Buddha] said that
> Form is like a ball of foam,
> Feeling is like a bubble,
> Discrimination is like a mirage,
> Compositional factors are like a banana tree,
> Consciousness is like an illusion.
>
> In the Mahāyāna [scriptural collection], conditioned phenomena are just without entityness, but they are per-

ceived in that way and are [wrongly] taught to be that way [by others]. Therefore, as an antidote to the afflictive obstructions and the obstructions to omniscience, it is said [in the *Diamond Cutter* (*Vajracchedika*)]:

> Products are to be viewed as like
> Stars, cataracts, butter lamps,
> Illusions, dew, bubbles,
> Dreams, lightning, and clouds.

Therefore, this is not something to be feared: the intelligent, having analyzed, should become forbearant.

Another [Buddhapālita] says:

> The Supramundane Victor set forth the categories of illusion, echo, reflection, mirage, dream, ball of foam, water bubble, and banana tree as examples of the selflessness of conditioned phenomena. There is nothing whatsoever real or non-mistaken in this. It is said that these are elaborations, these are falsities. In the statement, "All phenomena are selfless," selfless means non-entityness because the term "self" is a word for entityness.

Regarding that, one who is not another [i.e., myself, Bhāvaviveka], says that here, since the appearance as self is a mistaken reality, and since the term "self" is a word for self [of persons and does not mean entityness], and since a self that is a separate entity does not exist in those [aggregates] and they themselves are not a self just as they are not Īśvara, that scripture, because of referring to the selflessness of persons which is to be specifically realized in the Hearer Vehicle, cannot indicate that phenomena are selfless. If it could, it would be meaningless [for the Buddha] to have taken up another vehicle [the Mahāyāna].[40]

Before exploring Bhāvaviveka'a argument in detail, the stanza he cites from the *Diamond Cutter Sutra* warrants explanation.

> Products are to be viewed as like
> Stars, cataracts, butter lamps,
> Illusions, dew, bubbles,
> Dreams, lightning, and clouds.

According to Jam-yang-shay-ba and the annotator of his *Great Exposition of Tenets*, Nga-wang-bel-den, this stanza sets forth nine examples that illustrate four characteristics of products.[41] The characteristic of nature is indicated by the examples of stars, cataracts, and a butter lamp. The characteristic of experience is indicated by the example of a magician's illusion. The characteristic of fault is indicated by the examples of dew and bubbles, and the characteristic of renunciation, by the examples of dreams, lightning, and clouds.

THE CHARACTERISTIC OF NATURE

The Nature of Products is Like Stars

Products' nature of being a composite of appearance and emptiness is illustrated by stars. All phenomena have two natures. Their emptiness of true existence is their final, ultimate mode of being that appears to a non-conceptual exalted wisdom (*nirvikalpakajñāna, rnam par mi rtog pa'i ye shes*). This ultimate mode of being, which is the mere elimination of true existence, is illustrated by the fact that during the day, only the clear sky appears and stars are not visible. In the same way, the exalted wisdom consciousness sees only the emptiness which is the negative of true existence and does not see any conventional elaborations whatsoever.

The other nature of products is their conventional mode of being that appears to a conventional conceptual consciousness. This conventional mode of being is posited through appearing to a non-defective awareness. Just as when the night is covered by darkness, the constellations of stars appear clearly, so the varieties of conventional phenomena appear to a conventional thought consciousness. For those with the obstructive covering of ignorance (like darkness), various mistaken appearances (like stars) are perceived. Nevertheless, not all appearances to conventional thought consciousnesses are mistaken in the Svātantrika system. Products appear correctly to factually concordant consciousnesses — conventional valid cognizers. The appearance of objects as truly established from their own side, without being posited through appearing to a non-defective awareness, exists only for mistaken minds. Phenomena do not exist in that way and appear so only through the force of predispositions for ignorance.

The example of stars, which do not appear during the day but do appear at night, illustrates the mode of apprehension of a non-conceptual exalted wisdom and a conceptual conventional consciousneess. For a non-conceptual exalted wisdom of those who have not achieved Buddhahood, only emptiness — the absence of true existence and the final mode of being of phenomena — appears. To a conceptual conventional consciousness the varieties of conventional truths appear. This appearance of conventional phenomena is not an object of abandonment of the path to Buddhahood, for conventionalities appear to a Buddha's exalted wisdom knowing the varicties (*yāvajjñāna, ji snyad gzigs pa'i ye shes*). Rather, it is the conception of these phenomena as truly existent, ultimately existent, without being posited through the force of appearing to a non-defective consciousness, which is abandoned on the path.

The Nature of Products is Like Cataracts

Due to ignorance, products appear to be truly established but, in fact, are empty of being established in the way that they appear. This nature of emptiness is exemplified by cataracts.

If a phenomenon were ultimately established, then the phenomenon itself would have to be its own final mode of being, its own essence. If this were the case, then a reasoning consciousness searching for the mode of being of that phenomenon would have to find the phenomenon itself at the conclusion of its analysis. However, a consciousness which analyzes with reasonings, such as the lack of being one or many, finds that the phenomenon under investigation is not ultimately one or many and, therefore, is not ultimately established. The reasoning consciousness finds that the mode of being of the phenomenon, rather than being the phenomenon itself, is its very lack of ultimate establishment, its emptiness of being established in the way in which it appears.

This is similar to the case of a person with cataracts who sees falling hairs. If the falling hairs actually existed, they would have to be seen even more clearly by a person with good vision. The fact that such a person does not see falling hairs indicates that they do not exist. Similarly, if phenomena were ultimately established, as they appear to be to an ignorant consciousness, that ultimate establishment would have to be ascertained by an analytical consciousness specifically investigating ultimate establishment. The fact that such a consciousness, after searching for ultimate establishment, does not find it indicates that phenomena are empty of ultimate establishment.

The Nature of Products is Like a Butter Lamp

Although phenomena do not ultimately exist, they do exist, and it is necessary to posit the factors of the category of appearance — conventional truths. This is illustrated by a butter lamp. Although the flame of a butter lamp does not naturally abide in the lamp, it is undeniable that the flame arises when such things as butter and a wick are assembled. In the same way, although no phenomenon whatsoever ultimately exists, all of cyclic existence and nirvana arise in dependence on the phenomena of the impure class, such as contaminated actions and afflictions, and the phenomena of the pure class, such as the six perfections, the eighteen emptinesses, and the four noble truths.

In this way, the nature of products is illustrated by the examples of stars, cataracts, and a butter lamp. The nature of emptiness is exemplified by cataracts, the nature of appearance by a butter lamp, and the nature of a combination of emptiness and appearance is illustrated by stars.

THE CHARACTERISTIC OF EXPERIENCE

The Experience of Products is Like that of a Magician's Illusion

A magician is able to take pebbles or sticks and, by rubbing them with a salve and casting a mantra, cause them to appear as various pleasant or unpleasant things. The audience, viewing these false appearances, reacts to them with attachment or fear even though, in fact, there is nothing there to bring benefit or harm. In the same way, sentient beings are tortured by the sufferings of cyclic existence due to misconceiving the nature of phenomena. They generate various attachments and hatreds through the force of being affected by the ignorance that conceives of true existence, whereas, in fact, phenomena are not truly existent, and they experience suffering as the result of desire and hatred. Being led like a dog who chases a stone thinking that it is food or tempting a child with an empty fist that it thinks holds candy, sentient beings manufacture various hopes and fears about things that do not truly exist. This suggests that one must reverse attachment and not follow after those objects, attempting to experience their taste.

THE CHARACTERISTIC OF FAULT

Products are viewed as faulty from the viewpoint of their nature of impermanence and from the viewpoint of their nature of suffering.

Products' Fault of Impermanence is Like Dew
A tiny dewdrop on the tip of a blade of grass immediately dries up at the slightest cause, such as being touched by sunlight. It has a nature of utter instability. In the same way, all conditioned phenomena, as soon as they are established, have an inner nature of disintegration, without depending on a later cause for them to fall apart. For this reason, the *Perfection of Wisdom in One Hundred Thousand Stanzas* (*Śatasāhasrikāprajñāpāramitāsūtra*) and Maitreya's *Ornament for Clear Realization* (*Abhisamayālaṃkāra*) refer to impermanence as the aspect of non-being and the aspect of non-existence (because of being the aspect of the non-existence of permanence).[42]

Products' Fault of Suffering is Like a Water Bubble
When water bubbles appear, they have a nature of water, when they disappear, they return to the nature of water. With regard to contaminated feelings, sutra says, "Whatsoever feeling here is a suffering." Feelings of suffering arise in the aspect of suffering as soon as they are produced. When contaminated pleasures cease, they become entities of suffering and are, therefore, called sufferings of change. Because feelings of equanimity are the basis of all suffering, they are explained to be pervasive sufferings of conditioning.

Thus, the three types of contaminated feelings — those of pain, pleasure, and equanimity are all identified as being types of suffering: the suffering of pain, the suffering of change, and the pervasive sufferings of conditioning respectively. Common beings (*pṛthagjana, so so skye bo*) (etymologically, those who take birth (*jana*) by the power of individual (*pṛthak*) contaminated actions and afflictions)[43] do not perceive the three types of feelings as having a nature of suffering. Rather, such beings, often derogatorily referred to as children (*balaka, byis pa*) by the Buddha, attribute qualities of pleasure and pain, pleasantness and unpleasantness to contaminated feelings. To the sight of Superiors, those who have achieved the path of seeing or above, it is said that "Pleasure never exists on the point of the needle of cyclic existence." That is, all experience in the cycle of existence has a nature only of suffering. This is something that can only be understood fully by Superiors; it cannot be understood by common beings. Therefore, the suffering nature of all contaminated feelings is called a truth for Superiors (*āryasatya, 'phags pa'i bden pa*).

CHARACTERISTIC OF RENUNCIATION

The characteristic of renunciation is the lack of true existence of products — that quality of products which, when realized, causes them to be renounced. This characteristic of non-true existence of past, present, and future products is illustrated by a dream, lightning, and clouds, respectively.

Past Products' Characteristics of Renunciation are Like a Dream

When remembering a dream, one may feel desire or hatred for objects that appeared in the dream. Even though the dream objects are not real, they are nonetheless capable of serving as the basis of desire and hatred. In the same way, although the effects of past actions are experienced, it is not necessary that the actions that cause those effects be truly established. The mere fact that an effect is experienced does not entail that its cause must truly exist. Past products, such as actions in former lifetimes, produce effects yet are empty of true establishment, much as past dream objects can cause desire and hatred.

Present Products' Characteristics of Renunciation are Like Lightning

Lightning appears with radiant whiteness just for an instant and then immediately becomes non-existent without one being able to say, "It first appeared there, then it remained here, and finally disappeared there." In the same way, when one searches for present things, whether it be from the viewpoint of object, agent, and action or cause, effect, and entity, one can find no nature that is more than an appearance to a non-defective awareness. Through merely seeking for a truly existent thing with a reasoning consciousness, this object sought is broken down and disappears; it cannot be found anywhere.

Future Products' Characteristic of Renunciation are Like Clouds

A pure empty sky does not have the capacity to produce rain, but rain falls from clouds gathered in the sky, and those clouds can continuously yield such effects as a ripened harvest. In the same way, contaminated actions, afflictions, and predispositions for assuming bad states gather in the natural clear light of the mind. These defilements are merely adventitious and are not the final nature of the mind; otherwise, liberation would be impossible because the mind could not be purified of defilement. The mind is naturally pure and empty of true existence. As the clouds are capable of producing harvests, contaminated actions, afflictions, and predispositions for assuming bad states are capable of producing a variety of fruitional effects in the future, such as rebirth as an animal. These future fruits are empty of true existence. If future things were ultimately established, they would have to exist at all times whereby all effects would have to abide in their causes, in which case it would absurdly follow that all the effects which arise in dependence on a cloud, such as a harvest, would have to exist in the cloud. Because future effects do not exist in their causes but rather arise gradually through a process of maturation, it can be inferred that future products lack ultimate establishment; they are empty of true existence.

Having examined the meaning of the stanza from the *Diamond Cutter*, it is now necessary to explore Bhāvaviveka's argument that this stanza in particular and the Mahāyāna scriptures in general teach the selflessness of phenomena, whereas the stanza from the Hīnayāna sutra which says, "form is like a ball of foam ..." and all other Hīnayāna sutras teach only the selflessness of persons.

The Buddha is ostensibly saying very nearly the same thing in the two stanzas, even repeating the two metaphors of bubbles and a mirage. On face value, there is nothing to point to that indicates that the passage from the Hīnayāna sutra merely teaches the selflessness of persons while the Mahāyāna passage teaches the more subtle selflessness of phenomena. Bhāvaviveka's assertion that the selflessness of phenomena is not taught in the Hīnayāna scriptural collection (*piṭaka*, *sde snod*) revolves around two essential points of disagreement between the Svātantrikas and Prāsaṅgikas: the meaning of the term self (*ātman*, *bdag*) and what constitutes the two obstructions — the afflictive obstructions (*kleśāvaraṇa*, *nyon sgrib*) and the obstructions to omniscience (*jñeyāvaraṇa*, *shres sgrib*). This becomes clear through reexamining his commentary to the thirty-fourth stanza of the seventh chapter of Nāgārjuna's *Treatise on the Middle Way:*

> Self and mine are without entityness, but they are perceived in that way. Therefore, as an antidote to the afflictive obstructions, the Supramundane Victor taught in the [scriptures of the] Hearer Vehicle:
>
> > The Seer of Reality, [the Buddha] said that
> > Form is like a ball of foam,
> > Feeling is like a bubble,
> > Discrimination is like a mirage,
> > Compositional factors are like a banana tree,
> > Consciousness is like an illusion.

In the Mahāyāna [scriptural collection], conditioned phenomena are just without entityness, but they are perceived in that way and are [wrongly] taught to be that way [by others]. Therefore, as an antidote to the afflictive obstructions and the obstructions to omniscience, it is said [in the *Diamond Cutter*]:

> Products are to be viewed as like
> Stars, cataracts, a butter lamp,
> An illusion, dew, a bubble,
> A dream, lightning, and clouds.

Therefore, this is not something to be feared; the intelligent, having analyzed, should become forbearant.

Another [i.e., Buddhapālita] says:

> The Supramundane Victor set forth the categories of illusions, echoes, reflections, mirages, dreams, balls of foam, water bubbles, and banana trees as examples of the selflessness of conditioned phenomena. There is nothing whatsoever real or non-mistaken in them. It is said that these are elaborations, these are falsities. In the statement, "All phenomena are selfless," selfless means non-entityness because the term "self" is a word for entityness.

Regarding that, one who is not another [i.e., myself, Bhāvaviveka], says that here, since the appearance as self is a mistaken reality, and since the term "self" is a word for self [of persons and does not mean entityness], and since a self that is a separate entity does not exist in those [aggregates] and they themselves are not a self just as they are not Īśvara, that scripture, because of referring to the selflessness of persons which is to be specifically realized in the Hearer vehicle, cannot indicate that phenomena are selfless. If it could, it would have been meaningless [for the Buddha] to have taken up another vehicle [namely, the Mahāyāna].[44]

Bhāvaviveka states that the self of persons lacks entityness but is falsely perceived to exist truly. This misconception of the nature of the person constitutes the chief of the afflictive obstructions, which prevent liberation from cyclic existence. Since Hīnayānists seek to be liberated from cyclic existence, they must overcome the afflictive obstructions, and, therefore, the Buddha taught the selflessness of persons — the thorough knowledge of which is the antidote to the afflictive obstructions — in the Hearer or Hīnayāna scriptural collection. For Bhāvaviveka, the stanzas, "Form is like a ball of foam ..." are an instance of a Hīnayāna scripture that teaches the selflessness of persons.

Bhāvaviveka goes on to say that all conditioned phenomena, persons and other things, lack entityness but are falsely perceived to exist truly. The conception of phenomena as truly existing by way of their own entity is the chief of the obstructions to omniscience preventing the achievement of the omniscient consciousness of a Buddha, which is able to perceive directly all objects of knowledge (*jñeya*, *shes bya*) simultaneously. This conception of phenomena as truly existent is more subtle than the conception of a self of persons, and therefore the wisdom realizing that phenomena do not truly exist serves as an antidote to the more coarse afflictive obstructions as well as to the obstructions to omniscience. It is Bhavaviveka's view that the Buddha taught that conditioned phenomena are without entityness in the Mahāyāna scriptural collections so that those with the Mahāyāna aspiration to achieve Buddhahood for the welfare of all sentient beings could realize the non-true existence of phenomena and overcome both obstructions. Bhāvaviveka cites the passage from the *Diamond Cutter* as an instance of a Mahāyāna sutra that teaches that conditioned phenomena are without entityness.

He then goes on to quote Buddhapālita's commentary to the *Treatise on the Middle Way* (VII.34) in which Buddhapālita states that the similes of illusions, balls of foam, banana trees, and so forth that the Buddha employs in the Hīnayāna sutras denote the selflessness of phenomena, not merely that of persons. This is due to the fact that, according to Buddhapālita, when the Buddha the says that all phenomena are selfless, the word selfless (*anātman*, *bdag med pa*) means non-entityness (*niḥsvabhāva*, *ngo bo nyid med pa*), that is, not being established by way of its own entity, because self (*ātman*, *bdag*) is another word for entityness (*svabhāva*, *ngo bo nyid*).

Bhāvaviveka disagrees, saying that the term self in this context refers only to a misconceived nature of the person. The Hīnayāna scriptures, by saying that form is like a ball of foam, feeling is like a bubble, discrimination is like a mirage, compositional factors are like a banana tree, and consciousness is like an illusion, are indicating that a self that is a different entity from the aggregates does not exist anywhere among the aggregates, nor are the aggregates individually or collectively the self. The passage discusses only the nature of the person in terms of the five aggregates and in no way refers to the lack of entityness of phenomena, as Buddhapālita contends. Hearer scriptures teach only the object of a Hearer's wisdom, namely, the selflessness of persons. If the object of a Bodhisattva's wisdom, the non-entityness of phenomena, were taught in the Hīnayāna scriptures, then the complete antidote for the removal of both obstructions would be available in the Hīnayāna canon and the Buddha's teaching of the Mahāyāna scriptures would be totally redundant.

This controversy between Bhāvaviveka and Buddhapālita rests on the disagreement between the Svātantrikas and Prāsaṅgikas on three fundamental issues: the meaning of self and selflessness, the nature of the two obstructions, and the distinguishing feature of Hīnayāna and Mahāyāna.

According to the Svātantrikas, Yogācārins, Sautrāntikas, and Vaibhāṣikas, the term "self" (*ātman*, *bdag*) in isolation, and not in phrases such as "selflessness of phenomena" (*dharmanairātmya*, *chos kyi bdag med*), refers only to an attribute falsely ascribed to the person (*pudgala*, *gang zag*); it does not refer to other phenomena. It should be noted that self, in this context, is not a synonym for person as it usually is; when these tenet systems refute the existence of self, they are not refuting the existence of persons. Rather, they are negating a special type of person, a person which can appear to the mind independent of the appearance of other phenomena.[45]

The Prāsaṅgikas apply the bare term "self" to a wider context than merely the false nature of the person.[46] Buddhapālita says that self is a word for entityness,[47] the inherent existence which is falsely ascribed to all phenomena, including persons. Candrakīrti says in his *Commentary to Āryadeva's "Four Hundred"* (*Catuḥśatakaṭīkā*):

> Regarding this, "self" is the entity of things that does not depend on another, [it is] inherent existence. The non-existence of that is selflessness. Through the division into phenomena and persons it is understood as twofold, the selflessness of phenomena and the selflessness of persons.[48]

Thus, for the Prāsaṅgikas, self does not refer merely to a falsely attributed quality of just persons, but refers to an independent entity, an entity which exists under its own power, the existence of an objective mode of subsistence which is not merely imputed by terminology.[49] A person's quality of being an independent, inherently existent entity is a self of persons. Such a quality superimposed on phenomena other than the person is a self of phenomena. The non-existence of those two false qualities of persons and phenomena is the selflessnesses of persons and the selflessness of phenomena. In the Prāsaṅgika system there is no difference in subtlety between the two selflessnesses. They are distinguished from the point of view of the bases that are selfless, that is, persons and phenomena.

The Svātantrikas assert a difference of coarseness and subtlety between the two selflessnesses and also assert different objects of negation by the two selflessnesses. The lack of being a substantially existent person in the sense of self-sufficiency is the subtle selflessness of persons. This selflessness is coarser and more easily realized than the selflessness of phenomena — that phenomena do not exist from their own side without being posited by the power of a non-defective awareness (see pp. 143-150). Thus, unlike the Prāsaṅgikas, the Svātantrikas do not negate the same quality when they establish the selflessnesses of persons and phenomena. When they say that the person is selfless, they are negating the person's substantial existence in the sense of self-sufficiency. When they say that phenomena are selfless, they are negating the existence of phenomena from their own side without being posited by the power of appearing to a non-defective awareness. Though the Prāsaṅgikas distinguish the two selflessnesses from the point of view of that which is selfless, the Svātantrikas distinguish the two selflessnesses from the point of view of how they are selfless.[50] Let us examine the Svātantrika presentation of selflessness of persons in more detail.

In the Svātantrika school, the conception of the self of persons (*pudgalātmagraha*, *gang zag gi bdag 'dzin*) takes three forms:

1 the conception of a substantially existent self in the sense of self-sufficiency, which is the conception of the existence of a self that is capable of being identified independently without relying on the identification of the aggregates. This is the innate (*sahaja*, *lhan skyes*) conception of a self of persons according to the Svātantrikas, present in the continua of all sentient beings.
2 the conception of a self that is of a different character from the aggregates, that is, the conception of the existence of a self that

does not share the aggregates' qualities of production, abiding, and disintegration.

3 the conception of a permanent, single, independent self which is permanent in the sense that it is without production and disintegration, single in the sense that it lacks parts, and independent in the sense that it does not rely on another.

The last two conceptions of a self of persons do not exist in the mental continua of persons whose minds have not been affected by the study of non-Buddhist systems of tenets that propound such a self, like Sāṃkhya or Vedānta. Because the latter two conceptions do not exist in the continua of all sentient beings, but exist only for those who have studied false systems, these conceptions are called artificial (*parikalpita*, *kun btags*) conceptions of a self of persons by the Svātantrikas.[51]

The first conception, that of a substantially existent self, is the subtle conception of a self of persons and must be abandoned in order to be liberated from cyclic existence. This subtle conception of the I holds the self and the aggregates to be like a master and his servants, with the self seen as the controller of the body, for example. This innate conception of self holds the I or person to be substantially existent because it conceives of the I as self-sufficient, not depending on the aggregates.[52] The self-sufficient person is conceived to have a character different from and independent of the aggregates in the sense of acting as their controller.

The existence of such a self-sufficient person is refuted by acknowledging that in order for the person to be identified, one must rely on the prior identification of some other phenomenon, namely one or more of the aggregates, in which case the person cannot be self-sufficient. For example, the mottle of colors on a butterfly's wing cannot be identified without reference to the colors that compose it; it does not exist separately from those colors.[53]

The Svātantrikas reject the existence of a substantially existent person that is something other than the aggregates and assert that the person is merely designated to the aggregates. They find support in this statement from sutra:

> Just as, for example, chariot is designated,
> To a collection parts,
> So, in dependence on the aggregates,
> Conventionally, a sentient being is named.[54]

Thus, the Svātantrikas reject the existence of a self-sufficient person but do not reject the existence of the person. Bhāvaviveka says in the eighteenth chapter of his *Lamp for (Nāgārjuna's) "Wisdom"*, "Thus, we also actually impute the term self to consciousnesses conventionally because, since consciousness takes rebirth, it is the self."[55] For scriptural support that consciousness is the self, Bhāvaviveka cites two statements:

> Oneself is one's own protector
> Who else can offer protection?
> Through taming the self well
> The wise attain high status.[56]

And:

> Taming the mind is good
> Taming the mind brings bliss.[57]

Since one sutra refers to taming the self and the other to taming the mind, the terms mind and self are, according to Bhāvaviveka, used interchangeably in this context. Bhāvaviveka reasons that consciousness is the conventionally existent self because consciousness is that which takes rebirth; it appropriates the other aggregates which, together with consciousness, serve as the basis of designation of the conventionally existent person in the new lifetime.[58]

Those who assert that the five aggregates are the person, citing the quotation above about the chariot, are not saying that all five aggregates are the person nor that the five aggregates individually are the person. Rather, they assert that the collection of the five aggregates is the person. Furthermore, when Bhāvaviveka states that the mental consciousness is the person, he is not implicitly denying that the collection of the aggregates is the person. Rather, he holds that the main mental consciousness is the traveller continuously migrating through cyclic existence and, therefore, is appropriately designed with the term "person."[59] The positions on the conventional status of the person of the non-Prāsaṅgika Buddhist schools may be summarized in a general way as follows:

School	*Conventionally Existent Person*
Kashmiri Vaibhāṣika	continuum of the aggregates
Sautrāntika Following Scripture	continuum of the aggregates
Sautrāntika Following Reasoning	mental consciousness
Yogācāra Following Reasoning	mental consciousness
Yogācāra Following Scripture	mind-basis-of-all (*ālayavijñāna*)
Sautrāntika-Svātantrika	mental consciousness
Yogācāra-Svātantrika	continuum of consciousness[60]

Dispensing with the qualification "continuum" (*saṃtāna*), which here refers to the possessor of a series of moments, (for example, the continuation of moments of the mental consciousness over time)[61] the non-Prāsaṅgika schools posit either the collection of the five aggregates or some form of the mental consciousness as the person. Their views are summarized by Candrakīrti in his *Supplement to (Nāgarjuna's "Treatise on the) Middle Way"* (*Madhyamakāvatāra*) when he says:

> [The Buddha said,] "There is no establishment of self
> which is other than the aggregates."
> Therefore, the object of observation of the view of self is
> only the aggregates.
> Some assert all five aggregates as the basis
> Of the view of self, some assert just the mind.[62]

The Prāsaṅgikas deny that the collection of the aggregates is the person and that the mental consciousness is the person. They reject the view that the collection is the person by analyzing the relationship between a chariot and its parts.

The Svātantrikas assert that the collection of the axle, nails, wheels, car, and so forth of the chariot is the chariot and that when one searches for the object designated by the term "chariot" the collection of the parts of the chariot is found.[63] They say that the chariot is not just imputed to its parts nominally; if the basis of the designation of the name "chariot" were not the chariot, then the chariot would not exist. In the same way, they assert that the collection of the aggregates, the basis of designation of the term "person," is the person.[64]

Candrakīrti, in his *Supplement to the Middle Way*, rejects the view that the collection of the parts of the chariot is the chariot and that the collection of the aggregates is the person.[65] Although the chariot is designated in dependence on its parts, the parts of the chariot are not the chariot. If the mere collection of the parts of the chariot were the chariot, it would absurdly follow that the pile of disassembled parts of the chariot would be the chariot itself because, as the Svātantrikas and so forth say, the collection of the parts of the chariot is the chariot.[66]

Someone might object that it is not being said that the mere collection of the parts is the chariot. Rather, the special shape of the arranged parts is the chariot. Candrakīrti rejects this view, saying that there is no difference in the shape of the axles, wheels, and so forth before and after assembly. Therefore, since the chariot does not exist among the disassembled parts, it also does not exist among the assembled parts. It is also not feasible that the parts' shapes somehow change after they are assembled because no such change is observed. Finally, the general shape of the collection of the parts cannot be the chariot because, according to the Svātantrikas, the chariot is substantially established (*dravyasiddha*, *rdzas su grub pa*), but the collection of the parts and its shape are imputedly existent (*prajñaptisat*, *btags yod*).[67]

The Prāsaṅgikas do not negate the existence of the chariot; they negate the existence of the chariot as the collection of its parts. They assert that the collection of the parts of the chariot is the basis of the designation of the term "chariot," but the chariot is merely imputed to those parts. No matter how thoroughly the parts are scrutinized, the chariot cannot be found. The basis of the designation — the collection of the parts — is not and cannot be the object designated — the chariot. The basis of a particular designation and the object of that designation are mutually exclusive.[68] Just as the collection of the parts of the chariot is not the chariot, the collection of the aggregates is not the person.

The later seventeenth and early eighteenth century Tibetan scholar, Jam-yang-shay-ba, argues that Bhāvaviveka's contention that the mental consciousness is the person demonstrates that he has not abandoned the conception of a substantially existent person in the sense of self-sufficiency because he asserts that the person has a character different from that of the aggregates. According to Jam-yang-shay-ba, the conception of the person as having a character different from that of the aggregates takes two forms. The first is exemplified by that of the master and servant in which the person is the appropriator, the owner of the aggregates, with the self or person having the character of permanence, in contrast to the impermanent nature of the aggregates. It is the view of Jam-yang-shay-ba that this conception of self, the type of self asserted by the non-Buddhists, is what Bhāvaviveka and the Svātantrikas refute. They are unable to refute the more subtle conception of a self of persons in which the person is seen to be like a head salesman and the aggregates as junior salesmen. Here, the head salesman and the junior salesmen are similar in being salesmen, but the head salesman stands apart as the controller and supervisor of the others and thus has a distinct character. When Bhāvaviveka asserts that consciousness is the person, he falls into this type of conception of a self of persons because consciousness is itself an aggregate, as the head salesman is a salesman, but is nonetheless set above the other aggregates as their controller. The fact that consciousness has a distinctive character that separates it from the other aggregates is implicit in Bhāvaviveka's statement that consciousness is the person; when one searches among the aggregates for the conventionally existent person, it is Bhāvaviveka's contention that one will find consciousness. Thus, there must be some special quality of consciousness which sets it apart.[69]

What then is the person? In Candrakīrti's sevenfold reasoning, the person is shown not to exist inherently because when the object designated by the term "person" is sought, it is not found to be inherently the same as the aggregates, different from the aggregates, the basis of the aggregates, based on the aggregates, the possessor of the aggregates, the shape of the aggregates, or the collection of the aggregates. According to the Prāsaṅgikas, the self or person is the mere I which serves as the basis for the generation of the awareness thinking "I" in dependence on the aggregates. The person is merely imputed in terms of the aggregates and is not established by way of its own entity but nonetheless exists, performing the functions of accumulating actions and experiencing the fruition of those actions.[70]

The Prāsaṅgikas assert that the conception of the person as existing by way of its own entity and not merely being posited conventionally is the subtle conception of a self of persons. In reality, the person is merely posited by the power of convention; when the object designated by the verbal convention "person" is searched for, it is not found because the person and the aggregates do not inherently exist in any of the seven ways, which are considered to be exhaustive. That is, if the person is not inherently the same as, different from, based on, the base of, the possessor of, the collection of, or the shape of the aggregates, then the person does not inherently exist, substantially exist, or exist by way of its own character. This non-existence of the person by way of its own entity is the very subtle selflessness of persons.

According to Prāsaṅgika, through directly seeing and meditating on the mere absence of a person that exists by way of its own entity without being designated by conventions, one is able to abandon the innate conception of a self of persons. This is because the wisdom directly realizing the person's non-existence by way of its own entity and the ignorant consciousness conceiving the person to be established by way of its own entity both observe the same object — the mere I designated to the aggregates. However, their mode of apprehension of that object is directly contradictory, with the wisdom consciousness apprehending the mere I as empty of inherent existence and the ignorant consciousness apprehending the mere I as inherently existent. Through directly seeing and then becoming accustomed to the emptiness of inherent existence of the person, this wisdom consciousness uproots and abandons the conception of a self of persons.

For the Prāsaṅgikas, the selflessness of persons taught by the Svātantrikas, the lack of being a substantially existent person in the sense of self-sufficiency, is not the subtle selflessness of persons, being coarser than the person's lack of inherent existence. Even though the Svātantrikas, at least in terms of their own assertions, realize the person's lack of being substantially existent in the sense of self-sufficiency, they are incapable of abandoning the conception of the person as established by way of its own character because they hold that the person does in fact exist by way of its own character conventionally in the sense that the person is analytically findable among the aggregates. Thus, according to the Prāsaṅgikas, the Svātantrikas retain the subtle conception of a self of persons.[71]

Let us reiterate the coarse and subtle conceptions of self according to the Svātantrikas and Prāsaṅgikas. For the Svātantrikas, the conception of a self of persons has coarse and subtle forms. The coarse conception of a self of persons is the conception of a permanent, single, independent self. This is also an artificial conception in the sense that it is present only in the continua of those whose minds have been affected by the study of false systems of tenets that propound the existence of such a self. The subtle conception of a self of persons is that of a substantially existent person in the sense of self-sufficiency. This conception is innate, existing in the continua of all sentient beings who have not abandoned it, but can also be artificial.

The selflessness of phenomena, which is more subtle than that of persons, has only one form for the Sautrāntika-Svātantrikas: a phenomenon's lack of being established from its own side without being merely posited through the power of appearing to a non-defective awareness (see pp. 143-150). For the Yogācāra-Svātantrikas, this becomes the subtle selflessness of phenomena, adding the emptiness of subject and object being different substantial entities as the coarse selflessness of phenomena to be the object of the wisdom of Solitary Realizers.

The conception of the person as substantially existent in the sense of self-sufficiency, the subtle conception of a self of persons for the Svātantrikas, is asserted to be the coarse conception of self by the Prāsaṅgikas. Further, this coarse conception has artificial and innate forms, the artificial coarse conception being like master and servant with the self having a character different from that of the aggregates. The innate coarse conception of a self of persons is that in which the self and the aggregates are conceived to be like a head salesman and junior salesmen, with the self sharing some of the qualities of the aggregates but still maintaining a special status, being identifiable as the mental consciousness when analyzed.

The Prāsaṅgikas contend that the Svātantrikas only refute the artificial coarse conception of a self of persons. They are, therefore, said to abandon only the conception of self asserted by the non-Buddhists. They do not abandon, nor are they aware of, the innate coarse conception of a self of persons, that of the head salesman-junior salesmen analogy.

Being incapable of recognizing and abandoning even this form of the coarse conception of a self of persons, which exists naturally in the continua of all sentient beings who have not found the Prāsaṅgika view, the Svātantrikas and other Buddhist tenet systems are afflicted further by the subtle conception of a self of persons, the conception of the person as inherently existent, or established by way of its own entity and existing by way of its own character. This is the very subtle conception of persons and is abandoned by the wisdom realizing the emptiness of inherent existence of the person.

The selflessness of phenomena is the emptiness of inherent existence of phenomena other than persons, according to Prāsaṅgika. There is no difference in subtlety nor in the object of negation of the two selflessnesses; they are distinguished merely by the substratum qualified by the emptiness of inherent existence, namely persons and phenomena.[72]

In summary, what the Svātantrikas assert to be the innate subtle conception of self, the Prāsaṅgikas call artificial and coarse. There is an innate coarse conception of self which the Prāsaṅgikas say is not identified by the Svātantrikas, but even this is coarse. The subtle conception of a self of persons is the conception of the person as inherently existent, and this conception is identified and abandoned only by the Prāsaṅgikas.

The Svātantrika-Prāsaṅgika schism on the question of self and selflessness relates directly to their assertions concerning the two obstructions. The obstructions to liberation, literally the afflictive obstructions (*kleśāvaraṇa, nyon sgrib*), are those factors preventing liberation from cyclic existence. The obstructions to omniscience, literally the obstructions to objects of knowledge (*jñeyāvaraṇa, shes sgrib*), prevent the achievement of a Buddha's omniscient consciousness which simultaneously cognizes all objects of knowledge (*jñeya, shes bya*).[73]

According to the Vaibhāṣikas, Sautrāntikas, Yogācārins, and Svātantrikas, the conception of the person as substantially existent in the sense of self-sufficiency, having a character different from the aggregates, is the conception of a self of persons and is the chief of the afflictive obstructions, the others being desire, hatred, pride, and so forth. By negating the referent object of that conception — a self of persons — and becoming accustomed to that negation over the path, one is liberated from rebirth in cyclic existence. The selflessness of persons is thus the chief object of meditation for Hearers and Solitary Realizers (except in Yogācāra-Svātantrika, where it is said that Solitary Realizers meditate on the emptiness of subject and object being different substantial entities).[74] For the Svātantrikas, the obstructions to omniscience (or subtle obstructions to omniscience according to the Yogācāra-Svātantrikas) are the conception of true existence together with its seeds — the conception that phenomena are established as their own mode of subsistence without being posited by a non-defective awareness.

Bodhisattvas meditate on the emptiness of true existence in order to overcome the obstructions to omniscience and achieve Buddhahood. Their motivation is this. It is said in sutra:

> Buddhas neither wash sins away with water, nor remove the sufferings of beings with their hands. They transfer not their realizations to others. Beings are freed through the teaching of truth, the nature of things.[75]

Thus, the benefit bestowed on sentient beings by Buddhas derives from their abilities as teachers. In order to teach effectively, it is not sufficient that they have a good motivation; they must know what to adopt and discard, as well as the individual capacities and interests of their students. Therefore, they must be omniscient, and this entails the abandonment of the obstructions to omniscience. The Prāsaṅgikas assert that Bodhisattvas must first abandon the obstructions to liberation — the afflictive obstructions — before beginning to work on the obstructions to omniscience, but the Svātantrikas assert that Bodhisattvas begin to abandon the two obstructions simultaneously, beginning on the first Bodhisattva ground (*bhūmisa*). The Sautrāntika-Svātantrikas hold that the afflictive obstructions are fully abandoned by the eighth ground, with the last three grounds devoted entirely to removing the remaining obstructions to omniscience. The Yogācāra-Svātantrikas hold that the abandonment of both obstructions and the achievement of Buddhahood are simultaneous.[76]

According to the Svātantrikas, Hīnayānists do not realize the emptiness of true existence. For the Prāsaṅgikas, the conception of true existence together with its seeds are the afflictive obstructions, and mistaken dualistic appearance — the false appearance of phenomena as truly existent — together with its predispositions are the obstructions to omniscience. In order to be liberated from cyclic existence, one must destroy the conception of true existence through repeated cognition of the emptiness of true existence of persons and phenomena. After the conception of true existence — the obstructions to liberation — has been destroyed, the false appearance of phenomena as inherently existent remains, even to the non-conceptual sense consciousnesses, despite the fact that Bodhisattvas do not assent to that false appearance, instead viewing phenomena as like illusions, appearing one way but existing another.

They then go on to abandon the obstructions to omniscience, removing this false appearance, until they are able to perceive the two truths simultaneously and directly at Buddhahood.[77]

Therefore, it is the position of the Prāsaṅgikas that anyone who wishes to be liberated from cyclic existence must realize the emptiness of inherent existence of persons and phenomena. The Svātantrika assertion that one merely needs to cognize the selflessness of persons is rejected, as is their explanation of what constitutes the subtle selflessness of persons. For the Prāsaṅgikas, the conception of inherent existence is the chief of the afflictive obstructions, the root of all the other afflictive emotions such as desire and hatred. The realization of a selflessness less subtle than the emptiness of inherent existence, such as the selflessness of persons realized by the Svātantrikas, does not destroy any afflictions because it has not penetrated to the final nature of the person. Candrakīrti says in his *Supplement to the Middle Way* (VI.131):

> [According to] you, yogis perceiving selflessness
> Would not realize the reality of forms and so forth.
> [Therefore,] due to seeing forms [as inherently existent] and
> relating [to them as such]
> Desire and so forth are produced because their nature has
> not been understood.[78]

The emptiness of being a substantially existent person in the sense of self-sufficiency is not the very subtle selflessness of persons because when the former is realized, one does not understand that the person is not established by way of its own entity, and the person's not being established by way of its own entity is the very subtle selflessness of persons. Furthermore, through merely seeing and then becoming accustomed to the person's emptiness of substantial existence in the sense of self-sufficiency, one is not able to abandon the desire that sees forms as real because such a realization does not entail an understanding of forms as empty of inherent existence; the conception of forms as inherently existent is the cause of that desire.[79] Therefore, Candrakīrti is saying that the Svātantrikas and all others who merely realize a coarse selflessness of persons are incapable of abandoning the afflictive emotions and being liberated from cyclic existence because they have not destroyed the conception of true existence, the chief of the obstructions to liberation. Candrakīrti says in his commentary to Nāgārjuna's *Sixty Stanzas of Reasoning:*

> The abandonment of the afflictive emotions simply does not occur for those who wish to abandon the afflictive emotions but who apprehend the inherent existence of forms and so forth.[80]

Merely realizing that the person lacks substantial existence in the sense of self-sufficiency is not enough to abandon the afflictive emotions. It is impossible to abandon desire without directly realizing that forms do not inherently exist.[81]

It is the Prāsaṅgika position, then, that everyone who seeks liberation from cyclic existence must realize the subtle selflessness — the emptiness of inherent existence of persons and phenomena — whether that liberation is sought for one's own sake, the Hīnayāna motivation, or for the sake of others, the Mahāyāna motivation. There is no difference between the objects of the wisdom of Hearers and Solitary Realizers on the one hand and Bodhisattvas on the other. Referring to this subtle selflessness, the Prāsaṅgikas master Śāntideva says in his *Engaging in the Bodhisattva Deeds* *(Bodhicaryāvatara,* IX.41cd):

> Scripture says that without this path
> There can be no enlightenment.

That is, it is said in scripture that without the path realizing the emptiness of inherent existence, one cannot achieve the enlightenment of a Hearer or Solitary Realizer Foe Destroyer (*arhan*, *dga' bcom pa*) or that of a Buddha. Candrakīrti stresses that the knowledge of both selflessnesses is necessary in order to be liberated from cyclic existence. He says in his *Supplement to the Middle Way:*

> For the liberation of transmigrators, this selflessness
> Was taught in two aspects, with the divisions of persons and phenomena.[82]

[He also cites the] *Sutra on the Ten Grounds* (*Daśabhūmikasūtra*) to support the Prāsaṅgika position that Hīnayānists — Hearers and Solitary Realizers — and Mahāyānists realize the same selflessness. The sutra states that Bodhisattvas on the seventh ground are able to outshine Hearers and Solitary Realizers in terms of their understanding of the non-inherent existence of phenomena. Bodhisattvas on the sixth ground and below are not able to outshine them. If Hearers and Solitary Realizers do not realize the subtle selflessness of phenomena, as Bhāvaviveka contends, then it would follow that even Bodhisattvas abiding on the first ground would outshine all Hearers and Solitary Realizers in terms of their understanding of the emptiness of inherent existence of phenomena. However, because the sutra states that they are only outshone on the seventh ground, Candrakīrti concludes that Hearers, Solitary Realizers, and Bodhisattvas all realize the same subtle emptiness of inherent existence.[83]

Because Candrakīrti identifies the conception of inherent existence as the root of the afflictive emotions, if Hearers and Solitary Realizers did not realize the emptiness of inherent existence, it would absurdly follow that they could not abandon any of the afflictive emotions and would never be liberated from cyclic existence. Furthermore, if Hearers and Solitary Realizers did not realize the subtle selflessness of phenomena, they would continue to apprehend the aggregates to be inherently existent, in which case they could not fully realize the selflessness of the person, because the aggregates are the basis of the designation of the I or the person. Nāgārjuna says in his *Precious Garland:*

> There is misconception of an 'I' as long
> As the aggregates are misconceived.
> When this conception of an 'I' exists,
> There is action that results in birth.[84]

Without refuting the referent object of the conception of inherent existence with respect to the aggregates, which are the basis of designation of the person, the referent object of the conception of an inherently existent person — the object designated to the aggregates — cannot be refuted.[85] In other words, without refuting the inherent existence of the aggregates, the basis of designation of the person, the inherent existence of the person cannot be refuted.

This raises a problem. It is the position of the Prāsaṅgikas that as long as one misconceives the nature of the aggregates, one misconceives the nature of the person because the aggregates are the basis of designation of the person; in order for the person to appear to the mind, the aggregates must appear first. Thus, if the basis of designation is conceived to be truly existent, the object designated, in this case the person, is conceived to be truly existent. The conception of a truly existent person arises from the conception of the aggregates as truly existent. However, in practice it is said that the emptiness of the person is to be realized before the emptiness of the aggregates.

Candrakīrti says in his *Clear Words:*

> Because the I is not observed, the mine, the basis of designation as the self, also would not be observed at all. Just as when a chariot is burned, its parts are also burned and thus are not observed, so, when yogis realize the selflessness [of the person], they will also realize the selflessness of the mine, the things that are the aggregates.[86]

How can this be, if the Prāsaṅgikas also wish to maintain that one continues to misconceive the nature of the person as long as the aggregates are misconceived and that without realizing the emptiness of the aggregates, one cannot realize the emptiness of the person? In answer, it is said that the consciousness realizing the emptiness of the person can, without relying on another consciousness, remove superimpositions, misconceptions about the aggregates, and thus induce ascertainment of the emptiness of inherent existence of the aggregates. However, as long as the consciousness actively misconceiving the nature of the aggregates has not been abandoned, it is impossible to generate a wisdom consciousness understanding the emptiness of the person.[87]

A more satisfying solution to the problem would be to say that Candrakīrti's contention that yogis first realize the selflessness of the person means that they initially realize the selflessness of the internal aggregates (*nang gi phung po*), which are the basis of designation of the person. They thereby come to understand that the person is also selfless, at which point they go on to investigate the selflessness of other phenomena. Such an interpretation supports Candrakīrti's statement that yogis begin with the person while at the same time remaining consistent with Nāgārjuna's assertion that the I is misconceived so long as the aggregates are misconceived; by understanding the selflessness of the internal aggregates, which serve as the basis of designation of the person, yogis destroy the misconception of the aggregates, whereby they cease to misconceive the I.[88] Candrakīrti also finds support for his contention that Hīnayānists realize the subtle selflessness in statements by Nāgārjuna. In his proof that the Mahāyāna sutras are the word of the Buddha, he says in his *Precious Garland* (*Ratnāvalī*):

> The teaching in the Mahāyāna of non-production
> And of extinction in the Hīnayāna [refer to] the same

Emptiness [since they show that inherent existence] is extinguished
And that nothing [inherently existent] is produced.
Thus, let the Mahāyāna be accepted [as the Buddha's words.][89]

The emptiness of inherently existent production taught in the Mahāyāna sutras and the extinguishment of products referred to in the Hīnayāna sutras refer to the same thing. Therefore, the subtle selflessness of phenomena is taught for the sake of Hīnayānists in their own scriptures.

Bhāvaviveka's contention that the selflessness of persons and the selflessness of phenomena differ in subtlety and that they are objects of the wisdom of Hīnayānists and Mahāyānists respectively is objectionable to the Prāsaṅgikas for several reasons. First, as we have seen, the Prāsaṅgikas assert that Hearers and Solitary Realizers realize the selflessness of phenomena. This assertion rests on the Prāsaṅgikas' identification of the conception of an inherently existent person as the subtle conception of a self of persons. This conception of inherent existence also applies to the aggregates, the basis of designation of the person. Having realized the non-inherent existence of the person through merely reflecting on the same reasoning (such as the sevenfold reasoning), but in this case, with regard to the aggregates, one is able to realize the non-inherent existence of the aggregates. One is thereby able to realize that phenomena do not inherently exist.[90] Because there is no difference in subtlety between the selflessness of persons and phenomena, having realized one, it is possible easily to realize the other by merely applying a similar form of reasoning, substituting a phenomenon such as "form" in place of the "I" as the subject of the consequence.

The Prāsaṅgikas are thus able to assert that anyone who realizes the selflessness of persons can realize the selflessness of phenomena by shifting the focus of the reasoning. Because Hearers and Solitary Realizers understand the subtle selflessness of persons — the non-inherent existence of the person — they are equally capable of penetrating the selflessness of phenomena. Through merely realizing the non-existence of a self that is substantially existent in the sense of being self-sufficient and that has a character different from that of the aggregates, one cannot realize the selflessness of phenomena because one has not fully refuted the conception of a self of persons.[91] Because the Svātantrikas refute only the coarse conception of a self of persons and have not penetrated the subtle selflessness, they are incapable of asserting that Hīnayānists can realize the selflessness of phenomena through having realized the selflessness of persons, in that they hold the two selflessnesses to differ in the subtlety of their object of negation.

Bhāvaviveka's contention that there is a difference in subtlety in the two selflessnesses and that only the coarser selflessness, that of persons, must be realized in order to be liberated from rebirth is attacked by Candrakīrti from another perspective as well. He argues that it is not correct that one can abandon the afflictions and their seeds and be liberated from cyclic existence by meditating on the person's lack of being substantially existent in the sense of self-sufficiency because that selflessness is not the final mode of being of phenomena. Bhāvaviveka agrees that the selflessness of persons is not the final reality, rather the more subtle selflessness of phenomena — their emptiness of true existence — is the final reality. Further, Bhāvaviveka holds that ultimately the root cause of cyclic existence is the conception of true existence. Candrakīrti argues that it is contradictory for Bhāvaviveka to assert on the one hand that sentient beings cycle in mundane existence through the force of the innate conception of a self, the conception of true existence, and yet hold on the other hand that through meditating on the selflessness of a substantially existent person one can be liberated from cyclic existence. In other words, Candrakīrti finds it senseless for Bhāvaviveka to assert that the conception of a self of phenomena is the root of cyclic existence but that one can be liberated from cyclic existence without using the antidote to the conception of a self of phenomena. According to Bhāvaviveka, one can be freed from suffering without uprooting the ultimate cause of suffering; one can be released from rebirth, which is caused by the conception of a self of phenomena, by abandoning something which, according to Bhāvaviveka, is less subtle and fundamental, namely, the conception of a self of persons. The Svātantrikas assert that the conception of a self of persons arises in dependence on the more subtle conception of true existence, yet they posit the conception of a self of persons as the root of cyclic existence.[92] Candrakīrti finds this to be unacceptable. He writes in his *Supplement to the Middle Way* (VI. 140-141):

> [You hold] that when selflessness is realized
> One abandons the permanent self, [but] it is not asserted

That it is the base of the conception of self. Hence it is
  fantastic to propound
That through knowing selflessness [of substantially existent
  persons], the view of self [i.e., true existence] is
  eradicated.
That while looking for a snake living in a hole in the wall of
  one's house,
One's qualms can be removed and the fear of the snake
  abandoned
By [someone's saying], "There is no elephant here,"
Is, alas, laughable to other [scholars].[93]

That is, Bhāvaviveka's contention that one can overcome the view of a self of phenomena by abandoning the less subtle view of a self of persons is like trying to calm someone who fears that there is a snake in his house by telling him that there is no elephant in the house.

Bhāvaviveka, however, has already considered this qualm and answered it. He accepts that sentient beings cycle in mundane existence through the force of the innate conception of a self of phenomena, the conception that phenomena truly exist. He also holds that the selflessness of persons is not the final mode of subsistence of phenomena. However, he argues that one does not have to meditate on the selflessness of phenomena in order to be liberated from cyclic existence. He says in his *Essence of the Middle Way:*

Some who are frightened
Mistake a rope for a snake,
The knowledge that it is a coiled vine
Is a mind classed as an antidote.[94]

That is, a person might see a coiled piece of speckled rope and think that it was a snake. If that person were told, "It isn't a snake, it's a coiled vine from a tree," the person's fear of a snake would be allayed. Despite the fact that a vine is not the mode of being a rope, one can nonetheless effectively remove the fear of a snake with an erroneous statement. In the same way, although the selflessness of persons is not the final mode oof subsistence of phenomena, it is not contradictory that by meditating on it one can abandon cyclic existence and its causes.[95] Bhāvaviveka cites a passage from sutra to prove that the Buddha used this technique of expedience: not telling the truth in order to more easily benefit others. The *Treasury of Tathāgata Sutra* (*Tathāgatakośasūtra*) says:

> Kāśyapa, it is thus. Some persons are pained by the unfounded doubt [that they have drunk] poison and say, "I drank poison! I drank poison!" and beat their breasts and wail. For them, one who is skilled in medical methods acts in such a way as to remove the unreal poison [by giving them a medicine to make them vomit so that they believe that the poison has been removed[96]]. Similarly, Kāśyapa, for childish beings who are beset by the afflictive emotions, I teach doctrines in an incorrect way.[97]

Bhāvaviveka is thus willing to go to considerable lengths to uphold his contention that the selflessness of phenomena is not taught in the Hīnayāna scriptures and, therefore, not realized by Hearers and Solitary Realizers. He asserts that statements in the Hīnayāna scriptures which state that all phenomena are selfless are teaching that phenomena lack a self of persons because, when the term "self" is used in those scriptures in referring to phenomena as selfless, it refers to a self of persons.[98] According to Bhāvaviveka, if the selflessness of phenomena — the emptiness of true existence — were taught in the Hīnayāna scriptures, then the teaching of the Mahāyāna would have been pointless. As noted before, Bhāvaviveka's position rests on his understanding of the two obstructions, an understanding not shared by the Prāsaṅgikas. For Bhāvaviveka, the conception of a self of persons is the chief of the obstructions to liberation. By realizing the selflessness of persons, one can achieve liberation from cyclic existence, the goal of the Hīnayānists. The conception of true existence, on the other hand, is the chief of the obstructions to omniscience. Through realizing the selflessness of phenomena, Bodhisattvas achieve Buddhahood. If the selflessness of phenomena, the object of a Bodhisattva's wisdom, were taught in the Hīnayāna sutras, the means of achieving Buddhahood would be fully accessible in their scriptures; any further exposition would be redundant. Therefore, Bhāvaviveka says that the Buddha's teaching of the Mahāyāna would have been meaningless. It is clear then that Bhāvaviveka distinguishes the disciples of the Hīnayāna and Mahāyāna by the object of their wisdom. Although the difference in motivation is clearly important, with Hīnayānists seeking mere liberation from cyclic existence and Bodhisattvas seeking Buddhahood for the welfare of others, motivation alone does not distinguish the two vehicles for Bhāvaviveka; he seems to imply that if the teaching of the selflessness of phenomena were available to Hearers, they would be capable of achieving Buddhahood. In order to defend the efficacy and purpose of the Mahāyāna scriptures, Bhāvaviveka is therefore willing to disregard or explain away any and all references to the selflessness of phenomena that appear in Hīnayāna sutras.

It is important to note that Bhāvaviveka is not arguing with Buddhapālita and the Prāsaṅgikas about the meaning of the selflessness of persons and phenomean. It is his belief that he and Buddhapālita, as Mādhyamikas, are in agreement on that point. He is apparently unaware that the selflessness of persons and the selflessness of phenomena that he propounds is something other than that held by the Prāsaṅgikas. Indeed, it is only in the works of Candrakīrti, and later Tsong-kha-pa, that we find this distinction elucidated. Thus, Bhāvaviveka from his standpoint has no quarrel with Buddhapālita about what the selflessness of phenomena is; his objection concerns where it is taught.

Candrakīrti argues strongly against Bhāvaviveka, holding that the non-inherent existence of phenomena is taught in the Hīnayāna and that method (*upāya, thabs*), not wisdom (*prajñā, shes rab*) is the distinguishing feature of the two vehicles. He writes in his commentary to Nāgārjuna's *Sixty Stanzas of Reasoning* that statements such as "All conditioned phenomena are false, having the character of deception," appear repeatedly in the Hīnayāna literature.[99] He interprets this deceptive nature to be that phenomena appear to exist inherently when in fact they do not.[100] The non-inherent existence of phenomena — the selflessness of phenomena — is therefore indicated by such statements in the Hīnayāna scriptures. He further holds that Nāgārjuna, the founder of the Mādhyamika school, asserts that the selflessness of phenomena is taught in the Hīnayāna. For support he cites this stanza from the *Treatise on the Middle Way* (XV.7):

> In the *Advice to Katyayana*
> "Exists," "not exists," and both
> Are rejected by the Supramundane Victor
> Knowing [the nature of] things and non-things.

Nāgārjuna states that the Buddha refuted inherent existence ("exists"), utter non-existence ("not exists"), and both inherent existence and utter non-existence in the *Advice to Katyayana*. Since that text is a Hīnayāna scripture included in the *Brief Scriptures on*

Discipline (*Vinayakṣudravastu*), non-inherent existence is taught in the Hīnayāna.[101]

Demonstrating that Nāgārjuna does not hold Bhāvaviveka's position that the selflessness of phenomena is not taught in the Hīnayāna constitutes a refutation with scripture (*āgama, lung*). Candrakīrti's refutation of Bhāvaviveka's position with reasoning (*yukti, rigs pa*) appears in the first chapter of the autocommentary to his *Supplement to the Middle Way*. His argument is expanded by Tsong-kha-pa in his *Great Commentry to (Candrakīrti's) Supplement* as follows:[102]

Bhāvaviveka has stated in his *Lamp for (Nāgārjuna's) "Wisdom"* that if the selflessness of phenomena were taught in the Hīnayāna scriptural collection, then the teaching of the Mahāyāna would be senseless. If he means by this that the teaching of the Mahāyāna would be senseless because the selflessness of phenomena is the only thing taught in the Mahāyāna sutras, then, according to Candrakīrti, he is not correct because the Mahāyāna sutras teach many topics essential for the achievement of Buddhahood. Candrakīrti says in his autocommentary to his *Supplement to the Middle Way:*

> The teaching of the Mahāyāna does not teach the selflessness of phenomena alone. Then what [else does it teach]? The Bodhisattva grounds, the perfections, prayers, great compassion, and so forth, complete dedications, the two collections, and the inconceivable reality [of the Truth Body].[103]

The ten Bodhisattva grounds, the practice of the six perfections, the great aspirational prayers and dedications of Bodhisattvas — the means for generating the altruistic aspiration to enlightenment — the two collections of merit and wisdom, and the Three Bodies of a Buddha all must be understood and cultivated in order to achieve Buddhahood, and they are not set forth in the Hīnayāna scriptural collection. Candrakīrti cites Nāgārjuna's Precious Garland:

> Since all the aspirations, deeds,
> And dedications of Bodhisattvas
> Were not explained in the Hearers' Vehicle, how
> Could one become a Bodhisattva [through the Hearer
>   Vehicle]?
>
> The subjects based on the deeds of Bodhisattvas

> Were not explained in the [Hīnayāna] scriptural collection
> But were explained in the Mahāyāna, therefore
> The wise should hold [it to be the Buddha's word].[104]

In the first stanza, Nāgārjuna enumerates some of the practices necessary for becoming a Bodhisattva and progressing to Buddhahood that are taught only in the Mahāyāna and do not appear in Hīnayāna scriptures. One cannot achieve Buddhahood merely by following the teachings of the Hīnayāna. The full path to Buddhahood is presented only in the Mahāyāna (which, therefore, should be accepted as the word of the Buddha, as Nāgārjuna states in the second stanza). Notable by its absence in the list of teachings unique to the Mahāyāna is any mention of the selflessness of phenomena. This lends significant weight to Candrakīrti's argument, for if Bhāvaviveka were correct in his assertion that only Bodhisattvas realize the selflessness of phenomena in order to achieve Buddhahood and that this selflessness is taught only in the Mahāyāna, then Nāgārjuna should have included the selflessness of phenomena among the topics taught only in the Mahayāna sutras. He does not.

Even if the debate is limited to a consideration of the exposition of the selflessness of phenomena, Candrakīrti still finds fault with Bhāvaviveka's assertion. The Prāsaṅgikas hold that the selflessness of phenomena is taught in the Hīnayāna scriptures, but it does not necessarily follow from that that the teaching of this selflessness in the Mahāyāna would be purposeless. According to Candrakīrti, even though the selflessness of phenomena is taught in the Hīnayāna scriptural collections, there is purpose in its being taught in the Mahāyāna because, whereas the selflessness of phenomena is taught briefly in the Hīnayāna, it is set forth extensively in the Mahāyāna. The reason for this is that Bodhisattvas take as their main object of abandonment the obstructions to omniscience such that they must greatly expand their awareness of suchness (*tathatā*, *de kho na nyid*). Hearers and Solitary Realizers, on the other hand, are able to abandon the afflictive obstructions and attain the state of a Foe Destroyer by meditating on emptiness with abbreviated reasonings. Candrakīrti says in his autocommentary to his *Supplement to the Middle Way:*

> It is suitable that the Mahāyāna was taught in order to elucidate the selflessness of phenomena because [the Buddha] wished to express the teaching extensively. The selflessness of phenomena is confined merely to a brief illus-

tration in the Hearer vehicle.[105]

Therefore, in the Mahāyāna scriptural collections, the selflessness of phenomena is taught completely, in limitless forms of reasoning, because Bodhisattvas must have a vast awareness of emptiness in order to abandon the more subtle obstructions to omniscience and achieve Buddhahood. Nevertheless, it is the position of the Prāsaṅgikas that liberation from suffering cannot be achieved without realizing the subtle emptiness, the lack of inherent existence of persons and phenomena. Therefore, the selflessness of phenomena must be taught in the Hīnayāna scriptures. Thus, according to Candrakīrti, the selflessness of phenomena is set forth in both the Hīnayāna and Mahāyāna sutras; there is a difference, however, in the way in which it is set forth.[106]

Again, Candrakīrti cites Nāgārjuna for support. His *Praise of the Supramundane (Lokātītastava)* says:

> You [the Buddha] said that without realizing signlessness
> There is no liberation.
> Therefore, you taught it completely
> In the Mahāyāna.[107]

The first two lines refer to the fact that it is impossible to achieve liberation from cyclic existence without cognizing signlessness — the emptiness of inherent existence. That emptiness must therefore be taught in the sutras of both vehicles. The last two lines state that the Buddha taught signlessness fully in the Mahāyāna; by implication it was not taught fully in the Hīnayāna.[108]

Thus, the selflessness of phenomena is taught completely in the Mahāyāna scriptural collections and meditated on completely on the Mahāyāna path. It is not taught completely in the Hīnayāna scriptural collection nor is it meditated on completely over the Hīnayāna path. What does it mean not to be meditated on completely, if Hīnayānists must directly realize the selflessness of phenomena again and again in order to be liberated from cyclic existence?

It might be suggested that in the Mahāyāna the non-inherent existence of all objects of knowledge is realized whereas Hearers and Solitary Realizers cognize the non-inherent existence of only some objects of knowledge. This is not correct because when the non-true existence of one object is understood with valid cognition, if one then analyzes whether or not another object truly exists, one is able to realize its non-true existence through the reasoning employed before.[109] That is, having realized the emptiness of one object, one can automatically infer the emptiness of any object to which one turns one's mind. Furthermore, it would be impossible for Hīnayānists to realize the emptiness of only a portion objects of knowledge because the emptiness of all objects of knowledge is directly realized in meditative equipoise (*samāhita, mnyam bzhag*) on the path of seeing and beyond.

According to Tsong-kha-pa, the difference between the two vehicles with regard to the selflessness of phenomena is that in the Mahāyāna it is set forth in limitless forms of reasoning and in the Hīnayāna it is set forth in abbreviated reasonings. Further, on the Māhāyāna path the selflessness of phenomena is meditated on using those limitless forms of reasoning whereas Hīnayānists only employ the abbreviated forms in their meditation. Tsong-kha-pa says in his *Great Commentary to (Candrakīrti's) Supplement:*

> Although [Hīnayānists] do not generate the wisdom that refutes the true establishment of the person with limitless forms of reasoning, they do completely cultivate the antidote to the seeds of the afflictive emotions; they do not completely cultivate the antidote to the obstructions to omniscience.[110]

Thus, Hīnayānists — those seeking to become Foe Destroyers — do not meditate on the selflessness of phenomena in such a way as to abandon the obstructions to omiscience. They do not meditate on the selflessness of phenomena in terms of limitless forms of reasoning. However, if it is asked whether Hearers and Solitary Realizers fully meditate on the selflessness of phenomena, it must be asserted that they do, because they abandon completely the conception of a self of phenomena, that phenomena truly exist.[111]

Bhāvaviveka's rejection of Buddhapālita's assertion that the selflessness of phenomena is taught in the Hīnayāna scriptures and Candrakīrti's subsequent attack against Bhāvaviveka's position bring into focus several fundamental differences between the Svātantrika and Prāsaṅgika schools. First, the selflessness of the person is identified by the Svātantrikas as the person's lack of being substantially existent in the sense of self-sufficiency. The Prāsaṅgikas label this selflessness as coarse and contend that meditation on it is not an antidote to the afflictive obstructions, as the Svātantrikas hold it to be. For the Prāsaṅgikas, the selflessness of persons is the person's emptiness of inherent existence. With respect to the selflessness of phenomena, Bhāvaviveka asserts that it is phenomena's lack of existing from their own side without being posited by the force of appearing to a non-defective awareness. This is again labelled as coarse by the Prāsaṅgikas, who assert that a phenomenon's lack of inherent existence is the selflessness of phenomena. Thus, the Svātantrikas present two selflessnesses with two different objects of negation and assert that there is also a difference in subtlety between them, with the selflessness of phenomenon being more difficult to penetrate than that of persons. The Prāsaṅgikas assert that the two selflessnesses are equally subtle and distinguish them by the basis of negation — persons and other phenomena; the object of negation — inherent existence — is the same.

The question of the coarseness and subtlety of the two selflessnesses extends into the Svātantrika and Prāsaṅgika presentation of the two obstructions. For Bhāvaviveka, the conception of a self of persons is the chief of the obstacles to be overcome in order to gain liberation from cyclic existence and thus is the chief obstruction which Foe Destroyers must eradicate; the more subtle conception of true existence is the chief obstruction to omniscience, overcome by Bodhisattvas. For the Prāsaṅgikas, the conception of self, of both persons and phenomena, equally subtle, is the chief of the obstructions to liberation and is abandoned by all Foe Destroyers. The appearance of phenomena as inherently existent is the obstruction to omniscience.

Since, according to Bhāvaviveka, only Bodhisattvas realize the selflessness of phenomena, he contends that it is only taught in the Mahāyāna scriptures. For him, this is the fundamental purpose of the Buddha's teaching the Mahāyāna. For the Prāsaṅgikas, everyone who achieves liberation from cyclic existence must realize the subtle selflessness of persons and other phenomena. They assert, therefore, that the Prāsaṅgika view is found in the Hīnayāna scriptures, that the emptiness of inherent existence of persons and phenomena is taught in the Hīnayāna scriptures.

In the end, the question of whether the selflessness of phenomena is taught in the Hīnayāna revolves around the conception of the root of cyclic existence and of what constitutes liberation. For Bhāvaviveka, the fundamental cause of cyclic existence is the conception of true existence yet one can be liberated through realizing the less subtle selflessness of persons. According to the Svātantrikas, the *final* root of cyclic existence is the conception of a self of phenomena whereas the root of cyclic existence is the conception of a self of persons. For the Prāsaṅgikas, the root of cyclic existence is the subtle conception of self, the conception of persons and phenomena as inherently existent, and it is this which must be overcome in order to be released from suffering. Eliminating the conception of true existence as identified by the Svātantrikas does not cut the root of cyclic existence. Not only do the Prāsaṅgikas assert that both conceptions of self must be eradicated for liberation, they posit a more subtle conception of self as the root of cyclic existence and assert that its antidote is taught in both the Hīnayāna and Mahāyāna scriptures — briefly in the Hīnayāna and extensively in the Mahāyāna.

The Prāsaṅgikas do not assert that every time the term "selflessness" appears in the Hīnayāna sutras does it mean the emptiness of inherent existence. They freely admit that the Buddha often taught the coarse selflessness for disciples who temporarily cannot realize the more subtle. Nor do they argue that everyone understood the same thing when the Buddha described phenomena as selfless; the differing conceptions of the meaning of that term gave rise, in part, to the various tenet systems. However, they do assert that there are coarse and subtle conceptions of self and coarse and subtle selflessnesses. Because there are two conceptions of self, there are two levels of afflictive emotions induced by those conceptions. According to the Prāsaṅgikas, the conception of the person as substantially existent in the sense of self-sufficiency is identified by the Svātantrikas who are thus able to abandon the afflictive emotions induced by that conception through realizing the emptiness of such as self. However, from the Prāsaṅgika perspective, the subtle conception of self, the conception of the person as inherently existent, is asserted to be a valid form of consciousness by the Svātantrikas; they do not identify it as an erroneous conception.[112]

The Prāsaṅgikas assert that when the understanding of the coarse form of selflessness is present, the more subtle conception of self may operate, but when the emptiness of inherent existence is understood, none of the coarser misconceptions of the nature of the person is possible. Since the Prāsaṅgikas identify the subtle conception of self — the conception of inherent existence — as the root of cyclic existence, they assert that the wisdom of selflessness taught by the Svātantrikas and the other schools are not antidotes to suffering and rebirth. The Prāsaṅgikas thus display a rather strict exclusiveness in their appraisal of the other schools of Buddhist philosophy in that they assert that only by realizing the most subtle selflessness, which is only taught in their school, can anyone be liberated from the cycle of mundane existence. At the same time, they demonstrate a catholicity in their assertion that everyone who is liberated from suffering and rebirth, whether they follow the Hīnayāna or Mahāyāna path, must realize the exact same thing, the emptiness of inherent existence.

4 Ultimate Existence

The Svātantrikas assert that the conception of ultimate existence is the final root of cyclic existence and that Bodhisattvas must realize that phenomena lack ultimate existence in order to achieve Buddhahood. Ultimate existence is thus the object of negation, the conception of which must be identified and destroyed in order to attain highest enlightenment. Although the Svātantrikas assert that ultimate existence has not, does not, and never will exist, the conception of it very much does, and that conception is the final root of cyclic existence. In order to destroy it, one must first identify its referent object — one must understand the meaning of ultimate existence. Śāntideva says in his *Engaging in the Bodhisattva Deeds*:

> Without contacting the imputed existent
> Its non-existence cannot be apprehended.[1]

For the Ge-luk-bas, there are two *loci classici* in the Svātantrika literature which most clearly identify the object of negation. The first appears in Bhāvaviveka's *Blaze of Reasoning*.

Bhāvaviveka says in the third chapter of his *Essence of the Middle Way* (III.26):

> Here, earth and so forth
> Are not entities of the elements ultimately
> Because of being produced
> And because of having causes, like a consciousness.[2]

In the autocommentary, the *Blaze of Reasoning*, he explains what he means by "ultimately":

> Regarding ultimate (*paramārtha, don dam*), with respect to "object" (*artha, don*), it is an object because of being that which is to be known; this is synonymous with "that which is to be examined (*parīkṣaṇīya, brtag par bya ba*)" and "that which is to be understood (*pratipādya, go bar bya ba*)." "Highest" (*parama, dam pa*) is a word [meaning] supreme. With respect to the compound *paramārtha*, because it is an object as well as being highest, it is the highest object. Or [it means] the object of the highest (*paramasya artha, dam pa'i don*); because it is the object of the highest non-conceptual wisdom (*nirvikalpajñāna, rnam par mi rtog pa'i ye shes*), it is an object of the highest [consciousness]. Or, it [means] that which accords with the highest object [that is, the highest consciousness]. Since the ultimate exists for a wisdom that accords with a realization of the ultimate, it accords with [that which directly realizes] the highest object.[3]

Thus, Bhāvaviveka interprets the compound *paramārtha* (translated here as "ultimate") in three ways. In the first, taking *paramārtha as a karmadhāraya* compound, both the terms "highest" (*parama*) and "object" (*artha*) refer to the object — emptiness — because it is both highest or supreme as well as an object, something which is known. In the second interpretation, he takes *paramārtha* as a *tatpuruṣa* compound meaning "object of the highest," with "highest" referring to a Superior's non-conceptual exalted wisdom of meditative equipoise (*samāhita, mnyam bzhag*) and object referring to emptiness, the object realized by that highest wisdom consciousness. He calls the third type of *paramārtha* a concordant ultimate, applying both "highest" and "object" to the subject, a wisdom consciousness. Interpreting *paramārtha* as a *bahuvrīhi* compound, he designates the wisdom that accords with a Superior's non-conceptual exalted wisdom directly realizing the ultimate with the term "ultimate."[4]

Thus, in Bhāvaviveka's three interpretations of the compound *paramārtha*, the first two refer to emptiness in that it is both the highest object and the object of the highest consciousness. In the third interpretation, a consciousness is identified with the term *paramārtha*. It is important to note, however, that Bhāvaviveka does not interpret *paramārtha* as a simple *bahuvrīhi* compound, "that which has the highest object," in which case it would refer to all consciousnesses realizing emptiness. He is careful to specify that the wisdom *that accords with* the realization of the ultimate is a concordant ultimate because it has the ultimate as its object. Jam-yang-shay-ba thus explains the third *paramārtha* as a wisdom of subsequent attainment of hearing, thinking, or meditation which realizes emptiness. Such a wisdom is similar to or concordant with the ultimate wisdom and thus is posited as the ultimate.[5] By identifying this third type of *paramārtha* as a wisdom of subsequent attainment (*pṛṣṭha-labdhajñāna, rjes thob ye shes*), which is a conceptual consciousness that follows after a direct cognition of emptiness, Jam-yang-shay-ba indicates that Bhāvaviveka wishes to restrict the third type of *paramārtha* to conceptual consciousnesses, excluding non-conceptual wisdom consciousnesses of meditative equipoise from the category. Bhāvaviveka makes this point himself later in the *Blaze of Reasoning*, in which a hypothetical opponent raises the objection:

> The ultimate is beyond all awareness, but the negation of the entityness of things is an object [expressed] by letters. Therefore, is it not the case that there is no negation?[6]

That is, the ultimate is free from all elaborations and cannot be conceived of just as it is by any conceptual consciousness. Therefore, the opponent argues, the presentation of refutations and proofs is inappropriate in the context of the ultimate. Yet, the opponent argues, when Bhāvaviveka seeks to refute that earth is an entity of the elements ultimately, he claims that the refutation by reasoning of the entityness of individual things is capable of being explicitly expressed by words composed of letters; however, because it is ultimate, that entityness cannot be negated by the power of verbal conventions. Therefore, the opponent claims, Bhāvaviveka's assertion that earth does not ultimately exist does not refute the entityness of things.[7]

The opponent sees the ultimate and conventional as two unconnected spheres. The ultimate is beyond all elaboration, beyond conception, beyond expression. Bhāvaviveka's hypothetical opponent finds a modern-day supporter in J. W. de Jong, who describes *paramārtha* in this way:

> But this absolute by its very nature is inaccessible to philosophical thought. One might try to approach it by indirect

> means, but all one could say or think about it would of necessity be false. It cannot be thought of as being or as nothingness.[8]

If this is the case, how can Bhāvaviveka bring the inconceivable into the conventional realm of his syllogism and assert that earth does not exist "ultimately"?

Bhāvaviveka specifies what he means by ultimate when he refutes ultimate existence:

> The ultimate is of two types. One is a supramundane non-contaminated [consciousness] free from elaborations which operates without activity. The second, possessing conceptual elaborations, is called a pure mundane wisdom which accords with the collections of merit and wisdom and operates with activity. Here [in the context of the passage from the *Essence of the Middle Way*], this is held as the qualification of the thesis ["does not ultimately exist"]; thus, there is no fault.[9]

That is, ultimate consciousnesses are of two types. The first is a supramundane, non-contaminated meditative equipoise of a Superior which operates without conceptual activity, that is without involvement with any object of thought. The second type of ultimate consciousness (the third type in the discussion above, p. 135) is an exalted wisdom of subsequent attainment which is a conventional mundane subject but which is pure in the sense that it does not come under the power of mistaken appearances. Such a consciousness accords with the trainings in the collection of merit and wisdom and operates with conceptual activity; it is involved with objects of thought. When Bhāvaviveka says that earth does not exist as the entity of the elements ultimately, "does not exist ultimately" in that thesis means not to exist for this latter type of ultimate consciousness. Since the entityness of phenomena does not exist in the face of such a wisdom consciousness, Bhāvaviveka is justified in saying that they do not ultimately exist, and the fault raised by the opponent is not incurred.[10]

This second type of ultimate consciousness, what Bhāvaviveka calls the concordant ultimate, is not restricted only to exalted wisdoms of subsequent attainment. Kamalaśīla says in this *Illumination of the Middle Way* (*Madhyamakāloka*):

> All wisdoms arisen from correct hearing, thinking, and meditation are non-mistaken subjects. They are called ultimates because their [object] is the ultimate.[11]

Thus, all wisdom consciousnesses ranging from those of hearing and thinking which analyze suchness through to inferential reasoning consciousnesses in the continuum of a Superior are categorized as concordant ultimates. A wisdom arisen from *hearing* is produced in dependence on a sign that arises from remembering the three modes due to hearing the statement of another person. Wisdom arisen from *thinking* refers to an inferential consciousness that understands the meaning to be inferred in dependence on a correct proof which is arrived at through the power of one's own correct thought without relying on its being set forth by someone else.[12] Thus, here, both the wisdoms arisen from hearing and thinking are inferential consciousnesses.

To summarize, an opponent challenges Bhāvaviveka's use of the term ultimate. On the one hand, he says, Bhāvaviveka wishes to assert that the ultimate transcends all awareness, that is, that ultimate truths are not within the sphere of any dualistic consciousness. At the same time, he asserts that the meaning of not existing ultimately is not existing in the face of analysis by a dualistic reasoning consciousness, thereby implying that the refutation of a truly established or ultimately existent nature must be accomplished using terms and thought consciousnesses. The opponent finds these two assertions contradictory, entailing the consequence that either the ultimate existence of phenomena cannot be negated because conventional, dualistic consciousnesses are incapable of dealing with the ultimate or that ultimate truths do not stand beyond the sphere of dualistic consciousnesses but rather are the objects of conventional, conceptual, dualistic awarenesses because the refutation of an ultimate entityness is posited in terms of terms and thought consciousnesses.[13]

Bhāvaviveka responds that there are two types of ultimate consciousnesses, one that directly realizes emptiness without taking an image of emptiness as its appearing object (**pratibhāsaviṣaya, snang yul*) and which is free from all dualistic appearance, and another that operates conceptually, through the medium of images, and is a mundane or conventional wisdom consciousness. It is this second type of wisdom that refutes ultimate existence. Thus, for Bhāvaviveka there are two types of reasoning consciousnesses that understand the lack of ultimate existence, conceptual and non-conceptual. A non-conceptual reasoning consciousness, despite the fact that it is not explicitly engaged in the process of reasoning, is so-called because it arises as a result of the process of reasoning. A conceptual or dualistic reasoning consciousness is not able to understand emptiness in the way in which a non-conceptual reasoning consciousness sees emptiness. In this sense, ultimate truths — emptinesses — transcend the sphere of dualistic awareness. However, when a conceptual reasoning consciousness properly analyzes the mode of being of an object, it finds that the object does not truly exist. This is the meaning of not existing ultimately according to Bhāvaviveka.[14]

By delineating these two types of ultimate consciousnesses, Bhāvaviveka is able to preserve the unique character of meditative equipoise, which realizes emptiness directly in a non-dualistic cognition. However, such a cognition is difficult to understand and does not occur until the path of seeing (*darśanamārga*, *mthong lam*). Also, a non-conceptual reasoning consciousness is not engaged in analysis; it does not refute ultimate existence. Therefore, Bhāvaviveka posits as his third type of ultimate that which accords with realization of the ultimate. Such a consciousness is ultimate (*paramārtha*), in that, since a conceptual reasoning consciousness of hearing, thinking, or meditation which realizes emptiness is realizing suchness, it is the highest (*parama*); and, since it is the object sought by those who wish to abandon the obstructions, it is an object (*artha*).[15]

However, by creating the category of the concordant ultimate and then further specifying that it is the conceptual wisdom consciousness which, through analyzing the mode of being of phenomena, determines whether an object ultimately exists or not, Bhavaviveka is not suggesting that a Superior's meditative equipoise is to be explicitly excluded from the determination that phenomena do not ultimately exist.[16] Rather, he is arguing that the understanding of the mode of being of phenomena need not wait for the attainment of the path of seeing. He is indicating that rational thought, a reasoning consciousness, is fully capable of analyzing and investigating the mode of being of an object and is further capable of ascertaining that that object does not exist in the fact of the reasoning consciousness, that the object does not ultimately exist. The conceptual reasoning consciousness is what actually carries out analysis of the object and discovers that it does not truly exist. Based on this analysis, direct cognition of the lack of true existence — emptiness — occurs on the path of seeing. Bhāvaviveka thereby emphasizes that the analysis of reality is to be undertaken by ordinary beings and that reasoning and analysis yield an understanding of the fact that things do not exist in and of themselves, but in fact are empty of ultimate existence. By giving the exalted name "ultimate" to conceptual reasoning consciousnesses in the continua of common beings, Bhāvaviveka emphatically upholds the place of reasoning and analysis on the path.

Bhāvaviveka's labelling of conceptual reasoning consciousnesses as ultimates flies directly in the face of T. R. V. Murti's claim, "Kalpanā is avidyā par excellence,"[17] and that "the viewing of it [emptiness] through thought-forms is avidyā."[18] For Bhāvaviveka, thought (*kalpanā, rtog pa*) is not ignorance (*avidyā, ma rig pa*). Thought consciousnesses can be ignorant consciousnesses, but a thought consciousness may also be a wisdom consciousness, an ultimate consciousness. Emptiness, the lack of ultimate existence, must initially be understood through "thought-forms" before it can be realized directly on the path of seeing. Indeed, according to the Mādhyamika presentation of the Bodhisattva path, the Bodhisattva spends at least one period of countless aeons viewing emptiness through "thought-forms" on the paths of accumulation (*sambhāramārga, tshogs lam*) and preparation (*prayogamārga, sbyor lam*) before his initial direct realization of emptiness.[19] Thus it is not the assertion of Bhāvaviveka that thought is necessarily a form of ignorance, which is defined as an active misconception of the nature of reality. As Bhāvaviveka makes so clear, conceptual reasoning consciousnesses are the indispensible tools of the Bodhisattva who is seeking to dispel all forms of ignorance. By designating conceptual reasoning consciousnesses with the term "ultimate," Bhāvaviveka certifies their place in the path.

Like Bhāvaviveka's hypothetical opponent, Murti sees the ultimate, which he calls "the Absolute," as utterly transcendent and totally beyond comprehension by thought and analysis. Bhāvaviveka on the other hand, recognizing the rigidity of such a view, is able to expand the category of the ultimate to include not only emptiness but consciousnesses by which it can be known.

Jang-gya provides a useful summary of the various meanings of the term ultimate in Svātantrika. He explains that there are ultimates that are objects and ultimates that are subjects and that each of these can be further divided into actual and concordant ultimates.

Emptiness — the lack of true existence — is an actual ultimate in that it is free from the elaborations of true existence as well as the elaborations of dualistic appearance when it is directly realized by a Superior's exalted wisdom of meditative equipoise. When emptiness is realized by a conceptual reasoning consciousness, it is free from the elaborations of true existence but appears dualistically, that is, emptiness and the conceptual consciousness realizing it remain separate. The conceptual consciousness is not directly realizing emptiness; it understands it through the medium of a generic image or meaning-generality (*arthasāmānya*, *don spyi*), which is the appearing object of that consciousness. Emptiness is its referent object. When emptiness serves as the referent object of a conceptual consciousness, it is called a concordant ultimate because, for that consciousness, it is not free from the elaborations of dualistic appearance. Thus, the two types of objective emptiness, actual and concordant, are differentiated from the point of view of the type of consciousness realizing them, non-conceptual and conceptual wisdom consciousnesses respectively.

As is clear from Bhāvaviveka, the two types of consciousnesses realizing emptiness may also be called ultimates. A Superior's non-conceptual exalted wisdom of meditative equipoise is capable of eliminating both the elaborations of true existence and dualistic appearance when it realizes emptiness. It is, therefore, called an actual ultimate within the ultimates which are subjects. The conceptual reasoning consciousness is able to remove the superimpositions of true existence but still has dualistic appearance. It is, therefore, called a concordant ultimate.[20] It is important to note that although all of these are called ultimates, only emptiness is an ultimate truth, and none of the ultimates, nor any other phenomenon for that matter, ultimately exists.

Having identified what Bhāvaviveka means by ultimate, it is now necessary to explore what he means when he says that phenomena do not ultimately exist. To conceive of a phenomenon as ultimately existent is to believe that it is its own mode of being; that it exists in and of itself such that the final nature of the object is the object itself. To conceive of a table as ultimately existent is to conceive that the ultimate or final nature of the table is the table itself.[21] The purpose of reasoning consciousnesses is to discover whether phenomena exist as their own final nature, whether they ultimately exist or not. A reasoning consciousness is searching for the final nature of the object under analysis; it is an awareness that comprehends the mode of being of the object it analyzes; it is an analyzer of the ultimate. Therefore, in order for a phenomenon to be ultimately existent, it must be found by or exist for an inferential reasoning consciousness analyzing the ultimate. If it does not exist for such a consciousness, it does not ultimately exist because it is the sole purpose of the reasoning consciousness to investigate the final mode of being of that phenomenon. If a table, for example, truly or ultimately exists, the reasoning consciousness will find that the table itself is the mode of being of the table.[22] If the table is truly established it must be found to be truly established by a reasoning consciousness because that consciousness analyzes whether phenomena truly exist or not. Through a process of reasoning (that will be described in the next chapter), the consciousness searches for the ultimate existence of the object and does not find it; it finds the mere absence of the object's ultimate existence, its emptiness of ultimate or true existence. The consciousness searches for the ultimate existence of the object and finds its non-ultimate existence. This non-ultimate existence of the object is its reality (*dharmatā, chos nyid*) and its final nature.[23]

Therefore, whatever is ultimately existent must necessarily exist for a reasoning consciousness analyzing the ultimate. Is it also true that whatever exists for a reasoning consciousness analyzing the ultimate is necessarily ultimately existent? No, because emptiness exists for a reasoning consciousness but does not ultimately exist. If the reasoning consciousness turns its light of analysis on the lack of ultimate existence that it has found when searching for ultimate existence and investigates that lack of ultimate existence in an effort to discover whether it ultimately exists, it will find that the lack of ultimate existence itself does not ultimately exist; emptiness is empty of true existence. Thus, although emptiness — the lack of ultimate existence — exists in the face of a reasoning consciousness, it does not ultimately exist.

If a phenomenon is truly established, it must be established for a reasoning consciousness. However, whatever is the mode of being of an object and exists for a reasoning consciousness is not necessarily truly established, because the emptiness of a table is both the final mode of being of the table and exists for a reasoning consciousness analyzing the table but is not truly established.[24] Still, it can be said that any phenomenon, including emptiness, which is analyzed by a reasoning consciousness investigating the mode of being of that phenomenon does not exist for that reasoning consciousness. The non-existence of that phenomenon for that consciousness analyzing the ultimate is the reality or final nature of the object.[25] It is, therefore, important to make a distinction between being the object found by a reasoning consciousness and being able to bear analysis by a reasoning consciousness. When such a consciousness analyzes an object in order to determine whether it ultimately exists, that object's lack of ultimate existence is the object found by the reasoning consciousness. This does not imply that the lack of ultimate existence itself ultimately exists. The object found by the reasoning consciousness is what that consciousness understands — which is the non-true existence of the object under scrutiny. Again, if that non-true existence is analyzed, it also is found to lack ultimate existence; it cannot bear analysis by a reasoning consciousness.[26]

Nothing is able to bear analysis by a reasoning consciousness. Therefore, to not exist ultimately is to not be established as capable of bearing analysis by a conceptual reasoning consciousness which properly analyzes the mode of being of phenomena.[27] Due to not recognizing that the object found by a reasoning consciousness cannot itself bear analysis by that consciousness, one may be led to the conclusion that the object found by a reasoning consciousness must truly exist. This was the opinion of the great Tibetan logician Cha-ba-chö-gyi-seng-gay (*Cha-pa-chos-kyi-seng-ge*), who asserted that non-true existence is truly established. On the other hand, if one wishes to assert that emptiness — the lack of ultimate existence — is itself empty but also believes that the object found by a reasoning consciousness must ultimately exist, one is forced to assert that emptiness is not found by a reasoning consciousness and hence is not an object of knowledge. According to this view, if emptiness were found by a reasoning consciousness, it would have to exist truly. This was the position of the great translator Lo-den-shay-rap (*bLo-ldan-shes-rab*).[28]

The conception that an object is able to withstand analysis by a reasoning consciousness is identified as the artificial conception of true existence by some Tibetan scholars. Such a conception of true existence is not present in the continua of all sentient beings; its cause is the study of wrong tenet systems that propound the ultimate existence of phenomena.[29] The innate conception of true existence, the final root of cyclic existence for the Svātantrikas, is identified in a passage from Kamalaśīla's *Illumination of the Middle Way* (*Madhyamakāloka*):

> An awareness that mistakenly superimposes the opposite onto things that are in reality without entityness is called the "concealer" (*saṃvṛti, kun rdzob*) because it obstructs [itself] from [perception of] suchness or because it veils [other awarenesses] from [perception of] suchness. As it says in the [*Descent into Laṅkā*] *Sutra:*
>
> > Things are produced conventionally;
> > Ultimately they are without inherent existence.
> > That which is mistaken about what does not
> > inherently exist
> > Is asserted to be a concealer of reality.
>
> Because [an artificial awareness] arises from that [conception of true existence], all false things which [such an artificial awareness] sees displayed by that [conception of true existence as if they are truly established] are called "mere conventionalities." Moreover, that [conception of true existence] arises through the maturation of beginningless predispositions for error, whereby all living beings see [phenomena] displayed as if [they had] a true nature in reality. Therefore, all entities of false things [which exist] through the power of those [sentient beings'] thoughts are said to "only exist conventionally."[30]

"An awareness that mistakenly superimposes the opposite onto things that in reality are without entityness" refers to the innate conception of true existence that superimposes ultimate existence onto phenomena that lack ultimate existence. Such an ignorant consciousness — the conception of true existence — is called a concealer or an obstructor because the ignorant consciousness obstructs other minds from seeing reality — non-true existence — and thus conceals the final mode of being from them. The ignorant consciousness itself is also obstructed from seeing suchness, as an eye obstructed by cataracts is prevented from clearly seeing forms.

"Because [an artificial awareness] arises from that [conception of true existence], all false things which [such an artificial awareness] sees displayed by the [conception of true existence as if they truly existed] are called mere conventionalities." This sentence indicates that due to the conception of true existence, phenomena appear to the thought consciousnesses of sentient beings to be truly existent. This is a false appearance; those phenomena do not truly exist, they exist only conventionally.

It is the opinion of Tsong-kha-pa that the consciousnesses to which the appearance of true existence is displayed are necessarily conceptual consciousnesses and are not sense consciousnesses because, in his view, the object of negation — true existence — does not appear to the sense consciousnesses in the Svātantrika system. There are a number of statements in the works of the Svātantrika masters that support his position, such as Jñānagarbha's comments that, "Just as what is seen by cowherds and above abides as conventional truths ...,"[31] "When a thing appears, real [that is, truly existent] production and so forth do not,"[32] and "No one has any quarrel concerning the factor which appears to the consciousnesses of the two parties [in a debate]."[33] The first quote implies that everything that common beings, such as cowherds, see is validly established in the way in which it appears. The second indicates that the truly existent production of an object, which is to be negated, does not appear when that object appears to the senses. The third quotation supports the Svātantrika assertion of a commonly appearing subject, which appears to the sense direct perceivers of the parties in a debate, those sense consciousnesses being non-mistaken with respect to the subject's existence by way of its character (*sva-lakṣaṇa-siddha, rang gi mtshan nyid kyis grub pa*). The fact that the Svātantrikas have no quarrel with the way that the subject appears to the parties in the debate indicates that they do not assert that the object of negation appears to the sense consciousnesses. This point will be discussed further in the context of the two types of conventional truths (pp. 210-212).

"Moreover, that [conception of true existence] arises through the maturation of beginningless predispositions for error, whereby all living beings see [phenomena] displayed as if [they had] a true nature in reality." This sentence indicates that the conception of true existence, which causes objects to appear falsely to thought consciousnesses, is the innate conception of true existence that has operated beginninglessly and that causes phenomena to appear falsely to the minds of all sentient beings, regardless of whether their minds have been affected by the study of tenets.

"Therefore, all entities of false things [which exist] through the power of those [sentient beings'] thoughts are said 'only to exist conventionally.' " This last sentence provides Kamalaśīla's understanding of the conventional status of phenomena. The entities of those phenomena which appear falsely due to the conception of true existence do validly exist though the power of sentient beings' thoughts. For a Svātantrika, it is not suitable to posit phenomena as existing through the power of the conception of true existence. There are valid consciousnesses that are not affected by ignorance which can posit the conventional existence of phenomena. Thus, conventional existence means existence which is posited by the power of appearing to a non-defective mind, the perception and conception of which has not been affected by the power of the conception of true existence. Such a non-defective mind may be non-conceptual or conceptual. Since the object of negation — true existence — does not appear to the non-conceptual sense consciousnesses, a sense consciousness is non-defective if it has not been affected by one of the superficial causes of error (see pp. 67-68). A though consciousness is non-defective if it is non-mistaken with respect to its determined or referent object (**adhyavasāyaviṣaya, zhen yul*), that is, if the thought consciousness is correct regarding the general characteristics of its object. A thought consciousness conceiving of a permanent sound would be considered mistaken. For the Svātantrikas, if the object of negation appeared to the sense consciousnesses, they would not be capable of positing the conventional existence of objects because ultimate existence would be certified by sense experience.[34]

Thus, it can be inferred from Kamalaśīla's statement that true existence or ultimate existence is a mode of subsistence that is established from the object's own side, without being posited through the power of appearing to a non-defective consciousness. What it means to be "posited through the power of appearing to a non-defective awareness" is elucidated with the example of a magician's illusion.

In India it is said that a magician could take an ordinary object such as a pebble or a twig, rub it with a certain salve, and then cast a mantra, thereby causing the pebble or twig to appear as some other object, such as a horse or an elephant. At that time, both the magician and the audience for whom he is performing the trick see a horse where the pebble once was. However, the ways in which the magician and the audience perceive the horse are different. The magician sees the horse but does not believe it to be a real horse, knowing that he has conjured the appearance of a horse from a pebble with the use of the salve and mantra. The audience sees the horse and believes that is is real. A person who arrives after the show has begun will only see the pebble because his eyes have not been affected by the mantra cast by the magician.

For both the audience and the magician, the appearance of the pebble as a horse comes about through the power of the mind affected by the mantra; the appearance is not produced naturally from the pebble without depending on that mind. The magician understands this, but, for the audience, it appears that a real horse is standing in front of them and that this appearance is not dependent on the power of the mind.

Since the magician actively intends for the pebble to appear as a horse, the way in which the horse appears to him is different from the way in which someone might mistake a coiled rope in a dark corner to be a snake. It is not because the rope is in any way a snake that the rope appears as a snake; it is merely due to the external condition of darkness which causes the rope to appear in that way. The same can be said about a pebble which has not been conjured with mantra and salve; it is the nature of the pebble not to appear as a horse. However, a pebble which has been affected by mantra and salve is said to gain an additional objective status which is its appearance as a horse. At the time of the magic show, it is as if the pebble becomes the entity of the illusory horse.[35]

Jang-gya makes this point when he says that for the magician, the pebble is merely posited as a horse through the power of the mind that was affected by the mantra; the pebble does not appear as a horse from its own side, independent of that mind. Nevertheless, there does exist an objective mode of being of the pebble itself which appears as a horse, a mode of being which is posited in dependence upon the awareness affected by the mantra. The appearance of the illusory horse must exist in order for it to be mistaken for a real horse by the audience.[36]

For the Svātantrikas, a consciousness innately conceiving true existence conceives of phenomena as existing from the side of their own objective mode of subsistence, without being posited through the force of appearing to a non-defective awareness. In the same way, the audience at the magic show believes that the horse that they see in front of them is a real horse and is not appearing to them through the power of their minds, which have been affected by the magician's spell. Ordinary beings who have not understood emptiness conceive things to be established from their own side without depending at all on being posited through the power of an awareness.

Someone who has understood emptiness, the lack of ultimate existence, understands that phenomena do not exist exclusively from their own side, that an object's mode of being depends on being posited by the non-defective awareness to which it appears. A person who has understood emptiness is like the magician who sees the appearance of the horse but knows that the horse is not real, that it is appearing through the power of the mind that has been affected by the mantra. The appearance of the horse is not merely a mental projection; it is a mode of subsistence of the pebble affected by the mantra and salve. However, the illusory horse does not exist until the magician or the audience have looked at the pebble. Thus, although there is an objective mode of subsistence, it does not exist until it is perceived by the mistaken sense consciousnesses affected by the mantra. In the same way, the Svātantrikas assert that all phenomena are merely posited through the power of appearing to a non-defective mind, but they do not assert that they are merely posited by the mind. There is an objective mode of subsistence of phenomena that exists from the object's own side and that is established by way of the object's own character. However, just as the illusory horse does not exist until it is perceived by the mistaken sense consciousnesses, the objective mode of subsistence of objects does not exist without appearing to a non-defective awareness.

Thus, for the Svātantrikas, two factors are essential. The first is the objective mode of subsistence of the object which exists from the object's own side but does not exist independently. If it did, it would be an extreme of permanence. This mode of subsistence is posited by appearing to a non-defective consciousness which is either conceptual or non-conceptual. Phenomena gain their entities through the power of the awarenesses to which they appear. However, such consciousnesses do not subjectively impute those phenomena without any objective basis; that would be an extreme of annihilation. They rather, more passively, posit that which appears to them. As Jang-gya says:

> According to these Mādhyamikas, the fact that things are

> posited through the power of an awareness that is not damaged by valid cognition and the fact that there also exists the thing's own mode of subsistence that is posited by the power of that [awareness] is not contradictory, just as a basis of conjuring [that is, a pebble] can be posited as appearing as a horse or elephant by the power of an awareness affected by mantra and salve, and there [also] exists a mode of subsistence which is the appearance of a horse or elephant even from the side of the basis of conjuring and which is posited through the power of that awareness.[37]

This mode of being which is established from the object's own side but which is posited through the power of appearing to a non-defective consciousness is the conventional mode of being of phenomena in the Svātantrika system. Their final mode of being is their lack of ultimate existence, their emptiness of being established from their own side without depending on being posited by a non-defective awareness. A Superior directly realizing this emptiness perceives only the lack of this ultimate existence; no conventionalities appear to his mind. He is like a latecomer to the magic show who neither sees the illusory horse nor conceives it to be real.[38]

Thus, in the Svātantrika system, when it said that phenomena do not exist ultimately, there are two types of non-ultimate existence. The first, deriving from Bhāvaviveka's *Blaze of Reasoning*, is the inability to bear analysis by an ultimate consciousness — a conceptual consciousness of hearing, thinking, or meditating that analyzes suchness. The second type of non-ultimate existence, described in Kamalaśīla's *Illumination of the Middle Way*, is the non-existence of an objective mode of subsistence that is not merely posited through the force of appearing to a non-defective awareness.[39]

For the Svātantrikas, true existence, ultimate existence, real existence, existence which is not posited by the power of an awareness, and existence which is capable of bearing analysis by a reasoning consciousness engaged in ultimate analysis are all objects of negation and do not exist even conventionally. Existence by way of the object's own character, inherent existence, existence by way of the object's own entityness, existence by way of its own entity, and existence capable of withstanding a search for the object designated are asserted by the Svātantrikas to be conventionally existent.[40] Bhāvaviveka holds that it is a deprecation of phenomena to refute inherent existence without affixing the qualification "ultimately." That is, for Bhāvaviveka phenomena inherently exist conventionally but not ultimately. In the fifteenth chapter of Bhāvaviveka's *Lamp for (Nāgārjuna's) "Wisdom"*, an opponent asks Bhāvaviveka:

> If entityness does not exist, how are there things? If there are things, it is not the case that entityness does not exist. Therefore, [your] thesis has the fault of deprecating that meaning.[41]

In response, Bhāvaviveka says:

> It has been asserted that things have entityness ultimately; it is not [our] thesis that they are just without entityness. Thus, since the meaning of the thesis is not a deprecation, it is not the case that the meaning of the reason is not established. Therefore, this [thesis] is without fault.[42]

Thus, Bhāvaviveka asserts that he is not deprecating or denying phenomena because he asserts that things are without entityness *ultimately*. It is, therefore, clear that he asserts that if phenomena lacked an entityness in the sense of establishment by way of the object's own entity conventionally, it would be a deprecation.[43] According to the Svātantrikas, phenomena are established by way of their own character and are established from their own side conventionally. Therefore, inherent existence cannot be refuted conventionally. It is only when the qualifications "ultimately" or "truly" are affixed to inherent existence or existence by way of the object's own character that they can be refuted; phenomena exist by way of their own character, they do not exist by way of their own character ultimately.[44]

The Prāsaṅgikas assert that phenomena do not inherently exist even conventionally, and, therefore, when they negate inherent existence or existence from the object's own side, they find it unnecessary, indeed redundant, to add the qualification "ultimately" or "truly" because, according to them, if something exists by way of its own character or inherently exists, it necessarily also truly exists and ultimately exists.[45] Whereas the Svātantrikas assert that phenomena exist by way of their own character, exist from their own side, and inherently exist while negating true existence, ultimate existence, and real existence, the Prāsaṅgikas assert that existence by way of the object's own character, existence from the object's side, inherent existence, ultimate existence, true existence, and real existence are synonymous and refute them all.[46]

In his *Supplement to (Nāgārjuna's) "Treatise on the Middle Way"* Candrakīrti attacks the Svātantrika assertion that phenomena exist by way of their own character conventionally, stating four absurd consequences that are entailed by that position:

1 If phenomena did inherently exist, then it would absurdly follow that the meditative equipoise of a Superior would destroy phenomena because if things were established from their own side, they would be established in reality, in which case they would be observed by a Superior's exalted wisdom of meditative equipoise — the consciousness that directly perceives reality. However, when emptiness is directly cognized, such an inherently existent nature does not appear, which means that either it did not exist in the first place or that the exalted wisdom consciousness destroyed it. Since the Svātantrikas assert that phenomena inherently exist, they incur the latter fault.[47]
2 If phenomena did inherently exist, it would absurdly follow that conventional truths would be able to withstand analysis by reasoning because they would ultimately exist.
3 If phenomena did inherently exist, it would absurdly follow that production from the four extremes of self, other, both, and neither would not be refuted because production from other would be findable under analysis and thus would ultimately exist.
4 If phenomena did inherently exist, it would absurdly follow that the Buddha was wrong when he said in the *Kāśyapa Chapter Sutra* (*Kāśyapaparivarta*) that phenomena are empty of themselves, that is, as being established as their own mode of being.[48]

Thus, the Prāsaṅgikas find it contradictory for the Svātantrikas to assert that phenomena are posited by an awareness on the one hand and are established by way of their own character on the other. Although it can be said that both the Svātantrikas and Prāsaṅgikas assert that phenomena are posited by the power of awareness, they differ greatly on what they mean by that. The Prāsaṅgikas assert that phenomena such as forms are posited by the power of a conceptual awareness that imputes verbal conventions, that designates an object to its basis of designation. Such a designation is completely subjective; the object designated cannot be found in its basis of designation. The mode of subsistence of the object that is posited by the designating consciousness is merely a nominal imputation. The Svātantrikas assert that phenomena are posited conventionally by the power of appearing to a non-defective consciousness such as a sense direct perceiver. While they hold that there is no mode of subsistence that is not posited by the power of appearing to an awareness, they also assert that this mode of subsistence which is posited by the power of appearing to an awareness is not merely nominally designated. The Prāsaṅgikas find this to be contradictory.[49]

For the Prāsaṅgikas, the awareness by which the object is posited is necessarily a designating thought consciousness which actively imputes the name and qualities of the object. For the Svātantrikas, the awareness which posits the object may be conceptual or non-conceptual as long as it is non-defective, for its function is to posit the inherently existent object that appears to it. The role of the awareness is more passive in the Svātantrika scheme because the awareness posits the entity of that which appears to it. For the Prāsaṅgikas, the analytically unfindable object is merely designated by terms and thoughts; it is utterly non-existent from its own side. The Svātantrikas cannot conceive of a valid mode of subsistence that is merely designated; for them, if something exists, it must exist by way of its own character.

To reiterate, for the Svātantrikas, objects are posited through the power of appearing to a non-defective awareness. The existence of the object depends both on the basis of designation and the designating consciousness. There is an objective mode of subsistence that is posited through appearing to an awareness. Thus, the consciousness is positing something that exists from the object's own side. They assert that there is no mode of subsistence that is not posited by appearing to such an awareness. A mode of subsistence that is not so posited is the meaning of true existence and is the object of negation of the Svātantrikas.

For the Prāsaṅgikas, the existence of the object is posited only by an awareness. The power to posit the existence of the object lies only with the awareness. The term "objective mode of subsistence" (*yul gyi sdod lugs*) suggests to the Prāsaṅgikas that the object exists from its own side, exists inherently. They thus concur with the Svātantrikas that there is no objective mode of subsistence that is *not* posited by an awareness, but they go further and take the more radical position that there is also no objective mode of subsistence that *is* posited by an awareness. The lack of such a mode of subsistence that is posited by awareness is the emptiness of inherent existence. From the Prāsaṅgika perspective, then, the Svātantrikas refute only a coarse self of phenomena but assert a subtle self of phenomena, inherent existence. The Prāsaṅgikas refute both.

Because the Prāsaṅgikas are able to refute the inherent existence that the Svātantrikas conventionally uphold while at the same time maintaining the viability of all phenomena within the emptiness of inherent existence, Tsong-kha-pa considers Prāsaṅgika to be the highest of the Indian schools of Buddhist philosophy.

The Tibetans brought their own approach to the study of Buddhist philosophy in that, in addition to cataloguing the Indian schools, they ranked them and compared their assertions on the basis, path, and goal, establishing a hierarchy the study of which provided a new insight into the various problems and solutions of Indian Buddhist philosophy. The hierarchy established by the Ge-luk-bas is as follows:

Prāsaṅgika-Mādhyamika
Sautrāntika-Svātantrika-Mādhyamika
Yogācāra-Svātantrika-Mādhyamika
Cittamātra (Yogācāra) Following Reasoning
Cittamātra (Yogācāra) Following Scripture
Sautrāntika Following Reasoning
Sautrāntika Following Scripture
Vaibhāṣika[50]

From lowest to highest there is an increase in the subtlety of the two extremes identified by the individual schools. The Vaibhāṣikas abandon the extreme of permanence by asserting that all conditioned phenomena are impermanent and abandon the extreme of annihilation by asserting that the past and the future are substantial entities (*dravya*, *rdzas*), that is, that the past of an object exists after its present existence and the future of an object exists before its present existence.[51] The Sautrāntikas abandon the extreme of permanence by asserting that uncaused phenomena are not substantially existent and abandon the extreme of annihilation by asserting that objects are naturally established as places for imputing designations and as bases of conception by thought. The Yogācārins abandon the extreme of permanence by asserting that objects are not naturally established as the bases of conception by thought and as places for imputing designations. For example, a table is not established by way of its own character as a basis for the affixing of the name "table". They assert that dependent phenomena and consummate phenomena are truly established, thereby abandoning the extreme of annihilation. As we have seen, the Svātantrikas abandon the extreme of permanence by asserting that no phenomenon is established from the side of its own objective mode of subsistence without being posited by the power of appearing to a non-defective awareness. They abandon the extreme of annihilation by asserting that all phenomena are established from their own side, that they exist by way of their own character. The Prāsaṅgikas abandon the extreme of permanence by asserting that phenomena are not established from their own side and under their own power, and abandon the extreme of annihilation by asserting that phenomena are imputedly existent, being mere designations by terms and thoughts.

In the progression from Vaibhāṣika to Prāsaṅgika, the middle way of the lower school becomes an extreme to be abandoned by the higher. The Vaibhāṣikas assert that everything is substantially established (*dravyasiddha, rdzas su grub pa*). The Sautrāntikas refute this by asserting that some phenomena are imputedly existent, by which they mean that these phenomena do not exist independently as a separate substantial entity, but rather are designated to other factors. The Sautrāntikas assert that all phenomena are established by the power of their own particular status as bases of conception by thought and as places for the imputation of designations. The Yogācārins refute this with reasoning, proving that imputations do not truly exist. The Yogācārins assert that the dependent and consummate natures are truly established. The Svātantrikas refute this by proving that phenomena lack a mode of subsistence that is not posited by the power of an awareness. Still, the Svātantrikas contend that all phenomena are established from their own side. This is refuted by the Prāsaṅgikas, who assert that when the object designated is sought among its bases of designation, there is nothing to be found.[52]

This is not to imply that in the Tibetan scheme the lower systems have no purpose other than to be refuted by the upper, serving as straw men for the upper schools' polemics. The tenets of the lower school are seen as a stepping stone to the higher, as means of understanding the increasingly profound philosophical positions of the upper systems. The structure of Tibetan doxographies reflects this appreciation in that they begin with the non-Buddhist systems and then proceed to Vaibhāṣika, Sautrāntika, Yogācāra, Svātantrika, finally culminating with the presentation of the Prāsaṅgika system. With this approach one is able to see a development and refinement of concepts and terminology that would be imperceptible if one began one's study with Prāsaṅgika.

This approach to the study of Buddhist philosophy allows one to discern a progression away from substantial existence, away from objects' existing in and of themselves, toward imputed existence, toward analytical unfindability. For the Vaibhāṣikas there are phenomena which substantially exist (*dravyasat, rdzas yod*) and phenomena which do not substantially exist, such as a table, but all are substantially established (*dravyasiddha, rdzas su grub pa*). For the Sautrāntikas, some phenomena are substantially established and some are not, but all are truly existent. For the Yogācārins, some phenomena are truly existent and some are not, but all phenomena are inherently established (*svabhāvasiddha, rang bzhin gyis grub pa*). The Svātantrikas refute the true existence of all phenomena but cannot refute their inherent existence, feeling that if phenomena did not inherently exist, they would not exist at all. The Prāsaṅgikas refute this inherent existence and assert that all phenomena are merely imputedly existent (*prajñātisat, btags yod*) and do not cover their bases of designation.[53] Phenomena thus become more and more nominal as one progresses from Vaibhāṣika to Prāsaṅgika.

There is also a discernible progression in their views on the nature of sense experience. Among the four tenet systems there are two explanations of how a direct perceiver knows a sense object. The Sautrāntikas, Yogācārins, and Mādhyamikas assert that the object casts an aspect (*ākāra, rnam pa*) toward the perceiving consciousness. The Vaibhāṣikas assert that no such aspect exists. According to the other systems, an eye consciousness perceiving a table cognizes that table by the eye consciousness being generated into the aspect of the table, as a mirror takes on the aspect of the object reflected in it. This does not mean that the consciousness becomes the object, but it can be said that it becomes like the object. These schools assert that all of the uncommon characteristics of an object, such as its subtle impermanence and its production, abiding, aging, and disintegration, *appear* to the sense consciousness perceiving it. However, these qualities are not necessarily *ascertained* by the sense consciousness because the consciousness was not generated in the aspect of those qualities. In order for an object to be ascertained, the object must appear to the consciousness and the consciousness must also be produced in the aspect of the object. This provides an explanation of how an object could appear but not be seen, as in the case of being deeply absorbed in a conversation while walking and thus being unaware of one's surroundings.[54]

The aspect into which the consciousness is generated is similar to the object but is of the nature of consciousness; the aspect and the consciousness are one entity. A sense consciousness knows an object through an aspect similar to the object being generated in the consciousness.[55]

In contrast, the Vaibhāṣikas assert that the eye consciousness and eye sense extend out to the object so that there is no need for the object to be reflected in the consciousness. They do not distinguish between a subjective aspect and the object itself; the appearance of the object is the object itself.[56]

The Buddhist schools' positions on aspected and aspectless sense perception have correlates to the various types of realism elaborated in Western philosophy. Here, realism is taken to mean the view that material objects exist externally and independently of sense perception.[57] In this scheme, the Vaibhāṣika position represents a form of direct realism, the view that sense perception is a direct, straightforward, and immediate contact of the consciousness and its object.[58] That the Vaibhāṣika view does not represent the simplest form of direct realism, naive realism, which holds that things exist exactly as they are perceived to, is evidenced by the Vaibhāṣikas' assertion that all gross objects, things that can be either physically or mentally broken down into parts, are conventional truths. They also assert that all impermanent phenomena with the exception of true paths (*mārgasatya*, *lam gyi bden pa*) are contaminated in the sense that they can serve as causes for the increase of the afflictive emotions because impermanent phenomena can be objects of desire or hatred.[59] Thus, although the Vaibhāṣika position may be classified as one of direct realism, it is not to be assumed that their approach to sense experience is non-analytical.

The Sautrāntikas criticize the Vaibhāṣika position, arguing that if direct perception were not aspected, either objects could not be perceived at all because there would be no way for the consciousness to perceive the object, or it should be possible to see through walls because a consciousness, being immaterial and going out to its object, would not be obstructed by matter.[60] The Sautrāntika introduction of the aspect into the process of sense perception represents a development away from the Vaibhāṣika view toward what would be classified in the West as a form of indirect realism, specifically representive realism, which states that actual perception is perception of sensa; to perceive an external object is to perceive the sensa caused by it so that sense perception is technically limited to the perception of sensa, not of the object itself.[61] The Sautrāntikas do indeed distinguish between the object and its aspect, but would balk at the suggestion that for this reason sense perception is somehow indirect. Although they assert that objects exist external to the mind perceiving them and cause the sensa or representations that we perceive, they would not be frightened by the notorious pitfall of representative realism — if sense experience is technically only of sensa and never of external objects, how are the objects to be ascertained? Are material objects not unobserved and thus finally unintelligible?[62] The Sautrāntikas assert that the aspect is similar to the object and thus allows the object to be directly perceived. The aspect is not mistaken for the actual object; it merely allows the object to be perceived. For the Sautrāntikas, a sense direct perceiver is a complete engager (**vidhipravṛttibuddhi, sgrub 'jug gi blo*) that is, everything that exists in the same substantial entity with the object, all of its specific characteristics, appears directly to a sense consciousness.[63]

Persuaded by the argument from illusion, that the same thing sometimes appears differently to different people, the Yogācārins sever the relationship between the external object and its aspect that the Sautrāntikas maintain, asserting instead that external objects are utterly non-existent and that the object is not a cause of the consciousness perceiving it. The Yogācārins hold that subject and object arise simultaneously, both arising from the same latency (*vāsanā, bags chags*) or seed (*bīja, sa bon*) that resides in the mental consciousness or mind-basis-of-all (*ālayavijñāna, kun gzhi rnam shes*). A seed is activated, causing the appearance of the object and the consciousness perceiving it. Subject and object are the same substantial entity, arising from the same cause; there are no objects that are not of the nature of consciousness. Thus, the Yogācārins maintain that there are sensa without objects external in entity to the perceiving consciousness and that these sensa are of the nature of the mind. In this way, their view approaches one of idealism or Berkeley's immaterialism, for the Yogācārins assert that objects composed of material particles do not exist.

The Sautrāntika-Svātantrikas, in the person of Bhāvaviveka, reacted strongly against the Yogācārin view, holding that external objects do exist as they appear to direct perception, although they do not truly exist. The Yogācāra-Svātantrikas assimilated the Yogācārin idealism, asserting that subject and object do not exist as separate entities conventionally, but rejected the Yogācārin contention that consciousness truly exists.[64]

Thus far, the process of perception has originated with the subject — consciousness — as in the assertion of the Yogācārins and Yogācāra-Svātantrikas, or with the externally existent object, as in the assertion of the Vaibhāṣikas, Sautrāntikas, and Sautrāntika-Svātantrikas. The Prāsaṅgikas incorporate elements of both the subjective and objective approaches, at once maintaining factors of realism and skepticism. The Prāsaṅgikas are realists in that they assert that external objects exist as separate entities from the perceiving consciousness. They are skeptics in that they deny the veracity of sense perception in terms of the appearance of inherent existence. From another point of view, they are not realists in that they do not accept that all of the characteristics of the object that appears to a sense consciousness are true; a sense consciousness correctly perceives the general object and its primary characteristics but misperceives the object as inherently existent. In this way, they go beyond the position of the critical realists, who hold that in veridical perception those characters that appear to the senses are the actual characters or properties of the external object.[65] The Prāsaṅgikas also are not skeptical in a certain sense in that they do not deny that indubitable information can be gained about the nature of things.[66] For them, external objects exist, but they do not exist in the way that they appear. Objects appear to exist inherently, and this false appearance is perceived by the non-conceptual sense consciousnesses. There are two factors that appear to the sense consciousness, the appearance of inherent existence and the mere appearance of the imputedly existent object. For common beings these two appearances are mixed.[67] There are thus true and false aspects present in the sensa which ordinarily cannot be distinguished. The Prāsaṅgikas turn to the other valid source of knowledge, inference, to discern and destroy with reasoning the conception of inherent existence by thought and the perception of inherent existence by the sense consciousnesses. Reasoning reveals that the object does not exist in and of itself but is empty of inherent existence. By becoming accustomed to this emptiness again and again from the viewpoint of many different reasonings, the false factor in sense perception can be identified and, through developing direct perception of emptiness and accompanying that practice with altruistic deeds, that false appearance can finally eliminated at Buddhahood.[68]

Thus, in the Prāsaṅgika system, reasoning and analysis provide the means for eliminating the deceptive factor in sense perception. The objects of the senses exist validly as external objects but do not exist in the way that they appear; they appear to exist in an of themselves when in fact they are merely subjectively designated. All of the lower schools assert that phenomena appear to exist inherently and do exist inherently.[69] The Prāsaṅgikas concur that phenomena do indeed appear to exist in and of themselves but argue that this is a false appearance, unfindable under analysis.

5 The Reasoning Consciousness

Heretofore the importance of the reasoning consciousness for Bhāvaviveka and for the Mādhyamika school in general has been noted, but the specific processes of reasoning have not been delineated. In this chapter, two of the many reasonings employed by the Svātantrikas will be analyzed. The two reasonings are those which receive the greatest emphasis from the founders of the two branches of Svātantrika, Bhāvaviveka and Śāntarakṣita.

As cited earlier, Bhāvaviveka says in the third chapter of his *Essence of the Middle Way* (III.26):

> Here, earth and so forth
> Are not entities of the elements ultimately
> Because of being produced
> And because of having causes, like a consciousness.[1]

Bhāvaviveka explains that "earth and so forth" are the subjects (*dharmin, chos can*) of the syllogism. "And so forth" refers to the other three elements — water, fire, and wind. "Are not entities of the elements ultimately" is the predicate (*dharma, chos*). Bhāvaviveka provides two reasons for the probandum or thesis that earth and so forth are not entities of the elements ultimately, "because of being produced" and "because of having causes." "Like a consciousness" is the example (*dṛṣṭānta, dpe*). Therefore, Bhāvaviveka's statement in syllogistic form is:

The subjects, earth and so forth, are not entities of the

> elements ultimately because of being produced, as is the case, for example, with a consciousness.

In the *Blaze of Reasoning*, a hypothetical opponent objects that by asserting that earth is not the entity of the element earth ultimately, Bhāvaviveka contradicts his own acceptance of the categories of phenomena set forth by the Buddha because he denies their existence.[2] Bhāvaviveka responds that the objection is unfounded because he is not asserting that earth and so forth are not the entities of the elements, but that they are not the entities of the elements *ultimately*. When the Buddha presented the entities and characteristics of phenomena, he did so conventionally and said that ultimately they lack entityness.[3] Bhāvaviveka thus makes clear that he is denying the ultimate existence of phenomena and is in no way attacking their conventional status.

In order to gain a fuller understanding of Bhāvaviveka's syllogism, it is necessary to place it within the framework of Buddhist logic. Ge-luk literature on the topic of Signs and Reasonings (*rtag rigs*) sets forth a sixfold division of correct signs, dividing them by way of the entity of the sign, the predicate of the probandum, the mode of proof, the probandum, the way the sign relates to the similar class, and the party.[4] Greatest attention is paid to the first, the division of correct signs by way of entity. In this division, signs are considered in terms of their relationship to the predicate of the probandum. When divided from the point of view of entity, correct signs are of three types: correct effect signs (*samyakkāryahetu, 'bras rtags yang dag*), correct nature signs (*samyaksvabhāvahetu, rang bzhin gyi rtags yang dag*), and correct signs of non-observation (*samyakanupalabdhihetu, ma dmigs pa'i rtags yang dag*).

Correct effect signs involve a relationship of cause and effect between the predicate of the probandum and the sign; an effect is stated as the sign of the syllogism and the cause of that effect is stated as the predicate of the probandum.[5] The most famous example of a correct effect sign in Indian logic is, "On a smoky mountain pass, fire exists because smoke exists," with the effect, smoke, stated as the sign and the cause of that effect, fire, being stated as the predicate of the probandum.

As suggested by the name, a correct nature sign is the same nature as the predicate of the probandum. In the example, "The subject, sound, is impermanent because of being a product," product and impermanent thing are synonyms and thus are of one nature.[6]

For the third type of correct signs, correct non-observation signs, the predicate of the probandum in the proof must be a negative phenomenon (*pratiṣedha, dgag pa*).[7] Bhāvaviveka's syllogism falls into this category in that the predicate of his probandum is a negative, "are not entities of the elements ultimately." There are numerous divisions and subdivisions of correct non-observation signs, the first division being into (1) correct non-observation signs of the non-appearing and (2) correct non-observation signs which are non-observations of that which is suitable to appear.[8] The former necessarily involves the special class of supersensory objects and thus is not relevant to the categorization of Bhāvaviveka's reason.

Correct signs which are a non-observation of that which is suitable to appear are of two types: correct signs which are a non-observation of a related object suitable to appear and correct signs which are an observation of a contradictory object suitable to appear. The reason in the syllogism, "On a lake at night, smoke does not exist because of the non-existence of fire," is an example of a correct sign which is a non-observation of a related object. On a dark night smoke is not visible on the surface of a lake. However, it would be suitable for fire, which is related to smoke as its cause, to appear since fire is visible at night. The absence of fire can therefore serve as a correct sign proving the non-existence of smoke on the lake.[9]

Correct signs which are an observation of a contradictory object suitable to appear are of two types: correct signs which are an observation of an object suitable to appear that is contradictory in the sense of not abiding together and correct signs which are an observation of an object suitable to appear that is contradictory in the sense of mutual exclusion. An example of the first is, "In an area covered by fire, tangible cold does not exist because of being an area covered by a large fire."[10] Someone might wonder whether cold is present in an area visible in the distance. The presence of cold cannot be directly perceived without relying on a sign, such as the presence of snow and ice. The absence of cold could be inferred by observing an object which is contradictory with cold and which is also suitable to appear. Because cold and fire are contradictory in the sense that they cannot be present in the same place simultaneously, the presence of fire serves as a correct sign in the proof of the absence of cold in a place covered by a large fire.

An example of a proof statement which employs a correct sign which is an observation of an object suitable to appear that is contradictory in the sense of mutual exclusion is, "The subject, sound, is not a permanent phenomenon because of being a product."[11] Product and permanent phenomenon are mutually exclusive; whatever is a product is necessarily not a permanent phenomenon and whatever is a permanent phenomenon is necessarily not a product. Thus, the observation of sound as a product, its being produced in dependence on causes and conditions, serves as a correct sign proving that sound is not permanent.

In seeking to discover which type of correct sign Bhāvaviveka employs in his syllogism, "The subjects, earth and so forth, are not entities of the elements ultimately because of being produced," it can first be deduced that the sign is one of non-observation because the predicate of the probandum is a negative phenomenon (*pratiṣedha, dgag pa*). In all proofs involving non-observation signs the predicate of the probandum must be a negative phenomenon.[12] Bhāvaviveka says in the *Blaze of Reasoning*, " 'Are not' is a phrase that indicates a negative."[13] Bhāvaviveka goes on to explain that in the proof that earth and so forth are not entities of the elements ultimately, the negative "are not" is to be taken as a non-affirming negative (*prasajyapratiṣedha, med dgag*) rather than an affirming negative (*paryudāsapratiṣedha, ma yin dgag*). A non-affirming negative does not imply any positive phenomenon or affirming negative in its place, but is a mere elimination of the object negated. Therefore, when Bhāvaviveka says that he is merely negating that earth and so forth are entities of the elements ultimately, this does not suggest that they are the entities of something else.[14]

Having ascertained that the sign in Bhāvaviveka's syllogism is a non-observation sign, it must still be determined which type of non-observation sign it is. Since that which is being negated in the predicate, the existence of earth and so forth as entities of the elements ultimately, is not a supersensory object, it cannot be a non-observation sign of the non-appearing, but must be a correct sign which is a non-observation of the suitable to appear. When this type of non-observation sign is divided into correct signs which are a non-observation of a related object suitable to appear and correct signs which are an observation of a contradictory object suitable to appear, the first type of sign is necessarily a non-affirming negative whereas the second is either an affirming negative or positive phenomenon.[15] Because Bhāvaviveka's sign, "being produced," is a positive phenomenon, it can be deduced that it is of the latter type, a correct sign which is an observation of a contradictory object suitable to appear.

Within this category, "being produced" is a correct sign which is an observation of an object suitable to appear that is contradictory in the sense of mutual exclusion because it is Bhāvaviveka's position that to be ultimately existent as the entities of the elements and to be produced from causes and conditions are mutually exclusive; no phenomenon can be both ultimately existent and a product. The implications of this view will be explored when the establishment of the pervasion is discussed.

In order for Bhāvaviveka's reason to be correct, the three modes must be established, the first of which is the property of the subject (*pakṣadharma, phyogs chos*). The property of the subject is established if the sign, "being produced." is a property of the subject, "earth and so forth." It is accepted by all four schools of Buddhist tenets that the four elements, earth, water, fire, and wind, are products because they arise in dependence on causes and conditions. The property of the subject is thus easily established.

A similar example (**sadṛṣṭānta, mthun dpe*) is used to facilitate understanding of the second mode of the sign, the forward pervasion (*anvayavyāpti, rjes khyab*). In Bhāvaviveka's syllogism, the forward pervasion is, "Whatever is a product is necessarily not an entity of the elements ultimately." The similar example is a consciousness. It is generally accepted by the schools of Buddhist tenets that a consciousness is a product because of being produced in dependence on an observed-object-condition (*ālambana pratyaya, dmigs rkyen*), an empowering condition (*asādhāraṇa-adhipati-pratyaya, bdag rkyen*), and an immediately preceding condition (*sama-nantarapratyaya, de ma thag rkyen*). A consciousness is also easily proved to be not the entity of the elements ultimately, the predicate of the probandum, because no one, Buddhist or non-Buddhist among the Indian schools, asserts that consciousness is any of the four elements. Even the Nihilists (*ayata, rgyang 'phen pa*) assert that consciousness is an elemental evolute; they do not assert that it is an entity of the elements.[16] Just as consciousness is a product and is not the entity of the elements ultimately, it is to be understood that other products, even the elements of earth, water, fire, and wind, are not entities of the elements ultimately.

The counterpervasion (*vyatirekavyāpti, ldog khyab*) in Bhāvaviveka's syllogism would be, "Whatever is the entity of the elements ultimately is necessarily not a product." In order for product to be a correct sign, it must be non-existent in the dissimilar class; it must be just non-existent in the class of that which is an entity of the elements ultimately. In order to clarify the meaning of the dissimilar class, a dissimilar example (**vidṛṣṭānta, mi mthun dpe*), a member of the dissimilar class of which the sign may not be a member is often given. A dissimilar example in this case would be something that is an entity of the elements ultimately and is not a product. However, because the dissimilar class, and hence a dissimilar example do not exist, Bhāvaviveka does not prove the counterpervasion and does not state a dissimilar example. There is nothing which is an entity of the elements ultimately. Bhāvaviveka writes in the *Blaze of Reasoning:*

> Here, from among the three modes of the sign, the mode in which [the sign] is opposed to the dissimilar class is not indicated. Here, only two modes of the reason that I wish to propound are designated. The property of the subject [i.e., that earth and so forth are products] is exhausted in that which exists only in the similar class [not being the entity of the elements ultimately]. With respect to the dissimilar class, not even a minute particle of the other — the existence of entityness — exists. Therefore, the dissimilar class does not exist. Thus, an example and reason of the counter [pervasion] from the dissimilar class are not indicated here.[17]

Bhāvaviveka thus concerns himself with the first two of the three modes, the property of the subject and the forward pervasion. Since the property of the subject, that earth and so forth are products, is accepted by all Buddhist schools, it is clear that Bhāvaviveka's argument hinges on the forward pervasion, that product only exists in the similar class of the predicate of the probandum, or, more simply stated, whatever is a product is necessarily not an entity of the elements ultimately. The pivot of Bhāvaviveka's argument is his assertion that whatever is produced from causes and conditions does not ultimately exist.

For example, in Buddhist literature, earth is defined as that which is hard and obstructive.[18] Bhāvaviveka says that earth is not an entity which is ultimately hard because of being an element, as is the case with wind.[19] His point is that just as wind is not ultimately hard, so earth, which is defined as that which is hard and obstructive, is not ultimately hard due to its being an element. Whatever is an element is necessarily not ultimately hard. If the elements were ultimately hard, they would be hard without depending on their causes, in which case even water and wind would have to be hard. If the elements ultimately existed, they would be established from their own side without being posited through the power of an awareness. If that were the case, there could be no valid cognizer which comprehends that earth is hard and water is not hard because earth and water would ultimately exist and would not depend on the valid cognizers which comprehend them as having different qualities. From another perspective, if smoke, for example, were truly established, it would arise without depending on specific causes, in which case it would absurdly either depend on all phenomena in the universe or it would not depend on anything, including fire.[20]

However, the elements do not ultimately exist because they are aggregations of the eight substantial particles — earth, water, fire, wind, form, odor, taste, and tangibility. If something is ultimately existent, it must not be an aggregation of its parts because it must abide uniquely, without depending on anything. For Bhāvaviveka, things do not ultimately exist because they are produced from the aggregation of their causes and conditions and because they do not arise without those causes and conditions; if they existed ultimately, they would not depend on anything.[21]

Bhāvaviveka thus draws out the absurd implications of ultimate existence. Phenomena sharing the same quality, such as hardness, would be indistinguishable because that hardness would exist in and of itself and would be the final mode of being of that phenomenon. In Bhāvaviveka's system, sentient beings conceive of phenomena as existing ultimately, as existing from the side of their own objective mode of being without depending on being posited through the power of appearing to an awareness. Bhāvaviveka seeks to destroy this conception by pointing out how things would have to exist if they did ultimately exist — they would have to exist in utter independence, without depending on any cause whatsoever, as if each phenomenon existed in and of itself in its own unique vacuum. Having drawn out the implications of ultimate existence in this way, Bhāvaviveka sees no need to resort to complicated reasonings to refute this ultimate existence. He can prove that earth and so forth are not entities of the elements ultimately merely by stating that they are products, they are produced by causes and conditions. That fact alone, accepted by all schools of Buddhist tenets, is sufficient to deny their ultimate existence. Being a product and being ultimately existent are contradictory in the sense of being mutually exclusive; whatever is one cannot be the other. Once earth, or any other impermanent phenomenon, is observed to possess a quality which is contradictory to ultimate existence, the possibility of earth being ultimately existent is removed. It is in this sense that Bhāvaviveka's reason is a correct sign which is the observation of a contradictory object in the sense of being mutually exclusive. Anything that is produced from causes cannot ultimately exist. Bhāvaviveka is thus able to point to the fundamental quality of impermanent phenomena, that they are products, as a proof of their emptiness of ultimate existence.

In the stanza from the *Blaze of Reasoning*, Bhāvaviveka provides two reasons why earth and so forth are not entities of the elements ultimately, "because of being produced" and "because of having causes." He explains that this second reason is provided to indicate other forms of the reason such as "because of being a [functioning] thing," "because of being an object of knowledge," and "because of being an object of expression." He says that whatever has causes, or is a thing, an object of knowledge, or an object of expression is not an entity of the elements ultimately.[22] In other words, nothing is ultimately an entity of the elements or anything else; nothing ultimately exists. Bhāvaviveka employs reasons for which the property of the subject is easily acceptable. Simplicity, however, does not imply that the reasoning is to be dismissed; the power of his approach derives from the simplicity of the reason when the forward pervasion is established.

Śāntarakṣita's Reasoning of the Lack of Being One or Many

The first stanza of Śāntarakṣita's *Ornament for the Middle Way* says:

> These things propounded by ourselves and others,
> Because they lack in reality
> A nature of unity or plurality,
> Do not inherently exist, like a reflection.[23]

When put in syllogistic form, Śāntarakṣita's stanza reads:

> The subjects, these things propounded by our own and other schools, do not inherently exist because of lacking a

> nature of unity or plurality in reality, as is the case, for example, with a reflection.

It should be noted that in the thesis, Śāntarakṣita uses the phrase, "do not inherently exist." This is one of the cases referred to by Tsong-kha-pa in which the Svātantrikas speak of phenomena as not existing inherently or not existing by way of their own character. It is Tsong-kha-pa's position that, despite such statements, the Svātantrikas assert that phenomena exist by way of their own character conventionally and inherently exist conventionally but refute that phenomena inherently exist ultimately. Thus, for the sake of clarity, Śāntarakṣita's syllogism may be restated as:

> The subjects, these things propounded by our own and other schools are not truly established because of not being either truly established unities or pluralities.

Kamalaśīla states in his *Illumination of the Middle Way* (*Mādhyamakāloka*) that Śāntarakṣita's stanza can be taken as either a consequence or a syllogism.[24] However, there are apparent problems with both approaches.

If the stanza is construed as a consequence, the following consequence might be stated to a Vaibhāṣika opponent:

> It follows that the subject, a minute partless particle, does not truly exist because of not being a truly existent unity or plurality.

In order for this to be a correct consequence, the sign must be accepted by the opponent, that is, the Vaibhāṣika must accept that minute partless particles are not truly existent unities or pluralities. However, the Vaibhāṣikas cannot accept the reason because they assert that partless particles are truly existent and are unities.[25]

This difficulty is acknowledged and answered by Kamalaśīla who says in the *Illumination of the Middle Way:*

> If [this reason is used] to prove a consequence, it is not the case that the reason is not established because, although the opponents have not asserted that things lack being either one or many, since they assert phenomena which are pervaded by that [i.e., the lack of being one or many], they just assert that [things lack being either one or many] implicitly as well.[26]

His point is that even though the opponents do not explicitly accept that the subject is not a truly existent unity or multiplicity, they implicitly accept it as such because they are logically forced to that position. The argument is best illustrated with an example.

The theistic Sāṃkhyas assert that the god Īśvara is permanent and unitary, by which they mean that all the factors of Īśvara which exist in the morning also exist in the evening; there is nothing present in Īśvara in the morning that is absent in the evening. All of the factors of Īśvara are mutually one at all times, and they, therefore, do not explicitly assert that Īśvara is not a truly existent one. However, they also assert that Īśvara creates different situations, in the morning causing some beings to be happy and in the evening causing others to be sad. From the Buddhist perspective, anything that creates different effects at different times, that is, whose activities are inconsistent, cannot be permanent and one. The Sāṃkhyas thus assert that Īśvara is a permanent unity but ascribe qualities to him that contradict that assertion.[27] They therefore come to assert implicitly that Īśvara is not a truly existent unity because it is not suitable to produce some effects at one time and not produce them at another.

Kamalaśīla argues that the use of the consequence is justified in that the pervader is implicitly asserted because the pervaded is explicitly asserted. To understand what this means it is necessary to examine the consequence in question:

> It follows that the subject, Īśvara, is not a truly existent unity because of creating different effects at different times.

The Sāṃkhyas explicitly assert the reason in this case. In a correct consequence, the pervasion must be validly established which means, in this case, that whatever creates different effects at different times is necessarily not a truly existent unity. The reason, "creating different effects at different times" is the pervaded, and the predicate "not being a truly existent unity," is the pervader; whatever is the reason A is a pervaded by the predicate B. Thus, t' Sāṃkhyas explicitly accept the reason of the above consequence and so explicitly accept the pervaded whereby they are logically forced to accept implicitly the pervader or the predicate, "is not a truly existent unity." Anything that creates different effects at different times is a member of the larger set of those things which are not truly existent unities. The Sāṃkhyas thus implicitly assert the predicate of the consequence that served as the reason of the prior consequence:

> It follows that the subject, Īśvara, does not truly exist because of not being a truly existent one.

The opponent thereby implicitly accepts the reason. In this way, it is suitable to take Śāntarakṣita's stanza as a consequence despite the fact that the reason is not explicitly accepted by the opponent.

The other qualm that is raised concerns the subjects set forth when Śāntarakṣita's stanza is put in syllogistic from. In the stanza, Śāntarakṣita identifies "these things propounded by ourselves and others" as the subjects of his syllogisms. Some of these things, such as the principal (*pradhāna, gtso bo*) asserted by the Sāṃkhyas, partless particles asserted by the Vaibhāṣikas, and the inexpressible person asserted by the Vātsīputrīyas do not exist according to the Mādhyamikas. Consequently, the question is raised as to whether it is possible to have a correct syllogism, the subject of which is a non-existent.

In Tibetan textbooks on Signs and Reasonings, three types of incorrect or facsimile reasons are set forth: contradictory reasons (*viruddhahetu, 'gal pa'i gtan tshigs*), indefinite reasons (*anaikāntikahetu, ma nges pa'i gtan tshigs*), and non-established reasons (*asiddhahetu, ma grub pa'i gtan tshigs*). Facsimile reasons are not correct signs because they are not all three modes of the sign in a particular proof. A contradictory reason in a particular proof is the property of the subject but is not the forward pervasion. It is the inverse forward pervasion which means that the sign exists only in the dissimilar class. "The subject, sound, is a permanent phenomenon because of being a product" is an example of a contradictory reason.[28]

An indefinite reason in a particular proof is the property of the subject but is not the forward pervasion. Unlike the contradictory reason, it is also not the inverse forward pervasion. An example would be, "The subject, the sound of a conch, arises through exertion, because of being impermanent." The sound of a conch is impermanent but the sign exists in both the similar and dissimilar class, that is, there are impermanent things which arise from exertion, such as a pot, and which do not arise from exertion, such as a rock. There are several types of indefinite reasons which need not detain us here.[29]

A non-established reason in a particular proof is not the property of the subject of that proof. Such reasons are of three types: non-established reasons in relation to the fact (*artha, don*), in relation to the mind (*buddhi, blo*), and in relation to the other party (*pakṣa, rgol ba*). Non-established reasons in relation to the fact are of seven types: non-established reasons due to (1) the non-existence of the entity of the sign, (2) the non-existence of the entity of the subject, (3) the non-difference of the sign and the predicate of the probandum, (4) the non-difference of the basis of debate (subject) and the sign, (5) the non-difference of the basis of debate and the predicate of the probandum, (6) the non-existence of the sign, in accordance with the mode of statement, with the subject sought to be known, and (7) the non-existence in the subject sought to be known of a portion of the reason.[30]

The names of these seven types of non-established reasons in relation to the fact are for the most part self-explanatory. We are concerned with the second type, a non-established reason due to the non-existence of the entity of the sign. An illustration of such a non-established reason is, "The subject, the horn of a rabbit, is impermanent because of being a product." In this case, the sign is not a property of the subject because the subject does not exist.

Returning to Śāntarakṣita's syllogism, it would seem that when non-existents such as the principal (*pradhāna, gtso bo*) or a self of persons (*pudgalātman, gang zag gi bdag*) are stated as subjects which do not truly exist because of not being truly one or many, the sign would be a non-established reason due to the non-existence of the entity of the subject because, for Śāntarakṣita, the principal and a self of persons are as equally non-existent as the horn of a rabbit.

However, the fault of a non-established reason due to the non-existence of the entity of the subject is incurred only when the sign and predicate of the probandum are positive phenomena. Despite the fact that the subject is a non-existent, it is not automatically the case that the reason is not established when the sign (the reason) and predicate of the probandum are non-affirming negatives.[31]

Objects of knowledge may be divided into positive phenomena (*vidhi, sgrub pa*) and negative phenomena (*pratiṣedha, dgag pa*). Any thing that exists is either a positive phenomenon or a negative phenomenon, with the latter being defined as a phenomenon which is an object realized through a mode of explicit elimination of its object of negation by the thought consciousness apprehending it. An example of a negative phenomenon is non-pot, which is realized through the explicit elimination of its objects of negation, pot. In contradistinction, a positive phenomenon is a phenomenon which is not an object realized through a mode of explicit elimination of its object of negation by the thought consciousness apprehending it. An example of a positive phenomenon is a pot, which is realized without the thought apprehending it having to resort to a process of explicit elimination.[32]

Negative phenomena are of two types, affirming negatives (*paryudāsapratiṣedha*, *ma yin dgag*) and non-affirming negatives (*prasajyapratiṣedha*, *med dgag*. The definition of an affirming negative is a negative that is expressed by a phrase indicating, in place of its own object of negation, another phenomenon which is either an affirming negative or a positive phenomenon. This means, first of all, that an affirming negative is a negative phenomenon. Secondly, the term that expresses the affirming negative must imply some positive phenomenon which the thought consciousness realizing the affirming negative understands in the place of the object of negation that is explicitly eliminated by the thought consciousness apprehending the affirming negative. A famous example of an affirming negative is expressed by the sentence, "The fat Devadatta does not eat during the day." The negative phenomenon is Devadatta's not eating during the day. The term expressing this implies a positive phenomenon — Devadatta's eating at night — for the thought consciousness realizing the object of negation — his not eating during the day. Due to the description of Devadatta as fat, the thought realizes that he must eat sometime and, therefore, realizes, in place of the fact that he does not eat during the day, the fact that he eats at night.

The definition of a non-affirming negative is a negative which is expressed by a phrase that does not indicate, in place of its own object of negation, another phenomenon which is either an affirming negative or a positive phenomenon. Thus, a non-affirming negative is a negative phenomenon which does not in any way imply a positive phenomenon in place of its object of negation. An instance is the lack of anything that is both a pot and non-pot. No positive phenomenon is implied.[33]

Non-affirming negatives are of two types, those whose object of negation occurs among objects of knowledge and those whose object of negation does not occur among objects of knowledge. An example of the first is the non-existence of the pot; the object of negation, a pot, occurs among objects of knowledge. An example of the second is the emptiness of true existence; true existence is a non-existent and thus does not occur among objects of knowledge.[34]

The reason and sign of Śāntarakṣita's syllogism, "The subject, the principal, does not truly exist because of not being truly one or many," are both non-affirming negatives of the latter type, those whose object of negation does not occur among objects of knowledge, because true existence and being a truly existent unity or multiplicity are both non-existents. That something which is a truly existent unity or multiplicity does not exist will be explored in the discussion of the establishment of the property of the subject.

Thus, Śāntarakṣita's reason is not non-established, even though the subject does not exist, because the sign and predicate of the probandum are non-affirming negatives. However, it would not be accurate to say that if the entity of the subject does not exist and the predicate of the probandum and the sign are not non-affirming negatives that the reason is necessarily not established due to the non-existence of the entity of the subject. For example, in the syllogism, "The subject, the horns of rabbit, are suitable to the expressed by the term 'moon' because of existing among objects of thought," the subject does not exist and the predicate of the probandum and the sign are positive phenomena, yet the reason is correct. Any object that can be thought of is suitable to be designated with any name because names do not inhere in objects; they are bestowed adventitiously.[35] Therefore, whatever exists among objects of thought, whether it exists or not, is suitable to be given the name "moon" or any other name. Because the horns of a rabbit can be conceived of, even though they do not exist, they can be called "moon." Because the three modes of the sign are established, it is a correct reason despite the fact that the subject does not exist and the predicate of the probandum and the sign are not non-affirming negatives.[36]

It would also be inaccurate to say that if the entity of the subject does not exist and the predicate of the probandum and sign are non-affirming negatives, then the reason is necessarily correct. For example, in the syllogism, "The subject, the horns of a rabbit, are the selflessness of phenomena because of being the consummate nature (*pariniṣpanna, yongs grub*)," the subject does not exist and the predicate of the probandum and the sign are both non-affirming negatives, but the reason is not established, and thus is not a correct reason. The selflessness of phenomena and the consummate nature are synonyms and are both non-affirming negatives because they are the mere absence of true existence, according to Mādhyamika. However, the horn of a rabbit is not the absence of true existence, the final nature of phenomena, and so the reason is incorrect, a fascimile.[37]

It is thus logically careless to assert that whenever the entity of the sign does not exist and the predicate of the probandum and the sign are non-affirming negatives that the reason is automatically correct, or that if the subject does not exist and the predicate of the probandum and the sign are not non-affirming negatives, then the reason is automatically a facsimile. The reason why the reason is not non-established in the syllogism concerning the horns of a rabbit being called by the name "moon" is that the predicate of the probandum — being suitable to be expressed by the term "moon" — and the sign — existing among objects of thought — are not necessarily existents; both existents and non-existents are suitable to be expressed by the term "moon" and exist among objects of thought. The reason why the reason is non-established in the latter syllogism concerning the horn of a rabbit being the selflessness of phenomena, despite the fact that the entity of the subject does not exist and the predicate of the probandum and the sign are non-affirming negatives, is that whatever is the predicate of the probandum and the sign must exist; whatever is the selflessness of phenomena and whatever is a consummate phenomenon must exist. Thus, whenever a non-existent is stated as the subject and either the predicate of the probandum or the sign must be existents, the reason will not be correct. When the predicate of the probandum and the sign do not have to be existents, the sign will not be a facsimile.[38]

When Śāntarakṣita states that, "The subject, the principal, does not truly exist because of not being either truly one or many," the entity of the subject does not exist and the predicate of the probandum and the sign do not have to be existents; nothing truly exists, whether it exists or not, and nothing is a truly existent unity or multiplicity, neither the horns of a rabbit nor the horns of a moose.

According to the logical system of Dignāga and Dharmakīrti, the subjects of syllogisms are of two types, basal subjects (*rang rten gyi chos can*) and mere subjects (*chos can 'ba' zhig ba*). In proving to a Sāṃkhya that, "the subject, sound, is impermanent because of being a product," sound is a basal subject because the predicate of the probandum, impermanence, is actually based on sound; sound is the actual basis of the syllogism. Basal subjects necessarily exist. When proving to a Sāṃkhya that, "The subject, the principal (*pradhāna*, *gtso bo*), does not exist as the substantial cause of the various manifestations because it is not observed as the substantial cause of the various manifestations," the principal is a mere subject or a merely stated subject in that one is not proving that the manifestations are not effects in terms of the principal itself because the principal does not exist. A non-existent cannot serve as the basis for even a negative predicate. A mere subject is only stated as the subject; it does not serve as the actual basis of the predicate of the probandum.[39]

If the mere subject does not serve as the basis of the predicate, what else could serve as the subject in order that the reason can be established and the thesis proven? The mental image or meaning-generality (*arthasamanya*, *don spyi*) of the non-existent subject, in this case the principal, serves as the basis of the predicate of the probandum and sign. It is this mental image, which exists for the Sāṃkhya and which is imagined to be the source of all transformations, that will serve as the actual basis of the syllogism. The Buddhist will seek to prove that the principal is not the substantial cause of the various transformations in an effort to destroy the false conception of the principal in the mind of the opponent. The Buddhist is not seeking to destroy the principal because it is utterly non-existent, it never has and never will exist. He is rather seeking to remove the conception of the principal from the opponent's mind. That false conception, rather than the non-existent principal, acts as the basis of the debate.

One might wonder whether it would not also be the case that the meaning-generality or generic image of sound would be the basal subject in the proof that sound is impermanent because of being a product. Inference, being a form of thought or conceptual consciousness, does not directly perceive impermanent phenomena such as sound, but rather understands them through the negative route of meaning-generalities. The appearing object of the thought consciousness realizing sound is the appearance as opposite from non-sound.[40] Thought is incapable of directly perceiving the subject, sound, and it would, therefore, seem that the meaning-generality of sound rather than sound itself would serve as the basal subject in the proof that sound is impermanent because of being a product; the generic image of sound is the only subject to which inference has access. However, the meaning-generality of sound is a permanent phenomenon which seems to preclude the possibility of it serving as the subject because it is impossible to prove the predicate of the probandum, impermanence, for a permanent subject.

Tsong-kha-pa addresses these problems in his *Notes to (Śānta-rakṣita's) "Ornament for the Middle Way"* (*dbU ma rgyan gyi zin bris*):

> There are bases which must be impermanent things; [for example] in the proof that sound is impermanent by [reason of being a] product and of fire existing on a [smoky] mountain pass by the sign of smoke, the two [subjects] sound and mountain pass [are impermanent things]. The images which are the appearance to thought as the opposite from these two are the actual bases of refutation and proof. Sound and mountain pass are not the actual bases because they do not actually appear to the thought that makes a refutation or proof. ... Nevertheless, the bases of the appearance of such images are sound and mountain pass. Therefore, the bases [of debate] are necessarily impermanent things.[41]

Tsong-kha-pa is making two important points here. First, in the proof that sound is impermanent because of being a product, the subject, sound, exists and is thus a basal subject. It is also the basis with respect to which the sign of being a product and the predicate of the probandum of being impermanent are established. As Tsong-kha-pa says in the same text:

> When one proves that sound is impermanent by [the sign of being a] product, the mere appearance which is the appearance as opposite from non-sound does not exist as an [impermanent] thing and thus the sign — product — is not established in relation to it; it must be established in relation to the sound which is the [meaning-generality's] basis of appearance. This is due to the fact that [impermanent] things are taken as the sign and predicate.[42]

Thus, sound itself is what is being proven to be impermanent, and it is in this sense that it serves as the basis of the debate.

The second point that Tsong-kha-pa makes is that the meaning-generality of sound serves as the actual basis for the functioning of the inferential consciousness. The appearance as opposite from non-sound, the appearing object (**pratibhāsaviṣaya*, *snang yul*) of the thought consciousness apprehending sound, is what actually serves as the basis of the proof that sound is impermanent. Inference, as a form of thought, is mistaken with respect to its appearing object in the sense that its appearing object, in this case the meaning-generality of sound, seems to be its object of engagement (**pravṛtti-viṣaya, 'jug yul*), sound itself. This does not imply, however, that thought is incapable of understanding its object; inference is an incontrovertible form of knowledge about its object of engagement.[43] Therefore, the inferential consciousness realizing that sound is impermanent because of being a product is not mistakenly thinking that the permanent meaning-generality of sound is impermanent, it is realizing that sound itself is impermanent.

In summary, because inferential consciousnesses are thought consciousnesses, they are incapable of directly perceiving their object of engagement and must operate through the medium of meaning-generalities. Therefore, in all cases of generating an inferential cognizer in dependence on a correct sign, the actual basis with which the conceptual awarenesses that realize the modes of the sign work is a meaning-generality, whether or not the stated subject exists. As Dharmakīrti says in his *Commentary on (Dignāga's) "Compendium on Valid Cognition"* (*Pramāṇavarttika*, IV.228):

> There are no external bases;
> It is asserted that all proofs and refutations
> Here depend on meaning-generalities.[44]

With this in mind, two types of stated subjects are distinguished, basal subjects and mere subjects. The former necessarily are existents, the latter, non-existents. In either case, however, they must be explicitly stated as the subject of the debate because they are what the opponent wants to know about. Despite the fact that the meaning-generality of the basal or mere subject will appear to the opponent's mind, it would be unsuitable to state the meaning-generality as the basis of the debate. When refuting the assertion of the opponent, the subject must be stated exactly as it is understood by the opponent.[45]

A basal subject exists and is the actual basis of the sign and the predicate of the probandum, although the meaning-generality of the basal subject is the actual basis for the operation of the inferential consciousness that understands the property of the subject and the predicate of the probandum, as Tsong-kha-pa explained above.

Regarding mere subjects, such as the self of persons or the principal, which are necessarily non-existents, there is disagreement between Tsong-kha-pa's two foremost disciples as to what serves as the basis of debate. Kay-drup writes that:

> Although [something] is not an established base, there is no contradiction in its being a subject under consideration and with respect to which the reason is ascertained.[46]

His position, then, is that even though the self of persons and the principal do not exist, they are to be taken as the subject of the syllogism; their meaning-generalities are not to be taken as the subject. His point is not that such non-existents are the appearing objects of a conceptual consciousness of the opponent, because he would concede that the meaning-generality of the principal, for example, would appear to the mind of a Sāṃkhya. Kay-drup is arguing that non-existents can serve as the basis of the sign and the predicate of the probandum.

Gyel-tsap offers another opinion:

> The sign is established by valid cognition in relation to the meaning-of-the-term [i.e., the meaning generality], which is a [mental] appearance. If the self-sufficient person [which does not exist] were not taken as the subject, the self of persons itself would not be refuted. Since the opponent is operating within apprehending [the self of persons] and its [generic image] as one, there is not the fault that the meaning-of-the-term would be unsuitable as the subject. Therefore, with regard to whatever is a correct sign, the subject under consideration is necessarily an established base, but whatever is the subject under consideration of a correct sign is not necessarily an established base.[47]

Gyel-tsap presents a more refined position. He begins by noting the commonly accepted view that the inferential valid cognizer establishes the sign in terms of the meaning-generality of the subject. He also concedes that the non-existent subject, in this case, a self-sufficient person, must be stated as the subject because that is the object of negation of the reasoning. Because the opponent conceives of his mental image of a self-sufficient person to be an actual self of person (which for the Buddhist does not exist), there is no reason why the meaning-generality of the non-existent subject cannot serve as the basis of the debate. He goes on to make the subtle distinction that in terms of the sign or reason, the subject always exists because the property of the subject is ascertained by an inferential consciousness in terms of a meaning-generality. However, the subject wanted to be known about is not necessarily an existent because there are mere subjects, such as the self-sufficient person. It seems, therefore, that for Kay-drup, all subjects are basal subjects because even non-existents can serve as the basis of the qualities of the sign and predicate of the probandum whereas for Gyel-tsap, the distinction between basal subjects and mere subjects is maintained.

Tsong-kha-pa's position is closer to that of Gyel-tsap or perhaps, more properly, Gyel-tsap's position is closer to Tsong-kha-pa's. He says in his *Notes to (Śāntarakṣita's) "Ornament for the Middle Way"*:

> Just such [an image] is designated as the subject in relation to which the predicate is posited as its predicate and [just such an image is designated as] the subject in relation to which the reason is posited as its property. Thus, there is no fault of the property of the subject not being established due to the mere subject's being refuted. ... When those bases of appearance are established as being those signs, even though [those bases or subjects] are refuted, the mere appearance [of the meaning-generality of the subject] serves as the subject on which the two qualities — the predicate being proven and the property of the subject — depend.[48]

It has thus been determined that non-existents can serve as, or more precisely, be stated as the subjects of correct syllogisms as long as the sign and predicate of the probandum are non-affirming negatives and as long as whatever is the sign and the predicate of the probandum need not be existents. The delineation of mere subjects has important implications in the practice of the path in that it allows the objects falsely imagined to exist by ignorance to serve as the bases of reasoning and be refuted. Ultimately existent persons and phenomena, although utterly non-existent, are the objects of negation by reasoning (**yuktipratiṣedhya, rigs pa'i dgag bya*). The mental images of those objects are the actual bases of the logical functions of reasoning. The ultimate goal is to destroy the ignorance that conceives of true existence. These concepts of true existence, unlike their objects, exist until they are destroyed by reasoning consciousnesses on the paths of seeing and meditation. The conceptions of true existence are thus called objects of negation by the path (*mārga-pratiṣedhya, lam gyi dgag bya*).[49]

Having established the suitability of non-existents' serving as the subjects of syllogisms, the three modes of Śāntarakṣita's reason may be considered. In establishing the first mode, the property of the subject, Śāntarakṣita breaks the reason down into two parts. To reiterate, the original syllogism is:

> The subjects, these things propounded by ourselves and others, do not truly exist because of not being truly existent unities or multiplicities.

The reason is divided into two parts. In other words:

> The subjects, these things propounded by ourselves and others, do not truly exist because of (1) not being truly existent unities and (2) not being truly existent multiplicities.

Śāntarakṣita considers each part of the reason separately, beginning with a refutation of those subjects that are asserted by non-Buddhist and Buddhist opponents to be truly existent unities. These subjects are included in five categories:

1 the permanent (*nitya, rtag pa*), such as the principal asserted by the Sāṃkhyas and analytical cessations (*pratisaṃkhyānirodha, so sor brtags 'gog*) asserted by the Vaibhāṣikas
2 the person (*pudgala,gang zag*), specifically the inexpressible person asserted by the Vātsīputrīyas
3 the pervasive (*vyāpaka, khyab pa*), such as space (*ākāśa, nam mkha'*) and time (*kāla, dus*) as asserted by the Nayaiyikas and Vaiśeṣikas[50]
4 the gross (*sthūla, rags pa*), that is, sense objects
5 the subtle, that is, minute particles (*paramāṇu, rdul phra rab*).

Before considering Śāntarakṣita's specific refutation of the first and last of these categories, his general argument bears consideration. The crux of his position is that nothing exists as a truly existent unity because everything has parts; there is no object of knowledge in the universe that is partless. Even permanent phenomena such as reality and uncaused space have parts. Reality or emptiness has many parts, such as the emptiness of a table, the emptiness of a chair, the emptiness of a pillar, and the emptiness of a pot.

Reality has the factor that is directly realized by Superiors and the factor that is inferentially realized by common beings. Uncaused space, which is defined as the lack of obstructive contact and which pervades everything, has parts such as that which pervades the inside of a building in the east and that which pervades the inside of a building in the west.[51]

There is also nothing impermanent that does not have parts. Physical particles are not partless, as will be seen. Gross objects composed of subtle particles obviously have parts. Consciousnesses are not partless because they have former and later moments. Also, whatever is a consciousness must be established as the factor which is produced from its own cause and the factor which produces its own effect.[52] Every phenomenon has three attributes: its meaning-generality, its qualities (*guṇa*, *yon tan*), and its factor of being itself.[53]

It might be argued that something could have parts and still be partless, but this is impossible because having parts and being partless are mutually exclusive. When something appears to the mind as having parts, the possibility of its appearing to be partless is eliminated and vice versa; there is no awareness to which one thing can appear both to have parts and be partless.[54]

Since all phenomena have parts, each phenomenon exists as a whole in relation to which its components are designated as parts. In the discussion of the reasoning of the lack of being one or many in his *Analysis of the First Chapter of* (*Maitreya's*) *"Ornament for Clear Realization"* (*Phar phyin mtha' dpyod skabs dang po*), Jam-yang-shay-ba examines the relationship between whole and part to provide a further reason why phenomena do not truly exist. Whole and part appear to be different entities with the whole being one thing and the parts another, whereas in terms of their mode of subsistence, whole and part are the same entity; they cannot be separated. If whole and part were different entities in fact in addition to appearing to be different entities, then whole and part would not exist because whole and part are designated in terms of each other. If whole and part appeared to be the same entity in addition to being the same entity in fact, whole and part also would not exist because they would be indistinguishable. Therefore, whole and part must appear to be different entities but must abide as the same entity. In other words, the way that whole and part appear and the way that they exist do not agree. Whatever appears one way and exists another is false and cannot be truly established. To be truly established means that an object's mode of appearance is established as its mode of being; the object must exist in the way that it appears.[55]

Śāntarakṣita argues that to be truly unitary means to be partless, and he logically proves that nothing is partless. It is easy to understand that phenomena with perceivable parts are not partless; this is evident to direct perception. But those phenomena imputed to be unitary and partless that are inaccessible to direct perception are more difficult to refute. For this reason, Śāntarakṣita's refutation of permanent unities and partless particles warrants special consideration.

Dharmakīrti's *Commentary on (Dignāga's) "Compendium on Valid Cognition* (II.204) says:

> That which has a nature of non-disintegration
> Is called permanent by the wise.[56]

The Sautrāntikas, Yogācārins, and Svātantrikas assert that a permanent phenomenon is one which has a nature of non-disintegration. These schools assert that the state of destruction of an object is permanent despite the fact that the state of destruction of a pot, for example, newly comes into being when the pot is smashed. The state of destruction of the pot is permanent in the sense that it does not change moment by moment as impermanent phenomena do.[57] Unlike the lower schools, the Prāsaṅgikas assert that the state of destruction of an object is a functioning thing because it depends on causes and is capable of creating effects.[58]

According to the Vaibhāṣikas and the non-Buddhist schools of Indian philosophy, if something is permanent, everything about it that exists at one moment must exist at a later moment and vice versa. Those factors that exist at those times are asserted to be one. It is this conception of permanence which Śāntarakṣita takes as his target when he refutes the permanent and unitary principal asserted by the Sāṃkhyas.[59] The Sāṃkhyas wish to uphold the permanent and unitary nature of the principal while asserting that it also produces various transformations at different times. If it were indeed permanent and unitary in the sense that the Sāṃkhyas define it, the principal could not produce different effects serially but would have to create the same effect constantly. Because the Sāṃkhyas do not assert this, the principal is not truly one because its nature of producing one effect in a former moment ceases when its nature of producing another arises in a later moment.[60]

The Vaibhāṣikas assert that analytical cessations, the mere absences of a particular afflictive emotion destroyed by wisdom, are permanent and unitary. They hold that analytical cessations are observed by consciousnesses arisen from meditation but that they do not serve as causes of the consciousnesses apprehending them. They assert that unconditioned phenomena (*asaṃskṛtadharma*, *'dus ma byas kyi chos*) such as analytical cessations have an unchanging, unitary nature at all times, but they would argue that they avoid the trap fallen into by the Sāṃkhyas because they do not assert that unconditioned phenomena produce effects.[61]

Nevertheless, Śāntarakṣita is able to prove that unconditioned phenomena do not have a unitary, unchanging nature. The Vaibhāṣika may be asked whether the analytical cessation that existed at the time when it was observed by an earlier consciousness exists at the time of a later consciousness. Since analytical cessations are permanent, he must say that it does. In that case, does the later consciousness know the analytical cessation at the time of former consciousness? Obviously, it does not. If it does not, then that analytical cessation must have a factor which is the object of knowledge of the former consciousness but not the object of knowledge of the later consciousness. In that case, it would follow that the analytical cessation that exists at the time of the former consciousness is never known by the later because its nature of not being known by the later consciousness at the earlier time is never lost since whatever is permanent never changes. If the Vaibhāṣika seeks to avoid these problems by saying that the analytical cessation that serves as the object of knowledge of a former consciousness does not exist at the time of the later consciousness, then it would follow that the permanent cessation would be impermanent and momentary because its former nature does not exist at a later time.[62]

The refutation of partless particles is important because if minute particles are proven to have parts, all physical phenomena will necessarily be proven to have parts, since they are composed of minute particles. The Vaibhāṣikas assert that physical forms (*rūpa*, *gzugs*) are aggregations of minute partless particles. In order to prove that the existence of partless particles is impossible, Śāntarakṣita takes as his subject a minute particle which is surrounded on all sides by other minute particles. If the minute particle positioned in the middle of ten other particles in the four directions, the four intermediate directions, and above and below did not have parts, it would be impossible for the other particles to be located around it because the central particle would occupy no space. It could not have an eastern surface or a western surface because it would have no parts; all of its sides would be the same. It would absurdly follow that all ten surrounding particles would contact the central particle in the same place, that is, all ten particles and, by extension, all particles in the universe would occupy the same place, in which case physical objects such as the earth would not exist; they would have no dimension. If it is admitted that the central particle has sides that face the surrounding particles, then it must be accepted that minute particles have parts.[63]

If minute particles are not truly existent unities, the objects composed of them are not truly existent unities. Also, if the objects of the five sense consciousnesses are not truly established, the sense consciousnesses themselves are not truly established because they depend on the sense objects for their production; as Bhāvaviveka argued, anything that depends on something else cannot be truly or ultimately established. Therefore, based on the refutation of partless particles, it can be inferred that sense consciousnesses and their objects do not truly exist. However, Śāntarakṣita goes on in the *Ornament for the Middle Way* to refute the truly existent unitary consciousnesses propounded by the Mimāmsakas, Sāṃkhyas, Vaiśeṣikas, Jainas, Cārvākas, and Vedāntins among the non-Buddhists, and the Vaibhāṣikas, Sautrāntikas, and Yogācārins among the Buddhists.[64]

The pivotal point in establishing that truly existent unities do not exist is that everything has parts, and Śāntarakṣita goes to some length to prove this. He shows that anything that can be asserted by a Buddhist or non-Buddhist can be logically demonstrated to be composed of physical parts, such as minute particles, or temporal parts, such as moments of consciousness. By refuting truly existent unity, that anything is truly one, Śāntarakṣita is not saying whole and part do not exist conventionally or that the terms "one" and "many" cannot be used. He is proving that there is nothing which is one that ultimately exists.

The proof that there is nothing which is truly many is accomplished more quickly. Śāntarakṣita says:

> When anything is analyzed
> It is without oneness.

> That which does not have oneness
> Also is without manyness.[65]

If a truly existent unity does not exist, a truly existent multiplicity cannot exist because if one does not exist, many cannot exist. A truly existent multiplicity would be composed of many truly existent unities. Therefore, once it can be shown that a truly existent unity does not exist, it is obvious that truly existent multiplicities do not exist. Kamalaśīla says in the *Illumination of the Middle Way:*

> If the lack of unitary entity is established, it is only obvious that the lack of multiplicity is also established because a multiplicity is an entity that is a composite of ones.[66]

If there are no trees there can be no forest.[67]

In order to ascertain the other two modes of the sign, the forward pervasion — the existence of the sign only in the similar class — and the counterpervasion — the definite non-existence of the sign in the dissimilar class — three valid cognizers are needed:

1 a valid cognizer which ascertains the instance or entity[68] of the sign,
2 a valid cognizer which ascertains that the predicate of the probandum and the object of negation are a dichotomy,
3 a valid cognizer which refutes that there is a common locus of the sign and the object of negation.[69]

To ascertain the instance or entity of the sign in this context means to ascertain the lack of a truly existent unity or multiplicity. This was accomplished with the establishment of the reason as a property of the subject.

It can be ascertained that the predicate of the probandum — non-true existence — and the object of negation — true existence — are a dichotomy by ascertaining that non-existence and existence are a dichotomy; there is nothing which both exists and does not exist. When non-existence is eliminated, existence is implied and vice versa. It can then be inferred that non-true existence and true existence are a dichotomy.

The third valid cognizer, that which refutes the existence of a common locus of the sign — not being a truly existent unity or multiplicity — and the object of negation — true existence — is perhaps the most important because it is this valid cognizer which realizes that whatever is not truly one or many does not truly exist. If something did truly exist, it would have to exist as either truly one or many because one and many are mutually contradictory and a dichotomy.

In Tibetan textbooks on reasoning, two things are defined as contradictory if they are mutually discordant. In others words, for two things to be contradictory it must be observed that they are different and that there is nothing which is both of them. There are two types of contradictories, those which are mutually contradictory and those which are contradictory in the sense of not abiding together, the former being defined as that which does not abide together in the sense of exclusion and inclusion. Mutual contradictories are divided into two, direct contradictories or dichotomies and indirect contradictories. A dichotomy is defined as that which is both mutually and explicitly discordant.[70]

One and many are mutually contradictory in the sense that the inclusion of one excludes the other and vice versa. Whatever is one is not many; if something is not many it must be one. Everything is either single or multiple, singular or plural; there is no third possibility. Śāntarakṣita says in the *Ornament for the Middle Way:*

> Things which have an aspect
> Other than one or many
> Are not feasible because
> These two are a dichotomy.[71]

If one and many are a dichotomy such that one excludes the other and there is no third category, truly one and truly many are also such a dichotomy. Having ascertained that if something exists, it is either one or many, it can be easily inferred that if something truly exists, it is truly one or truly many. The existence of a common locus of the sign and object of negation is thereby refuted. That is, there is nothing that is not truly one or many and truly exists.

The forward and counterpervasions are established by the valid cognizer which ascertains that truly one and truly many are a dichotomy in combination with the valid cognizer which ascertains the property of the subject. Tsong-kha-pa explains that:

> The valid cognizer which ascertains that being inherently the same and being inherently different are a dichotomy based on their being mutually contradictory ascertains the

> pervasion of the object of negation by the opposite of the sign. [This valid cognizer] in combination with the valid cognizer ascertaining the property of the subject ascertains the sign as opposite from the dissimilar class and the forward pervasion — the existence of the sign in only the similar class.[72]

The valid cognizer which ascertains that truly one and truly many are a dichotomy acts in combination with the valid cognizer which ascertains that the subject is neither truly one or truly many to establish the forward and counterpervasions because they ascertain that the sign — not being truly one or many — exists only in the similar class of that which is not truly existent and does not exist in the dissimilar class of that which is truly existent.[73] That is, by knowing that truly one and truly many are a dichotomy in the sense that there is no third category and nothing can be both, and, in addition, ascertaining that the subject of the syllogism is not truly one or many, one can ascertain that not being truly one or many exists only in the class of that which does not truly exist — whatever is not truly one or many necessarily does not truly exist — and that not being truly one or many does not exist in the class of that which truly exists — whatever truly exists is necessarily either truly one or truly many.

Jang-gya raises two important objections regarding the establishment of the pervasion in this syllogism. Someone might decide that the sign — not being truly one or many — exists in the dissimilar class of that which truly exists because true existence lacks being truly one or many.

Jang-gya answers that the mere fact that true existence is not truly one or many (because it does not exist) does not mean that the sign exists in the dissimilar class. Rather, there must exist a common locus of the dissimilar class and the sign, that is, there must exist something which both truly exists and is not truly one or many. Because no such thing exists, the sign does not exist in the dissimilar class.[74]

The second objection considered by Jang-gya is more complicated. When the valid cognizer ascertaining the pervasion realizes that whatever is not truly one or many is necessarily not truly existent, is it specifically realizing that each phenomenon which is not truly one or many does not truly exist? If so, it would be purposeless and redundant for the valid cognizer that subsequently realizes the thesis to ascertain that the subject does not truly exist, because the valid cognizer ascertaining the property of the subject would already have realized that the subject is not truly one or many and the valid cognizer ascertaining the pervasion would have realized that whatever is not truly one or many does not truly exist. In other words, the valid cognizer realizing the thesis would not be understanding anything new; it would merely be confirming what had already been established by the valid cognizer ascertaining the pervasion. If, on the other hand, it is asserted that the valid cognizer ascertaining the pervasion does not realize that all phenomena which are not truly one or many do not truly exist, this is also unsuitable because, if it is ascertained that the generality of that which is not truly one or many does not truly exist, it must be asserted that it is ascertained that the particularities of the generality do not truly exist.[75]

Based on statements by Tsong-kha-pa, Kay-drup, and Gyel-tsap, Jang-gya formulates the following response. The valid cognizer ascertaining the three modes of the sign in the syllogism, "The subject, a table, does not truly exist because of not being truly one or many," does not implicitly or explicitly realize that the table does not truly exist nor does it remove the misconceptions that conceive of the table as truly existent. Thus, it can be said that although the valid cognizer ascertaining the pervasion realizes that all instances of not being truly one or many do not truly exist, it does not realize this *specifically* in terms of the subject, a table. Rather, the valid cognizer which ascertains the three modes of the sign sets the table, as it were, for the realization of the thesis. Having ascertained the three modes, the mind is ready to ascertain the thesis immediately and without further cogitation. Although the valid cognizer ascertaining the three modes does not itself realize the thesis, it is capable of generating an awareness that realizes the thesis without the need for another intervening valid cognizer and without the need to state another reason. In other words, having ascertained the three modes of the sign, one needs merely to turn one's mind to the subject in order to realize the thesis.[76]

The classification of the sign in Śāntarakṣita's syllogism may now be considered. It will be remembered that the first type of correct sign from among the sixfold division is that of correct signs by way of entity, which are of three types: correct effect signs, correct nature signs, and correct signs of non-observation. Because the predicate of the probandum in Śāntarakṣita's syllogism is a negative phenomenon, the sign falls into the last category. In that the object of negation of the predicate is not a supersensory object, the sign can be further classified as a correct non-observation sign which is a non-observation of that which is suitable to appear. Such signs are of two types: correct signs which are a non-observation of a related object suitable to appear and correct signs which are an observation of a contradictory object suitable to appear. The sign of Bhāvaviveka's syllogism fell into the latter category; Śāntarakṣita's falls into the former because being truly one or many is related to true existence and would be suitable to appear if true existence existed, but being truly one or many is not observed.

The definition of a correct sign which is a non-observation of a related object suitable to appear is that which is a common locus of (1) being a correct sign which is a non-observation of the suitable to appear and (2) being a non-affirming negative. Such signs are of four types: correct signs which are a non-observation of (1) a cause suitable to appear, (2) a pervader suitable to appear, (3) a nature suitable to appear, and (4) a direct effect suitable to appear.[77]

The meanings of names of the four types are evident when illustrations of each are considered. An illustration of the first, a correct sign which is a non-observation of a cause suitable to appear is, "With respect to the subject, on a lake at night, smoke does not exist because of the non-existence of fire." The cause of smoke — fire — is not observed. An illustration of a correct sign which is a non-observation of a pervader is "With respect to the subject, on a craggy cliff where trees are not observed by valid cognition, a pine tree does not exist because of the non-existence of trees." The existence of trees pervades the existence of pine trees. An illustration of the third type, a correct sign which is a non-observation of a nature suitable to appear is, "With respect to the subject, on a place where pot is not observed by valid cognition, pot does not exist because of the non-observation of pot by valid cognition." The existence of pot and the observation of pot by valid cognition are of one nature. An illustration of the fourth type of correct sign which is a non-observation of the suitable to appear, that of a direct effect suitable to appear, is, "With respect to the subject, a walled circle devoid of smoke, the direct cause of smoke does not exist because of the non-existence of the direct effect, smoke."[78]

Ge-luk scholars have classified the reason of the lack of being truly one or many as either a correct sign which is a non-observation of a pervader suitable to appear, or as a correct sign which is a non-observation of a nature suitable to appear, or as both.[79] It would seem valuable to consider the reasoning as both in that each classification has potent implications for the refutation of true existence.

The illustration of a correct sign which is a non-observation of a pervader suitable to appear was "With respect to the subject, on a craggy cliff devoid of trees, a pine tree does not exist because trees do not exist." In this case, the generality, tree, was stated in the sign and the particularity, pine tree, was stated in the predicate of the probandum. The generality, tree, pervades all of its particularities, including the subclass of pine trees. Hence, the pervader is not observed, with, in this case, the pervader representing a wider class than the pervaded. However, in order to have a correct sign which is a non-observation of the pervader, it is not necessary that the pervader be the generality and the pervaded the particularity because pervasion also occurs with two coextensive categories. This is the case with the reason of the lack of being truly one or many where being truly one or many pervades true existence in that no third category of true existence could occur that was neither truly one or many. Therefore, the sign is a non-observation of a pervader, the non-observation of being truly one or many. Tsong-kha-pa supports this classification when discussing Candrakīrti's sevenfold reasoning in his *Great Exposition of the Stages of the Path*. He says, "Ascertainment is induced that the pervaded — inherent existence — does not pass beyond the pervader — the seven aspects such as same and different."[80] Classifying the reason of not being truly one or many as a correct sign of the non-observation of a pervader means that being truly one or many pervades all cases of true existence. This has obvious implications for the establishment of the forward and counterpervasions, but it also gives power to the ascertainment of the property of the subject in which the subject is found not to be truly one or many. Such a classification thus provides conviction to the meditator or debater who is seeking to prove to himself or another that phenomena do not truly exist.

Because whatever truly exists is either truly one or many, it is also suitable to classify the reason — not being truly one or many — as a correct sign which is the non-observation of a nature. Being truly one or many is the very nature of true existence because there is no third category. Therefore, by refuting truly existent unity and multiplicity one can be confident that true existence has been refuted.

Ge-luk scholars further classify the reason of the lack of being truly one or many according to the third of the original sixfold division of correct signs, that by way of the mode of proof. In this division, correct signs are analyzed according to whether the phenomenon being proved is an expression (usually a definiendum) or a meaning (usually a definition). Correct signs by way of the mode of proof are of five types: those proving the meaning, the expression, only the meaning, only the expression, and both the meaning and the expression.[81]

The reason of the lack of being truly one or many is classified by Tsong-kha-pa as proving only the expression.[82] That is, the predicate of the probandum — non-true existence — is a definiendum. Furthermore, the sign is proving only the expression or definiendum because the definition has already been ascertained.[83] That the sign proves only an expression is supported by Śāntarakṣita who says in his autocommentary to the *Ornament for the Middle Way*, "The reason does not have a thesis in the meaning class because of proving the subjective consciousness, term, and expressions of the object being proved."[84]

When a person has ascertained the property of the subject — that the subject is not truly one or many — and has ascertained the counterpervasion — whatever truly exists is either truly one or many — there is no possibility that the person could think that even though the subject is not truly one or many, there is some third type of truly existent subject. In other words, having ascertained the three modes of the sign, the person has fully understood the meaning of non-true existence. The meaning of true existence is derived completely from the sign of not being truly one or many. The person need only turn his mind to the subject to understand that it does not truly exist. The proof of a verbal or mental expression of non-true existence depends entirely on the modes of the sign in terms of the subject.[85]

Thus, by categorizing the sign of not being truly one or many as a sign proving only an expression, Śāntarakṣita indicates that not being truly one or many is the meaning of non-true existence. Therefore, by ascertaining the three modes of the sign one gains full understanding of what it means to be empty of true existence. This is a further indication of the capacity which the Svātantrikas find in the reasoning consciousness.

6 *The Two Truths*

Buddhist philosophical literature enumerates many different ways of dividing and categorizing phenomena. They may be divided into the conditioned (*saṃskṛta*, *'dus byas*) and the unconditioned (*asaṃskṛta*, *'dus ma byas*), into the positive (*vidhi*, *sgrub pa*) and the negative (*pratiṣedha*, *dgag pa*), into the contaminated (*sāsrava*, *zag bcas*) and uncontaminated (*anāsrava*, *zag med*), into the generally characterized (*sāmānyalakṣaṇa*, *spyi mtshan*) and the specifically characterized (*svalakṣaṇa*, *rang mtshan*) (a category not accepted by the Prāsaṅgikas), into the permanent (*nitya*, *rtag pa*) and the impermanent (*anitya*, *mi rtag pa*), and into the imaginary (*parikalpita*, *kun btags*), the dependent (*paratantra*, *gzhan dbang*), and consummate (*pariniṣpanna*, *yongs grub*). All of these categories are accepted by the Mādhyamikas, but the division that they most emphasize is that of the two truths (*satyadvaya*, *bden pa gnyis*). Nāgārjuna says in the twenty-fourth chapter of his *Treatise on the Middle Way:*

> Doctrines taught by the Buddhas
> Entirely depend on the two truths:
> Conventional worldly truths
> And ultimate truths.
>
> Those who do not comprehend the differences
> Between these two truths
> Do not know the nature
> Of the Buddha's profound doctrine.[1]

Bhāvaviveka echoes Nāgārjuna in his *Essence of the Middle Way:*

> Relying wholly on the two truths
> The Buddha taught the doctrine—
> Worldly conventional truths
> And ultimate truths.[2]

Śāntideva says in his *Engaging in the Bodhisattva Deeds* (*Bodhi[sattva]caryāvatāra*):

> The Subduer set forth all these branches
> For the purpose of wisdom.
> Therefore, those wishing to pacify sufferings
> Should generate wisdom.
>
> The conventional and the ultimate
> Are asserted to be the two truths.[3]

That which is divided into the two truths is objects of knowledge (*jñeya, shes bya*).[4] Although "existent" (*sat, yod pa*) and "phenomenon" (*dharma, chos*) are synonyms of "object of knowledge," they are not identified as the basis of division into the two truths in order to emphasize the fact that the two truths are objects that must be known in order to achieve liberation and Buddhahood.[5] It might be thought that "truth" is the basis of division of the two truths, but this is not the case, because conventional truths are not truths, as will be seen. Not only are objects of knowledge the basis of division of the two truths, all objects of knowledge are exhaustively included in the two truths; everything is either a conventional truth or an ultimate truth, as is stated in the *Meeting of the Father and Son Sutra* (*Pitāputrasamāgamasūtra*):

> It is thus: the Tathāgata comprehends the two [truths], conventional and ultimate. Furthermore, objects of knowledge are thoroughly exhausted in these conventional and ultimate truths.[6]

There is no third truth because, like one and many, the two truths are a dichotomy and mutually exclusive. Two things are a dichotomy if it can be said that something does not exist if it is not one or the other of them. A dichotomy includes all phenomena such that there is no third category, there is nothing which is both, and there is nothing which is neither.[7] Kamalaśīla says in his *Illumination of the Middle Way:*

> Regarding phenomena which have the character of mutual abandonment, if [something] is refuted as one and is not established as the other, it does not exist. Therefore, even the conception of a class which is neither is infeasible. ... Those which have the character of mutual abandonment pervade all aspects. Those which pervade all aspects eliminate another category, for instance, physical and non-physical.[8]

The reason why the two truths are considered a dichotomy is that ultimate truths are truths whereas conventional truths are falsities, truths only for ignorance, as will be explored. If something is identified as a deceptive object, it is impossible that is also a non-deceptive truth. If something is non-deceptive, it cannot also be a falsity. Therefore, deceptive object and non-deceptive object are mutually exclusive and a dichotomy; every phenomenon is either one or the other.[9] That there are only two truths and not a third is set forth in the sutra which says:

> The Knower of the World, without listening to
> others
> Taught by way of just these two truths.
> The conventional and, likewise, the ultimate.
> There is no third truth whatsoever.[10]

Ultimate truths (*paramārtha-satya, don dam bden pa*) are ultimate (*paramārtha, don dam*) or literally "highest objects" because they are the supreme object that can be known, as well as because they are objects of the highest consciousness, the non-contaminated meditative equipoise of a Superior. They are truths because they are non-deceptive in that they do not appear one way and exist another. Emptiness exists in the way in which it appears to a mind directly realizing emptiness.[11]

The definition of an ultimate truth, according to Jang-gya, is an object found by a valid reasoning consciousness analyzing the ultimate.[12] The reasoning consciousness searching for an object's final nature finds the emptiness of true existence of that object. That emptiness is an ultimate truth. Another well-known definition of an ultimate truth is an object realized by a direct valid cognizer which directly realizes it in a manner of the vanishing of dualistic appearance.[13] When emptiness is directly realized on the path of seeing and above, all forms of dualistic appearance have disappeared.

This latter definition ostensibly presents problems for the Yogācāra-Svātantrika-Mādhyamikas, who assert self-knowers (*svasamvedana, rang rig*). The definition of a self-knowing direct perceiver is that which is non-conceptual, non-mistaken, and has the aspect of an apprehender.[14] Self-knowers are a specialized type of consciousness that perform the function of knowing other consciousnesses. The Sautrāntikas, Yogācārins, and Yogācāra-Svātantrikas assert the existence of self-knowers in order to account for the memory of the subjective aspect of experience. We are able to remember not only what we saw in the past but our seeing of it. If there were no self-knower to experience the consciousness apprehending an object, memory of that consciousness would not be possible. In the example of an eye consciousness perceiving a patch of blue, the patch of blue is the apprehended (*grāhaka, bzung ba*), and the eye consciousness is the apprehender (*grāhya, 'dzin pa*). The eye consciousness sees the aspect (*ākāra, rnam pa*), and thus is said to have the aspect of the apprehended. The self-knower directly perceiving the eye consciousness apprehending blue experiences the apprehender and hence is defined as that which has the aspect of an apprehender.[15] When self-knowers experience consciousness, the appearance of all objects other than that consciousness vanishes. In this sense it can be said that an eye consciousness perceived by a self-knower valid cognizer is an object realized by a direct valid cognizer which directly realizes it in a manner of the vanishing of dualistic appearance, in which case an eye consciousness would fulfill the latter definition of an ultimate truth. To avoid this fault, the meaning of dualistic appearance must be explored further.

Three types of dualistic appearance are delineated:

1 the appearance as something different from the perceiver
2 the appearance of true existence
3 the appearance of conventionalities.[16]

In the case of a self-knower directly perceiving an eye consciousness, only the first type of dualistic appearance has vanished; the self-knower does not perceive the eye consciousness as if it were a separate entity. Since self-knowers are necessarily non-conceptual and the object of negation does not appear to sense consciousnesses according to the Svātantrikas, it can be speculated that the second type of dualistic appearance does not appear to a self-knower, although it would be misleading to go so far as to say that the appearance of dualistic appearance had *vanished*. A self-knower directly perceiving an eye consciousness has the third type of dualistic appearance because the eye consciousness is a conventionality; it is not an object found by a reasoning consciousness analyzing the ultimate.

However, a consciousness directly realizing emptiness has none of the three types of dualistic appearance. Emptiness and the mind directly realizing it are indistinguishable for that consciousness, being mixed like pure water poured into pure water.[17] For such a consciousness, all elaborations of true existence have ceased, and so there is no appearance of true existence. There is also no appearance of conventionalities; only emptiness appears. Therefore, the latter definition of an ultimate truth is accurate within the understanding that the phrase "in a manner of the vanishing of dualistic appearance" is understood to include all forms of dualistic appearance. Describing the wisdom realizing emptiness, Bhāvaviveka says in his *Essence of the Middle Way:*

> It establishes the negation
> Of all nets of conception,
> It is peaceful, individual knowledge,
> Non-conceptual, and without letters.
>
> It is free from sameness and difference
> And enters without [dualistic] entry
> Into reality, stainless like space.
> It is the wisdom that knows the ultimate.[18]

Despite the fact that emptinesses are the objects of ultimate consciousnesses, they do not ultimately exist. Emptinesses are ultimate truths because they are objects of ultimate consciousnesses and because they exist in the way that they appear. They do not ultimately exist in either of the senses of ultimate existence identified in Chapter Four. The form of ultimate existence identified by Bhāvaviveka takes the ultimate to be a conceptual reasoning consciousness of hearing, thinking, or meditating that analyzes the final mode of being of phenomena. A phenomenon that is analyzed by such an ultimate consciousness and exists in the face of it, is able to withstand analysis by it, would ultimately exist. In this case, what is identified as the ultimate (the reasoning consciousness) exists, but nothing ultimately exists because nothing can bear analysis by such a reasoning consciousness. It can be said that emptiness exists for a reasoning consciousness in that it is the object found by a reasoning consciousness. However, because the emptiness of a particular phenomenon under investigation cannot itself bear analysis, it is not contradictory to say that emptiness exists for or in the face of an ultimate consciousness but does not ultimately exist.[19]

The second type of ultimate existence, identified by Kamalaśīla, is the existence of an objective mode of subsistence that is not posited by the power of appearing to a non-defective awareness. Nga-wang-bel-den explains that whatever is established as ultimate in terms of this latter type of ultimate existence is necessarily established for the former because whatever existed by way of its objective mode of subsistence without being posited by the power of appearing to a non-defective consciousness would truly exist and thus would be found by a reasoning consciousness analyzing the ultimate; if something ultimately existed, it would be its own mode of being and that mode of being would be found by a reasoning consciousness investigating the final mode of being of phenomena. Whatever is established for the former type of ultimate is not necessarily established for the latter, that is, whatever is established by or found by a reasoning consciousness does not necessarily ultimately exist because emptiness — non-true existence — is found by a reasoning consciousness but, like all phenomena, is empty of ultimate existence.[20] Therefore, Jang-gya says that if this is understood, one can see that it is not contradictory to say on the one hand that nothing exists as its own mode of being or exists ultimately and to say on the other hand that emptiness exists, emptiness is the final mode of being, and emptiness is the ultimate.[21]

Ultimate truths can be divided in two ways; in terms of the bases that are empty and terminologically. In the first type of division, there are various enumerations of twenty-four emptinesses,[22] sixteen emptinesses, four emptinesses, and two emptinesses — the selflessness of persons and the selflessness of other phenomena.[23] A terminological division of ultimates into subjective and objective ultimates is elaborated in the texts of the Svātantrika masters. Jñānagarbha says in his *Two Truths* that a non-deceptive reasoning consciousness is an ultimate.[24]

Kamalaśīla says in his *Illumination of the Middle Way:*

> All consciousnesses arisen from correct hearing, thinking, and meditation are non-mistaken subjects, whereby they are called "ultimate" due to being the ultimate among them [i.e., consciousnesses].[25]

Subjective ultimates are the consciousnesses realizing emptiness and objective ultimates are the objects of those consciousnesses. Subjective ultimates are of two types, actual and concordant. An actual subjective ultimate is a non-conceptual wisdom of meditative equipoise directly realizing emptiness. Such a consciousness is able to eliminate all elaborations of true existence and all types of dualistic appearance. A concordant subjective ultimate is a conceptual reasoning consciousness of hearing, thinking, or meditation realizing emptiness, since it accords in aspect with an actual subjective ultimate. A conceptual consciousness realizing emptiness is able to stop the elaborations of true existence but realizes its object dualistically in the sense that the appearance of subject and object does not disappear, as it does in the case of a direct realization. A reasoning consciousness that understands emptiness conceptually also has dualistic appearance in the sense that a conventionality appears to it, namely, the meaning-generality or generic image of emptiness; a conceptual reasoning consciousness understands emptiness, which is its apprehended object (*grahya, bzung yul*), but is appearing object (**pratibhāsaviṣaya, snang yul*) is an image of emptiness, that image being a conventional truth.[26]

Objective ultimates, emptinesses, are also said to be of two types, actual and concordant. An actual objective ultimate is an emptiness that is realized in direct cognition and thus is an object devoid of the elaborations of true existence and dualistic appearance. A concordant objective ultimate is also an emptiness, but is called concordant because it is realized by a concordant subjective ultimate, a conceptual reasoning consciousness. Because such a consciousness is incapable of removing the elaborations of dualistic appearance, that emptiness is realized in a way different from how it would be realized by a non-conceptual wisdom of meditative equipoise. Thus, although the object, emptiness, remains the same, two types of objective ultimates are posited in terms of two types of consciousnesses realizing emptiness. Actual and concordant objective ultimates are designated from the point of view of how they appear to two types of reasoning consciousnesses, non-conceptual and conceptual.[27]

It is important to note that although there are actual and concordant subjective ultimates and actual and concordant objective ultimates, only emptinesses of true existence are ultimate truths; all consciousnesses realizing emptiness are conventional truths.

There is some question as to whether the negative of truly existent production is an ultimate truth or a conventional truth. This must be considered in the context of the works in which it is stated that the non-existence of production ultimately is a conventionality. When Śāntarakṣita says in his autocommentary to his *Ornament of the Middle Way* that the negation of ultimate production is a real conventionality, he is interpreted to mean by the term "negation" the reasoning consciousness which refutes ultimate production and the lack of ultimate production which that consciousness understands. When the reasoning consciousness and its object of comprehension are not differentiated, it can be said that the negation of ultimate production is a real conventionality. When subject and object are distinguished, the reasoning consciousness is a real conventionality and its object of comprehension, the non-existence of ultimate production, is an ultimate truth.[28]

When "Śāntarakṣita"[29] says in his *Commentary to (Jñānagarbha's) "Two Truths"*, "When [emptiness] is analyzed by reasoning, it is just a conventionality,"[30] he is interpreted to mean that the emptiness which is the negation of a self of phenomena does not ultimately exist; it, like all phenomena, exists conventionally. He is not asserting that emptiness is a conventional truth.[31]

Finally, that same text refers to the negation of real or ultimate production that appears to the sense consciousnesses. As discussed in an earlier chapter, the Svātantrikas assert that the object of negation does not appear to sense direct perceivers. Jñānagarbha says in the autocommentary to his *Two Truths*, "Real production and so forth do not appear."[32] This is interpreted to mean that the lack of real or ultimate production appears to sense consciousnesses that directly perceive their objects, such as forms, which lack ultimate production. Thus, the Svātantrikas assert that an eye consciousness directly perceiving a form apprehends all of the qualities that are the same substantial entity as the form, and, therefore, the negative of truly existent production (which is a quality of that form) appears to the eye consciousness. This negation of truly existent production is an affirming negative (*paryudāsapratiṣedha, ma yin dgag*) and is not an emptiness, which is necessarily a non-affirming negative (*prasajyapratiṣedha, med dgag*). Because this affirming negative negates real production, it is a concordant ultimate, but because it appears to the sense direct perceivers of common beings and is not a non-affirming negative, it is a conventional truth.[33]

A more difficult question is whether the selflessness of persons (*pudgalanairātmya*) is an ultimate truth or a conventional truth. It is the position of Kay-drup that the selflessness of persons is not an ultimate truth.[34] If an ultimate truth is defined as an object realized by a direct valid cognizer that directly realizes it in a manner of the vanishing of dualistic appearance, then all three types of dualistic appearance — the appearance of the object as different, the appearance of true existence, and the appearance of conventionalities — must not appear to a direct perceiver of an ultimate truth. Unlike the Prāsaṅgikas, who assert that there is no difference in subtlety between the selflessness of persons and the selflessness of phenomena and that Hīnayānists realize both, the Svātantrikas assert that the selflessness of persons is more easily understood than the selflessness of phenomena and that Hearers only realize the selflessness of persons — the person's lack of being substantially existent in the sense of self-sufficiency. This selflessness of the person is realized in terms of the four noble truths: true sufferings, true origins, true cessations, and true paths. Each of the four truths has four attributes, with those of true sufferings being impermanence, misery, emptiness, and selflessness. The four aspects of true origins are cause, origin, strong production, and condition and the four aspects of true cessations are cessation, pacification, auspiciousness, and definite emergence. The attributes of the last of the four truths, true paths, are path, knowledge, achievement, and deliverance.[35] On the path of seeing, Hearers directly realize that the four truths are empty of a self-sufficient person.[36] It should be noted that the object of the Hearer's wisdom is only selflessness and not the four truths because an exalted wisdom of meditative equipoise on the path of seeing of a Hearer is defined a Hearer's manifest realizer of the truth which is in one-pointed equipoise on the subtle selflessness of the person, which is its object.[37] This direct realization of the selflessness of persons may occur in the smallest unit of time in which an action can be accomplished.[38]

Based on the fact that Hearers realize the selflessness of persons in terms of the four truths, Jam-yang-shay-ba argues in support of Kay-drup's contention that the selflessness of persons is not an ultimate truth. Taking "an object realized in a manner of the vanishing of dualistic appearance by the direct valid cognizer which directly realizes it" as the definition of an ultimate truth, Jam-yang-shay-ba concedes that the uninterrupted path of a Hearer's path of seeing is a wisdom of meditative equipoise in which subject and object are mixed like poured into water, that is, that there is no dualistic appearance of difference. He argues, however, that the third type of dualistic appearance, the appearance of conventionalities is present because Hearers understand the selflessness of persons in terms of the sixteen aspects of the four truths, which are conventionalities. (There is some question as to whether true cessations are ultimate truths in this system, as will be discussed.) He cites two sutras for support, one which explains that an observable perfection of wisdom is one which involves duality and another which states that practices of the sixteen aspects of the four truths involve observation and therefore are facsimile perfections of wisdom and that in order to practice a real or natural perfection of wisdom, one must take the unobservable emptiness as the object. The sutra states:

> This is a facsimile perfection of wisdom; they are taught, "Form is impermanent." Similarly, they are taught, "[Form is] miserable, selfless, and impure." ... What are not facsimile perfections of wisdom? Those [perfections] taught in this way: Come here, child of good lineage. Cultivate the perfection of wisdom; do not view [all phenomena] from forms to knowers of all aspects (*sarvākārajñāna, rnam pa thams cad mkhyen pa*) as miserable, selfless, or ugly. Why? Form is empty of the entityness of form. That which is the entityness for form does not [truly] exist. That which does not [truly] exist is the perfection of wisdom.[39]

Thus, Jam-yang-shay-ba concludes that because the Hearer's realization of the selflessness of persons involves the sixteen aspects of the four truths, the Hearer realization entails the observation of conventionalities. Because the appearance of conventionalities does not vanish on the Hearer's path of seeing, dualistic appearance has not disappeared. Hence, the selflessness of persons as cognized by Hearers is not an ultimate truth.[40]

Jam-yang-shay-ba makes this argument in the first chapter of his textbook on Maitreya's *Ornament for Clear Realization* (*Abhisamayālaṃkāra*). In the third chapter of the same text he seems to contradict his position that the selflessness of persons is not an ultimate truth when he says that both the selflessness of phenomena and the selflessness of persons are asserted to be suchnesses (*tathatā, de kho na nyid*). He writes that, "Although Hearer and Solitary Realizer Superiors do not realize the selflessness of phenomena, it is asserted that they realize suchness and the emptiness which is the selflessness of persons."[41] Since he asserts that the selflessness of persons is an emptiness and a type of suchness, it would seem that it must also be an ultimate truth. He writes:

> There is no difference in the two selflessnesses in the sphere of reality (*dharmadhātu, chos dbyings*), which is like the sky. However, since there are three different modes of realization, three lineages [that of Hearers, Solitary Realizers, and Bodhisattva] are posited. For example, the sky is differentiated into the path of birds, the path of the wind, and the path of the sun.[42]

There is ample support, both from the statements of the Indian Svātantrika masters, as well as from Tsong-kha-pa, to support the assertion that the selflessness of persons is an ultimate truth. Kamalaśīla says in his *Illumination of the Middle Way:*

> Suchness, which has the character of the selflessness of phenomena and persons, because of possessing reason, is highest (*parama, dam pa*). It is also an object (*artha, don*) because it is the object sought for the purpose of realization by those who seek to abandon the obstructions (*avaraṇa, sgrib pa*). Also, it is the meaning, that is, the object of the unmistaken highest exalted wisdom. Thus, [for these two reasons] it is called the highest object [or ultimate] (*paramārtha, don dam*).[43]

Tsong-kha-pa says in his *Golden Rosary of Good Explanations* (*Legs bshad gser 'phreng*), "The two emptinesses — the selflessness of persons and the selflessness of phenomena — are explained in the sixteen emptinesses."[44] It is thus clear that according to Kamalaśīla,

Tsong-kha-pa, and Jam-yang-shay-ba the selflessness of persons is an emptiness. The question can be raised, however, as to whether it is possible for the selflessness of persons to be an emptiness and not be an ultimate truth. This question seems to be settled by Tsong-kha-pa in a discussion of Svātantrika in his commentary on Nāgārjuna's *Treatise on the Middle Way:*

> Therefore, the selflessness of the phenomena of the aggregates and the selflessness of persons — these being the mere elimination of elaborations that are the objects of reasoned negation — are the objects found by the uncontaminated exalted wisdom knowing the mode [of being]. Even elaborations of dualistic appearance of persons and the aggregates are pacified in the face of that [wisdom]. Hence, they are ultimate truths.[45]

Tsong-kha-pa thus concludes that the selflessness of persons is an ultimate truth in the sense that it is an object of a Buddha's omniscient consciousness that knows the final mode of being of phenomena. Because that exalted wisdom is, in terms of its realization of the ultimate, non-dual in all ways such that there is no appearance of the object as different, no appearance of true existence, and no appearance of conventionalities to it, the selflessness of persons, which is an object of that exalted wisdom, cannot be a conventional truth. However, Jam-yang-shay-ba's argument that the selflessness of persons is not an ultimate truth was cast in terms of how it is realized by a Hearer on the path of seeing, not in terms of a Buddha's omniscient consciousness. Although both positions are persuasive, it seems that those who assert that the selflessness of persons is not an ultimate truth remain obliged to demonstrate in what way the four noble truths are involved in a Hearer's momentary cognition of the mere vacuity of a self of persons.

The Ge-luk scholar Lo-sang-gön-jok (*bLo-bzang-dkon-mchog*) contributes this analysis of the question. Bhāvaviveka explains that the subtle selflessness of the person, which is the lack of being substantially existent in the sense of self-sufficiency, is an emptiness but does not assert that it is an ultimate truth. If it were an ultimate truth, it would have to be definitive, (*nītārtha*, *nges don*), but the selflessness of the person must be interpreted otherwise; the final mode of being of the person is not its emptiness of being substantially existent in the sense of self-sufficiency, but its emptiness of true existence. When Bhāvaviveka debates with lower systems about ultimate existence, he identifies that which is established for a reasoning consciousness analyzing the ultimate as the object of negation, he does not identify a substantially existent person which suggests that the lack of such a person is not the negative of ultimate existence and hence is not an ultimate truth. Bhāvaviveka also freely admits that the selflessness of persons is not the final mode of being when he says that Hearers do not realize the final mode of being yet abandon the afflictive emotions, implying with his example of the coiled vine that one can be mistaken about the nature of reality and still be liberated. One is still faced with the statement from Kamalaśīla that refers to "suchness, which has the character of the selflessness of phenomena and persons," but the selflessness of the person in this context may be taken as referring to the emptiness of true existence of the person and not to the emptiness of substantial existence.[46]

Another question is whether true cessations are ultimate truths. The path of seeing, whether of Hearers, Solitary Realizers, or Bodhisattvas, can generally be divided into two parts: exalted wisdoms of meditative equipoise (*samāhitajñāna*, *mnyam bzhag ye shes*) and exalted wisdoms subsequent to meditative equipoise (*pṛṣṭalabdhajñāna*, *rjes thab ye shes*). Exalted wisdoms of meditative equipoise are further divided into uninterrupted paths (*ānantaryamārga*, *bar ched med lam*) and paths of release (*vimuktimārga*, *rnam grol lam*). The definition of an uninterrupted path of a Mahāyāna path of seeing is a Mahāyāna clear realizer of the truth that serves as an actual antidote to the artificial conception of true existence, which is its corresponding object of abandonment.[47] That is, an uninterrupted path on this level is the wisdom consciousness directly realizing emptiness that destroys the artificial conception of true existence. The uninterrupted path is followed immediately by the path of release, which is the state of having abandoned the artificial conception of true existence.[48] Thus, the artificial conception of true existence is actually abandoned by the uninterrupted path; the path of release is the state of having abandoned that artificial conception. The second follows directly upon the first, and the two may take place in two of the smallest units of time in which an action can be performed. The object of the Bodhisattva's uninterrupted path is emptiness, the mere absence of true existence. The path of release, as a division of meditative equipoise, also directly realizes emptiness, but also has as its object a true cessation, the mere absence of the conception of true existence. Are these true cessations ultimate truths? Pan-chen Sö-nam-drak-ba (*Pan-chen bSod-nams-grags-pa*, 1478-1554), the author of the textbook literature of Lo-sel-ling (*bLo-gsal-gling*) and Gan-den (*dGa'-ldan*) colleges, argues that in the Svātantrika system, true cessations are not ultimate truths because they are not emptinesses. His rationale is: The object of negation of an emptiness must necessarily not exist. For example, the object of negation of the emptiness of true existence is true existence, which is utterly non-existent. However, although a true cessation is a non-affirming negative, it is not an ultimate truth because its object of negation — the conception of true existence — exists among objects of knowledge since it is a consciousness.[49]

Kay-drup presents the majority position among Ge-luk scholars, arguing that true cessations are ultimate truths. The path of release is a consciousness that actualizes the state of having abandoned the respective afflictions, and to actualize the cessation means that the path of release directly realizes that cessation. For Kay-drup, whatever is directly realized by an exalted wisdom of meditative equipoise must be an ultimate truth. It would be inappropriate for the object of the two parts of the exalted wisdom of meditative equipoise to change from an ultimate truth to a conventional truth.[50]

Conventional truths are all objects of knowledge other than emptinesses. To explain the meaning of the term *saṃvṛti*, Kamalaśīla cites a passage from the *Descent into Laṅkā Sūtra:*

> Things are produced conventionally;
> Ultimately they are without inherent existence.
> That which is mistaken about what does not
> inherently exist
> Is asserted to be a concealer (*saṃvṛti, kun rdzob*) of
> reality.[51]

A conventional truth (*saṃvṛtisatya, kun rdzob bden pa*) is a truth for a concealer. The concealer is an ignorant consciousness that misapprehends the nature of phenomena. Kamalaśīla says in his *Illumination of the Middle Way:*

> An awareness that mistakenly superimposes the opposite onto things that are in reality without entityness is called the "concealer" because it obstructs [itself] from [perception of]

> suchness or because it veils [other awarenesses] from [perception of] suchness.[52]

Thus, a concealer is a consciousness that obstructs the understanding of reality and which is itself obstructed from realizing the nature of phenomena. Jñānagarbha's *Two Truths* says:

> That by which or which is
> Obstructed from the real is asserted to be a
> concealer.
> Thus, all of these are truths;
> They are not truths that are objects of the highest
> [consciousness].[53]

Thus, conventional truths are not truths in the sense that ultimate truths are. Ultimate truths, emptinesses, are truths because they exist in the way in which they appear to a wisdom consciousness. Conventional truths are truths only for a concealer (*samantādvaraṇa, sgrib byed*). They are displayed by the conception of true existence as ultimately existent to ignorant conceptual consciousnesses. These consciousnesses conceive phenomena to exist truly, to exist in the way in which they are displayed by the conception of true existence. In this way, phenomena which appear to exist truly are truths only for ignorance, they do not in fact exist in the way they appear.

Phenomena other than emptinesses do, however, validly exist as is indicated by two other etymologies of *saṃvṛti*. When the *Descent into Laṅkā Sutra* says above that "Things are produced conventionally," *saṃvṛti* does not mean that production exists only for ignorance; rather it means that production exists for worldly convention and interdependently.

In general, there are three meanings of the *saṃvṛti* of *saṃvṛti-satya*.[54] The first is the ignorant consciousness for which truths for a concealer are true. The second meaning of *saṃvṛti* refers to objects that are mutually interdependent (*parasparasaṃbhavana, phan tshun rten pa*). In this sense, one may say that emptiness exists conventionally because emptiness is a dependent arising. T. R. V. Murti correctly identifies this meaning of *saṃvṛti* but misunderstands its meaning. He writes:

> It may also mean the mutual dependence of things — their relativity. In this sense it is equated with phenomena, and is in direct contrast with the absolute which is by itself, unrelated.[55]

Here, Murti implies that emptiness — reality — is not a phenomenon (*dharma*) and that it is unrelated to anything else, that is, is not a dependent arising. In that case emptiness itself would truly exist whereas it is the position of the Mādhyamikas — Svātantrika and Prāsaṅgika — that emptiness itself is empty. The third meaning of *saṃvṛti* is "conventions of the world" (*lokavyavahāra, 'jig rtan pa'i tha snyad*).[55] It is this meaning of the term that is used to translate *saṃvṛtisatya* as "conventional truth," although truth for a concealer is a more evocative translation.

Jang-gya defines a conventional truth as an object found by a conventional valid cognizer,[56] that is, an object found by a direct perceiver or inferential cognizer that is not affected by an internal or external cause of error. Thus, non-existents such as the horns of a rabbit are not conventional truths because they are not objects of valid cognizers. Emptinesses also are not conventional truths because they are objects only of ultimate consciousnesses: exalted wisdoms of meditative equipoise and reasoning consciousnesses of hearing, thinking, or meditation analyzing the ultimate.

There are two types of conventional truths, real conventional truths (*tathyasaṃvṛtisatya, yang dag kun rdzob bden pa*) and unreal conventional truths (*mityāsaṃvṛtisatya, log pa'i kun rdzob bden pa*). Jang-gya defines a real conventional truth as a phenomenon that is an object, found by a conventional valid cognizer, that is able to perform a function in accordance with its appearance to the awareness perceiving it. He defines an unreal conventional truth as an object, found by a conventional valid cognizer, that is not able to perform a function in accordance with how it appears to the awareness perceiving it. Jang-gya has clearly based his definitions on this passage from Jñānagarbha's *Differentiation of the Two Truths:*

> Since they are able and unable
> To perform functions as they appear,
> The division of real and unreal
> Conventionalities is made.[57]

There are problems with the Jang-gya's definition of real and unreal conventional truths, as Nga-wang-bel-den points out. He argues that the passage cited above from the *Two Truths* is not intended to provide definitions of the two types of conventional truths but merely to provide illustrations. Water is a real conventional truth because it appears to be able to perform the function of being drinkable and is. A mirage is an unreal conventional truth because it appears to be water but is not. It would be unsuitable, however, to define the two types of conventional truths in terms of their ability or inability to perform functions because, in that case, unconditioned space would be an unreal conventional truth because it is permanent and thereby unable to perform a function.[58]

It is also important to distinguish between unreal conventionalities and unreal conventional truths. Jñānagarbha says in his *Two Truths:*

> Those mere things that lack being imputed objects
> And [that are] dependently produced
> Should be known as real conventionalities.
> Those which are not real are imputations.[59]

His autocommentary to the stanza says:

> Imputed objects are real production and so forth, the appearance of consciousness [as external objects as asserted by the Yogācārins], the principal (*pradhāna*) [asserted by the Sāṃkhyas, the mind] which is an evolute of the elements [asserted by the Cārvākas], and so forth. [Real conventionalities] are devoid of [being] those because that which is a mere thing is able to perform a function in the way in which it appears. That which is produced in dependence on causes and conditions should be known as a real conventional truth. For, whatever appears from causes commonly to the consciousnesses of children and above is suitable to be a real conventionality because things abide in accordance with [their] appearance to consciousness.[60]

In addition to its explanation of real and unreal conventionalities, this passage is significant because the last sentence provides further evidence that the Svātantrikas assert that things exist in the way that they appear to sense consciousnesses, that the existence by way of the object's own character which appears to the senses is the conventional mode of being of phenomena, and that the object of negation — true existence — does not appear to the sense consciousnesses. However, returning to the discussion of the two types of conventional truths, Jñānagarbha in the passage above identifies real production, the principal, and so forth as imputations. These, like the horns of a rabbit, the son of a barren woman, a self of persons, and a self of phenomena are not unreal conventional truths because they do not exist, they are merely unreal conventionalities. Examples of unreal conventional truths would be the reflection of a face in the mirror which appears to an eye consciousness to be a real face but is not and the apprehended or appearing object of a thought consciousness — the meaning-generality or generic image of an object which appears to thought to be the actual object but in fact is the appearance as non-non-object.[61]

Forms, sounds, odors, tastes, objects of touch, the emptiness of true existence which appears to sense consciousnesses, and unconditioned space are all real conventionalities. Whatever is a real conventionality is necessarily a real conventional truth.[62]

Nga-wang-bel-den, in his *Annotations* to Jam-yang-shay-ba's *Great Exposition of Tenets* offers more refined definitions of real and unreal conventionalities. In fact, he provides two sets of definitions, one for the Sautrāntika-Svātantrika-Mādhyamikas and one for the Yogācāra-Svātantrika-Mādhyamikas. For the former, the definition of a real conventionality is a phenomenon that is renowned in the world to be a non-perverse object in that it accords with how it appears to the conventional consciousness that clearly perceives it. An example is water. An unreal conventionality is defined as an object which is posited from the viewpoint of its being a phenomenon renowned in the world as a perverse object in terms of how it appears to the conventional consciousness that clearly perceives it. An example is a mirage.

For the Yogācāra-Svātantrika-Mādhyamikas, the definition of a real conventionality is an object which appears to the conventional consciousness that clearly perceives it and is renowned in the world to be a non-perverse object. An unreal conventionality is defined as an object which appears to a conventional consciousness that clearly perceives it and which is posited by way of being renowned in the world to be a perverse object. The Yogācāra-Svātantrikas must eliminate the qualification that a real conventionality is an object that exists in the way that it appears to the consciousness perceiving it and the qualification that an unreal conventionality does not exist that way because they assert that external objects — objects that are a different entity from the consciousnesses perceiving them — do not exist. Therefore, for them, no sense object exists in the way that it appears to a sense consciousness. If they maintained that an object must accord with how it appears to the conventional consciousness perceiving it, no form, sound, odor, taste, or object of touch could be a real conventionality because the Yogācāra-Svātantrikas assert that these objects appear to exist as entities separate from consciousness but do not exist that way. However, because the Sautrāntika-Svātantrikas assert that external objects exist, they are able to hold that a real conventionality must exist in the way in which it appears to the conventional consciousness.[63]

Both sets of definitions mention that the object is "renowned in the world." This does not mean that the object must be known to ordinary beings, otherwise, objects that are inaccessible to direct perception by sentient beings, such as the subtle cause and effect of actions, would be neither real nor unreal conventionalities because they would not be renowned in the world as either perverse or non-perverse objects. Rather, to be "renowned in the world" merely means to be established by a valid cognizer that does not analyze the ultimate.[64]

In the Svātantrika system, only objects are classified as real or unreal conventional truths; all consciousnesses are real conventional truths because they appear to exist by way of their own character and thus, for the Svātantrikas, exist in the way in which they appear.[65]

The fact that the Svātantrikas assert that phenomena are established by way of their own character allows them to define real and unreal conventionalities in terms of whether they exist or do not exist in the way that they appear to consciousnesses. If they did not assert that phenomena are established by way of their own character, they could not hold, for example, that water is a real conventionality because it can perform the functions that it appears to be able to while a mirage is an unreal conventionality because it cannot perform those functions; water would also have to be an unreal conventionality because it appears to be established by way of its own character but is not.[66]

The Prāsaṅgika presentation of real and unreal conventionalities is very different. The Prāsaṅgikas assert that no conventional phenomenon is established in the way in which it appears and that all conventional consciousnesses are mistaken consciousnesses in that they are mistaken with respect to their appearing objects; objects appear to them to be inherently existent. Therefore, the Prāsaṅgikas do not distinguish between real and unreal conventionalities. Furthermore, for a reasoning consciousness, real conventionalities do not exist because such a consciousness ascertains that real establishment does not exist; in terms of the mode of analysis by a reasoning consciousness, all phenomena are established as falsities. They cannot differentiate real and unreal conventionalities, as the Svātantrikas do, in terms of whether or not objects exist in the way in which they appear to the consciousnesses perceiving them because all objects appear falsely to the sense consciousnesses of common beings; no sense object exists in the way in which it appears. However, within this false appearance, the Prāsaṅgikas distinguish real and unreal conventionalities. Candrakīrti says in his *Supplement to the Middle Way* (VI.24-25):

> Also, two types of perceivers of the false are
> asserted:
> [Those with] clear senses and [those with] defective
> senses.
> Consciousnesses having defective senses
> Are said to be wrong relative to consciousnesses
> having good senses.
>
> Objects realized by the world and apprehended
> By the six non-defective senses are true only from
> A worldly point of view, the rest are presented
> As unreal only from the viewpoint of the world.[67]

In terms of conventional valid cognizers, subjects that perceive the false — truths for a concealer — are of two types, real subjects and false subjects. The six consciousnesses when they are not affected by the superficial causes of error are real subjects. The six consciousnesses when they are affected by the superficial causes of error are unreal subjects. They are asserted to be real and unreal in relation to each other. The objects of those consciousnesses are also posited as real and unreal. An object of one of the six consciousnesses, which has not been damaged by a superficial cause of error, is a real conventionality relative to the sphere of conventional valid cognizers. An object of one of the six consciousnesses, which has been affected by a superficial cause of error, is an unreal conventionality relative to the sphere of conventional valid cognizers. Thus, the Prāsaṅgikas hold that there are no real conventionalities as understood by the Svātantrikas, but in order to conform with the world, they concede the categories of real and unreal in terms of conventional usage. Water is real, a mirage is not. However, because the Prāsaṅgikas are merely reflecting ordinary experience, such things as a self of persons, which is utterly non-existent but which is also accepted by the world to be true, is classed as a real conventionality, whereas for the Svātantrikas it is necessarily an unreal conventionality because it does not exist.

The Svātantrika division into real and unreal conventionalities is based on their assertion that phenomena are established by way of their own character. The fact that the Prāsaṅgikas do not make such a distinction even conventionally is based on their rejection and refutation of existence by way of the object's own character. For the Prāsaṅgikas, when forms and so forth are designated as real, that reality is damaged by the reasoning consciousness realizing the emptiness of forms and so forth; there are no real conventionalities for a reasoning consciousness. Thus, the Prāsaṅgikas do not distinguish between real and unreal in terms of a reasoning consciousness; for them, it is only suitable to make such a distinction in terms of a conventional consciousness. For a reasoning consciousness, there is no difference in truth or falsity between an illusory horse and a real horse; both are false in that they appear to exist truly to the consciousness perceiving them but do not. It is, however, suitable to use the convention "truth" for the real horse and "falsity" for the illusory horse in terms of conventional consciousnesses.

Nga-wang-bel-den provides a story illustrating the Prāsaṅgika position. Two villagers went to a temple to look at the paintings of deities on the walls. One of the villagers said, "The deity with the trident in his hand is Narayana and the one with a wheel in his hand is Maheśvara." The other villager said that it was the other way around and they began to argue. They asked a wandering holy man nearby to settle their dispute. The mendicant knew that the paintings were not the real deities, and thus, from that perspective, there was no difference in the truth or falsity of the villagers' claims. However, he also knew that in conformity with their minds, he could say that one was right and the other wrong, thereby fulfilling their wish to know without having told a lie.

Thus, when the Prāsaṅgikas say that in the Mādhyamikas' own system, *real* and unreal conventionalities are not asserted despite their asserting that there is a difference of *real* and unreal in terms of a worldly consciousness, the meanings of "real" in those two contexts are very different. The first refers to existence by way of the object's own character. The second refers to an object which is suitable to be called "true" in terms of ordinary worldly thought.[68]

Finally, the relationship of the two truths bears consideration. It is the position of the Mādhyamikas — both the Svātantrikas and Prāsaṅgikas — that the two truths are neither exactly the same nor completely different.

Four reasonings that refute the position that the two truths are different entities are set forth in the *Sutra Unravelling the Thought* (*Saṃdhinirmocana*). If conventional truths and ultimate truths were different entities, then the reasoning consciousness realizing the final mode of being of an object could not eliminate an ignorant consciousness conceiving that object to be truly existent because the final nature of the object — an ultimate truth — and the object itself — a conventional truth — would be different entities such that the emptiness of the object could not be the final mode of being of the object itself. In other words, understanding the final nature of the object — its emptiness — would have nothing to do with understanding the object itself, whereby it would be possible to understand the object's final nature while conceiving the object to be truly existent. It would thus be impossible to overcome the conception of true existence and highest enlightenment would be impossible. The *Sutra Unravelling the Thought* says:

> If the nature of conditioned things and the nature of the ultimate were different, then even those who see the truth would not be free from the signs of [the true existence of] conditioned things. Due to not being free from the signs of conditioned things, seeing the truth would not release them from the bonds of signs. If they were not released from the bonds of signs, they would not be released from the bonds of assuming bad states. If they were not released from those two bonds, those who see the truth also would not achieve nirvana, which is the unsurpassed attainment of bliss. They would also not become completely purified in the unsurpassed perfect complete enlightenment.[69]

The second consequence of the two truths being different entities is that an object's emptiness of true existence would not be the object's final mode of being; the emptiness would be one thing and the final mode of being of the object would be another, just as a pot is not the mode of being of a piece of cloth. The sutra says:

> Also, if the natures of conditioned things and the nature of the ultimate were different, then the nature of the ultimate would not be the general nature of all conditioned natures.[70]

An elaboration of the first two consequences is the third consequence that if the two truths were different entities, then the mere elimination of true existence with respect to the object would not be the reality of the object because the absence of true existence — an ultimate truth — and the reality of the object would be unrelated. The sutra says:

> If the natures of conditioned things and the nature of the ultimate were different, then the mere selflessness and entitynessless of conditioned things would not be the ultimate nature.[71]

Finally, the fourth consequence of the two truths being different entities is that the conception of true existence and the wisdom realizing non-true existence would exist simultaneously in the mental continuum of a Buddha because realizing the emptiness of true existence of phenomena would in no way have eliminated the conception of those objects as truly existent. Thus, a Buddha would have both wisdom consciousnesses and ignorant consciousnesses. The sutra says:

> Also, thoroughly afflicted natures and very pure natures would be established as different natures at the same time [in the continuum of a Buddha].[72]

All four of these consequences are intended to suggest that the two truths are not different entities. If they are not different entities, are they exactly the same? The *Sutra Unravelling the Thought* puts forth four more consequences that would be entailed if the ultimate truths and conventional truths were exactly the same.

If an object and its final nature, its emptiness of true existence were exactly the same, then anyone who perceived the object would perceive emptiness; directly perceiving a tree would be a direct cognition of emptiness. Thus, everyone would be liberated from cyclic existence. The sutra says:

> If the natures of conditioned things and the nature of the ultimate were not different, then all childish common beings would see the truth. As only common beings, they would attain nirvana, which is unsurpassed enlightenment and bliss. They would become completely purified in the unsurpassed, complete, perfect enlightenment.[73]

Second, if the two truths were exactly the same, it would follow that ultimate truths would be the objects of afflictive emotions, such as desire and hatred. Pleasant forms, for example, are often objects of desire, and if the emptiness of that form were exactly the same as the form, the emptiness would also be an object of desire in which case the observation of emptiness would not be an antidote to suffering, but a cause of suffering. The sutra says:

> If the natures of conditioned things and the nature of the ultimate were not different, then just as the natures of conditioned things are included in thoroughly afflicted natures, the nature of the ultimate would also be included in thoroughly afflicted natures.[74]

The third consequence of the two truths being exactly the same is that the different varieties of conventionalities would not exist because there are not different types of emptinesses; since all ultimate truths are similar, conventional truths would also have to be similar. The sutra says:

> If the natures of conditioned things and the nature of the ultimate were not different, then just as the nature of the ultimate is without particularities in all conditioned things, so all natures of conditioned things would be without particularities.[75]

Finally, a corollary of the first consequence is the fourth consequence that if the two truths were not different it would be unnecessary to seek the truth; there would be no truth beyond what appears to the senses. The sutra says:

> Yogis would not seek an ultimate higher than how conditioned things are seen, how they are heard, how they are differentiated, and how they are known.[76]

Thus, the sutra presents four absurd consequences that would be entailed if the two truths were different and four absurd consequences that would be entailed if the two truths were not different. Gyel-tsap notes that all eight of these are consequences that imply the opposite. Thus, the first four imply that the two truths are not different and the last imply that they are different. Is this one of the so-called "paradoxes" that allegedly abound in Buddhist literature, leaving us exactly where we started? The sutra has explained why the two truths must be the same and why they cannot be exactly the same. According to Ge-luk, the relationship of the two truths is one of being the same entity but different reverses (*ngo bo gcig dang ldog pa tha dad*).[77] For two phenomena to be the same entity means that they do not appear to be different to direct perception (*pratyakṣa, mngon sum*); they are indivisible. If this is the case, an apparent problem arises when it is asserted that the two truths are the same entity. According to Mādhyamika, when emptiness — an ultimate truth — is directly perceived by a non-Buddha, the phenomenon which is the basis of that emptiness — a conventional truth — does not appear. When a conventional truth is directly perceived by a non-Buddha, emptiness does not appear. The two truths are only perceived simultaneously by a Buddha. In this case, how can the two truths be the same entity if they appear separately to direct perception? The answer given is that to be the same entity means that the two phenomena in question do not appear *to be different* to direct perception. This does not imply that they must appear simultaneously to all direct perceivers. Form does not appear to a sentient being directly realizing the emptiness of a form. Emptiness does not appear to a sentient being directly perceiving a form. This does not mean, however, that the two appear to be different. When both a conventional truth and its emptiness appear to a direct perceiver, that is, when they appear to a Buddha, they do not appear to be different. Form and emptiness are the same entity, but this does not imply that they both must appear to all consciousnesses directly perceiving one or the other.

The wisdom consciousness directly realizing emptiness is the culmination of a process of reasoning investigating the final mode of being of the object. The reasoning consciousness is analyzing a form, for example, searching for the entity of the form to determine whether or not it truly exists. If the reasoning consciousness finds the form to be its own final nature, then the form would truly exist. However, the reasoning consciousness searching for the final nature of the form does not find the entity of form, it finds its absence. Form does not appear to the reasoning consciousness; if it did, it would truly exist. Thus, it is said that form does not exist in the face of the reasoning consciousness. That consciousness realizes only the emptiness of form, the lack of true existence of form. It does not perceive form. This is the reason why form, which is the same entity as its emptiness, does not appear to the wisdom consciousness realizing the emptiness of form. This does not imply that form does not exist; it means that it does not exist in the face of a reasoning consciousness realizing emptiness in the continuum of a person who has not achieved Buddhahood.

Whereas a sameness or difference of entity is posited in terms of direct perception, a sameness or difference of reverse is posited in terms of thought (*kalpanā, rtog pa*). Reverse (*vyatireka, ldog pa*) refers to the opposite of the negative. The two truths are different reverses, different opposites of the negative. Two phenomena which are different reverses are nominally different, different for thought, that is, they appear differently to thought. For example, sound and impermanent thing are different reverses. When the mind considers whether they are different, it does so through a negative route: are there non-sounds which are impermanent things and non-impermanent things which are sounds? There are non-sounds which are impermanent things, such as shapes. There are no non-impermanent things which are sounds because all sounds are impermanent. Since non-sound is different from non-impermanent thing, non-non-sound is different from non-non-impermanent thing; they are different opposites of the negative. Sound and impermanent things are thus different reverses. They are, however, the same entity because all sounds are impermanent things. When a sound is directly perceived, its impermanence does not appear differently. The two truths are different reverses because they appear differently to thought; non-non-conventional truth does not appear to thought in the way that non-non-ultimate truth does. They are not exactly the same. Because they have different reverses they are given different names.[78]

There is a mode of being beyond the appearance of conventional truths, and that mode of being is, for the Mādhyamikas, the final nature of reality, which when understood brings an end to suffering. To say that this final mode of being is the same entity as the conventional truth it qualifies means that the two abide together simultaneously. The emptiness of true existence of a conventional truth is its final nature. That the two truths are the same entity means that reality is present as the very nature of the objects of ordinary experience.

7 *An Overview of the Svātantrika School*

This chapter will present a summary of the essential positions of the Svātantrika school as perceived by the author of the best known Tibetan tenet text, Jam-yang-shay-ba. The root text of his *Great Exposition of Tenets* (*Grub mtha' chen mo*) presents in poetry the systems of Indian philosophy, both Buddhist and non-Buddhist. He then expands on the stanzas in the body of the text, providing copious quotations from primary materials to support his presentation. There are two excellent commentaries to the root text of Jam-yang-shay-ba's *Tenets*, one by the Mongolian scholar Nga-wang-bel-den (*Ngag-dbang-dpal-ldan*)[1] and the other by the Amdo scholar Lo-sang-gön-chok (*bLo-bzang-dkon-mchog*).[2] Their commentaries to the Svātantrika chapter of Jam-yang-shay-ba's *Tenets* provide the basis of this chapter. Most of the points discussed have been considered in detail in the preceding chapters. Others, such as the interpretation of scripture and the structure of the path to enlightenment, which are considered topics unto themselves in the Ge-luk curriculum, are discussed briefly here but must await further studies for their full exposition.

THE MEANING OF SVĀTANTRIKA

An autonomous sign (**svatantraliṅga rang, rgyud kyi rtags*), a sign which is established by way of its own power (**svairīsiddhaliṅga, rang dbang gis grub pa'i rtags*), and a sign which is established from its own side (**svarūpasiddhaliṅga, rang ngos nas grub pa'i rtags*) are synonyms. A Svātantrika is a Mādhyamika who asserts that signs proving the probandum are stated from the viewpoint of three modes — the property of the position,the forward pervasion, and the counterpervasion — and a subject which are established by way of their own power as they commonly appear to the minds of the two parties in the debate.[3]

DIVISIONS OF SVĀTANTRIKA

Svātantrika is divided into two: Sautrāntika-Svātantrika-Mādhyamika and Yogācāra-Svātantrika-Mādhyamika. The former prove the existence of external objects and the latter refute the existence of external objects.[4]

SAUTRĀNTIKA-SVĀTANTRIKA

The Three Natures

The Sautrāntika-Svātantrikas assert that the three natures are established by way of their own character. However, they assert that impermanent things, which are the bases of the emptiness of true existence, are dependent natures because they are not produced by their own power but are produced by the power of other causes and conditions. The factor of true existence which is imputed to dependent natures is an imaginary nature because it is merely a superimposition (*āropa, sgro 'dogs*). Dependent natures' emptiness of the imputed true existence is the consummate nature because it is the final mode of being. Each of the three natures lacks entityness (*svabhāvatā, ngo bo nyid*). Impermanent things, which are the bases of emptiness, are produced from others and are not produced by their own power ultimately. Thus, dependent natures lack the entityness of production. The factor of true establishment that is imputed to forms and so forth is a superimposition which is not the actual mode of being of those phenomena and is a character which ultimately is imagined. Therefore, imaginary natures lack the entityness of character. The reality which is the emptiness of true establishment is consummate without being a superimposition, is the mode of being, is the object of the highest reasoning consciousness, and lacks the entityness of true establishment. Thus, consummate natures are the ultimate and without entityness.[5]

The Selflessness of Phenomena is Not Taught in Hīnayāna Scriptures

The selflessness of phenomena is not explicitly taught in the

Hīnayāna scriptural collections (*piṭaka*, *sde snod*) because, if it were, there would have been no purpose in Buddha teaching the Mahāyāna scriptures. Furthermore, it is not necessary for Hīnayānists to realize the selflessness of phenomena — the emptiness of true existence — in order to be liberated from cyclic existence, even though the conception of true existence is the final root of cyclic existence. For example, the fear that arises from seeing a coiled rope and thinking that it is a snake can be removed by being told that it is not a snake but a coiled vine. In the same way, one who has realized and cultivated the selflessness of persons can destroy the afflictive obstructions (*kleśāvaraṇa*, *nyon sgrib*) and be liberated from cyclic existence. It is therefore unnecessary to realize the final nature of phenomena — the emptiness of true existence — in order to abandon the afflictive obstructions and achieve liberation.[6]

Refutation of Yogācāra

There are numerous statements in Mahāyāna sutras that seem to indicate that external objects do not exist and that everything is of the nature of consciousness. Bhāvaviveka argues emphatically that such statements do not indicate the non-existence of external objects. The statement in sutra, "External objects do not exist," is interpreted to mean external objects do not exist ultimately. The statements by the Buddha, "I propound mind only," and "These three realms are mind only," refute that there is a permanent self or that there is a performer of actions that is other than the mind; the meaning of these sutras is not that there are no external objects.[7]

Bhāvaviveka refutes the Yogācārin assertion that subject and object are produced from the same seed (*bīja*, *sa bon*) and are thus simultaneous by arguing that objects and their apprehenders are in a relationship of cause and effect and are thus produced sequentially. Therefore, an object is a separate entity from the consciousness which perceives it.[8]

The Yogācārins argue that there are no external objects because the minute particles (*paramāṇu*, *rdul phra rab*) of which such objects are said to be composed are too subtle to be perceived by the sense consciousnesses and because aggregations of minute particles are not suitable as the objects of sense consciousnesses because they do not substantially exist. Bhāvaviveka counters the argument by drawing a distinction between aggregations (*saṃghata*, *'dus pa*) and composites (*saṃcita*, *bsags pa*). An aggregation is a collection of many entities of dissimilar type, such as a forest or an army, and does not substantially exist. Individual particles as well as multiple particles of similar type that exist on one base are composites and substantially exist. Bhāvaviveka asserts that the minute particles of a composite can serve as the observed-object-condition (*ālambanapratyaya*, *dmigs rkyen*) of a sense consciousness.[9]

To support their claim that all appearances of external objects are false, the Yogācārins point to the fact that objects which do not exist, such as a double moon, appear to the sense consciousnesses. Bhāvaviveka responds that the appearance of a double moon is a false appearance to a consciousness that misperceives a single moon, and a single moon exists. Thus, consciousnesses depend on objects for their production; if there were no external objects, apprehending subjects could not be produced. If there were no external objects, direct perception (*pratyakṣa*, *mngon sum*) would be denied.[10]

Bhāvaviveka denies the existence of a self-knowing awareness (*svasaṃvedana*, *rang rig*) that perceives an apprehending consciousness, saying that an ordinary consciousness cannot appear without its object appearing, in which case a self-knower that perceives only the consciousness and not its object does not exist.[11]

The Reasoning Consciousness

Whatever is truly established must exist for a reasoning consciousness that analyzes the ultimate because the reasoning consciousness is that which seeks to discover whether an object is truly established or not; what it is seeking is true establishment. However, whatever exists for a reasoning consciousness is not necessarily truly established; reality — emptiness — is found by a reasoning consciousness but does not truly exist. Although there is an object, namely emptiness, which is found by a reasoning consciousness but which does not truly exist, if something is capable of bearing analysis by a reasoning consciousness, it must be truly established. Being able to bear analysis by a reasoning consciousness is the meaning of true existence and is the object of negation.[12]

Because it is easy to prove a similar example that possesses both the sign and the predicate of the probandum (*sādhyadharma*, *bsgrub bya'i chos*), Bhāvaviveka, in his *Essence of the Middle Way* (*Madhyamakahṛdaya*)and *Blaze of Reasoning* (*Tarkajvālā*), for the most part states syllogisms with negative signs, specifically, signs that are observations of a contradictory object. For example, he states, "The subject, an eye sense, does not ultimately see forms because of being a sense, as is the case, for example, with a nose sense."[13]

The Two Truths

Objects of knowledge (*jñeya*, *shes bya*) are the basis of division into ultimate truths (*paramārthasatya*, *don dam bden pa*) and conventional truths (*saṃvṛtisatya*, *kun rdzob bden pa*). In the term "ultimate truth" (literally, "highest object truth"), "highest" refers to a Superior's uncontaminated wisdom of meditative equipoise (*samāhita*, *mnyam bzhag*) realizing non-true existence. "Object" refers to the object found by that awareness, emptiness. It is a "truth" because of existing as it appears; it appears undeceivingly.

Conventional phenomena, phenomena other than emptiness, are truths for a concealer. The concealer is the ignorance that conceives of true existence and which is so-called because it conceals or obstructs reality. Conventionalities are of two types: (1) phenomena renowned in the world, illustrated by those that are able to perform functions in accordance with their appearance to a mind to which they appear clearly, these being real conventional truths (*tathyasaṃvṛtisatya*, *yang dag kun rdzob bden pa*) and (2) objects posited from the viewpoint of being renowned in the world as unreal, illustrated by those that are unable to perform a function in accordance with how they appear, these being unreal conventionalities (*mityāsaṃvṛti*, *log pa'i kun rdzob*). Real and unreal conventionalities are differentiated in terms of their truth or falsity within the conventional. Reàl conventional truths are things such as forms and sounds. Unreal conventionalities are, for example, reflections, the self of persons (*pudgalātman*, *gang zag gi bdag*), the self of phenomena (*dharmātman*, *chos kyi bdag*), and the principal (*pradhāna*, *gtso bo*) asserted by the Sāṃkhyas.[14]

Valid Cognizers

Like all Buddhist schools, the Svātantrikas assert that there are two valid cognizers (*pramāṇa*, *tshad ma*), direct perceivers (*pratyakṣa*, *mngon sum*) and inferential consciousnesses (*anumāna*, *rjes dpag*). The Sautrāntika-Svātantrikas assert that there are three types of direct perceivers: sense direct perceivers (*indriyapratyakṣa*, *dbang po'i mngon sum*), mental direct perceivers (*manasapratyakṣa, yid kyi mngon sum*), and yogic direct perceivers (*yogipratyakṣa, rnal 'byor mngon sum*). The Yogācāra-Svātantrikas add a fourth type which is rejected by the Sautrāntika-Svātantrikas, self-knowing direct perceivers, making a total of four in their system.[15]

The Paths and Fruits

A person definite in the Mahāyāna lineage exhausts the two obstructions — the predispositions (*vāsanā, bag chags*) of the afflictive emotions (*kleśa, nyon mongs*) and the conception of true existence — and achieves complete Buddhahood simultaneously. The afflictive obstructions are abandoned on the first seven Bodhisattva grounds (*bhūmi, sa*).

The three bodies of truth (*dharmakāya, chos sku*), enjoyment (*saṃbhogakāya, long spyod sku*), and emanation (*nirmāṇakāya, sprul sku*), the three secrecies of body, speech, and mind, the three hundred unshared qualities of a Buddha, and so forth are qualities of the fruit of Buddhahood.

Regarding the objects of abandonment, the three poisons of desire, hatred, and ignorance are the afflictive obstructions and the nine cycles of the conception of true existence are the obstructions to omniscience (*jñeyāvaraṇa, shes sgrib*).

The paths of Hearers (*śrāvaka, nyan thos*) and Solitary Realizers (*pratyekabuddha, rang sangs rgyas*) are similar in that both realize the selflessness of persons. They differ in the length of time needed to complete the path; it may take a Hearer three lifetimes to complete the path whereas a Solitary Realizer may take one hundred eons. They also differ in that Hearers rely on the instructions of a teacher in their last lifetime whereas Solitary Realizers do not. Solitary Realizers attain a similitude of a Buddha's major and minor physical marks; Hearers do not. Hearers teach others using sounds whereas Solitary Realizers may not.[16]

YOGĀCĀRA-SVĀTANTRIKA-MĀDHYAMIKA

True and False Aspectarians

There are two schools of Yogācāra-Svātantrika, those who accord with the True Aspectarians (*satyākāravādin, rnam bden pa*) and those who accord with the False Aspectarians (*alīkākāravādin, rnam rdzunpa*). The former, who include Śantaraksita and Kamalaśīla, assert that the aspect of blue, for example, which is the factor experienced as blue by an eye consciousness apprehending blue, is a functioning thing and a real conventionality. The Yogācāra-Svātantrikas who accord with the False Aspectarians, such as Haribhadra, assert that the nature of the aspect of blue does not exist as a functioning thing as it appears. Both the true and false aspectarians agree that the factor of blue that appears to be an external object is false; they disagree on the status of the mere appearance of blue as blue, with the former asserting that it is true and the latter that it is false.

The False Aspectarians are further divided into those who assert that the entity of the mind is tainted and those who assert that it is untainted. Among the Yogācāra-Svātantrikas, Jetāri accords with the tainted False Aspectarians and Kambala accords with the un-untainted False Aspectarians.[17]

Scriptural Interpretation

Faced with the vast corpus of sutras, the four schools of Buddhist tenets were faced with the problem of reconciling conflicting doctrines set forth in different sutras and internal inconsistencies within sutras. The Hīnayāna schools who, for the most part, did not accept the Mahāyāna sutras as the word of the Buddha, accepted the teachings of their smaller canon as definitive.[18] The Yogācārins and Mādhyamikas, accepting a far larger body of literature as authentic, developed a system of hermeneutics by which sutras were divided into the definitive (*nītārtha, nges don*) and interpretable (*neyārtha, drangs don*) and the literal (*yathāruta, sgra ji bzhin pa*) and non-literal. They looked chiefly to two sutras for their criteria, the *Sutra Unravelling the Thought* (*Saṃdhinirmocana*) and the *Teaching of Akṣayamati* (*Akṣayamatinirdeśasūtra*).[19]

In the *Sutra Unravelling the Thought*, the Buddha explains to Paramārthasamudgata that he turned the wheel of doctrine three times. The first turning of the wheel of doctrine took place in the deer park in Vārāṇasī where the Buddha taught the doctrine of the four truths to followers of the Hearer Vehicle (*śrāvakayāna, nyas thos kyi theg pa*). The Buddha states that the doctrines taught in the first turning of the wheel are interpretable.

In the second turning of the wheel of doctrine, the Buddha taught the doctrine of emptiness to those who had entered the Mahāyāna, explaining that all phenomena are without entityness. The teachings of the second wheel are also identified as interpretable in this sutra.

In the third and final turning of the wheel of doctrine, the Buddha explained to those of all vehicles what he meant when he said that all phenomena are without entityness in the second turning of the wheel. He distinguished three types of non-entityness in terms of the three natures: imaginary natures are without an entityness of character, dependent natures are without an entityness of production, and consummate natures are without an entityness and are ultimates. Imaginaries are not established by way of their own character. Dependent phenomena and consummate phenomena are. This doctrine of the third wheel is said to be definitive.[20]

The *Teaching of Akṣayamati* also divides sutras into the definitive and interpretable but uses different criteria. Sutras that teach conventionalities require interpretation to arrive at the final mode of being of the phenomena taught. Sutras that teach ultimates are definitive because emptiness, the final mode of being, is definite; there is nothing to be interpreted beyond that.[21]

The Yogācārins base their interpretation of scripture on the *Sutra Unravelling the Thought* classifying Hīnayāna sutras — first wheel sutras — and Mahāyāna sutras, such as the Perfection of Wisdom sutras — middle wheel sutras — as interpretable. For the Yogācārins, the division into definitive and interpretable is made in terms of how the doctrine is expressed; if a particular sutra can be taken literally it is definitive, if its meaning must be explained it is interpretable.[22]

The Mādhyamikas accept the difffrentiation of the three turnings of the wheel of doctrine but do not classify the sutras of the mddle wheel as interpretable. They draw the distinction between definitive and interpretable, not in terms of how the doctrine is expressed, but in terms of what the doctrine is, taking their lead from the *Teaching of Akṣayamati*. If the sutra teaches emptiness it is definitive, if it does not it is interpretable. They do not equate being literal with being definitive and being non-literal with being interpretable, as do the Yogācārins. The definitive is the true — ultimate truths — and the interpretable is the false — conventional truths.[23]

Within this rubric, the Svātantrikas and Prāsaṅgikas differ slightly. For the Svātantrikas, for a sutra to be definitive, it must both teach emptiness and be able to be taken literally. Therefore, the statement in the *Heart Sutra* (*Prajñāpāramitāhṛdayasūtra*) that "Form does not exist," although it teaches emptiness, is interpretable because it cannot be taken literally. The meaning of the sutra is not that form does not exist but that form does not truly exist. Other

Perfection of Wisdom sutras that teach that phenomena do not ultimately exist are definitive because they teach emptiness and can be taken literally.

The Prāsaṅgikas do not require that the negation be so qualified in the sutra; if it teaches ultimate truths it is definitive; if it teaches conventional truths it is interpretable.[24]

Bhāvaviveka accepts sutras of the final wheel, such as the *Sutra Unravelling the Thought*, as definitive but rejects the Yogācārin interpretation of those sutras. For example, he accepts the doctrine of the three non-entitynesses, but gives it his own Mādhyamika interpretation, as explained above. The Prāsaṅgikas classify sutras of the final wheel as interpretable, accepting that they are intended for Yogācārin disciples.[25]

The Object of Negation and Reasoning Consciousness

Both branches of Svātantrika agree that the object of negation (*pratiṣedhya, dgag bya*) is existence by way of the object's own mode of subsistence without being posited through the force of appearing to an awareness. This awareness is one which is not damaged by another valid cognizer in terms of its perception of existence by way of the object's own character.

In the autocommentary to his *Ornament for the Middle Way* (*Madhyamakālaṃkāra*), Śāntarakṣita states the reasoning of the lack of being one or many, citing the *Descent into Laṅkā* (*Laṅkāvatārasūtra*) and the *Meeting of Father and Son Sutra* (*Pitāputrasamāgamasūtra*) as scriptural sources. An example of a syllogism using that reasoning is, "The subjects, things such as forms, do not truly exist because of not being a truly established unity or a truly established multiplicity, as is the case, for example, with a reflection." The pervasion is established because whatever is truly established must be ascertained as being truly one or truly many. The property of the position is established because form and so forth are not truly established unities because of having parts; they are not truly established multiplicities because a truly established unity does not exist. In addition to the reasoning of the lack of being one and many, the Svātantrikas prove non-true existence mainly using the diamond slivers, the refutation of production of the existent and non-existent, the refutation of production by the four alternatives, and the sign or dependent arising.[26]

The Two Truths

The presentation of the selflessness of the person is shared by both branches of Svātantrika. The explanation of the basis of division of the two truths, their definitions, and divisions are also common.[27]

The Path

The Yogācāra-Svātantrikas assert that the obstructions to omniscience are of two types, coarse and subtle. The coarse obstructions are the conception of subject and object as being different substantial entities, together with the seeds of that conception. The subtle obstructions to omniscience are the conception of true existence and its seeds. The afflictive obstructions are the three poisons. The subtle obstructions to omniscience are the main object of abandonment by the Mahāyāna, the coarse obstructions to omniscience are the chief object of abandonment of the Solitary Realizer Vehicle, and the afflictive obstructions, the chief object of abandonment of the Hearer Vehicle. Thus, the three vehicles have different types of realization, with Hearers realizing the sixteen aspects of the four truths, Solitary Realizers understanding the emptiness of duality of subject and object, and Mahāyānists realizing the emptiness of true existence.

TRANSLATION
OF
THE SVĀTANTRIKA CHAPTER
OF
JANG-GYA'S *PRESENTATION OF TENETS*

Introduction to the Translation

Jang-gya Röl-bay-dor-jay *(lCang-skya Rol-pa'i-rdo-rje)*, also known as the Second Jang-gya Hu-tuk-tu *(Hu-thog-thu)* was born in modern Xinghai province in 1717. In 1721 he was recognized as the incarnation of Jang-gya Nga-wang-lo-sang-chö-den *(Ngag-dbang-blo-bzang-chos-ldan)*. At the age of nine he was taken to China, where he began his monastic studies and the study of Manchu, Chinese, and Mongolian. During this period, one of his fellow students was the fourth son of the Yung-cheng emperor who would later become the Ch'ien-lung emperor. In 1735, Jang-gya went to Tibet where he studied under the Seventh Dalai Lama and took his final monastic vows from the Second Panchen Lama. Upon his return to China in 1736, his boyhood friend, now Emperor, appointed him Lama of the Seal, the highest Tibetan clerical post in China. With imperial encouragement, Jang-gya began to compile an extensive Tibetan-Mongol dictionary. Upon its completion, he oversaw the translation and revision of the Mongolian edition of the Indian treatises *(bstans 'gyur)*. Completed in 1749, the translation into Mongolian comprises 108, 016 folios. In 1744, the Emperor and Jang-gya established the Gan-den Jin-chak-ling *(dGa'-ldan Byin-chags-gling)* in Peking, a teaching monastery modeled after the Ge-luk monastic universities of Tibet. Between 1736 and 1746 he composed his best known work, the *Presentation of Tenets (Grub mtha'i rnam par bzhag pa)*. Between 1772 and 1779 Jang-gya supervised the translation of the entire Word of the Buddha *(bka' 'gyur)* into Manchu. He died in 1786.[1]

Jang-gya was a prolific author, his collected works filling seven volumes. In addition to the *Presentation of Tenets,* his other well-known works include the *Song of the View (lTa ba'i mgur),* his commentary to the *Deeds of Samantabhadra (Bhadracarī),* and his commentary to Tsong-kha-pa's *Praise of Dependent Arising (rTen 'brel 'bstod pa).*

The *Presentation of Tenets* begins with discussions of what constitutes a tenet *(grub mtha')* and how Buddhists are distinguished from non-Buddhists. He then goes on to set forth briefly the tenets of nine non-Buddhist schools: Ayata (Cārvāka), Sāṃkhya, Brāhmana (which includes Vedānta), Vaiśṇava, Mīmāṃsaka, Aiśvara, Vaiśeṣika, Naiyāyika, and Nirgrantha (Jaina). The second section of the *Presentation,* which begins with a brief history of the Buddhist doctrine, is devoted to the two Hīnayāna schools, Vaibhāṣika and Sautrāntika. The third section provides a rather extensive treatment of the Cittamātra school, after dealing briefly with the rise of the Mahāyāna. The final section is devoted to Mādhyamika and concludes with a short presentation of Mantrayāna. Roughly half of the final section (and one fourth of the entire *Presentation of Tenets*) is translated here, beginning with Jang-gya's discussion of Mādhyamika in general and proceeding through his presentation of Svātantrika.

In the first chapter (chapter divisions and titles have been interpolated by the translator), Jang-gya provides a brief biography of Nāgārjuna, drawn primarily from Bu-dön's (*Bu-ston,* 1290-1364) *History of the Doctrine (Chos 'byung).* Jang-gya follows the traditional view that Nāgārjuna lived for 600 years. Tibetan scholars are not unaware of apparent disparities among the views set forth in the many works that they attribute to Nāgārjuna, which they account for by explaining that his work encompasses three periods or "great proclamations of the doctrine." These disparities have caused Western scholars to posit the existence of at least two Nāgārjunas. Jang-gya goes on to list Nāgārjuna's major works.[2] The chapter concludes with a listing of the major works of the followers of Nāgārjuna: Āryadeva, Buddhapālita, Bhāvaviveka, Candrakīrti, Śāntarakṣita, Kamalaśīla, and Śāntideva.

After briefly explaining Bhavaviveka's etymology of *madhyamaka,* Jang-gya devotes the remainder of the second chapter to a discussion of various ways of dividing the Mādhyamika school. The first is the division into the Mādhyamikas of the Model Texts *(gZhung phyi mo'i dbu ma pa)* and the Partisan Mādhyamikas *(Phyogs 'dzin pa'i dbu ma pa)* with the former including Nāgārjuna and Āryadeva and the latter, all later Indian Mādhyamikas.

Nāgārjuna and Āryadeva are Mādhyamikas of the Model Texts because their writings either do not make reference to or are ambiguous with respect to the doctrinal positions upon which the later Mādhyamikas parted company. Consequently, their works can be accepted as valid by all later Mādhyamikas, thereby serving as models or prototypes for their systems. Jang-gya states the Ge-luk position that although the writings of Nāgārjuna and Āryadeva cannot be classified as Prāsaṅgika or Svātantrika, their final opinion or thought *(dgongs pa)* is Prāsaṅgika. That is, although the writings of Nāgārjuna and Āryadeva were commented upon cataphatically by Prāsaṅgikas such as Buddhapālita and Candrakīrti, Svātantrikas such as Bhāvaviveka, and even Yogācārins such as Sthiramati, the correct interpretation of Nāgārjuna's writings, that is, the interpretation that accurately represents Nāgārjuna's own view, is that provided by Buddhapālita and Candrakīrti. Tsong-kha-pa says in his *Great Exposition of Special Insight (lHag mthong chen mo):*

> Which of those masters should one follow in seeking the thought of the Superior [Nāgārjuna] and his [spiritual] son [Āryadeva]? Seeing that the great elder [Atīśa] took the system of Candrakīrti to be chief, the great early lamas of these precepts also held that system to be chief. Candrakīrti saw that, from among the commentators on the *Treatise on the Middle Way (Madhyamakaśāstra),* it was the master Buddhapālita who elucidated completely the thought of the Protector [Nāgārjuna]. He [Candrakīrti] commented on the thought of the Superior, taking that system as his basis, while also taking many good explanations from the master Bhāvaviveka but refuting those that appeared to be slightly incorrect. Because I see the commentaries of those two masters [Buddhapālita and Candrakīrti] to be most excellent in explaining the texts of the Superior and his son, here the thought of the Superior will be delineated following the masters Buddhapālita and Candrakīrti.[3]

Tsong-kha-pa reached this conclusion after extensive study of the commentaries of Buddhapālita, Bhāvaviveka and Candrakīrti. It is reported in his biography that his decision to follow the Prāsaṅgika interpretation was confirmed in a vision in which Nāgārjuna and his five chief disciples appeared to Tsong-kha-pa. Buddhapālita blessed Tsong-kha-pa by placing his commentary to the *Treatise on the Middle Way* on Tsong-kha-pa's head.

Three ways of dividing the Partisan Mādhyamikas are referred to by Jang-gya. The first and most important is that of Prāsaṅgika and Svātantrika, made from the point of view of the means employed to cause an opponent to understand and accept the Mādhyamika position. Jang-gya digresses to consider what it means to be a founder *(shing rta srol 'byed)* of a system, an important question since none of the Indian Mādhyamikas called themselves Prāsaṅgikas or Svātantrikas or seem to have considered themselves to be founders or members of a given "system" apart from their being Mādhyamikas. Jang-gya argues that although Buddhapālita was the first to use consequences in commenting on Nāgārjuna, Candrakīrti is the founder of Prāsaṅgika. To be the first person to hold a view does make that person a founder. A founder must consciously distinguish his system from that of another. In support of his position that Candrakīrti rather than Buddhapālita founded Prāsaṅgika, Jang-gya notes that Bhāvaviveka discerned no fundamental difference between Buddhapālita and himself; he believed that Buddhapālita's use of consequences was merely a misuse of autonomous syllogisms. Bhāvaviveka did not conceive of Buddhapālita as establishing a new school. Jang-gya concludes that it is therefore difficult to hold that Buddhapālita is the founder of Prāsaṅgika.

Two other ways of dividing the Partisan Mādhyamikas are mentioned by Jang-gya. The first is into those who assert the existence of external objects *(bahyārtha, phyi don)* and those who do not. This division is not coextensive with Prāsaṅgika and Svātantrika; the Prāsaṅgikas and Sautrāntika-Svātantrikas hold that external objects exist conventionally whereas the Yogācāra-Svātantrikas assert that they do not. This division was current in Tibet prior to that of Prāsaṅgika and Svātantrika, which only came into use during the period of the second dissemination *(phyi dar)*. During the earlier dissemination *(snga dar)*, the translator Ye-shay-day *(Ye-shes-sde,* c. 800) referred to the Sautrāntika-Mādhyamikas, who assert the conventional existence of external objects, and the Yogācāra-Mādhyamikas who teach that external objects do not exist conventionally.[4]

The third and most nebulous of the divisions is that into the

Mādhyamikas who propound an establishment of illusion through reasoning *(māyopamādvayavādin, sgyu ma rigs grub pa)* and the Mādhyamikas who propound a thorough non-abiding *(apratiṣṭhāna-vādin, rab tu mi gnas pa)*. These terms were used by Advayavajra in the eleventh century.[5] According to some Tibetan scholars, those who propound an establishment of illusion through reasoning assert that an ultimate truth is a composite of two things — a basis, such as the aggregates, and the appearance of that basis' lack of true existence. This composite is established by an inferential reasoning consciousness. This position is ascribed to the Yogācāra-Svātantrikas. Tsong-kha-pa rejects this, arguing that there is no Mādhyamika who holds that such a composite is an ultimate truth; an ultimate truth is a non-affirming negative that is the mere lack of true existence and that appears non-dualistically to a wisdom consciousness in meditative equipoise. There is no appearance of the basis that is empty — a conventional truth — whatsoever.

Tsong-kha-pa also rejects the definition of a thoroughly non-abiding Mādhyamika as one who asserts that emptiness is the mere elimination of elaborations. It is correct that emptiness is said to be free from elaborations *(prapañca, spros pa)* in the sense that all webs of the conception of true existence are pacified in the face of the wisdom realizing emptiness. However, it is not the eliimination of all elaborations, that is, it is not the absence of everything. Tsong-kha-pa rejects the view that emptiness is the mere negation of all qualities and cannot be known by any consciousness. If this is the position of the thoroughly non-abiding Mādhyamikas, there are no such Mādhyamikas. Tsong-kha-pa thus rejects the use of the terms "establishment of illusion through reasoning" and "thoroughly non-abiding" as they were defined by earlier Tibetan scholars.[6]

Jang-gya begins the third chapter with an important question: How do the myriad schools of Tibetan Buddhism correspond to the classical Indian Mahāyāna schools of Cittamātra and Mādhyamika? Specifically, he asks if all the sects of Tibetan Buddhism are either Cittamātra or Mādhyamika. If so, why are there so many different names? If not, how can they be proponents of the Mahāyāna? Jang-gya's "brief" answer constitutes the remainder of the chapter.

He begins by noting that the Tibetan sects do not take their names from their philosophical views; some are named after the place where they originated, some are named for a particular teacher, and some are named for a practice emphasized by the school. Jang-gya goes on to survey the important sects and masters from the time of Śāntarakṣita in the eighth century to Tsong-kha-pa in the fourteenth century in an attempt to classify their philosophical views as Cittamātrin, Svātantrika, or Prāsaṅgika. Although this if often difficult to determine with certainty, his general conclusion is that the Svātantrika position dominated during the period of the first dissemination due to the influence of Śāntarakṣita and Kamalaśīla and that the Prāsaṅgika position prevailed from the time of the second dissemination onward due to the efforts of Atīśa, Ba-tsap-nyi-ma-drak, and their followers.

The chapter concludes with a paean to Tsong-kha-pa, revealing Jang-gya's Ge-luk perspective.

In the fourth chapter, Jang-gya defines Mādhyamika and explains why only the Mādhyamika school truly holds to the middle way; all other schools fall to one or both of the two extremes of ultimate existence or utter non-existence.

Only the Mādhyamikas are capable of asserting that all phenomena are empty of ultimate existence while upholding the conventional, valid existence of all phenomena. Jang-gya argues that dependent arising means being empty of true existence and vice versa. That is, something that lacks ultimate existence cannot be independently established; it must be dependently established, a dependent arising. Furthermore, something that is a dependent arising cannot be ultimately established; it must be empty of ultimate existence. The very phenomena that are empty of ultimate existence are also dependent arisings and validly existent. This is what is meant by the compatibility of emptiness and dependent arising.

The chapter closes with a consideration of why the Svātantrikas are considered Mādhyamikas if they assert that all phenomena exist by way of their own character *(svalakṣana, rang gi mtshan nyid)*, something that the Prāsaṅgikas reject. Jang-gya explains that although the emptiness posited by the Svātantrikas is less subtle than that of the Prāsaṅgikas, it is nonetheless accurate and universal, applying to all phenomena. This cannot be said for the emptiness asserted by the Cittamātrins, for example. The Svātantrikas are able to uphold the compatibility (as they understand it) of emptiness and dependent arising and are able to refute the two extremes of true existence and utter non-existence. They therefore fulfill Jang-gya's definition of Mādhyamika.

The fifth chapter is devoted to a brief consideration of scriptural interpretation in Mādhyamika. The Mahāyāna philosophical schools accepted a vast body of literature as the word of the Buddha *(buddhavacana, sangs rgyas kyi bka')* and consequently were faced with the problem of interpreting a formidable corpus of sacred scripture. Their task was complicated by a number of factors. First, it is a fundamental tenet of Buddhism that just as a physician does not prescribe the same medicine to cure all maladies, the Buddha did not teach the same thing to everyone; rather he taught doctrines appropriate to the interests and capacities of his listeners. Furthermore, his approach seems to have been facultive rather than dogmatic with regard to the acceptance of his teachings. It was the conviction of the various philosophical schools of Indian Buddhism that the Buddha was not an agnostic, that the antinomic character of his teaching was only apparent, and that his final view could be ascertained. Disagreements concerning that final view provides, to a great extent, the *raison d'etre* for the Mahāyāna schools in India.

Tsong-kha-pa takes this question of how to determine which sutras are of definitive meaning *(nītārtha, nges don)* and which sutras require interpretation *(neyārtha, drang don)* as the starting point of his *Essence of the Good Explanations (Legs bshad snying po)*. This work is Jang-gya's source here, where he focuses primarily on the Mādhyamikas' use of interpretative principles provided in the *Teaching of Akṣayamati (Akṣayamatinirdeśasūtra)* The principles are rather straightforward. Those statements in sutra whose subject is emptiness are definitive and those statements whose subject is a conventional truth require interpretation. The Svātantrikas and Prāsaṅgikas both accept this criterion but differ slightly over how the statements concerning emptiness must be expressed.[7]

The structure and practice of the path to enlightenment are generally dealt with only cursorily in the Ge-luk tenets texts, the structure of the path being delineated in great detail in monastic textbooks based on Haribhadra's two major commentaries to Maitreya's *Ornament for Clear Realization (Abhisamayālaṃkāra)* and the practice of the path set forth in a varity of "stages of the path" *(lam rim)* and "training of the mind" *(blo sbyong)* literatures. Jang-gya's presentation of the general practice of the Mādhyamika path in the sixth chapter is characteristically brief, employing a vocabulary well-known to his audience. He speaks of beings of the three capacities, a typology employed by Atīśa in his *Lamp for the Path to Enlightenment (Bodhipathapradīpa)*. Beings of small capacity are those persons who seek happiness within the cycle of birth and death. Those of middling capacity seek their own liberation from rebirth, the Hīnayāna motivation. Beings of great capacity seek enlightenment for all beings. He emphasizes the importance of the six perfections of giving, ethics, patience, effort, concentration, and wisdom. The progression to enlightenment, whether Hīnayāna or Mahāyāna, takes place over five paths. The first is the path of accumulation *(saṃbhāramārga, tshogs lam)* which, in the case of the Mahāyāna, begins with the creation of the altruistic aspiration to achieve Buddhahood for the welfare of all sentient beings. The second path, the path of preparation *(prayogamārga, sbyor lam)*, begins with the initial inferential realization of reality (with the various schools of tenets disagreeing as to the nature of that reality and by whom it is realized). The path of seeing *(darśanamārga, mthong lam)*, the third path, marks the initial direct realization of selflessness. On the Bodhisattva path it also corresponds to the beginning of the first of the ten Bodhisattva grounds *(bhūmi, sa)*. From this point on, the path is comprised of periods of meditative equipoise *(samāhita, mnyam bzhag)* in direct realization of selflessness and periods of subsequent attainment *(pṛṣṭhalabdha, rjes thob)*, states following direct realization devoted to the accumulation of the perfections other than wisdom. These periods occur over the course of the fourth path, that of meditation *(bhāvanāmārga, sgom lam)*, which culminates with the attainment of the fruition on the path of no more learning *(aśaikṣamārga, mi slob lam)*, the fruition of the Mahāyāna path being Buddhahood, of the Hīnayāna path the state of an Arhat.

As mentioned, the Mahāyāna and Hīnayāna paths are laid out in far greater detail in other Ge-luk commentaries and textbooks. Here Jang-gya follows a format that occurs in other tenet texts, drawing a correspondence among the bases, paths, and fruitions. The bases are the two truths, the paths are wisdom and method, and the fruitions are the Truth and Form Bodies of a Buddha.

The chapter on the path concludes Jang-gya's general presentation of Mādhyamika.

Before turning to the presentation of the specific assertions of the two branches of Svātantrika, Jang-gya discusses the etymology of the terms *svatantra* and *svātantrika* and the reasons why this particular group of Mādhyamikas came to be designated in Tibet as the Svātantrika or Autonomy school. He provides a summary of the Ge-luk position as to why the use of autonomous syllogisms *(svatan-*

tra prayoga, rang rgyud kyi sbyor ba) implies the assertion that phenomena exist by way of their own character *(svalakṣana, rang gi mtshan nyid)*.

Jang-gya's eighth chapter is devoted to a long exposition of Bhāvaviveka's refutation of the Yogācāra, drawn from the fifth chapter of his *Essence of the Middle Way (Madhyamakahṛdaya)* and the autocommentary *The Blaze of Reasoning (Tarkajvālā)*. Bhāvaviveka lived in a period of lively debate among the various Buddhist schools and seems to have been familiar with a number of Yogācāra texts, notably the *Discrimination of the Middle and Extremes (Madhyāntavibhāga)*. In the fifth chapter of the *Essence of the Middle Way* and *Blaze of Reasoning*, he launches a strident attack on the Yogācāra, dealing with each of their major assertions in turn. Bhāvaviveka sets the tone for the chapter in the first stanza (not included in Jang-gya):

> Others, boasting of their wisdom,
> Proud of their own system say,
> "Entry into the ambrosia of reality
> Is set forth well by the Yogācārins."[8]

Bhāvaviveka then goes on to refute the basic assertions of the Yogācārins: the three natures, the mind-basis-of-all *(ālayavijñāna, kun gzhi rnam shes)*, the non-existence of external objects, the existence of self-knowing awareness *(svasaṃvedana, rang rig)*, and the presence of the doctrine of mind-only in the teachings of the Buddha. A thorough exposition and analysis of Bhāvaviveka's arguments would require a separate monograph. He contends that the Yogācārins' assertions are contradicted by scripture and reasoning, their assertions falling to one or the other extreme. But he also argues that the Yogācāra positions are contradicted by worldly renown; displaying a pragmatism evident in all of his writings, he finds the idea that external objects do not exist to be counterintuitive and hence untenable.

Jang-gya turns in the ninth chapter to the meaning of ultimate existence, the object of negation for the Svātantrikas. Jang-gya seeks to distinguish between something being ultimate and something being ultimately existent. The wisdom consciousness of hearing, thinking, or meditation is an ultimate, according to Bhāvaviveka, because it is the highest consciousness. It also exists. Emptiness is the object found by such analysis and is the ultimate truth. For something to ultimately exist, it must be able to withstand analysis by such a consciousness and it is Bhāvaviveka's position that nothing can withstand such analysis. The mode of that analysis is the subject of the tenth chapter, in which Jang-gya summarizes the various reasonings used by Bhāvaviveka to prove that nothing ultimately exists.

In chapter 11, Jang-gya takes up the general topic of the two truths and considers a number of primary and secondary issues such as the relationship of ultimate truths and conventional truths, the division of ultimate truths into actual and concordant ultimates, the question of whether the selflessness of persons *(pudgalanairātmya, gang sag gi bdag med)* is an ultimate truth for Bhāvaviveka, the question of whether true cessations *(nirodhasatya, 'gog bden)* are ultimate truths, and the Svātantrika division of conventional truths into the real and the unreal. All of these issues have been discussed in chapter 6 of Part I of this work.

Jang-gya concludes his presentation of the Sautrāntika-Svātantrika in chapter 12 with a brief discussion of their uncommon tenets concerning the structure of the Hīnayāna and Mahāyāna paths. As discussed at some length in chapter 3 of Part I, Bhāvaviveka identifies the conception of a self of persons *(pudgalātman, gang sag gi bdag)* as the chief of the afflictive obstructions *(kleśāvaraṇa, nyon sgrib)* preventing liberation from suffering and rebirth. He identifies the conception of a self of phenomena *(dharmātman, chos kyi dbag)* as the chief of the obstructions to omniscience *(jñeyāvaraṇa, shes sgrib)* preventing the attainment of Buddhahood. Persons traversing either of the Hīnayāna paths must simply abandon the afflictive obstructions to achieve nirvana; Bodhisattvas must abandon both types of obstructions to become Buddhas. Jang-gya alludes to differences among the Sautrāntika-Svātantrikas, the Yogācāra-Svātantrikas, and the Prāsaṅgikas regarding the manner in which the two obstructions are abandoned. According to both branches of Svātantrika, Bodhisattvas begin to abandon both obstructions upon the attainment of the path of seeing and the first Bodhisattva ground. The Sautrāntika-Svātantrikas assert that Bodhisattvas complete the abandonment of the afflictive obstructions at the end of the seventh ground and proceed to then abandon the remainder of the obstructions to omniscience, whereas the Yogācāra-Svātantrikas assert that both obstructions are finally abandoned simultaneously with the achievement of Buddhahood. Differing from both of these views are the Prāsaṅgikas, who hold that Bodhisattvas work exclusively to abandon the afflictive obstructions during the first seven grounds and then turn their efforts toward the abandonment of the obstructions to omniscience on the eighth, ninth, and tenth grounds. Jam-yang-shay-ba, in his *Great Exposition of Tenets (Grub mtha' chen mo)*, provides Indian sources to support this differentiation.

Jang-gya begins his section on the Yogācāra-Svātantrikas with a discussion of the role played by the mind-only view in Śāntarakṣita's philosophy. The syncretic character of the Yogācāra-Svātantrika, the last great development of Indian Buddhist philosophy, is evident here. Śāntarakṣita took a far more accomodating view of the Yogācārins' position and their interpretations of the sutras that seem to teach mind-only than did Bhāvaviveka who, in his strident critique of Yogācāra, had gone to some length to demonstrate that the non-existence of external objects was not the message of any sutra. Candrakīrti took a less radical view. He says in the *Supplement to the Middle Way (Madhyamakāvatāra*, VI.96):

> The Buddhas said that when there are no objects of consciousness
> One easily finds the refutation of consciousness.
> If there are no objects of consciousness, the refutation of consciousness is established.
> Therefore, initially objects of consciousness are refuted.

The autocommentary says:

> The Supramundane and Victorious Buddhas cause their disciples to approach non-inherent existence *(niḥsvabhāva, rang bzhin med)* gradually. Because it is a method for entering into reality *(dharmatā, chos nyid)*, they talk initially about giving and so forth so that those accumulating merit may enter easily into reality. In the same way, the refutation of objects of consciousness is a method for fully understanding selflessness. Therefore, the Supramundane Victor spoke first only of the refutation of objects of consciousness so that those who understand the selflessness of objects of consciousness might easily enter into the selflessness of consciousness. Sometimes those who have understood that objects of consciousness do not inherently exist will come to realize that consciousness does not inherently exist through

> only [the teaching that objects do not inherently exist] itself; sometimes they will come [to realize it] by being taught just a little more. [Therefore] just the refutation of objects of consciousness is spoken of at first.[9]

Hence, rather than denying the presence of the doctrine of mind-only in the Mahāyāna sutras, Candrakīrti upholds its value as a propaedeutic for the understanding of the emptiness of inherent existence, the final nature of reality. Jam-yang-shay-ba seems to suggest that Śāntarakṣita was influenced by Candrakīrti's explanation in the formulation of the Yogācāra-Svātantrika view.[10] Indeed, Śāntarakṣita seems to echo Candrakīrti's position when he says in the *Ornament for the Middle Way* (92):

> The non-existence of external objects should be known
> Through relying on mind-only.
> [Then] relying on this [Mādhyamika] mode, it should be known
> That this [mind] too is completely selfless.

Jang-gya discerns a threefold progression. First, one understands the selflessness of persons, the reality set forth in the Hīnayāna; second, one realizes the non-existence of external objects taught in Yogācāra; finally, one realizes the final view, the Mādhyamika view, that consciousness also is empty.

Jang-gya raises the knotty problem of whether Śāntarakṣita is being true to the Mādhyamika tradition, that is, following Nāgārjuna, in his assertion that external objects do not exist. Whereas Jang-gya earlier had called Nāgārjuna a Mādhyamika of the Model Texts because he did not express a clear position on such questions as the existence or non-existence of external objects, here he provides a stanza from the *Sixty Stanzas of Reasoning* and construes it as evidence that Nāgārjuna denies the existence of the physical elements as objects separate from consciousness.[11]

In the fourteenth chapter, Jang-gya discusses the object of negation for the Yogācāra-Svātantrikas, to the extent that it can be discerned from a passage from Kamalaśīla's *Illumination of the Middle Way*. He provides a lengthy analysis of the metaphor of the magician's illusion to demonstrate what it means for something "to exist by way of its own mode of subsistence which is established from the object's own side without being posited through the power of appearing to a non-defective awareness." This phrase has been unpacked in chapter 4 of Part 1. Ultimate existence is a mode of being independent of a perceiving consciousness. Conventional existence must then be dependent. In the phrase, "through the power of appearing to a non-defective awareness," "appearing to" implies the existence of some objective status to which consciousness passively assents. A non-defective consciousness can be either a sense consciousness or a conceptual consciousness that is free from superficial and deep causes of error. Only valid consciousnesses can posit the existence of objects, objects about which those consciousnesses are, by definition, non-mistaken; what appears to such consciousnesses conventionally exists. Thus, two elements can be identified as necessary for positing the conventional existence of an object: the object itself and the positing consciousness; through the appearance of the object to a non-defective consciousness, the object may be said to attain its mode of being. A phenomenon gains its entity through the force of its appearance to a non-defective mind; its objective mode of subsistence does not exist independently of the consciousness to which it appears. Thus an object's objective mode of being inheres in the object itself but is dependent on a mind to perceive it.

Jang-gya's lengthy delineation of the reasoning of the lack of being one or many in chapter 15 is one of two largely original contributions he makes to the Ge-luk study of Svātantrika, the other being his summary of Bhāvaviveka's refutation of Yogācāra. Much of the rest of the Svātantrika chapter is a compilation and elaboration of statements made by Tsong-kha-pa in a variety of works.

He uses his brief chapter on the two truths in Yogācāra-Svātantrika to discuss the division of that school into the those that accord with the True Aspectarians *(satyākāravāda, rnam bden pa)* and False Aspectarians *(alīkākāravāda, rnam rdzun pa)*, two subschools of Yogācāra.[12] Jang-gya also uses this chapter to comment briefly on a number of miscellaneous topics.

Jang-gya concludes the section on Yogācāra-Svātantrika in chapter 17 with a discussion of the paths and fruitions. Haribhadra, whose delineation of the structure of the path is considered orthodox by the Ge-luk-bas, is classified by them as a Yogācāra-Svātantrika. As with the Sautrāntika-Svātantrikas, Jang-gya's description of the path is extremely brief, touching on a number of disconnected points of controversy. A full description of the Yogācāra-Svātantrika path would require a separate volume. There are several major points that may be mentioned here. The first is the alignment of the three selflessnesses with the three paths. According to Haribhadra, Hearers meditate on the selflessness of persons, Solitary Realizers meditate on the absence of a difference of entity of subject and object, and Bodhisattvas meditate on the emptiness of true existence. Second, toward the end of his *Ornament for the Middle Way*, Śāntarakṣita draws a distinction that was later incorporated into Tibetan "stages of the path" *(lam rim)* literature, that of Bodhisattvas of sharp faculties and Bodhisattvas of dull faculties. The former come to an understanding of emptiness before vowing to free all sentient beings from suffering while the latter are initially moved by the sufferings of others, vow to free them, and only later seek the knowledge of reality.

Jang-gya's presentation of Svātantrika is extremely rich; it is impossible here to elaborate on all of his points. The major issues in the Ge-luk view of Svātantrika have been considered in Part 1 of this study. The following translation is provided to document the structure, method, and style of the work of one of the greatest Tibetan doxographers.

There are two available editions of the *Presentation of Tenets*, one published by the Pleasure of Elegant Sayings Press in Sarnath, India in 1970 and the other edited by Lokesh Chandra and published by Sharada Rani in New Delhi in 1977; they differ only in scribal errors. Both editions have been used in the translation of the Svātantrika-Mādhyamika chapter that follows. Page numbers in the notes refer to the Sarnath edition.

Part One
Mādhyamika

The System of the Mādhyamikas, the Proponents of No Entityness

This section has two parts, the texts on which they rely and a presentation of the tenets which appear in those texts.

1 The Life and Works of Nāgārjuna

THE TEXTS ON WHICH THEY RELY

As was explained earlier [in a section not translated here], the founder of the Mahāyāna in general is the protector Nāgārjuna. Thus, the *Descent into Laṅkā Sutra (Laṅkāvatārasūtra)* says:

> If the vehicle of individual knowledge
> Is not accessible to logicians,
> I beseech you to explain who will bear [this teaching]
> After the Protector has passed away.[1]

That is, the object of the exalted wisdom, known by individual meditative equipoise *(samāhita, mnyam gzhag)*, is itself the vehicle that pacifies all terminological and conceptual elaborations *(prapanca, spros pa)*. Because it is very profound, it is asked who will bear [this profound vehicle] after the Teacher [Buddha] has passed into nirvana. In answer to this question, the Teacher said:

> Mahāmati, you should know that
> After the Sugata has passed away
> There will appear after some time
> One who will uphold the ways.
> In the south, in the land of Veda
> A monk renowned as Śrīmān,
> Called by the name of Nāga,
> Will destroy the positions of existence and non-existence.

He will fully explain to the world
My vehicle, the unsurpassed Mahāyāna.
He will then achieve the Joyful *(pramuditā, rab tu dga' ba)*
Ground
And go to the Land of Bliss *(sukhāvatī, bde ba can)*.[2]

Hence it was clearly prophesied that just this master [Nāgārjuna] would comment accurately on the vehicle of definitive meaning *(nītārtha, nges don)*, free from the extremes of [true] existence and [utter] non-existence. He is similarly prophesied in the *Great Cloud Sutra in Twelve Thousand Stanzas (Dvādaśasāhasrikāmahāmeghasūtra)*, the Action Tantra *Mañjuśrī Root Tantra (Mañjuśrīmūlatantra)*, and the *Great Drum Sutra (Mahābherīhārakaparivartasūtra)*.

In some sutras it is explained that this master is a first ground *(bhūmi, sa)* Bohisattva and in some, a seventh ground Bodhisattva. [However] the glorious Candrakīrti states in his *Brilliant Lamp Commentary (Pradīpoddyotana)* that this master manifested the state of Vajradhara in that same lifetime by means of the Mantra path. [Still,] it is explained in the *Great Cloud Sutra* and the *Great Drum Sutra* that in the future Nāgārjuna will become the Conqueror called Jñānākarāloka. Although there are many such disparate explanations, they are not contradictory. For example, many different presentations appear in sutras regarding the time at which our Teacher created the aspiration to enlightenment, became fully enlightened, and so forth because [such presentations] were made in terms of common and uncommon modes of appearance and actuality. This was stated by the foremost great being Tsong-kha-pa.

Regarding [the life of] this master [Nāgārjuna], four hundred years after the Buddha passed away, in the southern country of Vedarbha a wealthy childless brahmin received in a dream a prophecy from a deity that if he invited one hundred brahmins to teach religion, he would have a child. He did so, and through his prayers, in the tenth [lunar] month a child was born. The child was shown to an astrologer who said that although the signs were auspicious, he would not live more than seven days. The parents asked him if there was anything that would help and were told that if they invited one hundred brahmins to teach religion, the child would live for seven months; if they invited one hundred [Buddhist] monks to teach religion, he would be able to live for seven years. Beyond this there was nothing they could do. This was done and as the seventh year approached, the father and mother could not bear to see their child's corpse and so sent him to wander, accompanied by a servant.

Eventually, they arrived before the doors of glorious Nālandā [monastery]. There the child recited hymns from the *Sāma Veda* that were heard by the great brahmin Saraha, who was living there. He was taken inside where he explained his situation. The master [Saraha] said that if he were able to go forth [from the household life, that is, become a monk] there was a means for prolonging his life. Thus, he became a monk. He was given instruction concerning the protector Amitāyus [the Buddha of long life] and, having practiced, became free from the Lord of Death.

There [at Nālandā] he heard many instructions on Mantra from that same master [Sahara], was ordained by the abbot of Nālandā, Rāhulabhadra, and was known as the monk Śrīmān. (This is in accordance with Bu-dön's *(Bu-ston) History*. A different name for this abbot appears in the statements of some scholars.) Acting as the steward of Nālandā's spiritual community *(saṃgha, dge 'dun),* he transmuted [iron into] gold and relieved the misery of thc spiritual community. Shortly thereafter, a monk named Śaṃkara wrote a text called *Ornament of Reasoning (Nyāyālaṃkāra)* of twelve hundred thousand stanzas[3] refuting everyone, but this master defeated him.

When he was teaching the doctrine, two children came to listen. Because he had seen them go under the ground, he asked them who they were. They replied that they were *nāgas*. The master asked them to bring him some *yakṣa* clay [which is apparently ideal for building temples and *stūpas*], and they reported his request to the king of the *nāgas*. The king replied that if he would come [to the land of the *nāgas*], he would offer [him the clay]. Thus, knowing that it would be useful, he went to the land of the *nāgas*. He taught the doctrine to many *nāgas* and brought much *nāga* clay and the *Perfection of Wisdom in One Hundred Thousand Stanzas (Śatasāhasrikāprajñāpāramitāsūtra)* and so forth to the world of humans. Therefore, he is renowned as Nāgārjuna.

He benefited many beings in such countries as Puṇḍravardhana and Paṭavesa. He also went to the northern continent of Kuru where he brought limitless benefits to transmigrators through performing miracles, teaching the doctrine, and so forth. He also erected many stupas and temples. [In Bodhgayā] he encircled the vajra seat with a railing having a latticework of vajras and also established and erected the glorious Dhyānakaṭaka *stūpa*.[4] Through the imprint of such activities he gave inconceivable aid to the teaching. In particular, he completely restored the declined teaching of the Mahāyāna and spread the teaching of the Conqueror Buddha with a kindness comparable to that of the Conqueror himself.

Some Chinese histories that were translated from an Indian language explain that this master also brought the *Garland Sutra (Avataṃsakasūtra)* from the land of the *nāgas*. Since Indian texts and ancient Tibetan treatises refer to [his bringing] "the *Perfection of Wisdom in One Hundred Thousand Stanzas* and so forth," it is clear that the Mahāyāna sutras that this master brought from the land of the *nāgas* were not confined to the Perfection of Wisdom class.

Although there are many different modes of explanation concerning how long he lived in the world of humans, [the explanation] that he lived for six hundred years accords with the scriptural prophecies. It is also taken to be the correct position by the omniscient Bu-dön and the omniscient Tsong-kha-pa.

It is explained that this great master made great proclamations of the doctrine three times, but a clear explanation of what the three great proclamations of the doctrine were does not appear in the early texts nor in the statements of Tsong-kha-pa and his spiritual sons. Some scholars of another sect explain that the first proclamation of doctrine refers to his defeat of some Hearer *(śrāvaka, nyan thos)* sectarians, such as the monk Śaṃkara; that the second proclamation refers to his composition of treatises that teach the profound emptiness, such as the Six Collections of Reasoning; and that the third proclamation of doctrine refers to such texts as the *Praise of the Sphere of Reality (Dharmadhātustrota)* which, relying on sutras such as the *Great Drum*, teach that a permanent sphere of reality *(dharmadhātu, chos dbyings)* — the Sugata essence *(sugatagarbha, bder gshegs snying po)* — pervades all sentient beings. This explanation [of the three proclamations of doctrine] appears to be based on several statements in the *Great Cloud* and the *Great Drum* sutras. The excellent venerable Jam-yang-shay-bay-dor-jay *('Jam-dbyangs-bzhad-pa'i-rdo-rje)* takes this mode [of explanation] to be the correct position and explains that although the last two proclamations of doctrine accord in being topics of the middle wheel [of doctrine, that of the Perfection of Wisdom sutras], the third proclamation is distinguished from the second by the fact that the third proclamation extensively teaches that the Buddha is permanent in the sense of his continuum [lasting forever] and that, in fact, he did not pass into nirvana.

This great being wrote many treatises setting forth the common and uncommon sciences. There are Tibetan translations of medical treatises such as the *Hundred Applications (Yogaśataka)* and treatises on political ethics *(nītiśāstra): Drop for Supporting the People (Janapoṣaṇabindu)* and the *Hundred Wisdoms (Prajñāśataka)*. In addition, there are works on the interpretation of omens, the preparation of incense, alchemy, etc. Regarding the Buddhist sciences, there are many commentaries on sutras, such as the *Rice Seedling Sutra (Śālistambusūtra)* and the *Sutra on Dependent Arising (Pratītyasamutpādasūtra)*. In particular, there is the *Compendium of Sutra (Sūtrasamuccaya)* which proves through scripture the profound path of the middle way — the final definitive meaning. For the proof [of the middle way] through reasoning, there are six works: the *Treatise on the Middle Way (Madhyamakaśāstra)*, the *Seventy Stanzas on Emptiness (Śūnyatāsaptatikārikā)*, the *Refutation of Objections (Vigrahavyāvartanīkārikā)*, the *Sixty Stanzas of Reasoning (Yuktiṣaṣṭikākārikā)*, the *Treatise Called "The Finely Woven" (Vaidalyasūtranāma)* and the *Precious Garland of Advice for the King (Rājaparikathāratnāvalī)*.

Although it is renowned that there were eight commentaries to the *Treatise on the Middle Way* in India, [only] four of them were translated into Tibetan: the *Akutobhayā (Mūlamadhyamakavṛtti-akutobhayā)*[5], the *Commentary by Buddhapālita (Buddhapālitamūlamadhyamakavṛtti)*, Bhāvaviveka's commentary *Lamp for (Nāgārjuna's) "Wisdom" (Prajñāpradīpamūlamadhyamakavṛtti)*, and the glorious Candrakīrti's commentary *Clear Words (Mūlamadhyamakavṛttiprasannapadā)*. In addition, there is the work by Avalokitavrata *(Prajñāpradīpaṭīkā)*, which is an explanatory commentary to Bhāvaviveka's *Lamp for (Nāgārjuna's) "Wisdom"*. The contention that the *Akutobhayā* is an autocommentary [by Nāgārjuna] is not correct according to the foremost great being Tsong-kha-pa.

There are autocommentaries to the *Seventy Stanzas on Emptiness*, the *Refutation of Objections*, and the *Treatise Called "The Finely Woven"*. Candrakīrti wrote a commentary to the *Sixty Stanzas on Reasoning (Yuktiṣaṣṭikavṛtti)* and paṇḍita Parahitabhadra wrote a commentary to the *Seventy Stanzas on Emptiness (Śūnyatāsaptativṛtti)*.[6] It was asserted by many in the past that the *Essay on the Mind of Enlightenment (Bodhicittavivaraṇa)* written by this great master [Nāgārjuna] is instructions on the perfections, but Tsong-kha-pa and his [spiritual] sons assert that it is a supplement to the text of the *Guhyasamāja Tantra (Guhyasamājatantra)*. [He composed] many texts on Secret Mantra such as the *Five Stages (Pañcakrama)*, but I will not elaborate on them here.

With respect to the followers of this great being, the master Āryadeva wrote several short works on Mādhyamika, such as the *Compendium on the Essence of Exalted Wisdom (Jñānagarbhasamuccaya)*, the *Establishment of the Reasoning and Logic Refuting Error (Skhalitapramathanayuktihetusiddhi)*, and the *Length of a Forearm (Hastavālaprakaraṇakārikā)*. However, his *Treatise of Four Hundred Stanzas on the Yogic Deeds of Bodhisattvas (Bodhisattvayogacaryācatuḥśatakaśāstrakārikā)* has all the topics. There is also a commentary to this by the glorious Candrakīrti *(Bodhisattvayogacaryācatuḥśatakaṭīkā)*.

Buddhapālita's commentary on the *Treatise on the Middle Way* has already been mentioned. Although he is known to have written many treatises, others do not appear in Tibetan translation.

The two independent works by Bhāvaviveka [in the sense that they are not commentaries on Nāgārjuna] are the *Essence of the Middle Way (Madhyamakahṛdaya)* and its autocommentary, the *Blaze of Reasoning (Tarkajvālā)*. Many specifics of non-Buddhist and Buddhist tenets appear in these texts, and the essential points of Mādhyamika view, meditation, and behavior are given at length. For this reason, the incomparable great master Atīśa lectured on the *Blaze of Reasoning* on many occasions in India and Tibet. The *Precious Lamp for the Middle Way (Madhyamakaratnapradīpa)* was written by one known as Bhāvaviveka the Lesser and is not a work by this master.

The great master Candrakīrti's independent work, the *Supplement to the Middle Way (Madhyamakāvatāra)* together with its autocommentary are very famous as excellent good explanations. The master Jñānagarbha wrote the *Discrimination of the Two Truths (Satyadvayavibhaṅga)* with an autocommentary; the explanatory commentary *(Satyadvayavibhaṅgapañjikā)* attributed to Śāntarakṣita is a case of someone borrowing his name [and is not by the Yogācāra-Svātantrika Śāntarakṣita].

The master Śāntarakṣita wrote the *Ornament for the Middle Way (Madhyamakālaṃkāra)* and its autocommentary. With reference to this, that which is known as the autocommentary is a composition of alternating poetry and prose and is the actual treatise — the *Ornament for the Middle Way*. That which is known as the root text is the poetry within that set apart; it is not a case of two treatises, with the root text written earlier and the commentary added later. This is the position of the foremost omniscient being Tsong-kha-pa. The *Commentary on the Difficult Points of the "Ornament for the Middle Way" (Madhyamakālaṃkārapañjikā)* which is attributed to Kamalaśīla is a fabrication according to Kay-drup-jay *(mKhas-grub-rje)*. There are several mistakes in the *Commmentary on the Difficult Points;* however, since the master Dharmamitra holds that Kamalaśīla is the author, it must be considered whether it was written at a time when the master's mind had not yet matured. This point is made by the foremost precious Tsong-kha-pa in his *Notes on the Ornament for the Middle Way (dbU ma rgyan zin bris)*. The master Dharmamitra wrote an explanatory commentarry to the *Ornament for the Middle Way (Madhyamakālaṃkāraṭīkā)*.

The master Kamalaśīla wrote the *Illumination of the Middle Way (Madhyamakāloka)* in which he very clearly sets forth the uncommon systems of the great charioteers of Mādhyamika and Cittamātra. His points of reasoning are very subtle, and the foremost great being Tsong-kha-pa valued them highly. Śāntarakṣita's *Ornament for the Middle Way*, Jñānagarbha's *Differentiation of the Two Truths of the Mādhyamika*, and Kamalaśīla's *Illumination of the Middle Way* are renowned as the three books illuminating Svātantrika *(rang rgyud shar gsum)*.

In addition, there are many explanations of reasonings delineating the [Mādhyamika] view scattered in Mantra treatises written by these masters, but I will not mention them here.

The great master Śāntideva's *Compendium of Trainings (Śikṣāsamuccaya)* and *Engaging in the Bodhisattva Deeds (Bodhisattvacaryāvatāra)* are superior works of Mādhyamika. The texts of the masters Śūra [Aśvaghoṣa], Nāgabodhi, Āryavimuktisena, Haribhara, Buddhajñānapāda, and Abhayākāragupta are also included in the Mādhyamika class. Most of the accomplished great beings, such as the lord of adepts Lūhipāda, Ghaṇḍāpāda, Kṛṣṇacārin, Nāropa, and the lord Maitrīpāda are only followers of the master, the Superior Nāgārjuna. I will explain briefly at a later point which of them are Prāsaṅgikas and which are Svātantrikas. This has been brief; it can be known in its entirety from [consulting] other [texts].

2 *Mādhyamika Schools in India*

The presentation of the tenets that appear in those texts has four parts: the etymology, divisions, definition, and assertions of the Mādhyamikas.

ETYMOLOGY OF MĀDHYAMIKA

The master Bhāvaviveka says, "It is the middle *(madhya, dbu ma)* because it is similar to a center that is free from two extremes. It is the very center or *madhyama,* [the *ma* being] a *tadhita* affix [which indicates just] that meaning." Thus, the very center that is free from the extremes of existence and non-existence is the middle. And because they express that [middle way], a treatise on the middle way, tenets of the middle way, and persons who propound the tenets of the middle way acquire the name "Madhyamaka." That same master says, "Because of teaching and proclaiming the path of the middle way, '*ka*' [is added]. In terms [of *ka* being] the verbal root [for 'proclaiming'], a treatise or one who has the name 'Madhyamaka' is a Madhyamaka. Or again, because of being expressed by the name 'ka' it is called Madhyamaka, that is, a tenet of the Madhyamaka."[1]

DIVISIONS OF MĀDHYAMIKA

This section has two parts, the actual divisions and, ancillarily, the history.

Actual Divisions

Among the students of the glorious Nāgārjuna, Āryadeva is held to be valid like the master himself by the others, such as Buddhapālita. Therefore, earlier scholars gave the designation "Mādhyamikas of the Model Texts" to both the father [Nāgārjuna] and the [spiritual] son [Āryadeva], and "Partisan Mādhyamikas" to the others. Tsong-kha-pa and his spiritual sons also assert that this is correct.

The reason for designating them as Models and Partisans is this: although the final thought of the father and son rests in the Prāsaṅgika system, in terms of what is taught in their texts, there is no clearly delineated presentation of whether they assert that things conventionally exist by way of their own character *(svalakṣaṇa, rang gi mtshan nyid)*, whether they assert the existence of external objects, whether it is possible to generate an inferential consciousness in another party from the viewpoint of what is merely renowned to others, and so forth. Therefore, since [their texts] remain as a generality [common] to both the Prāsaṅgika and Svātantrika factions, they are called "Models." Although a brief refutation of Cittamātra appears in Nāgārjuna's *Essay on the Mind of Enlightenment*, there is no detailed explanation of whether or not he asserts external objects in his own system.

The great master Buddhapālita, in his *Buddhapālita, Commentary on the "Treatise on the Middle Way"* stated many consequences *(prasaṅga, thal 'gyur)* in commenting on the meaning of the reasonings set forth in the *Treatise on the Middle Way* and did not use autonomous reasons *(*svatantrahetu, rang rgyud kyi gtan tshigs)*. After that, the master Bhāvaviveka found many faults with Buddhapālita's commentary and explained many reasons why autonomous reasons must be stated. Thus, he founded the system of commenting [on the thought of Nāgārjuna] as Svātantrika. Later the glorious Candrakīrti explained that the faults [ascribed] to Buddhapālita did not apply, did much damage to the assertion of autonomous signs, and put forth many proofs of the unsuitability of asserting [autonomous reasons], thus founding the system of commenting on the thought of the Superior Nāgārjuna as Prāsaṅgika-Mādhyamika. Therefore, these [masters — Buddhapālita, Bhāvaviveka, and Candrakīrti] — are known as Partisan Mādhyamikas.

Kay-drup-jay's *Thousand Doses, Opening the Eyes of the Fortunate (sTong thun skal bsang mig 'byed)*[2] says, "Later, the master Buddhapālita wrote a commentary on the *Treatise on the Middle Way* which interprets the thought of the Superior father [Nāgārjuna] and his [spiritual] son [Āryadeva] in the manner of consequences *(prasaṅga, thal 'gyur).*" Some scholars of our own [Ge-luk] sect say that this means that Buddhapālita is the founder of Prāsaṅgika. However, this is not the opinion of the foremost great being Tsong-kha-pa. Although Buddhapālita did not use autonomous reasons and commented on the meaning of the text only through consequences, this alone is not sufficient to make him the founder of Prāsaṅgika. For in order to be designated as the founder of this or that system, one must clearly delineate proofs for the correctness of that system and [prove] why interpretation in any other way is unsuitable. For at the point of identifying founders in general, Tsong-kha-pa's *Essence of the Good Explanations (Legs bshad snying po)* says:

> One must seek out the thought of the scriptures of definitive meaning *(nītārtha, nges don)*, following one who has delineated their meaning well with reasoning damaging interpretation in any other way and reasoning proving that that meaning is certain, it being impossible to be interpreted otherwise.[3]

That mode [of delineating a distinct system] is similar here as well. Similarly, Gyel-tsap's *(rGyal-tshab-dar-ma-rin-chen) Heart Ornament, An Explanation of the Root Text and Commentary of the "Ornament for Clear Realizations" (mNgon rtogs pa'i rgyan gyi rtsa ba 'grel pa dang bcas pa'i rnam bshad snying po'i rgyan)*[4] and Kay-drup's *Thousand Doses* explain the meaning of founding a system in that [same] way, but fearing excessive length I will not write [about their explanations]. If the meaning of founding a system is identified in this way, it is easy to understand that the venerable Maitreya should not be designated as the founder of the Mādhyamika, and that only the protector Nāgārjuna is the founder of Mādhyamika.

Furthermore, if Buddhapālita were the founder of Prāsaṅgika, there would be no reason whatsoever for Bhāvaviveka's assertion that there is no difference between himself and Buddhapālita in terms of their being Svātantrikas. If it asked how it is evident that Bhāvaviveka asserted this, the foremost great being Tsong-kha-pa clearly speaks to this in his *Essence of the Good Explanations:*

> Even Bhāvaviveka did not think that there was disagreement between Buddhapālita and himself regarding the

> assertion or non-assertion of autonomous [syllogisms] *(svatantraprayoga, rang rgyud kyi sbyor ba);* [Buddhapālita's] system appears to [Bhāvaviveka] as one in which the use of autonomous syllogisms is unavoidable. Consequently, he did not assert that there is a difference between himself and Buddhapālita regarding the object of negation *(pratiṣedhya, dgag bya)* in the inherent existence *(svabhāva, rang bzhin)* of phenomena and persons.[5]

Thus, what could one say that would be more senseless than that the master Bhāvaviveka asserted that the founder of Prāsaṅgika was a Svātantrika!

That the founder of Prāsaṅgika is the glorious Candrakīrti is stated very clearly by the foremost great being Tsong-kha-pa:

> In the *Clear Words* [Candrakīrti] showed that Buddhapālita did not assert autonomous syllogisms and set forth many proofs that it is unsuitable for a Mādhyamika to use autonomous syllogisms and he did much damage to the opposite position, thereby founding [Prāsaṅgika].[6]

With respect to this, some have said that the meaning of this passage is that Candrakīrti demonstrated the damage [to the opposite position], but Buddhapālita is the founder. It is easy for those with intelligence to understand that this is totally meaningless.

Question: Then what is the meaning of the statement in Kay-drup's *Thousand Doses* that Buddhapālita wrote a commentary on the *Treatise on the Middle Way* that comments on the thought of the Superior [Nāgārjuna] in the manner of consequences?

Answer: As was explained before, this refers to his not using autonomous reasons when explaining the meaning of the text, but rather commenting on the meaning of the text only through consequences. [Kay-drup] is not explaining that [Buddhapālita] is the founder of Prāsaṅgika.

The king Indrabhuti and the great brahmin Saraha were holders of the Mādhyamika view who came before Nāgārjuna, and even though they composed texts that set forth the final view, they are not designated as the founders of Mādhyamika. Also, prior to Bhāvaviveka there was the master Devaśarman who held the Sautrāntika-Svātantrika-Mādhyamika view, and prior to the master Śāntarakṣita there were masters who held the Yogācāra-Svātantrika-Mādhyamika view, such as Āryavimuktisena, who, even though they wrote texts [on the view], are not designated as the founders of those systems. Please think well about the reason for this.

The great scholar and adept Jam-yang-shay-ba put forth an explanation that accords with the earlier statements [about Buddhapālita being the founder] in some places, but it is certain that in his own mind he held that just Candrakīrti is the founder of Prāsaṅgika. The root text of his *Tenets (Grub mtha' chen mo)* says, "Candrakīrti refuted [Bhāvaviveka] well and established [the Prāsaṅgika system] as uncommon"[7]; the commentary explains that only the glorious Candrakīrti clearly distinguished the uncommon Prāsaṅgika system.[8]

The glorious Śūra, Nāgabodhi, and so forth are also clearly Prāsaṅgika-Mādhyamikas as can be known through Śūra's *Cultivation of the Ultimate Mind of Enlightenment (Paramārthabodhicittabhāvanākramavarnasaṃgraha)* and Nāgabodhi's *Ordered Stages of the Means of Achieving Guhyasamāja (Samājasādhanavyavasthāli)*, and so forth. The foremost great being Tsong-kha-pa says that the great Child of the Conqueror, Śāntideva, accords with the glorious Candrakīrti. That the peerless great elder Atīśa is a Prāsaṅgika-Mādhyamika can be known from the root text and commentary of his *Lamp for the Path to Enlightenment (Bodhipathapradīpa)* and the root text and commentary of his *Quintessential Instructions on the Middle Way (Madhyamakopadeśa)*, and [the fact that he is a Prāsaṅgika] is explained more than once by Tsong-kha-pa and his sons.

The divisions of Mādhyamika are definitely two from the point of view of their assertions on conventionalities — those who assert and do not assert external objects. The former are Bhāvaviveka and the glorious Candrakīrti together with their followers. The latter are Śāntarakṣita, his [spiritual] son [Kamalaśīla], and so forth. If [Mādhyamika] is divided from the viewpoint of how the view ascertaining the ultimate — emptiness — is generated in one's continuum, [the divisions] are definitely two — Svātantrika and Prāsaṅgika. Svātantrika has two divisions, Sautrāntika-Svātantrika-Mādhyamika and Yogācāra-Svātantrika-Mādhyamika. The former [includes] the father Bhāvaviveka and his [spiritual] sons, and the latter, the father Śāntarakṣita and his [spiritual] sons. The difference between Prāsaṅgika and Svātantrika will be explained later.

Some earlier Tibetan scholars designated two Mādhyamikas: those who propound an establishment of illusion through a reasoning consciousness *(māyopamādvayavādin, sgyu ma rigs grub pa)*, who assert that a composite of appearance and emptiness is an ultimate truth and the proponents of thorough non-abiding *(apratiṣṭhānayādin, rab tu mi gnas par smra ba)* who assert that the mere elimination of elaborations with respect to appearance is an ultimate truth. The great translator Lo-den-shay-rap of Ngok *(rNgog bLo-ldan-shes-rab)* refutes this in his letter *Drop of Ambrosia (bDud rtsi'i thigs pa)*, saying that the position that [Mādhyamika] is twofold from the point of view of assertions on the ultimate is an obscured presentation causing amazement. The foremost great being Tsong-kha-pa also says, "This statement by the great translator from Ngok is very good because there is no Mādhyamika whatsoever who asserts that merely the object comprehended by an inferential reasoning consciousness is an ultimate truth." However, the foremost great being is explaining that it is incorrect to assert the meaning of propounding a reasoned establishment of illusion in that way; he is not asserting that the mere designations "reasoned establishment of illusion" and "thoroughly non-abiding" are incorrect for Mādhyamika, because such designations are clearly used by the master Śūra in his letter *Cultivation of the Ultimate Mind of Enlightenment*. This was stated by the great scholar and adept Nor-sang-gya-tso *(Nor-bsang-rgya-mtsho)* and I think that it is probably good. There are many reasons for these [points] yet to be explained but I will leave [the topic] for the time being.

3 History of Mādhyamika in Tibet

Question: In the Snowy Land [of Tibet] are these great path systems of the chariots of Mādhyamika and Cittamātra confined to just those divisions explained above or are there many divisions other than those? The first option cannot be correct because in the Land of Snow Mountains there are many names of schools of tenets that were not mentioned here. The second option is not correct because if [the Tibetan tenet systems] were explained in a manner other than these [Indian systems], it would not be suitable for them to be proponents of Mahāyāna tenets; yet, if they are not explained in some other manner, the use of other names for these tenet systems would be meaningless.

Answer: I will explain this briefly. The various names of schools of tenets in Tibet appear to have been designated by way of geographic area or the name of a master, as was the case with the eighteen Vaibhāṣika subschools. Also, some received certain instructions from an Indian scholar-adept *(paṇḍitasiddha, pan grub)* and primarily practiced those [instructions], due to which they were designated as separate schools with the names of those systems of instruction. Therefore, it does not seem certain that the names of the schools were designated only through philosophical view, as was the case with the schools of Mahāyāna tenets in the Land of Superiors [India]. For example, there are many cases of designating a name from the viewpoint of geographic area, such as Sa-gya-ba *(Sa-skya-pa)* and Dri-gung-ba *('Bri-gung-pa)*, from the viewpoint of a master, such as Karma-ba *(Karma-pa)*, and from the viewpoint of a system of instruction, such as the Great Completion *(rDzogs-chen-pa)* and the Great Seal *(Phyag-chen-pa, mahamūdrika)*.

However, this is an occasion for analyzing the differences in view only. That being the case, with regard to the time of the earlier dissemination of the doctrine in Tibet, the greatest propagation of the complete explanation and achievement of the Conqueror's entire system occurred around the time of the mighty god [King] Tri-song-day-dzen (*Khri-srong-lde-bṭsan*, reigned 755-797). At that time many great Indian scholars and adepts, such as the great master Padmasambhava, the mantra-bearer Dharmakīrti, Vimalamitra, and Buddhaguhya, came [to Tibet]. However, the one who bore the burden of explaining the excellent doctrine, from monastic discipline *(vinaya, 'dul ba)* through Mādhyamika, and who spread the system of lecturing on and listening to the doctrine was the great master Śāntarakṣita. This appears clearly in the ancient records.

The great master Padmasambhava subdued the gods and demons of Tibet and gave initiation and instruction in Secret Mantra to a small group, which included the king and his children, and it appears that Dharmakīrti also bestowed initiation in the Vajradhātu mandala of Yoga [Tantra]. However, accounts do not appear of their doing such things as explaining the great philosophical texts, and since they were very strict at that time regarding the Mantra class, it appears that they did not disseminate Secret Mantra widely.

Regarding view and behavior, it is explained [in the early histories] that by order of the king a law was proclaimed that in view and practice one must act in accordance with the system of the Bodhisattva Abbot [Śāntarakṣita]. Thus, since it is indisputable that the abbot Śāntarakṣita was a great charioteer following the Superior Nāgārjuna, the view at that time was none other than that of Nāgārjuna's system. In *Purifying Forgetfulness of the View (lTa ba'i brjed byang)* by the great translator Ye-shay-day *(Ye-shes-sde)*, who was a student of both the master [Padmasambhava] and the abbot [Śāntarakṣita], the system of Nāgārjuna is mainly followed, and in that [text the view] also appears to accord with the Yogācāra-Svātantrika-Mādhyamika system.

Later, after the master [Padmasambhava] had left and the great abbot [Śāntarakṣita] had passed away, a Chinese abbot named Hva-shang Mahāyāna spread his own system, composing many treatises that primarily taught the view of not applying the mind to anything.

Consequently, many of the people of Tibet, such as Queen Dro-sang-jang-chup (*'Bro-bzang-byang-chub*), entered his religious system. The king then saw that this system, which deprecated the factor of method (*upāya, thabs*), was not a pure religious system because it did not accord with the system of the former abbot [Śāntarakṣita] and that it was a cause of indolence in the Tibetan people in the practice of virtue. In accordance with the last will of the abbot, he invited the great master Kamalaśīla, who defeated the Chinese abbot well with scripture and reasoning. Kamalaśīla composed many treatises, such as the three *Stages of Meditation in Mādhyamika (Bhāvanākrama)* which praise analytical wisdom, and he spread the stainless system of lecturing and listening. At this time it also appears that the king proclaimed that thenceforth the view must accord with the system of the master Nāgārjuna and that views which accorded with the system of Hva-shang would be eliminated through punishment.

Therefore, although in the earlier dissemination of the teaching, a few *paṇḍitas* who bore the Cittamātra system came [to Tibet], the main system was that of Śāntarakṣita and Kamalaśīla, and thus it appears that only the Svātantrika-Mādhyamika view was widespread.

It is explained [in the histories] that in the later dissemination of the teaching, the great translator Rin-chen-sang-bo (*Rin-chen-bzang-po*, 958-1055) relied on many great scholars and adepts, studied the doctrines of Mantra and philosophy a great deal, and translated much of the word [of Buddha] as well as treatises (*śāstra, bstan bcos*). He delineated [the doctrine] through hearing and explanation, and his view was that of a Thoroughly Non-Abiding Mādhyamika. This great translator subdued [the demon] *nāga* Gar-gyal (*sKar-rgyal*), put an end to mistaken Mantra practices, and with great kindness filled the people of the snowy mountains with the pure teaching.

The divine lamas Ye-shay-ö (*Ye-shes-'od*) and Jang-chup-ö (*Byang-chub-'od*) could not tolerate the pollution of the teaching by coarse Tibetan practitioners of Mantra and invited the glorious, incomparable, great elder Dīpaṃkara Śrījñāna [Atīśa] (982-1054).[1] Because they entreated him to purify the teaching, he wrote texts such as the *Lamp for the Path to Enlightenment (Bodhipathapradīpa)* and spread the teaching of the Conqueror with a kindness comparable to that of the Conqueror himself. This incomparable, great elder held the view of the system of the Prāsaṅgika-Mādhyamika:

Through whom should one realize emptiness?
Candrakīrti, Nāgārjuna's student,
Prophesied by the Tathāgata,
And who saw the true reality.
One should realize the true reality
From instructions transmitted from him.[2]

Thus, he held the system of Candrakīrti to be chief.

When the Foremost Elder [Atīśa] came to Tibet, the Tibetan teachers offered him their own understanding of the view, but the Elder was not pleased and said, "No matter what your view is, cultivate the altruistic aspiration to enlightenment *(bodhicitta, byang chub kyi sems).*" Later, the Elder was pleased when Drom-dön *('Brom-ston,* 1005-1064) presented his realization of the view of the master Candrakīrti to him. He joined his hands at his heart and said, "Amazing! Now, to the east of India, only this view is to be held."

Thus, in the expositions of the stages of the path and in the statements of those renowned as the three brothers — the spiritual friend Bo-do-wa *(Po-to-ba)* and so forth [Jen-nga-ba *(sPyan-lnga-pa)* and Pu-chung-wa *(Phu-chung-ba)*] — which appear in the final, pure biographies of the Ga-dam-bas *(bKa'-gdams-pa)* stemming from the Great Elder, the Mādhyamika view is for the most part in accord with the system of Candrakīrti.

Regarding the great translator from Ngok [Lo-den-shay-rap] and his spiritual sons, despite the fact that many citations from the works of Bhāvaviveka and Candrakīrti are found [in their writings], it appears that their mode of sustaining the view [in meditation] accords for the most part with that of Śāntarakṣita and his [spiritual] son [Kamalaśīla].

The development of the view in several mind-training texts deriving from Dharmakīrti of Suvarnadvīpa [present-day Sumatra] appears to accord with the system of the False Aspectarian *(alīkākāravāda, rnam rdzun pa)* Cittamātrins.[3] However, it was rare for any of the followers to know how to explain the Indian texts without mixing their meaning [with that of other systems].

The originator of the view known as Jo-mo-nang-ba *(Jo-mo-nang-pa)* is renowned to be the great adept Yu-mo *(Yu-mo)* who was born in the vicinity of Gang-day-say *(Gangs-te-se),* who had a little meditative stabilization *(samādhi, ding nge 'dzin)* and clairvoyance *(abhijñā, mngon shes),* and who wrote some textbooks on Kālacakra. The disseminator of the system was the omniscient Shay-rap-gyal-tshen

(Shes-rab-rgyal-mtshan) of Dol-bo *(Dol-po);* later there arose many who held the lineage, such as Jo-nang Gun-ga-dröl-chok *(Jo-nang Kun-dga'-grol-mchog,* 1495-1566). With regard to the system's view, they assert that the ultimate truth is positive, permanent, and independent, and they assert that an element *(dhātu),* which is the Sugata-essence [Buddha nature] that is permanent, stable, eternal, and adorned with the thirty-two marks, naturally exists in the continua of all sentient beings. This [assertion] stands outside the system of all the Mādhyamika and Cittamātra charioteers and is refuted with hundreds of scriptures and reasonings by the preeminent scholars of the Snowy Land, such as Rin-chen-dok *(Rin-chen-tog)* of Yar-drok *(Yar-'brog),* the foremost Ren-da-wa *(Red-mda'-ba,* 1349-1412), and the foremost great being Tsong-kha-pa and his spiritual sons.

The great, omniscient being of the age of disputation, the all-knowing Bu-dön *(Bu-ston,* 1290-1364) was an unrivalled scholar who studied all of the systems of tenets; the view as explained in his own system accords greatly with the Ga-dam-bas, and he takes the texts of Candrakīrti to be chief.

Also, at an earlier time, the great translator Ba-tsap-nyi-ma-drak *(Pa-tshab-nyi-ma-grags,* born 1055) studied in Kashmir for twenty-three years and invited the great *paṇḍiṭa* Kanakavarman to Tibet. He translated many Mādhyamika treatises and listened and lectured. Many students came [to study with him], such as those renowned as the four sons of Ba-tsap. It appears that they spread the explanation of the Mādhyamika system of the master Candrakīrti more widely in Tibet than he [Ba-tsap] did.

Gö-rin-bo-chay Kuk-ba-hlay-dzay *('Gos-rin-po-che Khug-pa-lhas-btsas)* went to India twelve times, met with seventy-two scholar-adepts, and appears to have given many explanations of tantras. He also held the Mādhyamika view to be chief, but from his statements it is difficult to determine whether he was Prāsaṅgika or Svātantrika. Since many great translators, such as the translator Kay-gay-kor-lo-drak *(Khe-gad-'khor-lo-grags)* appear to have been students of the great scholar Abhayākaragupta (c. 1100), one wonders whether they relied on him for their view; there does not appear to be a clear explanation. Similarly, the majority of the great translators, such as the three, Ra *(Rva Do-rje-grags),* Dro *('Bro Shes-rab-grags),* and Nyen *(gNyan Dar-ma-grags),* appear only to have declared themselves to be Mādhyamikas; it seems difficult to decide such things as whether they were Prāsaṅgikas or Svātantrikas.

Drok-mi Shakya-ye-shay (*'Brok-mi Shakya-ye-shes*, 992-1072) went to India and heard the three Hevajra tantras together with their branches, etc., from the master Vīravajra, an actual student of the master called Durjayacandra who held the lineage of Ḍombiheruka, student of the master Virūpa. He stayed in India for twelve years. Returning to Tibet, he disseminated Mantra doctrines. Later, he met the *paṇḍiṭa* Gayādhara and studied the Mother Tantra cycles. Many Sa-gya doctrines derive from him. The view of their system of path and fruition *(lam 'bras)* is explained as being that of the great Mādhyamika [Prāsaṅgika], but their manner of identifying the view appears to be slightly different from that of other systems in that it is related to Mantra precepts; it is renowned as the view of the union of manifestation and emptiness. Nonetheless, since it presents the thought of the great adept Virūpa, it does not pass beyond Prāsaṅgika, although the followers' mode of explanation is not unequivocal.

Regarding the great *paṇḍiṭa*, skilled in the five sciences, Jam-yang-gun-ga-gyel-tsen (*'Jam-dbyangs-kun-dga'-rgyal-mtshan*, 1182-1251) [known as Sa-gya Paṇḍiṭa], his view [when explaining] the Mantra class [of texts] appears to be just that [of the union of manifestation and emptiness], and his explanations of the view for the Sutra class greatly praise the Thoroughly Non-Abiding Mādhyamika. A later Sa-gya, the great venerable Ren-da-wa *(Red-mda'-ba)*, who completed the path, gained supreme ascertainment of the system of the honorable Candrakīrti, and his commentary to Candrakīrti's *Supplement (Madhyamakāvatāra)* and instruction manuals on the view accord in essence with the foremost great being Tsong-kha-pa.

The view renowned as the Shi-jay *(Zhi-byed)* system stems from the protector of transmigrators, Paramapitṛbuddha. This Paramapitṛbuddha is generally renowned as having been an actual student of the protector Nāgārjuna, and in the history surrounding that teaching, it is explained that Parama listened to the doctrine relying on eighty male and female adepts [as teachers]. When they enumerate the lamas of their lineage, they begin with the master Nāgārjuna and go through the students of Nāropa and Maitripāda. Although some widely renowned scholars who wrote histories of doctrine give accounts which agree with the earlier histories, it seems difficult to be certain.

Some explain that Parama and the great Kashmiri paṇḍiṭa Śākya-śrī were the same person, but no reasons for this are evident. Be that as it may, it is probably true that he was an actual student of the protector Nāgārjuna because this appears to accord with several Chinese histories. The source for the Shi-jay system's view is the sutras of the Perfection of Wisdom class, and in their essays of instructions, Nāgārjuna is held to be valid. In addition, the statements of Ma-ji-lap-drön *(Ma-cig-lab-sgron)* are in great agreement with the Prāsaṅgika position, although since then, the bearers of the instructions seem to a large extent to be confusing fish and turnips.

The great bearer of the practice lineage in the Snowy Range, Mar-ba-chö-gyi-lo-drö of Hlo-drak (*Lho-brag Mar-pa-chos-kyi-blo-gros*, 1012-1096) went to India three times and Nepal four times. He met with one hundred and eight gurus who were scholars and adepts, such as the great *paṇḍiṭa* Nāropa, the lord Maitripāda, the glorious Jñānagarbha, and the great adept Śāntibhadra. He studied in detail the explanation, instructions, and practices of the majority of the father and mother [Highest] Yoga Tantras, such as the glorious *Guhyasāmaja*. After his return to Tibet, there were many bearers of the lineage, such as the "four students of the transmission," and since his activities of Secret Mantra were extremely vast, many lineages of his percepts have continued to spread, even to the present. With respect to the view of the Foremost One himself [Mar-ba], there appear to be many lineages of Mādhyamika and Cittamātra instructions, because he listened to many gurus who were scholars and adepts. However, the Foremost One himself says in a song that the teacher who destroyed superimpositions *(āropa, sgro 'dogs)* in the view was just Maitripāda. Also, whenever he explained view, meditation, behavior, or tantra, he took Nāropa and Maitripāda as his principal [sources]. Not only was the lord Maitripāda a Mādhyamika, he took only the system of the glorious Candrakīrti to be chief. He says in his *Ten Stanzas on Suchness (Tattvadaśaka)*:[4]

> Not Aspectarians, not Non-Aspectarians,
> Even Mādhyamikas who are not adorned
> With the guru's speech are only mediocre.

Thus, both True [Aspectarian, *satyākaravāda, rnam bden pa*] and False Aspectarian *(alīkāravāda, rnam 'dzun pa)* Cittamātrins do not realize the meaning of suchness *(tathatā, de kho na nyid)*, and even among Mādhyamikas, those who are not adorned with the quintessential instructions of the guru are said to be mediocre Mādhyamikas. The *paṇḍita* Sahajavajra, an actual student of [Maitripāda] himself, says in a commentary that the instructions of the guru are only the instructions of the glorious Candrakīrti.[5]

The great *paṇḍita* Nāropa also holds only the system of the glorious Candrakīrti because he says in his commentary to the continuation [that is, the eighteenth chapter] of the *Guhyasāmaja Tantra:*

> This commentary on the continuation of the tantra
> Following the *Brilliant Lamp* of Candrakīrti
> Describes Nāgārjuna's quintessential instructions.

And:

> Relying on the stages of instruction
> Of the masters Nāgārjuna, Āryadeva,
> Nāgabodhi, Śākyamitra,
> Candrakīrti, and so forth ...

Also, his description of the view appears to be like that [of Candrakīrti] alone. Therefore, the statement of some earlier and later logicians that Maitripāda was a Cittamātrin because he was a student of Ratnākaraśānti is simply to be discarded; it is like a stone thrown too late.

Thus, the view of the king of adepts Mar-ba is unquestionably that of the Great Mādhyamika — Prāsaṅgika. Nevertheless, in the instructions on the view deriving from Mar-ba, there are systems using terminology that accord with the Cittamātra system as well. However, as was explained before, the foremost Mar-ba had many gurus who were scholars and adepts and also had many instructions transmitted from them. Therefore, it is not necessary that all the instructions deriving from the lama Mar-ba be of the Mādhyamika system.

In the *Hundred Thousand Songs (mGur 'bum)* of the venerable Mi-la-re-ba (*Mi-la-ras-pa*, 1040-1123) as well, the type of statements on the view which appear in the teaching to Tse-ring-ma *(Tshe-ring-ma)* accord with the Prāsaṅgika view.[6] The foremost great being Tsong-kha-pa also said that the meaning of that song accords with Mādhyamika. Furthermore, in some songs the four yogas are identified, and even these can be suitably explained as either [belonging to] the Mādhyamika or Cittamātra view. Since these are not treatises designed as presentations of the general teaching, but are statements of a particular view, meditation, or behavior appropriate for a particular questioner, even someone with dull faculties can understand that it would be meaningless if these [teachers] had to explain everything they knew to that person. So although the terminology of the four yogas comes from the master Ratnākaraśānti's *Ornament of the Cittamātra (Cittamātrālaṃkāra)*,[7] it does not appear that the four yogas of the Ga-gyu *(bKa' rgyud)* have to be those of the Cittamātra system.

The person who widely spread the name "Great Seal" *(Mahāmudrā, Phyag rgya chen po)* in instructions [on the view] was the incomparable Gam-bo-ba (*sGam-po-pa*, 1079-1153). The identification of the view in his statements appears in both the Perfection Vehicle system and Mantra system, and for both he uses the name "instructions on the Great Seal." He wrote treatises which prove, citing many sutra passages, that emptiness is called the Great Seal in the Perfection Vehicle system. Pa-mo-drup-dor-jay-gyel-bo (*Phak-mo-grub-rdo-rje-gyal-po*, 1110-1170) and Dri-kung-gyu-ra-rin-bo-jay (*'Bri-gung-skyu-ra-rin-po-che*, 1143-1217) appear to have been his followers. They also seem to have a system that values dependent arising in the class of appearance and does not discard investigation by the wisdom of individual analysis. However, their collected works are fraught with many contradictory notes added by a variety of wise and unwise students and thus are unreliable.

The term "One Pure Power" *(dKar-po-chig-thub)* was not disseminated widely after Shang-tsel-ba (*Zhang-tshal-pa*, 1123-1194) who wrote a treatise which is concerned mainly with the One Pure Power. It appears that this was the main object refuted by Mañjunātha Sa-gya Paṇḍiṭa.[8] Later, many of our own and other [sects] refuted this position. If Shang-tsel-ba's own assertion rests in the position that the mind is not to be directed to anything, then these refutations are accurate; I do not wish to elaborate on it in detail.

Thus, I have written the foregoing explanations having sought our sources for the individual systems of tenets. Generally speaking, although the Tibetan transltors met with impeccable Indian scholars, it does not seem to be certain that they sought to discover those scholars' assertions on the view. Even [when they] sought to discover [their positions], these scholars and adepts taught an essential point concerning view or meditation that was appropriate for the mind of the questioner; it is doubtful that they explained everything they knew to that person. This is the procedure of the good spiritual guides of the Mahāyāna. They are not like the lecturers of today who, when offered a piece of dried meat, will bore you with all they know.

Therefore, with the exceptions of the Jo-nang system and, later, the system of the view of the translator Dak-tsang Shay-rap-rin-chen (*sTag-tshang Shes-rab-rin-chen*, 1405-?), the instructions on the view of the majority of the early scholars and adepts had some Indian scholar or adept as their source. However, among their followers, some had a little experience but did not know reasoning, others had studied a little but did not differentiate tenet systems, a few wanted to repeat what had been said before but did not even know how to repeat the words, and the majority mixed all the teachings they saw into those of their own system. It would be difficult to express [all the ways that they made mistakes].

The Jo-nang-ba view is one which appeared adventitiously from its own place; it has no source whatsoever in a scholar or adept. Dak-tsang divided [the path] into the three stages of the unanalyzed, the slightly analyzed, and the highly analyzed and then explained a view in which the former states are negated by the latter. [This explanation] is amazing because, instead of another opponent needing to set out contradictions to his system, he himself destroys his own presentation of the two truths. Those who, despite having such a nature, tire themselves trying to contradict the undisputed great charioteers are only objects of the supreme compassion of the excellent.

Also, from [consulting] the ocean-like scriptures of the foremost father Tsong-kha-pa and his [spiritual] sons one can see the many mistakes made regarding the essentials of the view in earlier times, even by those who claimed to be Mādhyamika scholars, such as Tang-sak-ba of Shang *(Zhang Thang-sag-pa)*. The many who claim to be followers of the Great Seal, Amanasikāroddeśa, and Cittapakṣa [?] are only [followers of] the system of the Chinese abbot Hva-shang, which denegrates the factor of method *(upāya, thabs)*. There appear to have been many who denegrated the class of method in all ways, or who said that the class of behavior was necessary but discarded individual analysis when seeking the view, or who said that analysis with wisdom was needed when initially seeking [the view] but discarded analysis when sustaining the actual session, and so forth. None of these pass beyond the system of Hva-shang. Since these wrong views spread widely, they appear to have mingled with the systems explained above.

My brief expression of the different views in the Snowy Land [above] is not motivated by the wish to develop something which is different from others, nor by partisanship, nor from a wish for fame. My intention is to benefit the many wise and unwise [persons] who deprecate things which are not to be deprecated and who stain the stainless texts by mixing together all the terminology of many discordant systems. Specifically, I have set this forth in order to delight greatly those who have authentic faith, induced by the path of reasoning, in this unconfused differentiation of the system of the great charioteers, free from all stains of error, by the foremost lama Tsong-kha-pa and his [spiritual] sons. And [I put this forth] in order to make known to those with good predispositions that the stainless, supreme path is this very system of the foremost second Conqueror, Tsong-kha-pa. Otherwise, what intelligent scholar would take great joy in putting the profound talk about scripture and reasoning in the ears of these transmigrators who [believe that they] have manifested the state of freedom from attachment and who think that the refined gold of good explanations and a pile of glass trinkets of wrong explanations are exactly the same!

Now, I will say this. There was one who completely filled all the regions of the earth with the faultless Conqueror's teaching until the end of time through expanding the force of [his] wish to bear the excellent doctrine of the Conqueror — [that wish being made] in the presence of the Conquerors not one time [but many times] — by proclaiming the great lion's roar of the proper mode of dependent arising, the profound middle path free from all extremes of existence and non-existence, the essence of the teaching. Our excellent leader whose name is difficult to express, the venerable all-knowing one, the glorious Lo-sang-drak-ba *(bLo-bzang-grags-pa)* [known as Tsong-kha-pa] whose banner of fame flies over the three worlds was that very person. Regarding which great charioteer the venerable one [Tsong-kha-pa] himself followed, it appears thus in the statements of the protector [Tsong-kha-pa] himself [from his *Praise of Dependent Arising (rTen 'grel bstod pa)*]:

> The mode of your [the Buddha's] unsurpassed vehicle
> Abandoning the extremes of existence and non-existence

Was explained just as it is in the texts
Of the prophesied Nāgārjuna, a garden of jasmine.

The vast sphere of stainless wisdom is the cause of
Freedom in the sky of scriptures,
Removing the darkness of the heart of extreme conceptions,
Outshining the lustre of the constellations of wrong
propositions.

[The definitive meaning[9]] is illuminated by the rosary of
white light
Of the good explanations of the glorious moon [Candrakīrti].
When, by the kindness of my lama,
I saw this, my mind rested.

As it says, he saw that just the tradition of the glorious protector — the Superior Nāgārjuna — and Candrakīrti was supreme, and he himself illuminated the unmistaken path for the fortunate. Therefore, the intelligent should know that although there are inconceivable common and uncommon biographical facts concerning this venerable great being, from among them all, the chief is this alone: he filled the world with the kindness of the complete fulfillment of the Subduer's precious teaching by ascertaining and teaching to others the meaning of the thought of all the Conqueror's scriptures of sutra and tantra, without even the tiniest error, by way of stainless scripture and reasoning without confusing the distinctions made by the great charioteers.

Thus, from the fine points of the practice of monastic discipline up to the great tenet systems and, in Mantra, from the fine points of rites and practices of mandalas up to the great commentaries on the tantras, this venerable one [Tsong-kha-pa] analyzed and gave certainty to everything with many scriptural citations and reasonings for every subtle point. He was never tainted by the fault of oversimplification or fabrication; he went back to the thought of each of the founding scholars and adepts and, in addition, went back well to the word of the Conqueror. In this way he arranged all of the teachings as causal factors in one person's [path to] becoming completely enlightened so that each one [of the teachings] becomes supportive to another without contradiction. He thereby upheld and spread both the explanation and practice of the teaching.

It is established by stainless reasoning that not only is there no such biography among the prior scholars and adepts of the Snowy Land, but also there is no way that even the biography of Nāgārjuna, for instance, in the Land of Superiors could surpass his. How could there be a chance of this [biography] being similar to the biography of someone which is taken to be authentic merely upon the prophecy of another, "The being who was prophesied by so and so."

More than the fact that he saw the faces of many personal deities *(yi dam gyi lha)*, attained many meditative stabilizations and clairvoyances, and so forth, the chief biographical fact is what was just explained. As the venerable lama himself said:

> In the beginning, I strove for vast hearing.
> In the middle, all the systems of texts appeared as
> instructions [for practice].
> In the end, I practiced day and night.
> All was dedicated for the sake of spreading the teaching.

Thus, at the very beginning he strove for detailed, vast hearing — without being rough or partial — of the word of the Conqueror and all the textual systems of the great charioteers, which explain his thought. In dependence on that, all the sutras and treatises from Guṇaprabha's *Stanzas on Discipline (Vinayakārikā)* to the glorious *Guhyasamāja Tantra* — all the textual systems — appeared as practical instructions in the sense that they were included as either principal aspects or branches of the path to one person's becoming completely enlightened. Through practicing the complete corpus of the path, which had appeared in this way, with constant, earnest achievement, the power of experience through stainless reasoning induced ascertainment of the essentials of the path. Thus, the proof [literally, "correct effect sign," *(*samyak-kārya-hetu, 'bras rtags yang dag)*] that he thereby drove the nail of non-confusion is, generally, his knowledge of how to uphold all the teachings without contradiction and, specifically, the foremost being's scriptures on sutra and mantra. For, no matter how much these texts are analyzed, direct perception establishes that there is not even an iota of a place to find blame for [his texts being] disjointed, redundant, contradictory, or overstepping the valid [Indian] texts.

Therefore:

> Though I have heard many textual systems on the path of
> reasoning,

Understanding comes through much exertion.
My collection of qualities is not worse that [that of] many
But even though I make effort, I remain without realization.
Having seen this well through the kindness of lama
  Mañjunātha [Tsong-kha-pa],
I have explained this with merciful intentions.

This is only an expression of the truth.

4 The Middle Way

DEFINITION OF A MĀDHYAMIKA

A member of one of our own [Buddhist] schools who refutes well the extreme of existence — that all phenomena are ultimately established *(paramārthasiddha, don dam par grub pa)* — and the extreme of annihilation — that phenomena do not exist even conventionally — and who asserts that [phenomena] are not truly established *(satyasiddha, bden grub)* is a Mādhyamika. Regarding the extremes, Nāgārjuna's *Treatise on the Middle Way* [XV.10] says:

> "Existence" is the conception of permanence.
> "Non-existence" is the view of annihilation.
> Therefore, the wise do not abide
> In existence or non-existence.

Thus, there are two, the extreme of existence and the extreme of non-existence. Extreme of existence *(astyanta, yod mtha')*, extreme of permanence *(śaśvatānta, rtag mtha')*, and extreme of superimposition *(āropānta, sgro 'dogs kyi mtha')* are synonyms. Extreme of non-existence *(nāstyanta, med mtha')*, extreme of annihilation *(ucchedānta, chad mtha')*, and extreme of denial *(apavādānta, skur 'debs kyi mtha')* are synonyms. Extreme *(anta, mtha')* and holding to an extreme are not the same because an extreme must be something that does not exist whereas holding to an extreme must be something that does exist.

Other [that is, non-Buddhist] schools never assert that any person or phenomenon is a dependent arising, a mere conditionality *(idam-pratyayatā, rkyen nyid 'di pa)* arising in dependence on causes *(hetu, rgyu)* and conditions *(pratyaya, ryken);* they assert that these [persons and phenomena] are only truly established. All of our own schools assert that they [i.e., the non-Buddhist schools] have fallen into the abyss of the views of permanence and annihilation.

Our two Hearer *(śrāvaka, nyan thos)* schools [Vaibhāṣika and Sautrāntika] assert the dependent arising of conditioned phenomena *(saṃskṛta, 'dus byas)* which arise in dependence on causes and conditions and assert that they thereby abandon the two extremes. They refute the extreme of permanence, such as an agent who is unchanging in nature, and the extreme of annihilation which [according to them] is the assertion that cause and effect, the four truths, and so forth are utterly incorrect.

The Proponents of Awareness Only *(vijñaptimātravādin, rnam par rig pa tsam du smra ba)* delineate a suchness *(tathatā, de kho na nyid)* which is the non-duality of object and subject. They assert that they abandon the extreme of permanence, such as the true existence of imaginaries *(parikalpita, kun brtags)*, and abandon the extreme of annihilation, which [for them] is the assertion that the other two natures [the dependent *(paratantra, gzhan dbang)* and the consummate *(pariniṣpanna, yongs grub)*] are utterly non-existent (as was explained earlier [in the Cittamātra chapter not translated here]).

The wise Mādhyamikas assert that dependent arising means being empty of true existence, and they assert that emptiness of true existence means dependent arising; it does not mean a non-entity that lacks the ability to perform a function. Therefore, they do not need two separate reasons to refute the two extremes, and they can present [cyclic existence and nirvana] in the context of those very bases upon which a nature of true existence is refuted. Thus, the reason "[because of being] a dependent arising" alone refutes the extremes of permanence [because whatever is a dependent arising does not truly exist] and annihilation [because whatever is a dependent arising conventionally exists].

Therefore, since among our own schools, the Cittamātrins and below [that is, the Sautrāntikas and Vaibhāṣikas] assert that phenomena have a truly existent nature, they come to have the view of permanence even though they do not propound that [things] are permanent. Also, since they assert that something [impermanent] that truly existed at an earlier time is destroyed in the next moment, even though they do not assert that its continuum is severed, they nevertheless come to have a view of annihilation. Therefore, once it is asserted that things have a nature of true existence, one never passes beyond the extremes of permanence and annihilation.

Specifically, the Yogācārins [Cittamātrins] assert that they abandon the view of non-existence because mentally arisen dependent phenomena *(paratantra, gzhan dbang)* truly exist [as the same entity as the consciousness perceiving them] and they abandon the view of permanence because dependent phenomena do not have an imaginary nature *(parikalpita, kun btags)* [which is a different entity from the perceiving consciousness. Thereby] they deny the conventional existence of subject and object in terms of external objects, and they superimpose [true existence] onto dependent phenomena, which [according to the Mādhyamikas] do not truly exist. Therefore, they fall to the extremes of both permanence and annihilation.

Hence, only the Mādhyamika view does not fall to the extremes of existence and non-existence and is free from the faults of permanence and annihilation; the others are not. This point [appears in] Candrakīrti's *Clear Words*, which says:

> According to those who assert that dependent phenomena are merely things which are minds *(citta, sems)* and mental factors *(caitta, sems las byung pa)* and that these do not have an imaginary entity [that is, a difference of entity between subject and object], they thereby abandon the view of existence [according to them]. And through the fact that these dependent things which are causes of the thoroughly afflicted *(saṃkliṣṭa, kun nas nyon mongs pa)* and the completely pure *(vaiyavadānika, rnam par byang ba)* do exist, [they say] that they abandon the view of non-existence. But because, [according to them] the imaginary does not exist and dependent phenomena do exist, they come to have both views of existence and non-existence. Therefore, how could they abandon the two extremes?[1]

Also:

> Thus, in that way it should be known that only the Mādhyamika view lacks the consequences of being views of existence and non-existence and that the views of others, such as the Vijñānavādins, are not [free of the consequences

of holding the two extremes].[2]

The protector Nāgārjuna says [in his *Precious Garland*]:

> Ask the worldly ones, the Sāṃkhyas, the son of Uluka,[3]
> And the Nirgranthas who propound that the person
> And the aggregates [substantially exist[4]]
> If they assert what passes beyond existence and
> non-existence.
>
> Thus, the ambrosia of Buddha's teaching
> Explains what is called "the profound"
> Passed beyond existence and non-existence.
> Know that it is an uncommon doctrine.[5]

Therefore, if one wishes to be free from the views of permanence and annihilation, one should assert that all dependently arisen persons and phenomena have the meaning of [their] emptiness of true existence, like a moon in water [that is, not truly existent but not utterly non-existent, for a moon in water does not exist as a moon but does exist as a reflection]. Nāgārjuna's *Sixty Stanzas of Reasoning* says:

> Those who assert that dependent things
> Are like a moon in water,
> Not real and not unreal
> Are not captivated by [wrong] views.[6]

Objection: The *King of Meditative Stabilizations Sutras* (*Samādhirāja*) says:

> Both existence and non-existence are extremes.
> Pure and impure are extremes as well.
> Therefore, having abandoned both extremes
> The wise do not abide even in the center.

Also, the revered Maitreya says in his *Ornament for Clear Realization* (*Abhisamayālaṃkāra*) [III.1]:

> Because of not abiding here or there
> Or even abiding in their center,
> And knowing the equality of the times,
> It is asserted that wisdom has gone beyond.

Do these passages not reject abiding even in a middle which is an abandonment of the two extremes?

Answer: Many mistaken statements, such as that the Mādhyamika system has no assertions, have arisen through this wrong idea; therefore, I will discuss it. These passages teach that one should not, like the Proponents of True Existence, abandon trifling extremes but then apprehend a middle free from them which is conceived to be truly existent and abide there. How could these [passages] teach that there is no middle free from the extremes!

Vasubandhu's *Reasonings for Explanation (Vyakhyāyukti)* says:

> *Anta* means completion, last part,
> Nearness, direction, and lowness.

Thus, *anta* [extreme] has many usages, but with regard to its meaning in this context, the master Kamalaśīla says [in his *Illumination of the Middle Way*]:

> If in Mādhyamika there were anything ultimate that was the nature of the mind's own entity, then how could the conceptions, "this is permanent" or "this is impermanent" be extremes? It is not reasonable to say that proper mental application that accords with the suchness of things is a case of falling [to an extreme].

Thus, *anta* here is a place that one falls into, just as in the world, a rocky abyss is called *anta* and falling into that is called falling into an *anta*.

Since real existence *(*samyaksat, yang dag par yod pa)* does not exist even conventionally, non-real existence must exist conventionally. Therefore, [to hold that phenomena] do not ultimately exist is not a case of holding an extreme of non-existence, and making the refutation "does not ultimately exist" is not a refutation of the extreme of non-existence. Still, conceiving that the non-existence which is the negation of the object of negation really exists [that is, to believe that the negation which is emptiness truly exists] is a case of falling to the extreme of non-existence. Hence, refuting that is a refutation of the extreme of non-existence. Therefore, that is a superimpositional extreme of non-existence [superimposing true existence on emptiness] whereas [holding that] such things as actions and their effects do not exist conventionally is a deprecational extreme of non-existence [denying conventional existence]. When phenomena are conceived to exist ultimately, those [ultimately existent] objects are extremes of superimposition, and the subjects conceiving such are [consciousnesses] conceiving of the extreme of superimposition. Because those who profess to be Mādhyamikas must know these things, I have explained them briefly. They should be known in detail from the statements of the foremost omniscient being Tsong-kha-pa.[7]

Thus, in order to lead those disciples who temporarily are unable to realize the profound path of the middle way, the Supramundane Victor *(bhagavan, bcom ldan 'das)* taught some that a self of persons *(pudgalātman, gang zag gi bdag)* exists. To others he gave teachings stemming [from the view that] a self of persons does not exist but subjects and objects exist. To some having the Mahāyāna lineage *(gotra, rigs)* he said that a non-duality which is an emptiness of the duality of subject and object exists. To those of ripened faculties and surpassing intelligence he taught the middle path free from the two extremes and having the essence of emptiness and compassion. Nāgārjuna's *Precious Garland* says:

> Just as grammarians
> [Begin with reading the alphabet,
> So the Buddha teaches doctrines
> That disciples can bear.
>
> To some, he teaches doctrines
> For the reversal of sins.
> To some, for the sake of achieving merit;
> To some, (doctrines) based on duality;
>
> To some, (he teaches doctrines) based on non-duality.
> To some, the profound, frightening to the fearful,
> Having an essence of emptiness and compassion,
> The means of achieving (highest) enlightenment.][8]

Aryadeva's *Four Hundred* says:

> The [Buddha] taught existence, non-existence
> Both existence and non-existence, and neither.
> Is it not that due to the illness
> All [of these] become medicine?

The *Four Hundred* also says,

> In the beginning non-merit is overcome.

In the middle self is overcome.
In the end all [wrong] views are overcome.
Those who understand this are wise.

Thus, that which is called the Mādhyamika view must be a combination of the two: (1) the non-existence of even the smallest particle of a truly established nature in all conditioned and unconditioned phenomena and (2) the compatibility of asserting all presentations of cyclic existence and nirvana, such as produced *(utpādya, bskyed bya)* and producer *(utpatti, skyed byed)* and negative *(pratiṣeda, dgag)* and positive *(vidhi, sgrub)* [phenomena] within that [non-true existence]. If one wishes to analyze whether the views of the many Tibetan systems are the Mādhyamika view, they must be analyzed from this very viewpoint alone. This mode [of assertion] is the fundamental tenet of both Mādhyamikas — Prāsaṅgika and Svātantrika — of the Land of Superiors. The Superior Nāgārjuna says [in his *Treatise on the Middle Way*, XXIV 18-19]:

We explain dependent arising
As emptiness.
That is dependent imputation,
That is the middle way.

Because there are no phenomena
That are not dependent arisings,
There are no phenomena
That are not empty.

Even those Mādhyamikas [the Svātantrikas] who assert existence by way of its own character *(svalakṣaṇa, rang mtshan)* conventionally do not, in any way, assert that phenomena are truly established. Therefore, they explain the synonymity of dependent arising and emptiness that was explained above [in the quotation from Nāgārjuna]. Bhāvaviveka's *Lamp for [Nāgārjuna's] "Wisdom"* says:

> The emptiness that is called "dependent arising" is dependently imputed. The convention is asserted for the mundane and the supramundane. Therefore, it is imputation in dependence on appropriation. It itself is the middle path because the middle is the abandonment of the extremes of production and non-production and existence and non-existence.

When one has gained certainty with respect to this unmistaken mode of settling the view of the basis [, the two truths,] in this way, then, at the time of path, the unmistaken essential of the inseparability of method *(upāya, thabs)* and wisdom *(prajñā, shes rab)* will come easily. One is then able to create in one's continuum the unmistaken causes of the fruition — the two bodies [the Truth Body *(dharmakāya, chos sku)* and the Form Body *(rūpakāya, gzugs sku)*]. Therefore, one must seek to ascertain this Mādhyamika view, which is extremely important on all occasions of the basis, path, and fruition in the Mahāyāna.

Now, this [qualm] must be analyzed: If, in order to be designated as a Mādhyamika, one's view has to be a realization of the meaning of the subtle dependent arising that is free from all extremes, then it would not be suitable for the Svātantrika-Mādhyamikas to be Mādhyamikas because they do not refute the subtle extreme of existence by way of [the object's] own character *(svalakṣaṇa, rang mtshan)* since upon searching with reasoning for persons and phenomena — the objects designated — they posit a particular base of designation as this or that particular [phenomenon]. If a Mādhyamika were posited not [because of] refuting all extremes regarding phenomena, but through asserting a middle way that destroys all extremes in terms of his own [mind], then it would [absurdly] follow that the Proponents of True Existence [the non-Mādhyamika schools] would be Mādhyamikas because they assert their own view as the middle path from the point of view of their [particular] refutation of the two extremes.

This must be explained. In general, [if] a mode of emptiness — the refutation of an object of negation in terms of [a false system's] tenets — is posited as the mode of being of phenomena, despite the fact that phenomena do not abide in that way, such is a mentally fabricated emptiness; it is not the meaning of the middle way. [On the other hand,] although a phenomenon abides in a way such that it is determined to be empty of an object of negation, [if] that mode of emptiness does not apply to all subjects, such is a trifling emptiness; therefore, it is not suitable to be the sphere of reality *(dharmadhātu, chos dbyings)*, suchness *(tathatā, te bzhin nyid)*.

Regarding that, the emptiness of forms being established as distant and cut off from the consciousness apprehending them or the emptiness [of forms] naturally being bases of conception for the thought consciousness apprehending them [asserted] in the system of the [Cittamātrin] Proponents of True Existence does not apply to all phenomena. Therefore, through those modes of emptiness one cannot realize the synonymity of dependent arising and emptiness for all phenomena, nor do those modes of emptiness apply to all phenomena. Therefore, they do not know how to posit well a refutation of the two extremes for all phenomena, nor [do they know how to posit] the compatibility of appearance and emptiness.

The Svātantrika-Mādhyamikas assert existence by way of its own character because [they say] that if existence by way of its own character is refuted conventionally, it is impossible to posit the conventional existence of an object. However, they do not assert that all phenomena are established by way of a mode of subsistence that does not depend on a non-defective awareness, and they refute (such a mode of subsistence] with numerous reasons. Because it is not the case that this type of emptiness which is such a negation [of a mode of subsistence that does not depend on a non-defective awareness] is inaccurate, it is not mentally fabricated. Also, because it applies to all conditioned and unconditioned things, it is not a trifling emptiness. Therefore, since that type of emptiness can be understood to be synonymous with dependent arising, this abandonment of the two extremes with respect to all objects is far more subtle than that of the Cittamātrins. Thus, Svātantrika-Mādhyamikas are fit to be called Mādhyamikas whereas the term Mādhyamika is not applicable to Cittamātrins. The foremost great being Tsong-kha-pa said, "These scholars also refuted the tenet of true existence of phenomena through many doors of reasoning and asserted non-true existence well. Hence, they are Mādhyamikas." It should be understood in this way. Avalokitavrata says:

> The knowledge that external and internal dependent arisings conventionally exist as mere illusions capable of performing functions and ultimately are without entityness is the mode of the perfection of wisdom taught by the proponents of the middle path, the Superior (Nāgārjuna] and his [spiritual] son [Āryadeva], Bhāvaviveka, Buddhapālita, and so forth.

However, those who realize the very subtle meaning of dependent arisings are only the Prāsaṅgika-Mādhyamikas.

5 Scriptural Interpretation

The presentation of the tenets of the Mādhymikas has two parts: (1) the division of definitive sutras and those requiring interpretation by Nāgārjuna and his spiritual sons and (2) the actual explanation of their tenets.

THE DIVISION INTO DEFINITIVE SUTRAS AND THOSE REQUIRING INTERPRETATION BY NĀGĀRJUNA AND HIS SPIRITUAL SONS

The section has two parts: citing what is said in the sutras and an explanation of the meaning of those [statements].

Setting Forth Statements from Sutras

An explicit statement by the protector Nāgārjuna [identifying] a sutra source by means of which he divided scriptures into the definitive (*nītārtha, nges don*) and those requiring interpretation (*nēyartha, drang don*) does not appear in the Superior's own works, such as the "Collections of Reasoning" and the *Compendium of Sutra*. However, an implicit indication exists in the way he explains the meaning of sutras. The glorious Candrakīrti establishes [the division of scriptures] citing the *Teaching of Akṣayamati (Akṣayamatinirdeśasūtra)*. Avalokitavrata also explains [the division] in that way in his explanatory commentary to Bhāvaviveka's *Lamp for (Nāgārjuna's) "Wisdom"*. In addition, the master Kamalaśīla in his *Illumination of the Middle Way* uses that same sutra as the source for the division into definitive sutras and those requiring interpretation. Thus, just the *Teaching of Akṣayamati* is the source for the division into the definitive and that requiring interpretation.

This is what the sutra itself says:[1]

> If it is asked, "What is a sutra of definitive meaning? What is a sutra whose meaning requires interpretation?" Sutras that teach the establishment of conventionalities are called [sutras] whose meaning requires interpretation. Those sutras that teach the establishment of ultimates are called [sutras] of definitive meaning. Sutras that teach by way of various words and letters are called [sutras] whose meaning requires interpretation. Those sutras that teach the profound — difficult to see and difficult to realize — are called [sutras] of definitive meaning. Sutras which teach things that must be expressed by way of various words [such as] self, sentient being, living being, the nourished, creature, person, born of Manu, child of Manu, agent, and experiencer in the manner of [there being a truly existent] controller, for instance, when there is no [truly existent] controller are called [sutras] whose meaning requires interpretation. Those sutras that teach the doors of liberation — emptiness, signlessness, wishlessness, no [truly existent] composition, no [truly existent] production, no [truly existent] birth, no [truly existent] sentient beings, no [truly existent] living beings, no [truly existent] persons, and no [truly existent] controllers — are called [sutras] of definitive meaning. This is called relying on sutras of definitive meaning and not relying on sutras whose meaning requires interpretation.

The Purpose of the Master's [Nāgārjuna's] Division Into the Definitive and the Interpretable

From among the doctrines taught by the Supramundane Victor *(bhagavan, bcom ldan 'das)* in many forms — existence and non-existence, truth and falsity, and so forth — some [persons] become doubtful as to which have true meanings and which have false meanings and some have mistaken ideas who, because of their own low intelligence, mistake the interpretable for the definitive and similarly mistake the definitive for the other [the interpretable. Nāgārjuna] clearly made the distinction between the interpretable and the definitive for them with the intention of fulfilling their purposes. The glorious Candrakīrti says [in his *Clear Words*]:[2]

> Some have the doubt, "Here, what is the teaching that has the meaning of suchness? Here, what is that which has a special intention?" Also, some due to having a weak intellect, think that interpretable teachings are definitive. In order to eliminate with reasoning and scripture the doubt and misunderstanding of both of those [types of people], the master [Nāgārjuna] composed this [*Treatise on the Middle Way*].

Regarding the way in which [Nāgārjuna] differentiated the definitive and interpretable, he stated all qualms that the meaning of definitive sutras should be interpreted in another way and refuted [those qualms] well, bestowing highest certainty regarding the path of purification from the point of view of many reasonings. He also established that meaning [of definitive sutras] by way of scripture, that is, with the word of the Supramundane Victor as witness. Thus, at the end of the passage [quoted above], the glorious Candrakīrti says:[3]

> Regarding that, reasonings are stated by [Nāgārjuna's] saying such things as [*MMK* I.1]:
>
> > From themselves, other,
> > [Both, or causelessly
> > Things are never produced
> > At all, anywhere].
>
> Statements of scripture are such [stanzas] as [*MMK* XIII.1]:
>
> > The Supramundane Victor said that deceptive
> > [Phenomena are falsities.
> > All products have the quality of deception.
> > Therefore, they are falsities].

With respect to the actual meaning of [the passage quoted from] the *Teaching of Akṣayamati*, the first two sentences which begin, "Sutras that teach the establishment of conventionalities ..." differentiate definitive and interpretable sutras from the point of view of their object of expression; they are not posited from the point of view of such things as the place and time [of the teaching. Those sentences] also briefly indicate that sutras that mainly teach conventionalities are categorized as interpretable and sutras that mainly teach ultimates are categorized as definitive. The next two sentences, which begin, "Sutras that teach by way of various words and letters ..." identify sutras that teach conventionalities and sutras that teach ultimates. Teachings of a variety of different objects with a variety of different words and letters are categorized as the former [sutras that teach conventionalities] and teachings of the meaning that is difficult to realize and that is of one taste [in the sense of being] an elimination of elaborations are categorized as the latter [sutras that teach ultimates]. The last two sentences that begin, "Sutras which teach things that must be expressed ..." indicate the mode of teaching of conventionalities by which [a sutra] comes to set forth conventionalities and the mode of teaching ultimates by which [a sutra] comes to set forth ultimates.

[The part of the sentence] from "a [truly existent] controller" through "experiencer" taken literally gives only synonyms for "person," but in fact does not refer only to persons; it must refer to all teachings of things that are objects and actions related to that agent as existent. For example, the chapter that is an analysis of coming and going [chapter II] and the chapter that is an analysis of action [chapter VII] in Nāgārjuna's *Treatise on the Middle Way* refutes all qualms that, if the goer who comes here from another worldly life and goes from this one to another exists, then the person must truly exist and [the qualm that] if the agent of virtuous and non-virtuous actions exists, then the person must truly exist. Therefore, although [these chapters] teach both agent and action, they must be taken as chapters that principally delineate the selflessness of persons [since agent and actions are phenomena directly related to the person]. In the same way, this [passage from the sutra] must be taken as having individual parts that indicate both phenomena and persons. The second sentence, from "emptiness" through "no [truly existent] birth" principally indicates the mode of the selflessness of phenomena *(dharmanairātmya, chos kyi bdag med)*. "No [truly existent] sentient beings" through "no [truly existent] controllers" principally indicates the mode of the selflessness of persons *(pudgalanairātmya, gang zag gi bdag med)*.

The *King of Meditative Stabilizations Sutra* (VII.5) says:[4]

> Instances of definitive sutras are known
> To accord with the Sugata's teaching of emptiness.

All doctrines teaching sentient being, person, or creature
Are known to require interpretation.

With respect to that, "interpretation" [literally: drawing or leading] in the sense of an interpretable scripture does not refer merely to teachings for the sake of leading disciples. Either (1) the meaning of the sutra is not suitable to be held in the way in which it is set forth and through explaining the [basis in Buddha's] thought, must still be interpreted otherwise, or (2) even though [the meaning of the sutra] is suitable to be taken literally, still, it alone is not the mode of being — the suchness — of those [phenomena discussed], due to which their suchness must be sought elsewhere. Thus, their meaning is interpretable — the meaning requires interpretation.

An example of the first is [the statement in the *Purposeful Statements* (*Udānavarga*, XXIV.23)[5]] "Father and mother are to be killed." Since the literal meaning of the statement to kill one's father and mother is not suitable to be taken as it is, it must be interpreted otherwise — [that one should destroy] the existence *(bhava, srid pa)* [the tenth link in the chain of dependent arising, the fully potentialized state of] karma and attachment *(tṛṣṇa, sred pa)* [the eighth link]. Such an interpretation is still interpretable in the latter sense [because the final mode of being of existence and attachment — their emptiness — still has not been set forth]. An example of the second is the teaching that resources arise from giving, despite the fact that its meaning is suitable to be taken literally. Someone might say that the production of resources through giving is the mode of being of that [giving] and that a mode of being of giving which is other than that does not exist. [In response to that qualm, one would] explain that the mode of being of giving is not merely that; its suchness must be sought elsewhere.

Definitive meanings are taught in the manner of eliminating elaborations of self, [truly existent] production, etc. with respect to phenomena and persons. Since the explicit meaning itself is the final mode of being, (1) it cannot be interpreted beyond that, (2) it is not suitable to be intrepreted as something other than that by another person, and (3) it also has valid proofs. Therefore, its meaning is definite — it is a definitive meaning. Although there are valid proofs for a statement such as that a sprout is produced from a seed, its meaning requires interpretation since [the statement] does not deal with the ultimate.

Kamalaśīla's *Illumination of the Middle Way* says, "What is the definitive meaning? It is that which has validity and is explained in terms of the ultimate because it cannot be interpreted otherwise by another."[6] Thus, he says that a definitive meaning must be a combination of that which has valid proofs and which teaches the ultimate. If the definitive and the interpretable referred merely to the existence or non-existence of a meaning which accords with how it is taught, having validity alone would be sufficient and it would not be necessary [for Kamalaśīla] to add the qualification "in terms of the ultimate." Thus, one must carefully distinguish the presence of special implications in portions of the statements of the great charioteers.

When the categorization into the definitive and interpretable is divided from the point of view of the means of expression, since the categorization must be made in terms of whether or not the meaning of a scripture must be interpreted in another way, only scriptures are to be taken as illustrations of the definitive or interpretable. Kamalaśīla's *Illumination of the Middle Way* says, "Therefore, it is to be understood that only that which expresses the ultimate is definitive and the opposite of that is interpretable. ... Also, the *Teaching of Akṣayamati* teaches that the non-[true] existence of production, etc. are definitive."[7]

When the definitive and interpretable are divided in terms of the object of expression, then the object itself which must or must not be interpreted otherwise has to be categorized as definitive or interpretable. Therefore, conventional truths (*saṃvṛtisatya, kun rdzob bden pa*) are categorized as interpretable, and ultimate truths (*paramārthasatya, don dam bden pa*) are categorized as definitive. The *Ornament Illuminating the Wisdom Engaging the Sphere of All Buddhas Sutra* (*Sarvabuddhaviṣayāvatārajñānālokālaṃkārasūtra*) which says, "That which is definitive is the ultimate," and the passage from the *King of Meditative Stabilizations Sutra* cited earlier [page 284] establish this.

Kamalaśīla's second *Stages of Meditation* says, "All of the words of the Supramundane Victor were spoken well because they directly or indirectly clarify suchness or flow to suchness." As he says, [all] doctrines whatsoever spoken by the Conqueror are for the purpose of attaining liberation. This is contingent on knowing that liberation cannot be attained through familiarity with conventional truths alone and that liberation must be attained through the force of meditation, having interpreted [conventional truths] and sought out suchness.

Qualm: Statements such as those in a Mother Sutra [a Perfection of Wisdom sutra] that "Form does not exist, the production of form does not exist," are not sutras of definitive meaning because they are not suitable to be taken literally.

Answer: These are not non-literal sutras because the *Extensive Mother Sutra* [the *Perfection of Wisdom in One Hundred Thousand Stanzas (Śatasāhasrikāprajñāpāramitāsūtra)*] affixes a qualification to the object of negation, saying "This is for the conventions of the world, not ultimately." The qualification of the object of negation in that way in one context applies to statements in other places in that Perfection of Wisdom text in which the qualification is not affixed. Therefore, although [the qualification "ultimately"] is not explicitly stated in this context [of saying that form does not exist], that does not make it non-literal.

With respect to this, according to the Svātantrikas, statements within sutras such as the *Perfection of Wisdom in One Hundred Thousand Stanzas* that explicitly apply the qualification "ultimately" to the object of negation are definitive and literal. [Statements] without words that clearly affix the qualification "truly" [or "ultimately"] to the object of negation in sutras such as the *Heart of the Perfection of Wisdom Sutra (Prajñāpāramitāhṛdaya)* cannot be taken literally and therefore are asserted to be interpretable, requiring interpretation in another way. Therefore, they assert that the statement in the *Sutra Unravelling the Thought (Saṃdhinirmocanasūtra)* that the middle wheel [of Buddha's teaching, the teaching of the Perfection of Wisdom sutras] requires interpretation is not saying that all [sutras] of the middle wheel [require interpretation].

The Prāsaṅgikas assert that the *Heart of the Perfection of Wisdom* and so forth are sutras of the middle wheel that do not explicitly affix the qualification "ultimately" to the object of negation. However, since they are similar in type to sutras that clearly affix the qualification "ultimately," such as the *Perfection of Wisdom in One Hundred Thousand Stanzas*, the qualification is implicitly affixed to the object of negation in those [sutras] as well. Therefore, they are only literal and definitive. That the words of the sutra, "Form does not exist, sound does not exist," and so forth teach that forms, sounds, etc., are utterly non-existent is not suitable even to be taken literally. Therefore, the words of a sutra, "Form does not exist," are necessarily not words of a sutra teaching that forms do not exist.

Thus, the protector Nāgārjuna set forth many faults, such as that dependence on causes and conditions is contradictory when internal and external causes and effects have a nature of true existence, and he established with many proofs that all presentations of bondage (*bandha, 'ching ba*) and liberation (*mokṣa, grol ba*) are feasible within the lack of a truly existent nature. [He thereby] proved that sutras that teach suchness, like the Mother Sutras, are definitive and sutras teaching what does not accord with those are interpretable. Therefore, Nāgārjuna's "Collections of Reasoning" such as the *Treatise on the Middle Way* open the way for distinguishing the definitive and interpretable. Furthermore, the fact that this mode of distinguishing the definitive and the interpretable relies on the *Teaching of Akṣayamati* can be known through Nāgārjuna's own mode of explanation.

Question: How does one interpret the statement in the *Sutra Unravelling the Thought* that if dependent natures are seen as not truly existent, it produces a view deprecating all three natures?

Answer: That statement is made in terms of the thoughts of disciples who, though having the Mahāyāna lineage, lack the supreme mind that realizes suchness, because for disciples who possess the supreme mind that realizes suchness, the very realization that dependent phenomena do not truly exist serves as a method of refuting the view of deprecation [because it aids realization of the conventional existence of phenomena].

Thus, in general, sutras of the middle wheel such as the *Perfection of Wisdom in One Hundred Thousand Stanzas* are definitive and sutras of the last wheel such as the *Sutra Unravelling the Thought* are interpretable. However, it is not contradictory that in terms of those disciples [who have not realized suchness], the final wheel becomes definitive and the middle wheel requires interpretation. For example, generally, between the teachings of self and selflessness, the latter is better, but it is not contradictory that the former is better for disciples who are temporarily not suitable vessels for the teaching of selflessness. Thus, as long as those disciples cannot understand the non-contradiction of the non-existence of even a particle of true establishment (**satyasiddhi, bden par grub pa*) and the suitability of making all presentations [of phenomena] within that [non-true existence], they must be taught doctrines which divide phenomena, with some being true [that is, truly established] and some being untrue. This is because they must be led in stages, being taught a portion of selflessness, and because the selflessness taught to them is not feasible for their minds if the basis in relation to which it is posited does not truly exist.

Therefore, this is the reason for statements refuting inherent existence *(svabhāva, rang bzhin)* in the person but not refuting it in the aggregates and statements refuting a difference of substantial entity *(dravya, rdzas)* between object and subject but not refuting the inherent existence of the emptiness of duality [of subject and object].

There are many points based on these that should be explained in detail, and knowing these well appears to be a supreme door for those with intelligence to generate firm, authentic faith in the word of the Conqueror and the valid treatises commenting on his thought.

6 *The Practice of the Path*

ACTUAL EXPLANATION OF THE MĀDHYAMIKAS' ASSERTION OF TENETS

In general, the Mādhyamikas who are followers of the Superior [Nāgārjuna] assert a Mahāyāna presentation of the basis, path, and fruition as follows. With respect to the basis, they have, first, a way of presenting the two truths, which are:

1 the non-existence of even a particle of a true nature in any person or phenomenon
2 and the suitability of positing all conventional presentations within that [non-true existence] without the slighest discrepancy.

With respect to the path, [they present] a path of inseparable method and wisdom which is a mutual union of:

1 the stages of the profound path, which is the unmistaken view — for a mind realizing suchness — of the non-existence of even a particle of that which is pointed to by a [consciousness mis-] apprehending signs [of true existence]
2 and the stages of the vast paths, which are included in (a) the genuine altruistic aspiration to highest enlightenment induced by love and compassion, preceded by training in the contemplations of beings of small and middling capacity,[1] (b) the deeds of the six perfections *(pāramitā, pha rol tu phyin pa)*,[2] as well as (c) the four ways of gathering students *(saṃgrahavastu, bsdu ba'i dngos po)*.[3]

[With respect to the fruition], in dependence on training in such a complete path, the fruition of enlightenment that does not abide in either of the extremes of cyclic existence *(saṃsāra, 'khor ba)* or [solitary] peace is actualized, with the two aspects of the Form Body *(rūpakāya, gzugs sku)* [the Complete Enjoyment Body *(sambhoga-kāya, longs sku)* and the Emanation Body *(nirmanakāya, sprul sku)*] effecting, as is appropriate, the welfare of disciples having the three lineages [the Hearer, Solitary Realizer, and Mahāyāna lineages]. This [assertion of the basis, path, and fruition] are the general tenets [of Mādhyamika].

The [Sautrāntika] Svātantrika-Mādhyamikas assert that those of the Hearer and Solitary Realizer lineages attain their enlightenment through becoming accustomed to just the selflessness of persons in conjunction with factors of methods for three lifetimes [for Hearers], one hundred eons [for Solitary Realizers], and so forth. However, the master Buddhapālita, who became an adept, the glorious Candrakīrti, and the venerable Śāntideva assert that those [Hīnayānists] also realize the selflessness of phenomena.

Question: What features must be complete in a person of sharp faculties having the Mahāyāna lineage who begins the path of three periods of countless eons?

Answer: Regarding the general structure of the path, the venerable Maitreya says [in his *Ornament for the Mahāyāna Sutras (Mahāyānasūtrālaṃkāra)*]:

> Faith observing the Buddha, and so forth
> Effort in the sphere of giving and so forth,
> Mindfulness that is marvelous contemplation,
> Non-conceptual meditative stabilization,
> And the wisdom knowing phenomena in all ways
> Are the five aspects.

Faith *(śraddhā, dad pa)* in this context is faith in everything included within the causes and effects of the Three Jewels, illustrated [in the stanza] by the faith observing the ethics and so forth of the Buddhas of the three times [past, present, and future]. Since such faith includes all the doctrines of the causes and effects of the Mahāyāna as its objects, when such faith is created, one is said to be skilled in faith. Regarding mindfulness, the chief of the marvelous contemplations is the creation of the altruistic aspiration to enlightenment *(bodhicittotpāda, byang chub tu sems bskyed)*, and all paths of the three vehicles become objects of that mindfulness. Therefore, when such mindfulness arises, one is said to be skilled in mindfulness. Regarding effort *(vīrya, brtson 'grus)*, if having created the aspiration to enlightenment, one lacks the earnestness to train in the deeds [of the perfections], enlightenment will not be achieved. Therefore, earnestness is to be generated for the deeds in general through armor-like effort. When such effort arises, one is said to be skilled in effort. Meditative stabilization *(samādhi, ting nge 'dzin)* and wisdom *(prajñā, shes rab)* [in the stanza] indicate the mode of training specifically in the last two perfections. The cultivation of the uncommon Mahāyāna calm abiding *(śamatha, zhi gnas)* and special insight *(vipaśyanā, lhag mthong)* is called being skilled in meditative stabilization and wisdom in this context.

Thus, one goes to the uncommon Mahāyāna refuge through having previously trained in the contemplations of beings of small and middling capacity. Then, through strongly seeking the welfare of others and [highest] enlightenment, one creates the aspiration [to enlightenment] — the basis of the [Bodhisattva] deeds — and trains in the powerful deeds of the Conqueror's Children. One becomes skilled in the general structure of such a path, and then, in accordance with, "thoroughly giving without signs, and so forth,"[4] one removes well, through hearing and thinking, superimpositions with respect to all types of clear realization *(abhisamaya, mngon par rtogs pa)* — the twenty-one divisions of non-contaminated wisdom *(anāsravajñāna, zag pa med pa'i ye shes)* which, when divided extensively, has one hundred forty-four divisions. When, through having cultivated them, one initially creates well-developed experience with respect to all [of these factors], one is said to have entered the beginning of the path to complete enlightenment in three periods of countless eons.

The development of the experience of emptiness through the wisdom arisen from meditation *(bhāvanāmayīprajñā, bsgoms pa las byung ba'i shes rab)* occurs at the time of the path of preparation *(prayogamārga, sbyor lam)*. However, there undoubtedly must be familiarization and so forth [with emptiness] by the wisdom arising from thinking *(cintāmayīprajña, bsam pa las byung ba'i shes rab)* at this time. It is said that until the attainment of the Mahāyāna path of seeing *(darśanamārga, mthong lam)*, those who have entered the path must cultivate intense familiarity with the types of clear realizations that are transcended through viewing them with knowledge at the time of the path of seeing. Therefore, one must make effort at meditation on the topics ranging from the importance of leisure and fortune[5] and the difficulty of finding it, through to the sixteen aspects of the four truths,[6] conjoining them with the uncommon [Mahāyāna] path. Even at the time of attaining a ground *(bhūmi, sa)*, one must perform both analytical and stabilizing meditation with respect to all types of clear realizations through a union of calm abiding and special insight. That is practiced by way of thirty-seven harmonies of enlightenment *(bodhipakṣadharma, byang chub phyogs kyi chos)*[7] and so forth.

In brief, there are no stages of practice other than sustaining any of the six perfections in states of meditative equipoise *(samāhita, mnyam gzhag)* and subsequent attainment *(pṛṣṭhalabdha, rjes thob)*. Therefore, one must gain ascertainment with respect to the statement by the excellent regent [Maitreya] that the six perfections are a great compendium of practice.

This is the general system of the great Mādhyamikas; the way for a beginner to take to mind the stages of the path, the way to enhance the path, remove obstacles, and so forth, and the way to identify and stop deviations from the path should be known in detail from one who has trained in the great systems of the path [presented by] the incomparable, great elder [Atīśa] and the foremost great being [Tsong-kha-pa] which illuminate well the quintessential instructions transmitted from the two charioteers [Nāgārjuna and Asaṅga, those instructions being] the final thought of the Conqueror. These should be known from the instructions on the stages of the path of the perfections written down by the foremost father [Tsong-kha-pa] and his spiritual sons [Gyel-tsap and Kay-drup] as well as a succession of excellent beings bearing their lineage. [The instructions should also be learned] by associating for a long time with a skilled spiritual guide who has mastered that system.

Differences appear in the texts of the great followers of the Superior [Nāgārjuna] regarding the presentations delineating the two selflessnesses — the mode of engendering in one's continuum the stages of the profound path, the view realizing suchness. Due to these, there are also slight differences in the presentations of the states of the paths and fruits. These [differences] should be known in very extensive form from the statements of the foremost father [Tsong-kha-pa] and his spiritual sons. I also wish to explain them elsewhere relying on their statements; I have given just a brief summary here.

7 *Svātantrika*

Explanation of the Svātantrika-Mādhyamika system has three parts: definition, divisions, and assertions.

DEFINITION

Amarasiṃha's Treasury (Amarakośa) says, "Own continuum [means] own power and self-power." Thus, own continuum *(svātantra, rang rgyud)*, own power *(svairī, rang dbang)*, and own nature *(svabhāva, rang bzhin)* are synonyms. Bhāvaviveka's *Lamp for (Nāgārjuna's) Wisdom*, in commenting on the thirteenth chapter of Nāgārjuna's *Treatise on the Middle Way* says:

> The thirteenth chapter was composed for the purpose of setting forth the non-entityness of conditioned phenomena in terms of another aspect, through the force of answers to the refutations [by opponents] and own-powered inferences.

Therefore, autonomous *(svatantra, rang rgyud)* means that an inferential consciousness *(anumāṇa, rjes dpag)* realizing the thesis *(pratijñā, bsgrub bya)* is produced without taking the lead merely from the opponent's assertions, but by his having ascertained the establishment of the modes of the sign *(liṅga, rtags)* with respect to a subject that is established as appearing commonly to non-mistaken valid cognizers *(pramāṇa, tshad ma)* of both parties in the debate through the force of an objective mode of subsistence from the side of its basis of designation. Mādhyamikas who assert the correctness of such a necessity are Svātantrika-Mādhyamikas.

In the Svātantrika system, non-defective sense consciousnesses are conventionally not mistaken with respect to their appearing objects (**pratibhāsaviśaya, snang yul*). The reason why they are not mistaken in that way rests on the fact that forms and so forth *appear* to non-defective consciousnesses to be established by way of their own entity, and they assert that forms and so forth *are* established by way of their own entity. Thinking of this, Tsong-kha-pa's *Great Exposition of the Stages of the Path to Enlightenment (Byang chub lam rim chen mo)* says:

> The reason why they assert autonomous signs (*svatantra-liṅga, rang rgyud kyi rtags*) in their system is this conventional existence of own-character (*svalakṣaṇa, rang mtshan*), that is, establishment by way of [the object's] own entity conventionally. Therefore, the [Svātantrikas'] positing and the [Prāsaṅgikas'] not positing of autonomous signs in their own systems derives from this very subtle object of negation.

Therefore, a Mādhyamika who asserts that the three modes of the sign proving non-true existence are established from their own side is the definition of a Svātantrika-Mādhyamika.

DIVISIONS

The Svātantrikas are definite as two, the Sautrāntika-Mādhyamikas[1] and the Yogācāra-Mādhyamikas. Regarding the reason why the first are called Sautrāntikas, since they assert that the observed-object-conditions (*ālambanapratyaya, dmigs rkyen*) of sense consciousnesses are external objects which are composites of subtle particles, their assertion of observed-object-conditions accords with the Sautrāntikas conventionally. Therefore, they are designated in that way.

Regarding the reason why the second are called Yogācārins, the master Śāntarakṣita's autocommentary to his *Ornament for the Middle Way* says:

> According to others:
>
> [Phenomena] which are causes and effects
> Are solely [the entity of] consciousness alone
> [Because] that which is established by it
>   [consciousness]
> Abides as [the entity of] consciousness.[2]

Also, "Hence, we accord with everything that appears in the *Sutra on the Heavily Adorned (Ghanavyūhasūtra)* and the *Sutra Unravelling the Thought*."[3] Thus, since they conventionally make assertions in accordance with the mode of Mere Knowledge *(vijñaptimātratā, rnam par rig pa tsam)*, which is an emptiness of external objects, they are called Yogācāra-Mādhyamikas. Therefore, Tsong-kha-pa's *Essence of the Good Explanations* says:

> Thus, it is good to [take it] in accordance with the assertion of the master Ye-shay-day that although such a system appeared here and there [prior to Śāntarakṣita], the master Śāntarakṣita extensively composed texts and founded the system of Mādhyamika tenets [teaching] the mode of the non-existence of external objects conventionally.

Objection: That etymology of Sautrāntika-Mādhyamika is incorrect, for Kay-drup's *Thousand Doses* says:

> Neither the master Bhāvaviveka nor Jñānagarbha accord with the Sautrāntikas in the presentation of conventionalities because there are many points of great disagreement, such as their not asserting self-knowers *(svasaṃvedana, rang rig)*, and because, if accordance is posited due to agreement on one position, then it would [absurdly] follow that everyone agrees with the tenets of everyone else.

Answer: There is no fault because this [statement by Kay-drup] is merely putting forth a point which refutes an etymology by earlier Tibetans that whatever the Sautrāntikas assert ultimately, these [Sautrāntika-Svātantrika] Mādhyamikas assert conventionally; he is not saying that in general it is unsuitable to etymologize Sautrāntika-Mādhyamika from the viewpoint of [their] according with the Sautrāntikas on one position. Also, there are many cases of an etymology or mere usage not having to contain all characteristics [of the object in question]. Furthermore, the glorious Candrakīrti, in his commentary to Āryadeva's *Four Hundred*, explains that Bhāvaviveka's mode of positing sense powers *(indriya, dbang po)* and objects *(viṣaya, yul)* in accordance with the Sautrāntikas is not correct. Also, that Bhāvaviveka asserts such is explained clearly in his commentary to his *Essence of the Middle Way*. Furthermore, Tsong-kha-pa's *Great Exposition of the Stages of the Path* and Kay-drup's *Thousand Doses* both explain [his position] as just that when they explain Bhāvaviveka's assertions.

Part Two
Sautrāntika-Svātantrika-Mādhyamika

The presentation of the Svātantrikas' assertions has two parts: the assertions of the Sautrāntika-Svātantrika-Mādhyamikas and the assertions of the Yogācāra-Svātantrika-Mādhyamikas. The first has two parts: a refutation of the system of the Proponents of True Existence and a presentation of the Sautrāntika-Svātantrika-Mādhyamikas' own system.

8 *Refutation of Cittamātra*

The refutation of the Proponents of True Existence has two parts: a demonstration of the incorrectness of their explanation of the three natures and a demonstration of the incorrectness of their explanation that external objects do not exist.

THE INCORRECTNESS OF THE [CITTAMĀTRIN] EXPLANATION OF THE THREE NATURES

Bhāvaviveka's *Essence of the Middle Way* [V.8-9] says:

> All the words of the Tathāgathas
> Explained here are valid for us,
> For they are believable, valid scriptures.
> The good assert that [these] are proven.
>
> Others who have doubt and wrong ideas
> From other scriptures do not accept them.
> Therefore, in order to engage in proving them
> The rational procedure should be sought.[1]

This explains that since the Vijñaptikas [Cittamātrins] ascribe faults to the Mādhyamikas that are not valid and [since] the [Mādhyamikas'] own system is valid, all the cases in which the Cittamātrins take the Mādhyamikas as the opponent should be refuted.

Regarding the mode of refutation, that same text says [V.10], "Non-dualistic things [are not reasonable] ..." This refutes the true establishment of consciousnesses which are empty of duality [of subject and object] and indicates the unreasonableness of refuting external objects. Bhāvaviveka also refutes the Cittamātrin presentation of the three natures with statements such as [at V.55], "The imaginary does not exist ..."

With respect to that, the Cittamātrins say:

> The subject, imaginary natures, lack entityness *(svabhāvatā, ngo bo nyid)* in the sense of lacking their own character *(lakṣaṇa, mtshan nyid)* because of being entities which are completely superimposed, as is the case, for example, with imagining a rope to be a snake.

[Bhāvaviveka says] that this is not correct because of the indefiniteness of the reason. Does the reason, "because of being entities which are completely superimposed," mean that an own-character *(svalakṣaṇa, rang mtshan)* of an imaginary entity is utterly non-existent, like a snake which is imputed to a rope? Or does it mean that because [imaginary natures] are objects of expression by terms and thought consciousnesses, the own-character of imaginary entities, like the entity of the rope, does exist? If you say that even the rope is not established by way of its own character, that [position] is damaged by worldly renown, because in the world it is renowned that there exists an entityness of rope, which is water and hemp twisted with the exertion of human hands. To explain this, Bhāvaviveka's *Essence of the Middle Way* [V.55] says:

> It is not asserted that "the imaginary does not exist
> Because of being imputed, like a snake [to a rope]"
> Due to indefiniteness concerning the entity of the rope.
> Or [if you say that the rope does not exist by way of its own
> character, your position] is damaged by [worldly]
> renown.[2]

Furthermore, in the example, the factor of wrong imputation — the snake — and the basis of imputation, the rope which exists by way of its own character, both exist. Similarly, in the case of the meaning [that is exemplified], the mistaken factor — the imputer — and the non-mistaken factor of the imputed entity, the basis of imputation, must both exist because, in the example, "like imputing a snake to a rope" stated by you, there are mistaken and unmistaken factors in the basis of imputation and the imputation, and there must be similarity between the example and the exemplified. However, you are not able to accept that [both exist] because you assert that entities of imputation do not exist by way of their own character, and since entities of imputation do not exist by way of their own character, they must not exist. Even incurring that fault, it is not correct that objects which are imputed as entities and attributes do not have an entityness of their own character because objects which are imputed as entities and attributes exist by way of an entityness of their own character conventionally. Thinking of this, Bhāvaviveka's *Essence of the Middle Way* [V.56ab] says:

> That [imputed entity] is not mistaken
> Because [the example] is seen to have many factors
> [erroneous and not erroneous].[3]

Furthermore, your explanation that entities of imputation are mistaken in all ways is not correct because, if that were the case, conventional phenomena would be denied, and because if conventionalities did not exist, it would be impossible also to realize ultimate entities — the objects of individual knowledge *(pratyātmavedya, so so rang gis rig pa)* — as well. Bhāvaviveka's *Essence of the Middle Way* [V.56cd] says:

> You deprecate things because
> Your refute objects in all ways.[4]

Also, Bhāvaviveka's *Blaze of Reasoning* says:

> If you say that things which are not literal entities are hardly like the objects of individual knowledge, it would still be contradictory to the presentation of conventional truths because sutra says, "It is impossible to realize the ultimate without conventional phenomena."[5]

The Cittamātrins also say:

> Although external objects do not exist, the appearance of the signs of [external] objects occurs in dependence on names and terminology. Since all conceptions are produced from that, it is correct that the imputations do not have an entityness of own-character.

[Bhāvaviveka responds that] this is also incorrect because animals such as birds and deer who do not know names, letters, etymologies, and terminology are seen to generate great afflictions *(kleśa, nyon mongs)*. Thus, external objects such as forms which are the objects [in relation to which] these afflictions are produced only exist. To explain this the *Essence of the Middle Way* [V.57] says:

> Even without names there are afflictions;
> It is not the case that objects appear from using names
> Because of the production of afflictions
> Even in animals who do not know speech.[6]

Also, the commentary following the stanza says, "It should be known that forms and so forth in dependence on which the afflictions are produced are only externally existent objects."[7]

Furthermore, you Cittamātrins' proving to us that dependent phenomena exist by way of their own character is meaningless because if you are proving [that they exist that way] conventionally, you would be proving what is already established, since we also assert that dependent phenomena are established by way of their own nature conventionally. If you are proving that they exist by way of their own character ultimately, then that is even more incorrect because an example which has the sign [reason] and predicate of the proof that dependent phenomena ultimately exist cannot be found.

The reason stated by you, "Things do not have entityness because of lacking a nature of expression" has the fallacy of being contradictory because the sign — lacking a nature of expression — eliminates that the subject — things — ultimately exist. To explain this, Bhāvaviveka's *Essence of the Middle Way* [V.71] says:

> To say that dependent phenomena exist conventionally
> Would be to prove what is [already] established [for us].
> If [you say that they exist] ultimately,
> There is no example and the reason is contradictory.[8]

This is also clearly explained in the commentary following this [stanza],[9] but fearing excess, I will not cite it.

Also, your assertion that the consummate nature — the suchness which is the emptiness of duality [of subject and object] — is ultimately existent is not correct because if consummate entities exist ultimately, freedom from the extreme of superimposition would not be possible, since they ultimately exist, and if the entity which is non-ultimate existence [itself] ultimately exists, one is not free from the extreme of deprecation. Furthermore, if consummate natures are ultimately established, it would follow that the exalted wisdom perceiving the modes *(yathāvajjñāna, ji lta ba gzigs pa'i ye shes)* would have observation [of signs of true existence], and [it would follow that] complete, perfect enlightenment *(samyaksaṃbodhi, yang dag par rdzogs pa'i byang chub)* would lack equality [since it would perceive both ultimate and non-ultimate existence]. In order to explain these fallacies, Bhāvaviveka's *Essence of the Middle Way* (V.95, 97] says:

> If an entity of the nature of existence and non-existence
> Were ultimate,
> How are you free
> From the extremes of superimposition and deprecation?[10]
>
> The Teacher would not be without observation [of true existence]
> Because he would observe [a truly existent] reality.
> Enlightenment would not be equal
> Because different natures would appear to it.[11]

The commentary following this says:

> If the observation [of the true existence] of the reality which is the consummate entity exists, then the Teacher — the Supramundane and Victorious Buddha — would not be without observation [of true existence] because of observing [an ultimately existent] reality. Hence, [your assertion] contradicts such scriptures as that which says:
>
> > The Buddha has the character of space
> > Space also has no character.
> > Homage to you who is without observation,
> > Free from illustration and definition.
>
> The enlightenment of the Teacher would also be unequal. Why? Because the two — the reality called the consummate entity and the exalted wisdom which perceives it — would be different. If they were two in that way, how could clear realization of the two entities be equal?[12]

[Bhāvaviveka's mode of] flinging the fallacy of the consequence that enlightenment would be unequal not only damages the Cittamātrins' assertion that consummate natures are truly established, but also damages their assertion that there manifestly exists a self-knower *(svasaṃvedana, rang rig)* which directly realizes the exalted wisdom at the time of meditative equipoise on suchness within the vanishing of dualistic appearance:

Also, you Cittamātrins assert that:

> The various appearances of objects, sense powers, and consciousnesses are established merely through the force of their respective potencies being deposited on the mind-basis-of-all *(ālayavijñāna, kun gzhi'i rnam par shes pa)*.

[Bhāvaviveka counters that] in that case, the generation of an awareness observing suchness in the continuum of common beings *(pṛthagjana, so so skye po)* would be very contradictory [that is, impossible] because the potency for a mind observing suchness could never have been placed on the mind-basis-of-all in the continua of those common beings earlier [without their actually having realized reality directly, in which case they would not be common beings, but Superiors *(ārya, phags pa)*]. If there is such production without that potency, then, in your system, the mind observing suchness would be causeless, like an awareness perceiving a flower in the sky. To explain this, Bhāvaviveka's *Essence of the Middle Way* [V.98] says:

> How can an awareness observing suchness
> Arise without the depositing of a potency?
> It is as infeasible as a mind seeing a sky-flower
> Without the depositing of its potency.[13]

Also, the commentary following that says:

> It is not feasible that a potency which was never deposited before on the mind-basis-of-all could be posited later. It is like the infeasibility of an awareness being produced which [actually] sees a flower in the sky.[14]

Regarding these reasonings, the opponents [Cittamātrins] assert that external objects do not exist but the appearance of objects arises only from the power of potencies on the internal basis-of-all, and they assert that the potencies are truly established as well. Therefore, [although] there is no fault within the context of conventionalities, within true establishment, reasoning entails that once a potency was not deposited [in the past], it cannot be deposited later. This is probably [Bhāvaviveka's position], for this discussion in the *Blaze of Reasoning* is prior to these passages where it says, "It [the consummate nature] is in all ways inexpressible because of being empty of entityness. Such an entity [i.e., a consummate nature] is treated as ultimate."[15] Also, the root text, the *Essence of the Middle Way* [V.95], says: "If an entity of the nature of existence and non-existence/Were ultimate."

These very extensive statements — in the root text and commentary of the *Essence of the Middle Way* — of the master Bhāvaviveka's refutation of the Cittamātrin presentation of the three natures do not seem to have been explained clearly by anyone. Since they are extremely subtle points of reasoning by a great charioteer, I have written what could be figured out with small intelligence hoping that this might serve as a cause for the intelligent to look at these texts. Thus, I ask them to look at length at the texts themselves.

This master [Bhāvaviveka] also set forth a brief refutation of the Cittamātrin presentation of the three natures in his commentary of Nāgārjuna's *Treatise on the Middle Way*, the *Lamp for (Nāgārjuna's) "Wisdom"*, which is kindly explained in the foremost great being Tsong-kha-pa's *Essence of the Good Explanations.* I want to explain that elsewhere.

THE INCORRECTNESS OF THE [CITTAMĀTRIN] EXPLANATION THAT EXTERNAL OBJECTS DO NOT EXIST

Bhāvaviveka's *Essence of the Middle Way* [V.15] says:

> If [you say] the awareness [perceiving] forms is not correct
> Because [you] assert that it perceives [them] as [external] objects,
> Then your reason is mistaken
> And your thesis falls apart.[16]

The commentary preceding that says:

> [The Cittamātrins] assert that any awareness which lacks the conception of object and subject accords with the fact in reality, but an awareness [apprehending] forms and so forth, although non-conceptual, is not correct because of

> perceiving [them as external] objects, as is the case with an awareness seeing the appearance of a double moon.[17]

With regard to the meaning of this, the reason stated by the Cittamātrins [is as follows]:

> The subject, a direct perceiver *(pratyakṣa, mngon sum)* [that is, a directly perceiving consciousness] apprehending blue which perceives blue as of a different nature from itself [that is, the awareness], is not non-mistaken as to what it perceives because of being a knower which perceives an object as other [than it is, i.e., as an external object], as is the case, for example, with a sense consciousness perceiving a double moon.

[In the quotation from Bhāvaviveka's commentary above], "although non-conceptual" indicates that the subject *(dharmin, chos can)* is a direct perceiver; "is not correct" indicates the probandum *(sādhya, bsgrub bya)* — mistaken with respect to appearance —, and "because of perceiving [them as external] objects" indicates the reason *(hetu, gtan tshigs)*.

With respect to [how Bhāvaviveka] expresses the fallacy in this [position], it is not a correct reason *(samyakhetu, gtan tshigs yang dag)* because the subject — an awareness [apprehending] forms — and the reason — a perceiver of objects — are not different because when the meaning of the reason is established, the entity of the subject is already established as false [because the establishment of the subject must be separate from the establishment of the reason]. The commentary following [the stanza] says:

> For, an awareness [apprehending] forms does not have an entity separate from a perceiver of apprehended objects, whereby a correct inference of [it as] a perceiver of apprehended objects is eliminated. Thus, since the entity of the subject is established as incorrect, it is contradictory [to your own theories of logic.][18]

Furthermore, the assertion of mind only, without external objects, is not correct because of being damaged through contradiction with [the Cittamātrins' own] assertion and through [worldly] renown. To explain this, Bhāvaviveka's *Essence of the Middle Way* [V.17] says:

If only mind is observed
And forms and so forth are not apprehended,
Your thesis is damaged
Through assertion and renown.[19]

The way that [their own] assertion is contradicted is that [the non-existence of external objects] contradicts [their] acceptance of the scripture which says, "An eye consciousness arises in dependence on the eye and form." The damage done by renown is that it is renowned in the world that without an object, such as a form, eye consciousnesses and so forth which apprehend them are not produced.

Also, the Cittamātrins say:

> Objects do not exist, but consciousnesses are produced, as is the case, for example, with a dream consciousness.

This is also incorrect. Even in dreams forms are seen by a conscious eye which is affected by beginningless predispositions (*vāsanā, bag chags*) for objects and subjects. Therefore, even a dream consciousness has an object of observation (*ālambana, dmigs pa*), like a consciousness remembering the blue seen before. Thus, the example is not similar [to the exemplified]. In addition, because [the Cittamātrins] abandon objective things, such as forms, they also deprecate objects. To explain this, Bhāvaviveka's *Essence of the Middle Way* [V.18-19] says:

Thus, because appearances are produced,
Like the awareness of forms and so forth in dreams,
Consciousness lacks [external] objects such as forms.
Saying such is unsuitable.

Since consciousnesses in dreams and so forth
Observe phenomena,
Even an example does not exist
And objects are deprecated.[20]

Though the commentary to this states, "with a conscious eye"[21] rather than "dream consciousness," it is not being asserted that sense consciousnesses are present in dreams, but rather it is being explained that, in general, consciousnesses which see dream forms have objects of observation.

Also, the Cittamātrins say:

> The existence of external objects is not feasible because it is incorrect if you assert that a single minute particle is an object [of a sense consciousness], and it is also incorrect if you assert that an aggregation of many minute particles is an object [of a sense consciousness]. The first [part of the reason] is established [since] a single minute particle is not an object of sense consciousnesses because of not appearing as a thing which is an object of a sense consciousness, as is the case, for example, with the physical sense powers *(indriya, dbang po)* [which are subtle matter and hence invisible to the senses]. The second [part of the reason] is established [since] an aggregation of many minute particles is not an object of a sense consciousness because of not being substantially established *(dravyasiddha, rdzas su grub pa)*, as is the case, for example, with the appearance of a double moon.

[Reporting the Cittamātrin position] in that way, Bhāvaviveka's *Essence of the Middle Way* [V.32-33] says:

> Regarding that, a single particle
> Is not an object of operation of an awareness of form
> Because of not appearing to it
> Just as a physical sense power is not an object of operation
> [of a sense consciousness].
>
> Many minute [particles of] form
> Are not held to be objects of operation of the mind
> Because of not being substantially existent
> Like, for example, a double moon.[22]

In answering this, [Bhāvaviveka says that] if you are proving that an individual minute particle, that is, a single minute particle which has not aggregated with [other particles] of a similar type, is not the object of a sense consciousness, then you are proving what is already established [for us], because we also do not assert that it is the object of a sense consciousness. To explain this, Bhāvaviveka's *Essence of the Middle Way* [V.34] says:

> Regarding that, if the opponent
> Is proving that a non-composite form
> Is not the object of operation of a mind,
> Then he would be proving what is already established.[23]

If you are proving that a form which is a composite of minute particles of a similar type is not an object of operation of a sense consciousness because of not being substantially established, then that reason is not established for us because we assert that a composite of conjoined minute particles is a substantially existent thing. We assert that such a composite object is an object of observation of a sense consciousness because it produces the sense consciousness apprehending it into having its aspect *(ākāra, rnam pa)*. To explain this, Bhāvaviveka's *Essence of the Middle Way* [V.35-36] says:

> [If (you say that objects do not exist because of being)
> composite forms,
> The reason would not be established]
> Because a composite of other [particles of] form
> Produces an awareness which perceives it.
>
> We assert that [composite] to be the object of observation
> Because it serves as the cause of the awareness perceiving it,
> As is the case with desire. Therefore,
> Your thesis is damaged by inference.[24]

Regarding the reason for this, the autocommentary says:

> A form which is a composite of minute particles of a similar type is asserted to be the object of observation itself. Why? Because such a composite of minute particles serves as the very thing which causes the awareness perceiving that composite form. That which serves as a cause for the awareness perceiving it is observed to be a composite, just as it is asserted, for example, that desire which has the character of attachment to an object observes just the composite of the form of a woman, and so forth. Therefore, your thesis, "A form which is a composite is not an object of observation," is damaged by this inference.[25]

[The Cittamātrin thesis is] contradictory to scripture [because] it contradicts the scripture which says that the abodes [sense powers] and objects of observation of the five collections of consciousness are composites.

If you [Cittamātrins] are proving that an aggregation of minute particles is not an object of observation of a sense consciousness, then we incur no fault because we also do not assert that an aggregation of minute particles is an object of observation of a sense consciousness. To explain this, Bhāvaviveka's *Essence of the Middle Way* (V.38cd] says:

> Since we do not hold the thesis that an aggregation [is an object of a sense consciousness],
> Your refutation of that does not damage [us].[26]

What is the difference between the two, a composite *(saṃcita, bsags pa)* and an aggregation *(saṃghata, 'dus pa)?* A collection of minute particles of a similar type with the same basis is called a composite. A pot, for example, is composed through combining many minute particles of a similar type which are its basis of composition. A collection in one place of minute particles of dissimilar types of substances with many bases, such as an army, a forest, or a rosary, is called an aggregation.

In addition, many [topics] are set forth, such as a refutation of the observed-object-condition *(ālambanapratyaya, de ma thag rkyen)* as explained in Dignāga's *Analysis of the Object of Observation (Ālambanaparikṣā)* and an analysis of whether minds *(citta, sems)* and mental factors *(caitta, sems byung)* are the same or different substantial entities *(dravya, rdzas)*. I will not elaborate on these here.

THIS MASTER'S REFUTATION OF SELF-KNOWERS *(SVASAṂVEDANA)*

The Cittamātrins say:

> When a consciousness meets an object, it is produced as an entity with two parts: an appearance having the aspect of the object apprehended and an appearance having the aspect of the apprehending subject.

[According to Bhāvaviveka] this is incorrect because, apart from the appearance in the aspect of the object, there is no appearance in the aspect of the subject itself. To explain this, Bhāvaviveka's *Essence of the Middle Way* [V.20cd] says:

> Except for the appearance as the object
> What other entity of the mind is there?[27]

[In answer] to this, [the Cittamātrins] say:

> It is not established that another [part] does not exist because the consciousness itself abides in its own entity and because it is produced as having the aspect of another

object, as is the case, for example, with a crystal jewel.

This means that when a lump of crystal is placed near an object, such as [something] blue, the crystal's own entity is clear, but through the power of being near that object it also possesses an aspect such as blue. Similarly, [the Cittamātrins] assert that when perceiving an object, a consciousness also has two aspects: an aspect of the apprehended which is the appearance as the object and the aspect of the apprehender which is the appearance as itself.

[Bhāvaviveka asserts] that this is not correct because the example is not similar to what is being proved. When a lump of crystal is placed close to an object, such as [something] blue, through the power of the object it loses the undefiled clarity of its own entity and comes to have an aspect such as blue. However, that which is a former moment of that clear crystal does not come to have the aspect, such as blue, because it has already ceased. Thus, the former moment of the clear crystal ceases by the power of being placed near the object and its later moments are produced so as to have the aspect of blue. Thus, to think that it is just the crystal of the former moment [that becomes blue] is mistaken. To explain this, Bhāvaviveka's *Essence of the Middle Way* [V.21-22ab] says:

> We do not assert that, like a crystal,
> The two [object and subject] appear because [the subject] is produced like the other [the object].
> For it is produced as that [object]
> Due to being placed nearby and is not the [former] moment of the crystal.
>
> We assert that, since it has ceased, it is wrong to think
> That it is produced as the other [the object].[28]

Furthermore, the aspects of apprehended and apprehender do not exist because the clarity of consciousness having an entity of self-illumination, which like the crystal when it is not close to, but is separated from, an object like blue, is never apprehendable in utter isolation.

Also, although it is suitable that a lump of crystal appears as having the aspect of blue when it is placed near a color such as blue, in no way is the crystal itself transformed into the entity of the color, such as blue, nor is the color transformed into the entity of the crystal. Otherwise, it would absurdly follow that the lump of crystal was the color or that the color was the lump of crystal. Similarly, when a consciousness is near a form, such as earth, the consciousness is produced as having the aspect of earth, but neither is consciousness itself transformed into the entity of form nor is the form itself transformed into the entity of consciousness. Otherwise, it would absurdly follow that earth and so forth would be sentient or that even mind would be mindless like earth and so forth. These [arguments] are stated in Bhāvaviveka's *Blaze of Reasoning*, but fearing excessive length I will not cite the sources.[29]

After that, he refutes the Cittamātrins' sign of the definiteness of simultaneous observation and refutes the Cittamātrin presentation of valid cognition *(pramāṇa, tshad ma)* and its effect. One should look there [in the *Blaze of Reasoning*] for an extensive treatment.

[REFUTATION THAT MIND-ONLY IS TAUGHT IN SUTRA]

The Cittamātrins say:

> Your refutation of mind-only is not correct because it is stated in a scripture of the Supramundane Victor [the *Sutra on the Ten Grounds (Daśabhūmika)*], "These three realms are mind only."

There is no fault because the meaning of this scripture is that this was said in order to refute the existence of an agent or enjoyer which is other than the mind, such as that imputed by the Forders *(tīrthika, mu stegs pa)* [non-Buddhists]; it was not so stated in order to refute external objects. In this way, the *Sutra on the Ten Grounds* says:

> A Bodhisattva on the sixth Bodhisattva ground viewing dependent arising in forward and reverse order thinks, "These mere aggregates of suffering, devoid of an agent or experiencer, arise from the twelve branches, ignorance and so forth, and the tree of suffering is manifestly established." O Children of the Conqueror, because it is definite that way, it is thus: the three realms are mind only, they are completely composed and written by mind; there is no agent or experiencer whatsoever other than mind.

Thus, the meaning of the passage is not a refutation of external objects.

Also, the Cittamātrins say that the emptiness of external objects is the intention of sutra because the "Questions of Maitreya Chapter"

(Maitreyaparipṛccā) of the *Perfection of Wisdom in Twenty-Five Thousand Stanzas (Pancaviṃsatisāhasrikāprajñāpāramitāsūtra)* says:

> What is the form of reality? It is that which is the permanent non-entityness of imaginary forms [imaginary natures] in imputed forms [dependent phenomena]; [it is] the selflessness of phenomena itself, the limit of reality, and so forth. It is not substantially existent and not non-substantially existent because the emptiness of superimposed objectivity and consciousness exist.

With regard to the meaning of this passage, [Bhāvaviveka replies] that it is a proof of the consciousness which perceives the emptiness of that which is superimposed; it is not establishing a consciousness without an object, because the object which is the form of reality — the object of a Tathāgata's individual knowledge — exists. Thus, since objects which are not superimpositions are not refuted, consciousness is in no way empty of objects which are a different substantial entity from it. To explain this, Bhāvaviveka's *Essence of the Middle Way* [V.29] says:

> If, due to the emptiness of superimposed objectivity,
> You are proving that consciousness [is devoid of external objects],
> Since objects which are not superimpositions exist,
> It is not the case that objects do not exist.[30]

The meaning of that is to be taken as explained above. I do not think that the thought of the passage is to be interpreted that, "... because if the object — the form of reality — which is the object of the individual knowledge truly exists, an object which is not a superimposition exists," for this master [Bhāvaviveka] asserts that there are external objects but does not assert that there are truly existent objects. Also, the statement in the autocommentary, "The object that is the form of reality exists," proves that an object which is a different substantial entity from consciousness exists but in no way proves that reality is an external object, nor does it imply that it [reality] truly exists. The statement in the autocommentary that, "Since that which is the thing that is not a literal entityness exists, [a non-imputed object exists]"[31] refers to the existence of an object which is empty of a superimposed entity; it should not be taken as an inexpressible thing, as is asserted by the Cittamātrins.

9 *The Meaning of Ultimate Existence*

The presentation of Bhāvaviveka's own system has four parts: an identification of the object of reasoned negation, the reasoning which refutes that, a presentation of the two truths delineated [by reasoning], and a brief presentation of the paths and fruits.

THE OBJECT OF NEGATION

In commenting on the passage from the *Essence of the Middle Way* [III.26] which says, "Earth and so forth are not elements ultimately *(paramārthataḥ, don dam par na)* [literally "for the highest *(parama, dam pa)* object *(artha, don)*], Bhāvaviveka sets forth three ways of positing the highest object *(paramārtha, don dam pa)* in answer to [the question of] what *paramārtha* refers to in that passage:

> With respect to object *(artha, don)*, it is an object because of being that which is to be known; this is synonymous with "that which is to be examined *(parīkṣaṇīya, brtag par bya ba)*" and "that which is to be understood *(pratipādya, go bar bya pa)*." Highest *(parama, dam pa)* is a word [meaning] supreme. With respect to the compound *paramārtha*, because it is an object as well as being highest, it is the highest object. Or [it means] the object of the highest *(paramasya artha, dam pa'i don)*; because it is the object of the highest non-conceptual wisdom *(nirvikalpajñāna, rnam par mi rtog pa'i ye shes)*, it is an object of the highest [consciousness].

> Or, it [means] that which accords with the highest object [that is, the highest consciousness]. Since the ultimate exists for a wisdom that accords with a realization of the ultimate, it accords with [that which directly realizes] the highest object.[1]

From among these, the first [explanation of *paramārtha*] goes from "With respect to object *(artha)*" to "because [it is an object] as well as being highest, it is the highest object." This explains *paramārtha* applying both "highest" *(parama, dam pa)* and "object" *(artha, don)* to the object [emptiness].

The second [begins], "Or [it means] the object of the highest." "Highest" refers to the uncontaminated non-conceptual wisdom, and "object" refers to its object [emptiness]. The two, object and highest, are treated separately as object [emptiness] and subject [non-conceptual wisdom].

The third [begins], "Or [it means] that which accords with the highest object." A wisdom of hearing, thinking, or above which analyzes suchness *(tathatā, de kho na nyid)* is a wisdom that accords with direct realization of suchness. This is taken as the highest object. In this case, both object and highest apply to the subject [that is, the consciousness realizing emptiness].

Question: To what does the *paramārtha* which is to be refuted in this context [of the passage from the *Essence of the Middle Way* above] refer?

Answer: Bhāvaviveka's *Blaze of Reasoning* says:

> Ultimate *(paramārtha, don dam pa)* [consciousnesses] are of two types. One is a supramundane non-contaminated [meditative equipoise] free from elaborations which operates without [conceptual] activity. The second, possessing conceptual elaborations, is called a pure mundane wisdom [of subsequent attainment] which accords with the collections of merit and wisdom and operates with [conceptual] activity. Since here [in the context of the passage from the *Essence of the Middle Way*] this [latter type of ultimate] is held as the qualification of the thesis ["does not ultimately exist"], there is no fault.[2]

Therefore, in this context, that which exists for an inferential reasoning consciousness, that is, a concordant ultimate — the third *paramārtha* of the earlier explanation — is said to be ultimately existent, and that which is non-existent for that [consciousness] is said not to ultimately exist.

Therefore, if a sprout is truly established, it must be truly established for a reasoning consciousness analyzing suchness, because if a sprout is truly established, just that [sprout] must be established as the mode of subsistence of the sprout and because just that reasoning consciousness is a mind which comprehends the mode of subsistence.

Objection: If that is the case, then it follows that the final nature of a sprout is ultimately established because it exists for a reasoning consciousness and because it is established as the mode of subsistence of the sprout.

Answer: There is no fallacy [in my position], for although whatever is truly established must be established as the mode of subsistence and must be established for a reasoning consciousness, whatever is established as a mode of subsistence and is established for a reasoning consciousness does not have to be truly established. The reason for this is that if a sprout were truly established, a reasoning consciousness would have to find the sprout as truly established, because just a reasoning consciousness analyzes whether or not true establishment exists. Although a reasoning consciousness finds that a sprout does not truly exist, such a discovery is a case of analyzing whether the sprout truly exists and finding that it does not truly exist. It is not a case of analyzing whether or not the non-true existence of a sprout truly exists and finding that it does.

This is a difficult point in this system. The foremost great being Tsong-kha-pa said that due to not making this distinction well many mistakes have arisen, such as the earlier great scholars like the translator from Ngok *(rNog bLo-ldan-shes rab)* and his spiritual sons' assertion that an ultimate truth is not an object of knowledge and the lord of reasoning Cha-ba-chö-gyi-seng-gay's *(Cha-pa-chos-kyi-seng-ge)* assertion that non-true existence is truly established.

In Tsong-kha-pa's *Essence of the Good Explanations* and *Great Explanation of (Candrakīrti's) "Supplement" ('Jug pa'i rnam bshad chen mo)* he says that an identification of the object of negation clearer than what was explained before [concerning the three meanings of *paramārtha*] is not set forth in [other] texts by Bhāvaviveka, in Jñānagarbha's *Two Truths*, or in Śāntarakṣita's *Ornament for the Middle Way* together with its autocommentary[3], and that since the existence which is the opposite of the mode of conventional existence explained in Kamalaśīla's *Illuminations of the Middle Way* is the mode of true existence, it must be explained in that way.

Regarding this statement, a member of another sect[4] says:

> The foremost lama Tsong-kha-pa said this thinking that the mode of ultimate establishment is not taught at all in the texts of Bhāvaviveka and so forth, but this is not correct. For Jñānagarbha's *Differentiation of the Two Truths* says:
>
> > Only these appearances to the mind
> > Are conventional. The other is the other one [i.e., ultimate].
>
> [Jñānagarbha] thereby indicates both the measure of conventional establishment and the measure of ultimate establishment.

The statement even by some earlier scholars of our own [Ge-luk] sect that this appears to be true is just the noise of not having analyzed well either the statement of the foremost lama Tsong-kha-pa or the meaning of the text.

To refute this, the great scholar and adept Jam-yang-shay-bay-dor-jay *('Jam-dbyangs-bzhad-pa'i-rdo-rje)* says:

> [The wrong position is: "Only these appearances to the mind/Are] conventional" explains that what is conventionally established are only these appearances to the minds of cowherds and above, and the rest ["the other is the other one"] indicates that the measure of ultimate establishment does not appear to cowherds and so forth, because the former part is established by the commentary and explanatory commentary and it is established by reasoning that they [cowherds] do not perceive the other.
>
> [Jam-yang-shay-ba refutes this interpretation:] Therefore, according to you, it [absurdly] follows that cowherds and so forth are already liberated because no phenomenon whatsoever appears to them as truly established. It [absurdly] follows that they have already found the Mādhyamika view because all phenomena appear to them as conventionally established. Therefore, that passage does not indicate the measure of conventional and ultimate establishment, but [rather] is a passage which identifies the two truths.[5]

Since this is the statement of a great scholar who mastered the great texts, it is very good, but I wonder whether it would be good to explain it as follows.

In general, there are two ultimates in the use of the qualification "ultimately" with respect to the object of negation:

1 a reasoning consciousness of hearing, thinking, or meditation is the ultimate and, as was explained earlier, being established by that is ultimate establishment
2 the existence of an objective mode of subsistence without being posited by the force of a non-defective awareness is designated as ultimately existing.

The mode of apprehending [phenomena] as true by the innate consciousness conceiving true existence, [that conception being] the opposite of the reasoning consciousness analyzing the ultimate is a conception of the latter [type]. Therefore, the main object of negation of signs proving non-true existence is just the latter true establishment. Consequently, when those ascertaining the view of this system initially identify the conception of true existence in their continua, they must identify the latter mode of the conception of true establishment.

Therefore, the foremost great being Tsong-kha-pa himself clearly explains that the former mode of true establishment is described extensively in the root text and commentary of Bhāvaviveka's *Essence of the Middle Way* as well as the root text and commentary of Śāntarakṣita's *Ornament for the Middle Way*, etc. Thus, what chance could there be that the foremost lama Tsong-kha-pa asserts that that [former] mode of ultimate existence is not explained clearly in any reliable Svātantrika text except for Kamalaśīla's *Illuminations of the Middle Way?* If a clear description of ultimate existence in terms of the second mode of interpretation occurs in these texts, please show it and I will support [you].

Objection: The passage which you cited from Jñānagarbha's *Two Truths* indicates ultimate establishment in terms of the second mode of interpretation.

Answer: Show by which words it is indicated.

Objector: It is indicated by "the other is the other one."

Answer: Then it [absurdly] follows that there exists no phenomenon which is established in accordance with the mode of establishment explained by those words because the ultimate of the second mode of interpretation must refer to true establishment, and there is no Mādhyamika who asserts the existence of true establishment.

Objector: I accept [that there are no phenomena which exist in accordance with the mode of ultimate establishment explained by the passage].

Answer: Then it [absurdly] follows that ultimate truths do not exist because the ultimate which is indicated at that point in the passage which says, "The other is the other one" is that [ultimate truths].

Objector: The reason is not established [that is, the passage does not indicate ultimate truths].

Answer: Then, indicate the meaning of the statement from [pseudo-Śāntarakṣita's] explanatory commentary which says, " 'The other' is other than how [phenomena] appear. Therefore, this indicates that what is so for reasoning is the ultimate truth"! If you assert that true establishment is the ultimate truth, you do not even have the scent of a Mādhyamika.

Thus, regarding the meaning of the passage from Jñānagarbha's *Two Truths*, "Only these as they appear/Are conventional" [indicates] that only these [phenomena] as they appear to and are seen by conventional valid cognizers in accordance with how the objects exist are conventional truths. The first part indicates the definition and the second part indicates the definiendum. Moreover, taking the meaning of "appear" as "be seen by," it is explaining that in just the way that phenomena seen by both those whose mind have and have not been affected by tenets, from cowherds on up, abide objectively, so they abide as conventional truths; it is not explaining that objects which are established in reality [truly existent objects] are conventional truths. The term "only" eliminates that [these are] found by a reasoning consciousness.

"The other is the other one" indicates that an object which is found or established by a reasoning consciousness and is other than those [conventional valid cognizers] is the definition of an ultimate truth; "The other" indicates the definition [of an ultimate truth] and "the other one" indicates the definiendum. Thinking of this, Gyel-tsap-jay says:

> The commentary following this line says that just as objects which are found by conventional valid cognizers are posited

> as conventional truths, so only objects found by a reasoning consciousness are ultimate truths.

Since the autocommentary and the explanatory commentary clearly mention ultimate truths, what person having a mind would propound that this passage indicates the measure of true existence that is the object of reasoned negation! Therefore, how could there be any fault in the statement of the foremost lama Tsong-kha-pa!

If [the passage] is explained in this way, it is in complete accord with the thought of the text, because the foremost lama Tsong-kha-pa's opinion is that between the two modes of positing the ultimate, the ascertainment of the latter is extremely important for settling the view and that the mode of the latter ultimate establishment does not appear clearly in any text other than Kamalaśīla's *Illumination of the Middle Way*. He made this statement [cited earlier, page 316] with this in mind. Also, the meaning of the passage from the *Two Truths* cannot be interpreted in any way other than what was just explained.

Question: How does a consciousness innately conceiving true existence conceive phenomena to be true, and what is the hypothetical measure of true existence in this context?

Answer: I will explain this in the section on the Yogācāra-Svātantrika-Mādhyamikas [pp. 349-355].

Thus, both the ultimate in which the reasoning consciousness is referred to as the ultimate and something which is established for that [ultimate consciousness, such as emptiness] exist, but neither the ultimate of the latter mode of interpretation nor something existing in that way exists. Due to not making these distinctions there arose the wrong ideas that just as the Cittamātrins assert that the immutable consummate natures are ultimate and whatever is that is ultimately established, so in this system also if the emptiness of true existence is the ultimate, it must be ultimately established and whatever does not ultimately exist cannot be the ultimate. If this is known well, one will come to know the essential points that (1) saying that nothing exists as its own mode of being or exists ultimately and (2) asserting that reality exists and propounding that just that [reality] is the mode of being and the ultimate are not contradictory.

10 Refutation of Ultimate Existence

THE REASONING REFUTING THAT [OBJECT OF NEGATION]

In general, the five great reasons[1] are asserted in this system because most of them are stated in Bhāvaviveka's *Blaze of Reasoning* and because the refutation of the four alternatives of production is emphasized in the root text and commentary of Jñānagarbha's *Two Truths*. However, in the interest of ease in proving the sign and similar example *(*sadṛṣṭanta, mthun dpe)*, they primarily use a reasoning of parallelism in which the reason is shared.

In the root text and commentary of Bhāvaviveka's *Essence of the Middle Way*, [all phenomena] are included in the five aggregates *(skandha, phung po)*, the twelve sources *(āyatana, skye mched)*, and the eighteen elements *(dhātu, khams)*, and from among those, going from coarse to subtle, he first analyzes the form aggregate *(rūpaskandha, gzugs kyi phung po)*, and within that, the elements *(bhūta, 'byung ba)*. Bhāvaviveka's *Essence of the Middle Way* [III.26] says:

> Here, earth and so forth
> Are not entities of the elements ultimately
> Because of being produced
> And because of having causes, like a consciousness.[2]

"Earth and so forth" identifies the specific subjects *(dharmin, chos can)* and the term "and so forth" identifies water, fire, and wind [also] as bases of debate. "Are not entities of the elements ultimately" indicates the predicate *(dharma, chos).* "Ultimately" indicates that the conventional entities [of the elements] are not refuted, and that an existence by way of the object's own mode of subsistence without being posited by the power of the awareness to which it appears is refuted. "Are not entities" indicates that between negative phenomena *(pratiṣedha, dgag pa)* and positive phenomena *(vidhi, sgrub pa)*, a negative phenomenon is held as the predicate, and that from among negative phenomena, only a non-affirming negative *(prasajyapratiṣedha, med dgag).* The commentary says, "Here, the negative 'is not' is taken to mean a non-affirming negative and is not taken to mean an affirming negative *(paryudāsapratiṣedha, ma yin dgag).*"[3] The combination of the predicate and the subject is the position *(pakṣa, phyogs).* "Because of being produced" indicates the reason *(hetu, gtan tshigs).*

Regarding the elimination of fallacies [ascribed to Bhāvaviveka's] position, [the following objection might be raised].

> Objection: Your proof that earth and so forth are not entities of the elements is not correct because of contradicting [your own] assertions, contradicting direct perception *(pratyakṣa, mngon sum)*, and contradicting [worldly] renown.
>
> The first [reason, that your position contradicts your own assertions] is established because a scripture of the Teacher says, "Brahmins, 'everything' is [included in] the five aggregates, the twelve sources, and the eighteen constituents," and "Similarly, the definition of form is that which is suitable as form." Such statements set forth phenomena such as the aggregates as well as their definitions, whereas you refute these phenomena while asserting those scriptures to be valid.
>
> The second [reason, that your position contradicts direct perception] is established because, when one engages in ascertaining the specific character of objects, a sense *(indriya, dbang po)* [consciousness] is renowned as a direct perceiver *(pratyakṣa, mngon sum)*, and there is no valid cognizer *(pramāṇa, tshad ma)* which surpasses its perception, and while you yourself perform actions such as seeing and apprehending with the eyes the shapes of the elements, forms, and so forth, you refute those [elements] and disavow direct perception.

> The third [reason, that your position contradicts renown] is established because earth and so forth as well as its hardness are renowned to everyone in the world, from the lowest class on up.

Answer: None of these three fallacies exists because we have affixed the qualification "ultimately" to the thesis. Furthermore, the first fallacy does not exist because the presentations of the entities and characters of phenomena were made by the Supramundane Victor in terms of the conventional and are said not to have entityness ultimately. *The Perfection of Wisdom* says:

> Kauśika, all phenomena lack entityness. That which is the lack of entityness in all phenomena is non-true existence. That which is non-true existence is the perfection of wisdom.

The second fallacy also does not exist because the sense consciousnesses are stupid with respect to seeking the nature [of phenomena], and because a person with cataracts does not have a capacity for [true] seeing and so forth, but he perceives falling hairs.

The third fallacy does not exist because worldly persons are incapable of investigating the nature [of phenomena] due to being under the influence of obscuration, whereas this is a case of analyzing the ultimate.

Regarding the meaning of the reason, "because of being a product," "product" is that which is established by causes *(hetu, rgyu)* and conditions *(pratyaya, rkyen)*. With respect to the statement of concomitance with the similar class *(sapakṣa, mthun phyogs)*, whatever is a product is not an entity of the elements ultimately, as is the case, for example, with a consciousness. Here, an example and reason for a proof [of product] as just not existing in the dissimilar class *(vipakṣa, mi mthun phyogs)* are not indicated because there does not exist even the smallest particle of a thing which has entityness and is [a member of] the dissimilar class in the proof of that.

"Because of having causes and so forth" indicates other forms of reasons, such as having causes, being a [functioning] thing *(bhāva, dngos po)*, being an object of knowledge *(jñeya, shes bya)*, and being an object of expression *(vākya, brjod par bya ba)*.

Here, the important point is that if something ultimately existed, it would have to exist by the power of the object's own mode of subsistence without being posited by the power of the awareness to which it appears. Thus, since it would have to exist under its own power, it could not depend on anything else. Therefore, as they are similar in being products, there would be no valid cognizer that could make the distinction that consciousness is not an element and that earth and so forth are elements [ultimately]. Thinking of this, [Bhāvaviveka] set forth a reasoning of parallelism in which the reason is shared, as [explained] before. Hence, this must be understood well.

Furthermore, in Bhāvaviveka's *Blaze of Reasoning*, the progression of reasoning is the same in setting forth many analyses, such as of instances of the elements, the other aggregates, the sources, the constituents, definitions (*lakṣana, mtshan nyid*), illustrations (*lakṣya, mtshan gzhi*), the functioning of production (*utpatti, skye pa*) and disintegration (*vināśa, 'jig pa*), and bondage (*bandha, bcing ba*) and liberation (*mokṣa, thar pa*).

Regarding the proof [that these do not ultimately exist] from the point of view of scripture, the Supramundane Victor said:

> Those which are internal earth constituents and those which are external earth constituents are for the Tathāgata non-dualistic objects, are non-dual, not to be treated as dualistic. For he is perfectly and completely enlightened with respect to no-character and sameness of character.

And:

> When analyzed with awareness,
> Forms do not actually exist.
> Therefore, I say that the elements do not exist
> And true existence does not exist.

The reasoning of the lack of being one or many is also stated; Bhāvaviveka's *Blaze of Reasoning* says:

> Even the Tathāgata does not ultimately exist because of not being observed to be the same as or different from his body, like self, sentient being, person, and so forth.

Regarding the scriptures which prove that [phenomena] exist like illusions conventionally, such statements are made in sutras as:

> The Tathāgata is a reflection
> Of uncontaminated virtuous qualities.
> Though there is no reality or Tathāgata in these,
> An image appears to all the world.

11 The Two Truths

The presentation of the two truths delineated [by reasoning] has two parts: the actual presentation and derivative topics.

ACTUAL PRESENTATION

The basis of division of the two truths is objects of knowledge *(jñeya, shes bya)*. The divisions are two, conventional truths *(saṃvṛtisatya, kun rdzob dben pa)* and ultimate truths *(paramārthasatya, don dam bden pa)*. With regard to their sameness or difference, it is asserted here, as it is stated in the *Sutra Unravelling the Thought*, that [the position that the two truths are] different entities is damaged by four reasonings and [the position that the two truths] are the same reverse *(*ekavyatireka, ldog pa gcig)* [i.e., exactly the same] is damaged by four reasonings.

Regarding that, the four reasonings refuting that [the two truths] are different entities are that:

1 it would absurdly follow that by realizing the mode of being of a sprout, superimpositions of the conception of true existence with respect to the sprout would not be eliminated,
2 it would absurdly follow that the reality of a sprout would not be the sprout's final mode of subsistence,
3 it would absurdly follow that the mere elimination of true existence with respect to a sprout would not be the reality of the sprout,

4 it would absurdly follow that the conception of true existence and the wisdom realizing non-true existence would operate simultaneously even in the mental continuum of a Buddha.

[These fallacies would be incurred] if the sprout and the reality of the sprout were different entities. All four of these consequences *(prasaṅga, thal 'gyur)* are consequences that imply the opposite [that is, that the two truths are not different entities and thus, by extension, that they are the same entity].

The four reasonings refuting that [the two truths] are the same reverse [i.e., exactly the same] are that:

1 it would absurdly follow that even common beings would directly realize ultimate truths,
2 it would absurdly follow that reality would be an object of observation of an affliction *(kleśa, nyon mongs)*,
3 it would absurdly follow that there would be no need to seek the path of Superiors *(āryamārga, 'phags pa'i lam)*,
4 it would absurdly follow that the varieties of different divisions of conventionalities would not exist.

[These fallacies would be incurred] if a form and its reality were exactly the same reverse. All four are consequences that imply the opposite [that is, that the two truths are not the same reverse and thus different reverses].

With respect to the definitions of the two truths, an object found by a conventional valid cognizer is the definition of a conventional truth, and an object found by a valid reasoning consciousness distinguishing the ultimate is the definition of an ultimate truth.

Here [in this system], two ultimates are explained, actual and concordant ultimate truths. Jñānagarbha's *Two Truths* says:

> Since the negation of production and so forth
> Accords with the real,
> We assert it to be ultimate.

Kamalaśīla's *Illumination of the Middle Way* says:

> Thus, since this non-production accords with the ultimate, it is called an "ultimate"; it is not actually [an ultimate] because the actual ultimate is passed beyond all elaborations.

In addition, in Jñānagarbha's *Two Truths* "a non-deceptive reasoning [consciousness]" is called an ultimate.

Also, Kamalaśīla's *Illumination of the Middle Way* says:

> Those statements that "production does not exist ultimately" and so forth are asserted to mean the following: All consciousnesses arisen from correct hearing, thinking, and meditating are non-mistaken subjects whereby they are called "ultimate" due to being the ultimate among them [i.e., consciousnesses].

Thus, reality — the object — is explained as the ultimate, and the reasoning consciousness — the subject — is explained as the ultimate, and each of them has two types. Emptiness — the object — is the actual ultimate which is free from both the elaborations of dualistic appearance and the elaborations of true existence for an uncontaminated exalted wisdom *(anāsravajñāna, zag med ye shes)* of meditative equipoise *(samāhita, mnyam gzhag)*. For a conceptual reasoning consciousness, [emptiness] is free from the elaborations of true existence but is not free from the elaborations of dualistic appearance; therefore, it is free from only one portion of elaborations. Hence, an emptiness — an object — is, in general, an ultimate although for a conceptual reasoning consciousness it is not the ultimate which is free from both [types of] elaborations. These are two ways of positing the ultimate which is an object.

When a Superior's non-conceptual exalted wisdom *(nirvikalpakajñāna, mi rtog ye shes)* of meditative equipoise is absorbed in suchness *(tathatā, de kho na nyid)*, it is able to eliminate both elaborations with respect to its object. Therefore, it is the actual ultimate. The conceptual reasoning consciousness which comprehends suchness in dependence on a sign *(liṅga, rtags)* is able to remove elaborations of true existence with respect to its object but is not able to eliminate elaborations of dualistic appearance. Therefore, it is a concordant ultimate which is posited as ultimate due to merely according in aspect with the former [non-conceptual wisdom consciousness]. These are two ways of positing the ultimate which is a subject.

In summary, one should know that reality — the object — is an actual ultimate truth and that the consciousness — the subject — is not an actual ultimate truth, but in terms of what is explained in the text, is also explained as an ultimate. One should also know that there are presentations of actual and concordant [types] for each of those [objective and subjective ultimates] as well [as given above].

The emptiness which is an affirming negative *(paryudāsapratiṣedha, ma yin dgag)* — the negation of ultimate production and so forth with respect to the aggregates, etc — is an imputed ultimate and an actual conventionality because that mode of emptiness appears only dualistically for an awareness which sees it directly; it in no way appears free from dualistic appearance. That is the case because that mode of emptiness must appear even to conventional valid cognizers such as eye consciousnesses that directly perceive those bases which are empty. Through this one can know that a Buddha's exalted wisdom which knows the varieties *(yāvajjñāna, ji snyed pa mkhyen pa'i ye shes)* and a learner Superior's exalted wisdom of subsequent attainment *(pṛṣthalabdhajñāna, rjas thob kyi ye shes)* are comprehenders of illusory-like objects which are affirming negatives, and that even these objects which are composites of appearance and emptiness are metaphoric ultimates; they are not actual ultimates.

Furthermore, Kamalaśīla's *Illumination of the Middle Way* says:

> The suchnesses which have the character of the selflessness of phenomena and persons, because of possessing reason are highest *(parama, dam pa)*. They are also objects *(artha, don)* because they are the objects sought for the purpose of realization by those who seek to abandon the obstructions *(avaraṇa, sgrib pa)*. Also they are the meanings, that is, the objects, of the unmistaken highest exalted wisdom. Thus, [for those two reasons] they are called the highest objects *(paramārtha, don dam pa)*.

In this way, he explains that the selflessness of persons and phenomena are ultimate truths. Also, the foremost great being Tsong-kha-pa says in his *Great Commentary to (Nāgārjuna's) "Fundamental (Treatise on the Middle Way Called) Wisdom" (rTsa she tik chen)* in the context of Svātantrika:

> Therefore, the selflessness of the phenomena of the aggregates and the selflessness of persons — these being the mere elimination of elaborations which are the object of reasoned negation — are the objects found by the uncontaminated exalted wisdom knowing the mode [of being]. Even elaborations of dualistic appearance of persons and the aggregates are pacified in the face of that [wisdom]. Hence, they are ultimate truths.

Thus, he says that this system asserts that even the selflessness of persons is an ultimate truth. His *Essence of the Good Explanations* also explains that the passage from Kamalaśīla's *Illumination of the Middle Way* [cited above] indicates that both selflessnesses are actual ultimates. The omniscient Gyel-tsap also similarly explains in his commentary to Jñānagarbha's *Two Truths* that both selflessnesses are ultimate truths.

In addition, it is well known that in this system, an object realized by a direct valid cognizer that directly realizes it in a manner of the vanishing of dualistic appearance is taken as the definition of an ultimate truth, and an object realized by an awareness that directly realizes it in a manner having dualistic appearance is taken as the definition of a conventional truth. In that case, since an uninterrupted path *(ānantaryamārga, bar chad med lam)* in the continuum of a Superior directly realizing the selflessness of persons does not pass beyond a meditative equipoise involving the vanishing of dualistic appearance with respect to its object, like water poured in water, it must be asserted that the selflessness of persons is an ultimate truth.

Others say:

> Dualistic appearance is explained as having three types:
> 1 the appearance of something different from itself,
> 2 the appearance of true existence,
> 3 the appearance of conventionalities.
> Although [in meditative equipoise on the selflessness of persons] the first [two] do not exist, the last does. Therefore, it is not contradictory that [the wisdom consciousness realizing the selflessness of persons] has dualistic appearance [of the third type, despite the fact that dualistic appearance of the first two types has vanished]. A *Perfection of Wisdom Sutra* says that the teaching of the selflessness of form is said to be a facsimile perfection, and that when one actually practices the perfections, one must practice the unobservable emptiness. Therefore, even the exalted knower directly realizing selflessness in the continuum of a Superior of the lesser vehicles does not pass beyond a perfection of wisdom of the observable, whereby it is posited as having dualistic appearance.

Also, Kay-drup's *Thousand Doses* says:

> The Cittamātrins and Svātantrika-Mādhyamikas do not

> assert that the selflessnesss of persons is an ultimate truth, and they assert that the reasoning refuting a self of persons is a reasoning analyzing a conventionality.

Regarding this, according to the former position [that the selflessness of persons is an ultimate truth], it is still to be proven that there is no appearance of conventionalities for the uninterrupted path in the continuum of a Superior; [the absence of dualistic appearance of subject and object] is not suitable as a reason [proving that conventional appearance has vanished]. Also, it appears to be suitable to explain the meaning of the passages [cited to support the position that the selflessness of persons is an ultimate truth] in another way.

Positing an object realized by a direct valid cognizer that directly realizes it in a manner of the vanishing of dualistic appearance as the definition of an ultimate truth must still be analyzed with respect to the Svātantrikas who assert self-knowers [see pp. 195-196].

Furthermore, is the reasoning which settles that the self-sufficient person is empty because of lacking sameness with and difference from the aggregates a reasoning which analyzes the mode of subsistence of an object that is not subsumed by being merely posited through the power of appearing to a non-defective awareness? If it is, does [something become] a reasoning which analyzes the ultimate merely by that [i.e., analyzing whether a self-sufficient person is empty of being the same as or different from the aggregates] or not? Though something does become [a reasoning] analyzing the ultimate, is the discovery of such a self-sufficient person as non-existent by that reasoning necessarily a discovery by a reasoning consciousness that analyzes the ultimate or not? With respect to that, are two factors — being the actual ultimate found by a reasoning consciousness or not — to be distinguished relative to the awareness [which realizes them]? Such [problems] are to be analyzed well.

If, having arranged the statements of the three — the father [Tsong-kha-pa] and his sons [Gyel-tsap and Kay-drup] — one comes to know a system for dispelling objections, it appears that it will be speech pleasing to scholars. However, it is not suitable to be easily satisfied by those who, from seeing only one portion of the scriptures, discard other portions and do whatever they can to make up their own interpretations.

Bhāvaviveka's *Lamp for (Nāgārjuna's) "Wisdom"* commenting on the eighteenth chapter of the *Treatise on the Middle Way* where it says [XVIII. lab], "If the self were the aggregates/It would have production and disintegration," says:

> Here the syllogism is: Ultimately the elements, the aggregation of the elements, the sense powers, the aggregation of the sense powers, consciousness, the body together with the senses, and the body together with consciousness are not the self because of just having the quality of production and disintegration, as is the case, for example, with the external elements.

Thus, he affixes the qualification "ultimately" to each reasoning proving the selflessness of persons.

At the point of commenting on [XVIII.4]:

> When [the view of] I and mine is extinguished
> With respect to the internal and external,
> Grasping ceases and through
> Extinguishing it, birth is extinguished.

[Bhāvaviveka says]:

> That liberation [i.e., the extinguishment of birth] occurs for Hearer and Solitary Realizer Superiors through their seeing the selflessness of persons. Those who proceed by the Buddha Vehicle achieve [liberation] by abandoning the afflictive obstructions *(kleśāvarana, nyon mongs pa'i sgrib pa)* and the obstructions to omniscience *(jñeyāvarana, shes bya'i sgrib pa)*. The methods for abandoning the afflictive obstructions are those which are indicated [in the chapter].

Thus, he says that the reasonings described in that chapter are objects of meditation for those who have the Hīnayāna lineage as well, and he describes that mode of emptiness of the self of persons as the meaning of emptiness. The commentary preceding the passage just explained says, "Thus, the yogis who make effort to realize the suchness of internal and external sources realize that those are empty." The "Introduction to the Reality of the Hearers" *(śravaka-tattvāvatāra)* chapter of Bhāvaviveka's *Blaze of Reasoning* speaks frequently in the same vein; I will not elaborate on it here. Due to these facts it is indubitable [that the selflessness of persons is an emptiness] in Sautrāntika-Svātantrika-Mādhyamika, but which of the two truths the Yogācāra-Svātantrika-Mādhyamikas assert the suchness which is the lack of duality of subject and object to be should be analyzed.

The statements in Kay-drup's *Thousand Doses* that also damage the position that in the Svātantrika system true cessations *(nirodha-satya, 'gog bden)* are asserted to be conventional truths appear to be overwhelmingly accurate. Specifically, he argues that it must be asserted without question that the path of release *(vimuktimārga, rnam grol lam)* of the path of seeing *(darśanamārga, mthong lam)* actualizes the cessation *(nirodha, 'gog pa)*, which is a state of having abandoned the objects to be abandoned on the path of seeing. Thus, the meaning of a cessation being actualized by a path of release is not suitable as anything other than that it is directly realized [by that path of release], and an object directly realized by that path must be asserted as an ultimate truth. Furthermore, when the eight forbearances *(kṣanti, bzod pa)* and the eight knowledges *(jñāna, shes pa)* of the sixteen moments of forbearance and knowledge[1] are posited as the uninterrupted path *(ānantaryamārga, bar chad med lam)* and path of release [respectively] — without interruption by another consciousness — the eight knowledges are the entities of the path of release which attain a stainless true cessation — a separation from adventitious defilements *(akasikmala, glo bur dri ma)*. If the generation [of those eight knowledges] did not actualize [or bring about] the quality which is the state of having abandoned the discordant class [artificial conceptions of true existence], they would not differ in any way from the eight forbearances. Also, it would be meaningless to say that a true cessation is actualized in the state of subsequent attainment *(pṛṣṭhalabdha, rjas thob)* when one rises from that [path of release]. Therefore, [if true cessations were not ultimate truths] the cessation which is the state of having abandoned the objects to be abandoned on the path of seeing would never be actualized.

There are many points to be analyzed with this reasoning with regard to the Nature Body *(svabhāvikakāya, ngo bo nyid sku)* [of a Buddha] as well. Therefore, the intelligent and meek should analyze this further.

Divisions of Conventional Truths

Jñānagarbha's *Two Truths* says:

> Those mere things which lack being imputed objects
> And [which are] dependently produced
> Should be known as real conventionalities.

Also [the same text says]:

> Those which are not real are imputations.

Thus, he mentions two, real conventional truths *(tathyasaṃvṛtisatya, yang dag kun rdzob bden pa)* and unreal conventional truths *(mityāsaṃvṛtisatya, log pa'i kun rdzob bden pa).*

Their definitions are indicated by a statement [from the same text]:

> Since they are able and unable
> To perform functions as they appear,
> The division of real and unreal
> Conventionalities is made.

With regard to that, in general, those things that are not established by valid cognition *(pramāna, tshad ma)* such as a double moon and such as the principal *(pradhāna, gtso bo)* imputed by other schools [such as Sāṃkhya] are merely unreal conventionalities; they are not unreal conventional truths because they are not established bases *(gzhi grub).* Therefore, the previous passage from Jñānagarbha's *Two Truths* [above] does not indicate that such things as ultimate production are unreal conventional truths.

It is not correct to assert merely that that which is able to perform a function in accordance with its mode of appearance is the definition of a real conventional truth and that which is not able to perform a function in accordance with its mode of appearance is the definition of an unreal conventional truth because there are many cases of establishing with valid cognition that a base *(aśraya, gzhi)* is able to perform a function in accordance with its mode of appearance without establishing with valid cognition the meaning of real conventionality. Otherwise, it would absurdly follow that even common beings whose minds have not been affected by tenets refute with valid cognition the meaning of true existence with respect to earth and so forth because they establish with valid cognition that these are conventionalities and it must be asserted that "conventionality" is taken to mean falsity [therefore, it would absurdly follow that common beings would have understood emptiness because they understand falsities, i.e., conventionalities].

Thus, it should be known that a phenomenon that is an object found by a conventional valid cognizer that is able to perform a function in accordance with its appearance to the awareness perceiving it is the definition of a real conventional truth, and a phenomenon that is an object found by a conventional valid cognizer that is not able to perform a function in accordance with how it appears to the awareness perceiving it is the definition of an unreal conventional truth.

The divisions of real conventional truths are easy to understand. Regarding unreal conventionalities, the reflection of a face in a mirror that appears to a non-conceptual *(nirvikalpaka, rtog med)* consciousness, the apprehended object *(grāhyaviṣaya, gzung yul)* of a thought consciousness *(kalpana, rtog pa)*, and so forth are both unreal conventionalities and conventional truths. The self of persons *(pudgalātman, gang zag gi bdag)* and the self of phenomena *(dharmātman, chos kyi bdag)*, etc. which are imputed by [false] tenet systems are unreal conventionalities but are not held to be unreal conventional truths because they are refuted by valid cognition.

Objection: Kamalaśīla's *Illumination of the Middle Ways* says:

> These things that some authors of treatises, in passing beyond renown, impute as real — imaginaries and so forth — are said to exist as unreal conventionalities because they are not even renowned to exist. Those that are thoroughly imputed in accordance with dependent arising, such as, for instance, "Here a self or a sentient being does not exist. These phenomena are caused," exist as real conventionalities.

Does this statement not indicate that the two selves and so forth are unreal conventional truths?

Answer: It is not so because that [passage] is indicating that objects that are imputed only through the power of [false] tenets exist as unreal conventionalities; it is not indicating that they are conventional truths. Otherwise, it would contradict the statement, "They are not even renowned to exist."

Except for objects, this system does not make the distinction of real and unreal with respect to subjects, based on the fact that they assert that own-character *(svalakṣana, rang mtshan)* is established by valid cognition. If they did not assert own-character, then within the context that apprehended objects are similar in appearing clearly to sense consciousnesses, it would not be correct to assert that water and so forth are real conventionalities which are able to perform functions as they appear and that a double moon, the appearance of a double moon, and so forth are unreal conventionalities which are not able to perform functions as they appear because, in that case, since water appears to the sense consciousness apprehending water to be established by way of its own-character, it would [absurdly] irreversibly follow that [water] would be an unreal conventionality which was not able to perform a function as it appeared [see pp. 209-210].

Furthermore, it would [absurdly] follow that the establishment of form by way of its own-character is asserted [in the Svātantrika system] as the quality of the object of negation — the opposite of non-true existence — because existence by way of its own-character would be the object of negation of the reasoning consciousness analyzing the final [nature of phenomena]. If you accept that [existence by way of its own-character is the object of negation], then it [absurdly] follows that the object of negation appears to sense consciousnesses because existence by way of its own-character is present in the apprehended objects of sense consciousnesses. You cannot accept that [the object of negation appears to sense consciousnesses] because Jñānagarbha's *Two Truths* explains that truly established production and so forth do not appear to sense consciousnesses and explains that appearances to sense consciousnesses are never refuted. [For a discussion of this argument, see pp. 73-76, 208-210].

Objection: Regarding the explanation in Jñānagarbha's *Two Truths* that the object of negation — true existence — does not appear to sense consciousnesses, the reasoning consciousness analyzing the ultimate [i.e., emptiness] is [taken as the referent of] the ultimate [in the term "ultimate establishment"] and being established for that [reasoning consciousness] is explained as ultimate establishment. That [ultimate establishment] is explained as not appearing to sense consciousnesses; true establishment [or ultimate establishment, that is, being established by way of the object's own mode of subsistence without being posited through the force of appearing to a non-defective consciousness] is not being referred to.

Answer: Such a statement is not a good explanation because in Jñānagarbha's *Two Truths* and its commentary, the fact that truly established production, the principal *(pradhāna, gtso bo)* imputed by the Sāṃkhyas, the [mind which is an] evolute of the elements imputed by the Cārvākas, partless moments of consciousness, and so forth do not appear to direct perceivers is stated as a reason why it is correct to refute [those things] that are thoroughly imputed by others to be really existent. Also, as a reason why it is incorrect to refute the appearances [to sense consciousnessess], it is stated that the refutation of appearances to sense consciousnesses that are not imputed to be true [that is, appearances that are not falsely imagined to be truly existent] would only damage us. The reason for that rests on the fact that, since the objects of non-conceptual sense consciousnesses are real conventional truths, if those [objects] appeared to be truly established to them [the senses], it would [absurdly] follow that true establishment itself would be a conventional truth. Furthermore, he explains that within the context of the truly established things asserted by others [the Proponents of True Existence], conventionalities that accord with the actual entities of the objects are not feasible, and the fact that not even a particle of true establishment appears to sense consciousnesses is stated [by Jñānagarbha] as a reason why factually concordant conventionalities are not feasible within true establishment. Therefore, the omniscient Gyel-tsap also states that this system asserts that true establishment does not appear to sense consciousnesses.

It is similar to Yogācāra-Svātantrika-Mādhyamika because the foremost great being Tsong-kha-pa says in his *Great Explanation of (Candrakīrti's) "Supplement"* at the point of explaining the assertions of the father Śāntarakṣita and spiritual son [Kamalaśīla]:

> The perceivers of the displays as truly existent by the conception of true existence are thought consciousnesses, not sense consciousnesses because the explanation in Jñānagarbha's commentary on his *Two Truths* that the object of negation does not appear to the sense consciousnesses is similarly [applicable] here.

If it is not taken that way, [but rather that Jñānagarbha] is referring to what is ultimate for a reasoning consciousness, it is difficult to explain the meaning of the "displays as truly existent by the conception of true existence." [See pp. 350-351.]

There are many points to be explained, such as how illusions are used as example, but I will leave these for the time being.

Derivative Topics

The Sautrāntika-Svātantrikas are similar [to other Buddhist schools] in asserting that there are two valid cognizers which ascertain the two truths: direct valid cognizers *(pratyakṣapramāṇa, mngon sum tshad ma)* and inferential valid cognizers *(anumānapramāṇa, rjas dpag tshad ma)*. The divisions of signs which are the bases of inference and so forth are also for the most part similar to the former [schools of

Buddhist tenets]. Regarding direct perceivers, since it was already explained earlier why they do not assert self-knowing direct perceivers *(svasaṃvedanapratyakṣa, rang rig mngon sum)*, the number of [direct perceivers] is definitely three: sense direct perceivers *(indriyapratyakṣa, dbang po'i mngon sum)*, mental direct perceivers *(mānasapratyakṣa, yid kyi mngon sum)*, and yogic direct perceivers *(yogi-pratyakṣa, rnal 'byor mngon sum)*.

Their presentation of the effect of valid cognition accords neither with the Cittamātrins nor with the Sautāntrikas Following Reasoning because they [the Sautāntrika-Svātantrikas] do not assert self-knowers.

Their presentation of the three conditions of a sense consciousness also does not accord with the Cittamātrins because they assert that each of the minute particles in a composite are causes of a sense consciousness. They also assert that minute particles are substantially existent *(dravyasat, rdzas yad)* because minute particles are established objectively and are posited in the context of being found at the end of searching for the imputed object.

The omniscient Kay-drup states in his *Thousand Doses*, his *Great Commentary Illuminating the Principles*, and so forth that Mādhyamikas who assert non-true existence never assert partless things. Therefore, the meaning of the statement in Tsong-kha-pa's *Great Exposition of the Stages of the Path* at the point of expressing the assertions of Bhāvaviveka that, "Since he appears to assert final minute particles, he asserts partless particles as observed-object-conditions," does not refer to a partlessness in which there is no divisibility whatsoever no matter how much it is analyzed by reasoning. Rather, [Tsong-kha-pa] has in mind minute particles a smaller part of which cannot be seen by a sense consciousness without relying on a reasoning consciousness. If [the meaning of Tsong-kha-pa's statement] is taken that way, it seems to fit together [with Kay-drup's assertion], but it should still be examined.

The glorious Candrakīrti's *Supplement to the Middle Way* says:

> Some say that whatever the Sautrāntika system propounds as ultimate, Mādhyamika propounds as conventional. It should be known that this is propounded by those who do not understand the suchness [explained in Nāgārjuna's] *Treatise on the Middle Way*.

Also, Candrakīrti's commentary to Āryadeva's *Four Hundred* says,

"Those of our own schools who, like the Vaiśeṣikas, assert substantial minute particles are not correct." These statements appear to be denegrating this [Sautrāntika-Svātantrika-Mādhyamika] system.

Although the Prāsaṅgikas assert external objects, their way of positing them is not similar to that [of the Sautrāntika-Svātantrikas]. I will explain this briefly [in the Prāsaṅgika chapter]; it should be known in detail elsewhere.

Furthermore, it also should be analyzed whether or not [the Sautrāntika-Svātantrika assertion on] mental direct perceivers accords with that of the Prāmāṇikas. I think that they also differ slightly from the Yogācāra-Svātantrika-Mādhyamikas [on this point].

It is easy to understand that they do not assert a basis-of-all *(ālaya, kun gzhi)* and an afflicted mind *(kliṣṭamanas, nyon yid)*.

These [Sautrāntika-Svātantrika-Mādhyamikas] assert that the non-existence of external objects is not the thought of any sutra whatsoever, due to which they also do not assert that there exists a yogic direct perceiver which realizes the suchness that is the emptiness of duality [of subject and object]. Therefore, it appears that this master's [i.e., Bhāvaviveka's] system must also differ from other schools with respect to how to comment on the thought of Maitreya's *Ornament for Clear Realization*.

12 Presentation of the Path

This school does not assert a difference in the entity [or nature] of the paths of Hearers *(śrāvaka, nyan thos)* and Solitary Realizers *(pratyekabuddha, rang gyal)*, but does assert that they are distinguished in terms of the length of cultivation [of the path] and the effect [they achieve]. With regard to Solitary Realizers, they make presentations of the great and small Congregators *(vargacārin, tshogs spyod)* and the Rhinoceros-like *(khaṅgaviṣāṇakalpa, bse ru lta bu)*. Because they assert that the selflessness of phenomena is not taught in the Hīnayāna, Hearers and Solitary Realizers who are definite in the lineage of their own path do not realize the selflessness of phenomena.

Objection: It must be asserted that there exists someone who, having entered the Mahāyāna, ascertains the selflessness of phenomena well and later falls to become a Hearer or Solitary Realizer. If that is so, then there must be an actualization of the selflessness of phenomena [on the path of seeing] by such a person through meditation and an accustoming [on the path of meditation] to what was seen. If you accept that, then, since you must accept that he abandons the artificial conception *(*parikalpitagrāha, 'dzin pa kun brtags)* of true existence on the path of seeing and abandons the innate *(sahaja, lhan skyes)* [conception of true existence] on the path of meditation, the positions that the conception of true existence is asserted as the obstructions to omniscience and that Hearers and Solitary Realizers do not abandon [those obstructions] are not correct.

Answer: There is no fallacy. Such a person relying on such a path could merely temporarily suppress the manifest conceptions of true existence but could not abandon the seeds of either the artificial or innate conceptions of true existence. Therefore, these cases of directly seeing the selflessness of phenomena and becoming accustomed to what was seen are not posited as the path of seeing and path of meditation that realize the subtle suchness. The reason for this is that in order to abandon the seeds of the conception of true existence, meditation on selflessness alone is insufficient; it must be accompanied by the limitless collections. Therefore, generating the wisdom realizing non-true existence into the entity of an uninterrupted path which is the antidote *(pratipakṣa, gnyen po)* abandoning objects of abandonment depends on the power of the special method, and even at the time of the uninterrupted path itself, [the wisdom] must be related with the power of special types of method. By this reasoning, at the very time of the uninterrupted path at the end of the continuum [as a sentient being before achieving Buddhahood], along with the exalted wisdom of meditative equipoise there must exist a complete capacity definitely to manifest in the next moment all the conventional and ultimate uncontaminated qualities of a Conqueror. Nevertheless, conventional aspects do not have to be manifest in that exalted wisdom of meditative equipoise.

This is a difficult point in the Perfection Vehicle *(pāramitāyāna, phar phyin theg pa)*. It is one essential [reason why] one must definitely add the Mantra path to the end of the Perfection Vehicle path in order to become fully enlightened.

This way of dispelling objections is similar in Yogācāra-Svātantrika-Mādhyamika as well, and this process of reasoning is very important in the context of Prāsaṅgika also. These too are unrivalled, great features of the good explanation by the foremost great being Tsong-kha-pa, and I have spoken relying on the statements of the Foremost One himeself. How could the likes of me explain these difficult points on his own?

Objection: Since the honorable master Bhāvaviveka stated that if the selflessness of phenomena were taught in the Hearer scriptural collection *(śrāvakapiṭaka, nyan thos kyi sde snod)*, the teachings of the Mahāyāna would be purposeless, then a Hīnayāna Superior could not possibly have realized the selflessness of phenomena because, otherwise, the teaching of the selflessness of phenomena would not be the only distinguishing feature of the Mahāyāna.

Answer: There is no fallacy. The wisdom realizing the subtle suchness is the antidote to the conception of true existence of phenomena, and since the conception of true existence is an obstruction to omniscience, the teaching of the selflessness of phenomena was set forth for the purpose of abandoning the obstruction to omniscience. Therefore, if the selflessness of phenomena were taught in the scriptural collection of Hearers, Hīnayānists would have to abandon the obstructions to omniscience. If that were the case, then, since the antidote for abandoning the obstructions to omniscience would have to be fully taught in that scriptural collection, [Bhāvaviveka] says that it would [absurdly] follow that the Mahāyāna scriptural collection would be purposeless. He is not asserting that the Mahāyāna has no distinguishing features apart from the selflessness of phenomena.

They [the two branches of Svātantrika] are similar in asserting that the obstructions — the objects of abandonment — are two: the afflictive obstructions *(kleśāvaraṇa, nyon sgrib)* and the obstructions to omniscience *(jñeyāvaraṇa, shes sgrib)*. Since it is explained in Bhāvaviveka's *Blaze of Reasoning* that when a person definite in the Mahāyāna lineage attains the eighth ground *(bhūmi, sa)*, the afflictive obstructions are consumed, he does not assert, as do the other Svātantrikas, that the two obstructions are abandoned simultaneously by the vajra-like meditative stabilization *(vajropamasamadhi, rdo rje lta bu'i ting nge 'dzin)* [at the end of the tenth ground]. However, he also does not assert, as do the Prāsaṅgikas, that one does not begin to abandon the obstructions to omniscience until the afflictive obstructions have been consumed.

The four doctrinal forbearances *(dharmakṣānti, chos bzod)* of the uninterrupted path of the path of seeing are divided from the perspective of comprehending the reality of the four truths, and the four subsequent forbearances *(anukṣānti, rjes bzod)* are posited from the perspective of realizing [the reality] of the four subjects [that is, consciousnesses], observing the four doctrinal forbearances to be selfless. The foremost Gyel-tsap asserts that this procedure of the higher knowledge [texts, such as Asaṅga's *Compendium of Knowledge (Abhidharmasamuccaya)*] regarding the way of making such distinctions with respect to the eight knowledges is similar for all Mādhyamikas — Prāsaṅgikas and Svātantrikas.

All Prāsaṅgikas and Svātantrikas agree that the reasoning consciousness directly realizing non-true existence does not establish the existence of non-true existence, but the Yogācāra-Svātantrika-Mādhyamikas assert that the self-knower experiencing the reasoning consciousness which realizes non-true existence establishes the existence of non-true existence implicitly from its explicit realization of the reasoning consciousness. The Prāsaṅgika-Mādhyamikas assert that the subsequent cognizer (**paricchinnajñāna, bcad shes*) induced by the non-conceptual reasoning consciousness establishes the existence of non-true existence, and they assert that conceptual subsequent cognizers (**kalpanāparicchinnajñāna, rtog pa bcad shes*) and direct valid cognizers (*pratyakṣapramāṇa, mngon sum tshad ma*) are not mutually exclusive. For the Svātantrikas of this [Sautrāntika-Svātantrika] system, positing either of those two is not feasible, nor does the reasoning consciousness implicitly realize the existence of non-true existence because the explicit object of the reasoning consciousness is a non-affirming negative. Thus, how [the existence of the emptiness of true existence] is certainly to be reflected upon. Beginning with these, there are many points to be talked about, but I will leave them for the time being.

Such presentations as those of the Three Bodies (*trikāya, sku gsum*) of the state of the fruition [Buddhahood] agree for the most part with the other Mādhyamikas. Although there are many different modes of explanation in the texts, they constitute differences only in form; they are not discordant systems.

Part Three
Yogācāra-Svātantrika-Mādhyamika

This section has two parts: a general explanation and a detailed explanation.

13 The Integration of Mind-Only

GENERAL EXPLANATION

Śāntarakṣita's *Ornament for the Middle Way* says:

> The non-existence of external objects should be known
> Through relying on mind-only.
> [Then] relying on this [Mādhyamika] mode, it should be known
> That this [mind] too is completely selfless.[1]

The commentary following that says:

> Through relying on mind-only, things that are asserted to be external to the mind, such as I and mine, subject and object, etc.,[2] are just effortlessly realized to be without a nature [of a difference of entity between subject and object].[3]

Thus, this indicates two steps: initially, one ascertains the selflessness of persons and then ascertains the suchness which is the emptiness of duality [of subject and object]. The same text also says:

> Regarding this mode [mentioned in the stanza above], though one has realized that the mind is without a nature [of a difference of entity between subject and object] because it is not self-arisen, in order to realize the middle path which is an abandonment of all extremes, one thoroughly realizes the absence of a nature [of true existence] due to [the mind's]

> being devoid of a nature of one or many.[4]

Thus, three stages of ascertaining suchness are explained. After the first two stages [of ascertaining the selflessness of persons and the emptiness of duality of subject and object], when those with very great intelligence and effort analyze whether that mind is inherently one or many, they see that not even a particle of ultimate establishment (*paramārthasiddhi, don dam par grub pa*) exists. They thereby realize the middle path which is an abandonment of all extremes.

Proof that this is the Thought of Sutras

A sutra [the *Chapter on the Supramundane (Lokottaraparivarta)*] says:

> Furthermore, O Children of the Conqueror, having realized that the three realms are mind only, realize that the three times [past, present, and future] are similar to mind as well. Understand that mind is also without extremes and middle.[5]

The *Compendium of Doctrine (Dharmasaṃgīti)* says, "Supramundane Victor, all phenomena are imaginary in essence. They are exhausted in mind only, without substance, like illusions, rootless."[6] The *Descent into Lāṅka Sūtra* says:

> Through relying on mind-only
> One does not conceive of external objects.
> Abiding in correct observation
> One passes beyond mind-only as well.
>
> Having passed beyond mind-only
> One passes beyond non-appearance [of true existence temporarily].
> A yogi who abides in non-appearance
> See the Mahāyāna.[7]

[The Yogācāra-Svātantrikas] assert that such statements are teachings that present the ascertainment of the modes of suchness in the stages explained above.

Thus, it is asserted that the Mahāyāna is attained by way of two modes:

1 of consciousness only, which is an emptiness of external objects conventionally,
2 of the non-existence of the entityness of all phenomena ultimately.

Śāntarakṣita's *Ornament for the Middle Way* says:

> Those who, having mounted the chariot of the two modes,
> Grasp the reins of reasoning
> Thereby attain the state of a Mahāyānist
> Exactly as it is.[8]

The attainment of the Mahāyāna through these two modes is also the thought of the Conqueror because the autocommentary [to this stanza] says:

> The *Descent into Lāṅka Sūtra* says that the brief teaching of the Mahāyāna is included into two modes as follows:
>
> > All of the Mahāyāna is included in
> > The five phenomena,[9] nature,
> > The eight collections of consciousness,
> > And the existence of the two selflessness.[10]

Nevertheless, the Yogācāra-Svātantrikas do not assert, as do the Cittamātrins, that consciousness is truly established, or that the suchness which is the emptiness of duality [of subject and object] is truly established even conventionally. The Yogācāra-Svātantrikas also do not assert a mind-basis-of-all *(ālayavijñāna, kun gzhi rnam par shes pa)* that is a separate entity from the six consciousnesses, and from this it can be understood that they also do not assert an afflicted mind *(kliṣṭamanas, nyon yid)*.

Question: Is this mind-only mode of the non-existence of external objects an assertion of the protector Nāgārjuna or not? If it is [his assertion], you must say which texts of the protector Nāgārjuna indicate this [mind-only] mode.

Answer: This is shown by his *Sixty Stanzas of Reasoning (34)* where it says:

> Those explained as the great elements and so forth
> Are completely included within consciousness.
> Knowing that, if they lack [true existence],
> Are they not wrongly imagined?

The first two lines indicate that the elements *(bhūta, 'byung ba)* and elemental evolutes do not exist as objects separate from consciousness and that they are posited just as the appearance of consciousness in the aspect of those [objects], whereby they are included in consciousness.

The commentary following the stanza in Śāntarakṣita's *Ornament for the Middle Way* that begins, "Those who, having mounted the chariot of the two modes," says:

> Those engaged in inference that works by the power of things realize that all things are without inherent existence through the Mahāyāna which is included within the expression of the two modes and by which the Tathāgatas go and will go. Like those mounted on great chariots grasping the reins well, they thoroughly attain the "meaningful Mahāyāna."[11]

Thus, he says that Bodhisattvas mount the chariot of the two modes — the mode of mind-only conventionally and the mode of the middle way of non-inherent existence ultimately — and grasping the reins of stainless reasoning, attain possession of the Mahāyāna that has the meaning of suchness.

Although in the system of these Svātantrikas there are many minor divisions which have different modes of assertion among themselves, all are similar in asserting the corpus of the presentation for ascertaining suchness as just explained. In Āryavimuktisena's *Illumination of the (Perfection of Wisdom in) Twenty-Five Thousand Stanzas (Pancaviṃśatisāhasrikālokā)*, Haribhadra's *Illumination of (Maitreya's) "Ornament for Clear Realization" (Abhisamayālamkārāloka), Eight Chapters (Le'u brgyad ma),*[12] *Commentary for Easy standing on the Difficult Points of the Condensed (Perfection of Wisdom Sutra) (Sañcayagāthāpañjikā-subodhinī)*, Buddhajñānapāda's texts on texts on the perfection [of wisdom], and Abhayākaragupta's *Moonbeams of Essentials (Marmakaumudī)* and *Ornament for the Thought of the Subduer (Munimatālaṃkāra)* the mode of ascertaining the view is presented in just this way. The foremost ominscient one, Tsong-kha-pa, asserts that although a few who asserted the system of these Svātantrikas appeared prior to Śāntarakṣita and his spiritual son [Kamalaśīla], such as Āryavimuktisena, the founder of the Mādhyamika tenet system of the mode of the non-existence of external objects is the master Śāntarakṣita.

14 The Meaning of True Existence

The detailed explanation has four parts: an identification of the object of reasoned negation, an explanation of the reasoning refuting that, a presentation of the two truths delineated [by reasoning], and a brief presentation of the paths and fruitions.

IDENTIFICATION OF THE OBJECT OF REASONED NEGATION

The three modes of positing the ultimate and the difference between positing or not positing what is established as those [three modes] as ultimately established was explained earlier [pp. 314-316]. Therefore, here I will discuss briefly the mode of identifying the measure of true existence — the object of reasoned negation.

Kamalaśīla's *Illumination of the Middle Way* says:

> An awareness that mistakenly superimposes the opposite onto things that are in reality without entityness is called the "concealer" *(saṃvṛti, kun rdzod)* because it is obstructs [itself] from [perception of] suchness or because it veils [other awarenesses] from [perception of] suchness. As it says in the *[Descent into Laṅkā] Sutra:*
>
> > Things are produced conventionally;
> > Ultimately they are without inherent existence.
> > That which is mistaken about what does not
> > inherently exist

Is asserted to be a concealer of reality.

> Because [an artificial awareness] arises from that [conception of true existence], all false things which [such an artificial awareness] sees displayed by that [conception of true existence as if they are truly established] are called "mere conventionalities." Moreover, that [conception of true existence] arises through the maturation of beginningless predispositions for error, whereby all living beings see [phenomena] displayed as if [they had] a true nature in reality. Therefore, all entities of false things [which exist] through the power of those [that is, sentient beings'] thoughts are said "only to exist conventionally."

Thus, the existence of that which is the opposite of the mode of conventional existence set forth [in the passage above] is the measure of true existence — the object of reasoned negation.

Regarding this, [the part of the passage] that reads, "An awareness that mistakenly superimposes the opposite onto things that in reality are without entityness" indicates the mistaken mode of superimposing ultimate existence onto that which ultimately does not inherently exist. "Is called the 'concealer' because it is obstructs [itself] from [perception of] suchness or because it veils [other awarenesses] from [perception of] suchness" explains *(saṃvṛti)* as [meaning] concealer in terms of the original Sanskrit; it is obstructed from seeing the mode of being of reality. "Because [an artificial awareness] arises from that, all false things which [such an artificial awareness] sees displayed by that are called mere conventionalities" indicates that because of arising from that conception of true existence, all false things that are seen displayed as truly existent by the conception of true existence exist only as conventionalities. The seer in this context is a thought consciousness, not a sense consciousness [because] the foremost omniscient being Tsong-kha-pa said, "This system asserts that the object of negation — true existence — does not appear to the sense consciousnesses" and it was clearly explained earlier [pp. 334-336] that both Svātantrika systems are similar [regarding this point].

"Moreover, that arises through the maturation of beginningless predispositions for error" indicates that such a conception of true existence is the innate *(sahaja, lhan skyes)* conception of true existence, which has operated beginninglessly. The "thought" of "by the power of their thought" is explained as having both conceptual and non-conceptual [forms]. Therefore, the assertion by some that it is only a non-conceptual consciousness is not correct because there are many phenomena that do not appear to a non-conceptual consciousness of a common being which must be posited only through a conceptual consciousness, and those [phenomena] are also asserted to be established by way of their own character in this [system]. Tsong-kha-pa's *Great Commentary to (Candrakīrti's) "Supplement"* says, "It is not a conceptual consciousness only but refers also to non-conceptual consciousnesses." The terms "only" and "also" clearly indicate the existence of both conceptual and non-conceptual consciousnesses. Do not hold that this passage indicates that conceptual awarenesses do not exist [in the referents of "thought" in Kamalaśīla's statement]!

It is incorrect to think that these words of [Tsong-kha-pa's] statement that thought in this context can be a non-conceptual consciousness probably explains that the object of negation — true existence — appears to the sense consciousnesses. For this passage is indicating the mode by which things are posited as existing by the power of conceptual and non-conceptual consciousnesses, and it is indicating that these [phenomena are established by way of their] own character within being merely posited through the power of those two [types of consciousness], implicitly eliminating ultimate existence. Also, [phenomena that are established by way of their] own character within being merely posited through power of those two are conventional truths and are not the object of reasoned negation. Tsong-kha-pa's *Explanation of (Candrakīrti's) "Supplement"* clearly says:

> That false things which do not exist ultimately but are posited as existing by the power of those two exist only conventionally is the meaning [of the verse from the *Descent into Laṅkā Sutra*], "The production of things [exists] conventionally"; it does not mean that these exist for the concealer which is the consciousness conceiving of true existence.

Therefore, to say that this statement which indicates the manner of positing conventionalities [instead] indicates the measure of true existence — the object of negation — is not to speak well.

Question: If this system conventionally asserts that things [have] an own-character that is posited by the power of an awareness and asserts that establishment as an objective self-characterized mode of subsistence which does not depend on being posited by the power of an awareness is the measure of true existence — the object of reasoned negation — what does it mean to be posited or not be posited by the power of an awareness?

Answer: I will explain this. When a magician conjures such things as a pebble or stick into a horse or an elephant, the magician perceives the pebble, stick and so forth as a horse or an elephant, but he does not conceive of them as [being a real] horse or elephant. The audience whose eyes have been affected by the mantra and salve[1] have both the appearance of the basis of conjuring [the pebble or stick] as a horse or elephant and the conception of such [that is, they both see the horse or an elephant and believe it to be real]. A person who arrives at the place late and whose eyes are not affected by the mantra and salve has neither the appearance of the basis of conjuring as a horse or an elephant nor such a conception.

For the magician, the basis for conjuring the illusion is merely posited as a horse or elephant through the power of an awareness affected by the mantra and salve; it does not appear as a horse or an elephant from the side of the pebble or stick's own mode of subsistence without depending on such an awareness. Nonetheless, there must exist some mode of subsistence which is the appearance as a horse or an elephant from the side of the pebble or stick itself and which is posited by the power of the awareness affected by the mantra and salve. Otherwise, if it were said that [a pebble or stick] merely appears as a horse or an elephant just for a mistaken consciousness *(bhrānti-jñāna, 'khrul shes)* and that, in general, the basis of conjuring does not appear as a horse or an elephant, then an awareness which was mistaken with respect to appearance would not occur, because in general even the mere appearance of a pebble or stick as a horse or an elephant would not occur.

Therefore, although the basis of conjuring can be posited as appearing as a horse or an elephant, it is posited in that way by the power of appearing to a mistaken awareness; it is not posited by the power of the mode of subsistence of the basis of conjuring. Like that example, according to these Mādhyamikas, the fact that things are posited though the power of an awareness which is not damaged by valid cognition and the fact that the thing's own mode of subsistence which is posited by the power of that [awareness] also exists are not contradictory, just as a basis of conjuring can be posited as appearing as a horse or an elephant by the power of an awareness affected by mantra and salve while there [also] exists a mode of subsistence which is the appearance of a horse or an elephant even from the side of the basis of conjuring and which is posited through the power of that awareness. Therefore, positing — through the power of an awareness — the production of a sprout from a seed and the sprout's being produced from the seed from its [the sprout's] own side are not contradictory. This should be known regarding all [cases of] positing conventional existence in this system.

For the audience whose eyes have been affected by the mantra and salve, the appearance [of the pebble or stick] as a horse or an elephant is not perceived as [having] a mode of subsistence which is posited through the power of an internal awareness; they apprehend from the start a real horse or elephant standing there covering the spot. In the same way, ordinary sentient beings apprehend things as established from the side of the object's own mode of subsistence without depending at all on being posited through the power of an internal awareness. That is the mode of apprehension by the innate conception of true existence. They [the Svātantrikas] assert that establishment in accordance with apprehension by that mode of conceiving [true existence] is negated by reasons such as the lack of being one or many, but a mere mode of subsistence which is posited through the power of awareness is not negated by those reasonings.

Thus, in this way one can know the point at which [a consciousness] becomes an analyzer of suchness for this system. If one is not satisfied with the mere name and designation, "In general, a sprout is produced from a seed," and merely analyzes whether or not a sprout is produced from a seed from its own side, this does not make [that investigation] an analysis of suchness. However, when one analyzes whether or not that production of a sprout is produced from the side of the object's own mode of subsistence without depending on being posited through the power of an awareness, this is posited as analyzing suchness. In the Prāsaṅgika system, even the former type of analysis [into whether the sprout is produced from the seed] qualifies as an analysis of suchness, and the conception of existence by way of [the object's] mode of subsistence without depending on being posited by an awareness is not the subtle innate conception of true existence.

Although the Proponents of True Existence posit objects of comprehension *(prameya, gzhal bya)* — the two, specifically characterized phenomena *(svalakṣaṇa, rang mtshan)* and generally characterized phenomena *(sāmanyalakṣaṇa, spyi mtshan)* — through the power of the two valid cognizers [direct and inferential valid cognizers], they assert that valid cognizers comprehend phenomena that exist in an objective mode of subsistence. They do not assert that what is posited subjectively through the power of appearing to a valid cognizer is the mode of subsistence of that object. Therefore, this is totally different in meaning from being posited through the power of an awareness in this [Svātantrika] system.

Tsong-kha-pa's *Great Commentary on (Candrakirti's) "Supplement"* says:

> With regard to the illusory appearance [created by a magician], according to the Yogācāra-Mādhyamikas it is established [i.e., certified as existing] by a self-knowing direct perceiver *(svasaṃvedanapratyakṣa, rang rig mngon sum)* whereas according to the Svātantrikas who assert external objects, it is established by the sense direct perceiver *(indriyapratyakṣa, dbang po)* that apprehends the base such as the area or space [where the illusion appears].

According to the Yogācāra-Mādhyamikas, since the illusory horse or elephant is merely a mental appearance, it is realized implicitly by the self-knowing awareness that comprehends it, and according to the Sautrāntika-Mādhyamikas, since the illusory horse or elephant is an external object and imaginary form-source *(parikalpitarūpa-āyatana, kun brtags pa'i gzugs kyi skye mched)*, it is established by the sense direct perceiver that apprehends either the area or the space. That this is the thought [of Tsong-kha-pa] is stated by the great scholar and adept Jam-yang-shay-bay-dor-jay.

A person whose eyes have not been affected [by the mantra] has neither the appearance of a pebble or stick as a horse or an elephant nor the conception of that. Similarly, when the non-conceptual exalted wisdom *(nirvikalpakajñāna, rnam par mi rtog pa'i ye shes)* is generated from analyzing well with properly contemplated reasoning and cultivation in meditation, all dualistic appearances are completely pacified in the face of that exalted wisdom, whereby there is neither the appearance nor conception of true existence.

In summary, the Svātantrika system asserts that things are posited through the power of awareness and that these [things] are posited by thought, but they do not assert that being posited by an awareness [means] necessarily to be posited only by a thought consciousness because they assert that positing by an awareness also includes being posited by a non-conceptual [sense] consciousness. Nevertheless, they do not assert that everything that is posited by any awareness conventionally exists. Therefore, [for something to exist it] must be posited through the power of an awareness that is not damaged by valid cognition. In that way, phenomena such as forms, from the appearance side, are established in a mode of subsistence which is merely posited through the power of appearing to a non-defective awareness and, from the emptiness side, are empty of being established from the side of the object's own mode of subsistence without being posited by an awareness. There must be a composite of these two [appearance and emptiness]. The term "merely" in the statement "merely posited through the power of awareness" eliminates establishment by way of an uncommon mode of subsistence; it does not eliminate the existence of a mode of subsistence that is not just posited by names and terminology.

If these [points] are known well, one will be able to delineate accurately the ways in which the Svātantrikas' way of positing the two truths is subtler than that of the Proponents of True Existence and coarser than that of the Prāsaṅgikas. Furthermore, having analyzed in detail the statements of the foremost father Tsong-kha-pa and his spiritual sons, [one's mind] will become an arrowhead of Dharma.

15 The Lack of Being One or Many

THE REASONING REFUTING TRUE EXISTENCE

In his *Ornament for the Middle Way*, the master Śāntarakṣita exhaustively explains just the reasoning of the lack of being one or many, which is an analysis of the entity [of objects]. In doing so, he is explaining the thought of such sutras as:

> When phenomena are mentally broken up,
> An entity is not apprehended.
> Therefore, these are explained to be without expression
> And also without entityness ...

Also, the *Meeting of Father and Son Sutra (Pitāputrasamāgamasūtra)* says:

> These phenomena [such as] trees should be known
> To be like the appearance of a reflection,
> Which does not inherently exist,
> [Appearing] in a very clear mirror.
> My explanation of "emptiness of inherent existence"
> Should [itself] also be viewed as empty.

And the *Descent into Laṅkā* says:

> The entities of things are like
> Appearances [of things] in a mirror
> Which do not exist there
> Because of lacking oneness or otherness ...

In his *Illumination of the Middle Way*, the great master Kamalaśīla set forth many ways in which the Cittamātrins oppose the Mādhyamikas, and in explaining answers to those [objections] he used many scriptures and reasonings. In terms of reasonings, he extensively set forth the diamond silvers, the refutation of production from the existent and non-existent, the refutation of the four extremes of production, the lack of being one or many, and the reason of dependent arising. Here, I will speak briefly just about the reason of the lack of being one or many.

Śāntarakṣita's *Ornament for the Middle Way* says:

> These things propounded by ourselves and others,
> Because they lack in reality
> A nature of unity or plurality
> Do not inherently exist, like a reflection.[1]

Thus, he states the sign, and with respect to proving the modes (*rūpa*, *tshul*), there are two parts: the proof of the property of the position (*pakṣadharma*, *phyogs chos*) and the proof of the pervasion (*vyāpti*, *khyab pa*). The first of these has two parts: the proof of the lack of true unity and the proof of the lack of true plurality. The first of these has two parts: the refutation of true pervasive unity: the refutation of true unity in permanent phenomena and impermanent things imputed by our own and other schools and the refutation of the true unity of the person imputed by the Vātsīputrīyas; and the refutation of true non-pervasive unity: the refutation of external objects that are composed of partless particles and the refutation of the true unity of consciousness imputed by the two Proponents of [External] Objects [the Vaibhāṣikas and Sautrāntikas].

For the proof of the lack of true plurality, the non-existence of the true unity itself is stated as the sign. The proof of the pervasion is accomplished just by proving that one and many are explicitly contradictory in the sense of being mutually exclusive.

If this were explained extensively in connection with the texts, it would indeed be good but would be far too much. Therefore, I will explain just the essence of the meaning.

Here, regarding what is held as the subject (*dharmin*, *chos can*), just things that are imputed by our own and other schools, such as the principal (*pradhāna*, *gtso bo*) and a self-sufficient person are permissible because it was explained in the Sautrāntika chapter [not translated here[2]] that it is permissible to hold a non-established base [a non-existent] as the subject when the sign *(liṅga, rtags)* and predicate *(dharma, chos)* being proven are mere eliminations [non-affirming negatives]. Also, from among the three types of non-established [reasons] *(asiddhahetu, ma grub pa'i rgyu mtshan)* in relation to a fact *(artha, don)*, in relation to an awareness *(buddhi, blo)*, and in relation to [another] party *(pakṣa, rgol pa)* — the explanation of the five types of non-established signs with respect to the first [those in relation to the fact], such as the reason's not being established due to the non-existence of the entity of the subject, refers to when the sign and predicate being proven have a positive aspect; it is not definite [that the reason is not established] when the sign and predicate being proven are non-affirming negatives. Specifically regarding this point, the master Kamalaśīla's *Illumination of the Middle Way* says:

> For one who does not wish to prove a phenomenon that is a thing to be an existent entity but wishes to express a mere proof of an elimination of a phenomenon that is a superimposition, the expression of faults, such as not being established, does not require, even conventionally, a subject that is a thing because it [the reason] is not a quality of it [the subject] and because [the subject] is not feasible as the possessor of the quality that is based on that [subject]. Even though it is not established [as such], a reason that has [the relationship] such that if [the predicate of] the probandum *(sādhyadharma, bsgrub par bya ba)* did not exist it would not occur, is not prevented from establishing the meaning being sought.

Thus, it is clearly stated that a subject which is an actuality is not necessary when the sign and the predicate being proved are mere eliminations. However, it was already analyzed earlier [in the Sautrāntika chapter] whether or not when generating an inferential cognizer, the meaning-of-the-term *(śabdhāartha, sgra don)* [generic image] of a mere subject is needed as the basis for establishing pervasion for the mind of the other party.

Objection: If the sign and the predicate of the probandum of this syllogism of the lack of being one or many are only non-affirming negatives, then it is not feasible that the probandum is proved because the entities of the sign and the predicate of the probandum themselves do not exist, and if they do not exist, then it is not feasible that they are the same entity, in which case there is no relationship of one essence [between them] whereby it is not suitable that they be the object understood and the means of understanding. If you say that the sign and the predicate of the probandum are affirming negatives, that is also not feasible because, if that were the case, there would have to exist an actuality *(bhāva, dngos po)* which is the lack of the nature of unity or plurality, and the Mādhyamikas do not assert that.

Answer: There is no fallacy because, since the relationship of one essence is not just for [impermanent] things, non-[impermanent] things also have it [and in this reasoning the predicate of the probandum and the sign are non-affirming negatives, permanent phenomena]. Kamalaśīla's *Illumination of the Middle Way* says, "Here, [one] essence is another way of saying that [two things] lack being different entities, and even these [two] non-entities [the sign and predicate] are also similar [in being] selflessnesses." His idea is that if a difference of entity is refuted with respect to existents *(sat, yod pa)*, they become the same entity, and, since it is also refuted that in general they [the sign — not being a truly existent unity or plurality — and the predicate of the probandum — not ultimately existing] are one, they have the relationship of one essence in the sense of being different within being one entity, and since the sign [not being a truly existent unity or plurality] and the predicate of the probandum [not ultimately existing] are both similar in being entities of selflessness, it is not contradictory that although they are non-affirming negatives, [the predicate of the probandum] is the object understood and [the sign] is the means of understanding. Also, Kamalaśīla's *Illumination of the Middle Way* says:

> That is not correct because [one] essence is another way of saying non-difference [of entity], and because those non-entitynesses are similar [in being] selfless, [this] is just non-contradictory.

Also:

> In the same way, when things are, in reality, in opposition to being a nature of unity or plurality [i.e., the sign], like a reflection, it is definite that they are also in opposition to being ultimate entities [the predicate of the probandum]. Therefore, [the reason and the predicate of the probandum] are different in relation to [different] particulars of opposi-

> tion, whereby [the predicate of the probandum and the sign] can serve as those things that are the object understood and the means of understanding.

Regarding this point, earlier Tibetan scholars have said that when the *appearance* of non-true existence is proved through the *appearance* of the lack of being one or many, an affirming negative is proved, and when the lack of being one or many proves the emptiness of the suitability of applying the verbal designation "ultimate thing," a non-affirming negative is proved. Such statements are due to their not having understood these points and due to their not understanding that it is a fundamental tenet of Nāgārjuna and his spiritual sons to hold that the predicate of probandum in the proof of non-true existence is only an elimination.

It is stated in Kamalaśīla's *Illumination of the Middle Way* that the reasoning set forth by the statement, "These things propounded by ourselves and others ..." [see p. 357] in Sāntarakṣita's *Ornament for the Middle Way* may be taken either as a statement of refutation — a consequence *(prasaṅga, thal 'gyur)* — or as a statement of proof — a syllogism *(prayoga, sbyor ba)*.

Objection: If it is taken as a consequence, it is not suitable to state, "Because they lack, in reality, /A nature of unity or plurality" as a reason for the lack of being either a truly existent unity or plurality because in a consequence an assertion of the opponent is stated as the sign, and then a consequence must be thrown that is not wanted by the opponent [but in this case, the sign is not asserted by the opponent].

Answer: There is no fallacy because although the sign, the lack of being a truly existent unity or plurality, is not explicitly asserted by the opponent, it is implicitly asserted. This is because the opponent explicitly asserts an object of pervasion by that sign and because, if he explicity asserts the object pervaded, he comes to assert implicitly the pervader as well. As Kamalaśīla's *Illumination of the Middle Way* says:

> Regarding this, if [this reason is used] to prove a consequence, it is not the case that the reason is not established because, although the opponents have not asserted that things lack being either one or many, since they assert phenomena that are pervaded by that, they just assert that implicitly as well.

Objection: It is not correct that, since the pervaded is explicitly asserted, the pervader is implicitly asserted because otherwise, even the Nihilists would come to assert former and later lifetimes and omniscience. This is because the Nihilists assert that this life's consciousness exists, and it is pervaded by being preceded by the consciousnesses of previous lifetimes. Also, they assert that the four elements exist, and their existence is pervaded by being seen by an omniscient consciousness. If you say that you are not propounding that those parties assert these but that they come to assert them implicitly, that is also incorrect because, if that were the case, when one phenomenon was expressed, that term would implicity express all phenomena which exist as pervaders of that [phenomenon] and the awareness which is induced by that term would implicitly ascertain those [phenomena].

Answer: I will discuss this. Here, if the way in which the pervader is implicitly asserted due to explicitly asserting the pervaded were merely a case of generally having to assert the pervader implicitly when the pervaded is asserted, then it is true that those faults would be incurred. However, the meaning of [Kamalaśīla's] text is stated in that way considering the opponent's explicit assertion of a special object pervaded by not being a truly existent unity, which is asserted implicitly. Thus, there is not fault.

This is illustrated with the example of a permanent Īśvara asserted by the opponent. Regarding their mode of assertion that Īśvara is permanent, they assert that everything about Īśvara himself that exists in the morning also exists in the evening. Therefore, they do not assert that some of Īśvara's factors that exist in the morning exist in the evening, but other factors do not exist in the evening; they assert that all the factors that exist at the earlier time exist at the later time and that there are not factors that exist at the later time that did not exist at the earlier time. Thus, their not asserting that the factors of being Īśvara are mutually different is the way they assert that Īśvara is permanent and one. Therefore, that is the reason for saying that they do not explicitly assert that Īśvara lacks a nature of unity.

Also, they assert many phases of such an Īśvara, producing effects, like happiness in the morning and suffering in the evening. One who asserts such a serial creation of effects implicitly asserts that [Īśvara] is not a truly exist one because, since there must be a serial existence of the Īśvaras at many different times of producing pleasure and pain, Īśvara must have many stages and these Īśvaras are partless unities. In this way, one can understand the manner in which an object pervaded by not being a truly established unity is also asserted with respect to other bases, such as the principal [of Sāṃkhya] *(pradhāna, gtso bo)*, time [of Vaiśeṣika] *(kāla, dus)*, and so forth.

Regarding these points, although a pot is posited as an illustration of a unity in our own system and in asserted to exist in both the morning and the evening, the pot of the morning is not asserted to be one with the pot of the evening, and those two are posited as illustrations of plurality. Also, blue is asserted to be one, and it serially produces many earlier and later consciousnesses apprehending blue. One must know the reasons why these fallacies [adduced to the opponent above] do not apply [to our own position].

These [points] are the meaning of [this statement from] Kamalaśīla's *Illumination of the Middle Way:*

> Regarding this, those who imagine Īśvara and so forth to be a permanent and single entity assert [that Īśvara has] the quality of creating the occurrence of his effects serially. Therefore, they implicitly assert [that Īśvara] lacks an entityness of unity because [if Īśvara were] one entity, due to Īśvara's not being different from the state of non-production, it is not suitable [for Īśvara] to be a producer at a later time, since he was not at a former time. If he is a producer [at a later time], since Īśvara would be an entity that is of a discordant character from the earlier state [of non-production], unity falls apart.

Permanent and single [phenomena] that are imputed by the non-Buddhist Proponents of Permanence — such as the person *(puruṣa, skyes bu)*, principal *(pradhāna, gtso bo)*, time *(kāla, dus)*, and Brahmā as well as the three unconditioned phenomena *(asaṃskṛta, 'dus ma byas)* that are propounded to be permanent things *(*nityabhāva, rtag pa'i dngos po)* by the Vaibhāṣikas among our own schools [those three being space *(ākāśa, nam mkha')*, analytical cessations *(pratisaṃkhyānirodha, so sor brtags 'gog)*, and non-analytical cessations *(apratisaṃkhyānirodha, so sor min pa'i brtags 'gog)*], the inexpressible person propounded by the Vātsīputrīyas, and the consciousnesses that is imputed to be a truly existent entity by the Cittamātrins are set forth extensively in that text [the *Illumination of the Middle Way*] in terms of their respective modes of asserting [some sort of] non-unity — the object pervaded that is [used as] the reason [why they implicitly assert] the lack of truly existent unity.

There are many different subtleties in logically forcing our own and other schools to assert implicitly the lack of truly existent unity. Also, with regard to our own schools, there are many subtle differences in how the demonstration of logical damage applies to the opponent's assertion for the system of the two Proponents of [Truly Existent External] Objects [the Vaibhāṣikas and Sautrāntikas] and the Vijñaptikas [Cittamātrins]. These should be known in detail.

If one investigates by striving for many causal collections, such as not being satisfied with detailed analysis of the texts of the great charioteers until one's intelligence is [as sharp] as the point [of a blade] of *kuśa* grass as well as properly relying on a skillful spiritual guide, one will find the essential points of the subtle path of reasoning of the great charioteers. Although one studies over months and years until the flesh is wasted at merely arranging statements that reveal nothing to oneself other than training the mouth to speak, it would seem to be difficult to understand [the essentials].

I will briefly explain how the modes of the sign of this reasoning are proved when it is treated as an autonomous [syllogism] and whether [this sign] proves a meaning or an expression. The proof of the modes has two parts, the proof that the reason is a property of the subject[3] and the proof of the pervasion. The first [that the reason is a property of the subject] has two parts, the proof of the lack of being a truly existent unity and the lack of being [a truly existent] plurality.

The Proof of the Lack of Being a Truly Existent Unity

The subjects, the principal *(pradhāna, gtso bo)* and so forth, are not established as a truly existent unity because of being involved in many series of assistance to many former and later series of effects. If one thinks that there is no fallacy because there are many different potencies that create many different former and later effects, then it follows that the subjects [the principal, etc.] are not truly permanent and unitary because, due to having a series of effects, their former and later natures arise and disintegrate. To explain this, Śāntarakṣita's *Ornament for the Middle Way* says:

> Because of being involved in series of effects
> The permanent does not have a nature of unity.

If there are different [potencies] for each of the effects,
Then their permanence would disintegrate.[4]

With regard to the refutation of the assertion by others of our own [Buddhist] schools that the three unconditioned phenomena that are objects known by a Superior's exalted wisdom of meditative equipoise arisen from meditation *(bhāvanāmayī, bsgom byung)* are truly existent unities, the subjects, the three unconditioned phenomena, are not truly one, because of being in the relationship of subject and object with many series of former and later consciousnesses arisen from meditation. To explain this, Śāntarakṣita's *Ornament for the Middle Way* says:

Also, for a system which propounds that
The three unconditioned phenomena
Are objects which are known by a consciousness arisen from meditation,
Those are not one because of being related with series of consciousnesses.[5]

If you say that it is not contradictory for these objects to exist as truly existent unities even though they are related to series of consciousnesses, then, if the object of knowledge that is the object of a former consciousness exists at the time of a later consciousness, the former consciousness must also exist at that [later] time because object and subject are simultaneous. If you accept that, then it [absurdly] follows that the former and later consciousnesses arisen from meditation are disordered.

If you say that the object of the former consciousness is not present at the time of the later consciousness, then it follows that the subjects, those unconditioned phenomena, are momentary because of being things whose former nature does not occur at a later occasion and whose later nature does not occur at a former occasion, like a consciousness arisen from meditation.

Or, the subjects, the later [moments of these] unconditioned phenomena, are not unconditioned phenomena because of arising in dependence on the power of the earlier unconditioned phenomena, as is the case, for example, with the minds and mental factors arisen from meditation. If you say that the reason is not established, then it follows that these subjects arise under their own power because of arising without depending on other causes. If you accept that, then it follows that [these unconditioned phenomena] either exist permanently or are utterly non-existent because of being things that do not follow from causes. In explanation, Śāntarakṣita's *Ornament for the Middle Way* says:

> If the nature of the objects known
> By the former consciousness follows later,
> The former consciousness would become later
> And the later would similarly become former.
>
> If their entities do not arise
> At the former and later times,
> It should be known that the unconditioned,
> Like consciousness, would be momentary.
>
> Since they arise through the power
> Of earlier moments
> They would not be unconditioned,
> Like minds and mental factors.
>
> If you assert that [the unconditioned]
> Arise by their own power in these moments,
> Then, since they do not rely on another,
> They exist permanently or do not exist.[6]

Concerning these modes of refuting the truly existent permanent unities asserted by our own and other schools, it is essential that one know well the way in which the opponent asserts [phenomena] to be unitary due to which they have the burden of the fallacy. Otherwise, if one refutes mere unity and mere permanence with those reasonings, all the fallacies stated about the others will undeniably apply equally to oneself, whereby it will be difficult to explain the texts of the great charioteers without error.

Refutation of the Truly Existent Unitary Person Asserted by the Vātsīputrīyas

It follows that the subject, the person, lacks being a truly existent unity or plurality because of inexpressible as permanent or impermanent, like a flower in the sky. It follows [that it is inexpressible as permanent or impermanent] because if it were momentary, it would have a plural nature, and if it were not momentary, it would be suitable as a single entity, but since [according to the Vātsīputrīyas] it is inexpressible as either [momentary or non-momentary], there is no difficulty in establishing that it is empty of a nature of unity or plurality. To explain this, Śāntarakṣita's *Ornament for the Middle Way* says:

> Since it is unsuitable [according to the Vātsīputrīyas] to indicate that the person
> Is momentary or non-momentary,
> It is clearly known that it lacks
> A nature of being one or many.[7]

Refutation of a Truly Existent Pervasive Unity

The subjects, space *(ākāśa, rnam mkha')*, time *(kāla, dus)*, and so forth are not truly existent unities, because of being related with a composite of directional parts, such as east, and temporal parts, such as the past. To explain this, Śāntarakṣita's *Ornament for the Middle Way* says:

> Because of being related with different directions,
> How can pervasives be one?[8]

The Refutation of Truly Existent Gross [Objects That Are] One

The subjects, gross objects such as pots, are not truly existent unities because of involving conjunctions of contradictions in terms of substance, such as being obstructed and not obstructed; in terms of activity, such as moving and not moving; and in terms of quality, such as being colored or not colored.. To explain this, Śāntarakṣita's *Ornament for the Middle Way* says:

> Because of factors such as being obstructed and not being obstructed,
> Gross phenomena also are not one.[9]

Refutation of Minute Particles That Are Truly Existent Unities

It follows that the subject, a minute particle that dwells in the middle of particles in the ten directions, does not have a different location from the eastern particle and the remaining nine particles because its side that faces the east and its sides that face the other nine directions are the same. If you accept that, then it follows that gross objects such as earth could not be formed [because they would have no extension]. If you assert that there are individual sides that face the ten directions, then it follows that the subject, that minute particle, is not a partless unity because of having many sides that face particles in the ten directions. To explain this, Śāntarakṣita's *Ornament for the Middle Way* says:

> [Particles] either abide in contact,
> Circling, or without interstice.
> What is the nature of the central particle
> That faces an [other] particle?
>
> If you say that that which faces other particles
> Is the same [side of the central particle],
> How would earth, water, and so forth
> Become extensive?[10]
>
> If the side facing another particle
> Is asserted to be other [than other sides]
> How could a particle
> Be a partless unit?[11]

Since partless minute particles are not established in that way, one can know that the ten physical constituents *(dhātu, khams)* [the five sense powers *(indriya, dbang po)*, and the five sense objects] propounded by our own schools and the substance *(dravya, rdzas)*, quality *(guṇa, yon tan)*, action *(karma, las)*, generality *(sāmānya, spyi)*, particularity *(viśeṣa, bye brag)*, and inherence *(samavāya, 'du ba)*, and so forth imputed by other schools are not truly established. Specifically, if one knows that the ten physical constituents propounded by our own schools do not truly exist, one knows that the five constituents that are consciousnesses also do not truly exist because they are produced in dependence upon the physical constituents. If the five constituents that are consciousnesses do not truly exist, it is not correct that the mental consciousness *(manovijñāna, yid kyi rnam par shes pa)*, which is established through [their] acting as [its] immediately preceding condition *(samanantarapratyaya, de ma thag pa'i rkyen)*, is truly established. If the six collections of consciousness are not truly established, it is not feasible that the mental constituent, [which is comprised of] those consciousnesses just passed, truly exists. If main minds *(citta, sems)* do not exist in that way, mental factors *(caitta, sems las byung ba)* such as feeling *(vedanā, tshor ba)*, discrimination *(samjñā, 'du shes)*, and intention *(cetanā, sems pa)*, which are non-different in establishment and abiding with that [main mind], are easily established as not truly existing. Therefore, non-associated compositional factors *(viprayukta-saṃskāra, ldan pa ma yin pa'i 'du byed)* and non-revelatory forms *(avijñāptirūpa, rnam par rig byed ma yin pa'i gzugs)*, which are propounded to be established through the great elements *(mahābhūta, 'byung ba chen po)* acting as causes, can be known to be not established as truly existent unities. Also, unconditioned phenomena *(asaṃskṛta, 'dus ma byas)* such as space have been refuted earlier.

Therefore, the autocommentary to the *Ornament for the Middle Way* states that it is easy to realize that all eighteen constituents are not established as truly existent unities. That is how to apply the reasoning refuting objects that are truly existent unities to the refutation of subjects as well.

Regarding the specific reasoning that refutes a truly existent unity with respect to consciousness, the root text and commentary of the *Ornament for the Middle Way* extensively explain the reasoning proving the lack of truly existent unity from the viewpoint of three modes of refutation and so forth in terms of the refutation of the Vaibhāṣika system, which asserts consciousness as aspectless *(anākāra, rnam med)*, and the refutation of the systems of the Non-Pluralists, Half-Eggists, and Proponents of an Equal Number of Subjects and Objects in the Sautrāntika system. With respect to the refutation of the non-Buddhist systems, there are refutations of the Vaiśeṣika and Naiyāyika systems, the Kṣayaṃkara [Jaina] system, the Cārvāka system, the Sāṃkhya system, and the Guhyavedānta system. The Cittamātra system is refuted from the viewpoint of the refutation of the True Aspectarians *(satyākāravādin, rnam bden pa)* and the False Aspectarians *(alīkākaravādin, rnam rdzun pa)*, and with regard to the former [the True Aspectarians], by way of how they assert aspect *(ākāra, rnam pa)*.

Regarding [these modes of refutation], it appears that the tradition of explaining and listening to the three texts illuminating Svātantrika [Śāntarakṣita's *Ornament for the Middle Way*, Kamalaśīla's *Illumination of the Middle Way*, and Jñānagarbha's *Two Truths*] was very widespread in the Land of Snow Mountains at the time of the earlier dissemination of the teaching as well as at the time of such [figures] as the great translator from Ngok (Lo-den-shay-rap) and his spiritual sons during the later dissemination. As a consequence, the tradition of explaining and listening to [these texts] was still widespread at the time of the foremost Tsong-kha-pa and his spiritual sons. Hence, this is the reason why, with the exception of a few essential points of reasoning that have not been dealt with by earlier [scholars], they [Tsong-kha-pa, Gyel-tsap, and Kay-drup] did not extensively explain each type of reasoning, aligning it with the Svātantrika texts. That this is the case can be known from some remarks of the foremost Tsong-kha-pa and from Kay-drup-ma-way-nyi-ma's *Thousand Doses.*

Nowadays it is as if the tradition of explaining and listening within the framework of these texts has disappeared. On the occasion of explaining the expression of worship of Maitreya's *Ornament for Clear Realization* with Haribhadra's *Clear Meaning Commentary (Sphuṭārthā)*, when the phrase "because of lacking an entity of one or many" comes up, people only repeat, like counting *[om] mani [padme hum]*, whether beginning and end are complete or not, [what] appears in the arrangements of words by earlier scholars, explaining a little about the lack of being one or many. Through this, their pride fancying that they know well the reason of the lack of being one or many becomes firm. Aside from that, it appears to be rare for anyone to direct his mind to how to expand the reasonings, how to seek understanding, and so forth in connection with the basic texts.

The foremost great being Tsong-kha-pa's *Differentiation of the Interpretable and Definitive (Drang nges rnam 'byed)* [also known as the *Essence of the Good Explanations*] says:

> It indicates that in whatever is asserted by our own and other schools, there does not exist anything partless that does not have many parts such as temporal series, or parts of the object, or aspects of an object of consciousness.

"Temporal series" [indicates] the principal, the person, Īśvara, a permanent self, and so forth as well as the three permanent unconditioned things propounded by the Vaibhāṣikas. "Parts of the object" [indicates] gross objects, such as pots, and partless particles. "Aspects of objects of consciousness" [indicates] consciousness in accordance with the five non-Buddhist systems, the two Proponents of [Truly Existent External] Objects [the Vaibhāṣikas and Sautrāntikas], and the two Cittamātrin systems [True and False Aspectarians]. Tsong-kha-pa is saying that one needs to know the adaptations of the reasoning proving that [these phenomena] individually have many parts.

After that, Tsong-kha-pa's *Essence of the Good Explanations* says:

> When [phenomena] are established as having many parts, it is not contradictory for one phenomenon to exist as an

> entity of many parts, within conventionalities. However, damage is done to ultimate establishment [due to the fact that] if parts and whole are different entities, they would be unrelated and if they are the same entity, the parts would become one [because the whole is one] or the whole would become many [because the parts are many].

This indicates the need to know how the adaptations of the reasoning refuting truly existent unity or plurality apply to the individual assertions about those phenomena by our own and other schools and the need to know the modes of refuting true existence with that [reasoning]. Furthermore, when refuting [them], one should affix the qualification "truly" [or "ultimately"] in relation to the thought of the opponent. Because, in general, [there are cases when the opponent's position] must be refuted in terms of both truths [ultimate and conventional], there are some cases in which it is not necessary to affix the qualification "truly." However, in most cases, the qualification "truly" must be affixed. Once either their [the opponents'] system asserts a permanent partlessness, or even though they do not explicitly assert it, they are logically forced such that it is impossible for them not to assert partlessness, one demonstrates logical damage upon putting together [their] contradictions with the general non-occurrence of the partless. There are many such distinctions.

These are the ways to refute the object of negation imputed by our own and other schools, but in order also to refute the object of the innate conception of true existence, one must know well how damage is done by these reasonings. For, if phenomena were established in the way that they are held to be by the conception of true existence, they would have to be established as the object's mode of subsistence, and that would be a mode of subsistence that did not rely on an awareness. Although I am capable of expounding in detail on the specifics of these, since I fear the burden of too many words, let us leave it just at that.

The Proof of the Lack of Being a Truly Existent Plurality

The subjects, those things propounded by ourselves and others, are not established as a truly existent plurality because of the lack of a truly existent unity. [If there is no truly existent unity, a truly existent plurality cannot be established] because a plurality has the character of a composite of ones. To explain this, Śāntarakṣita's *Ornament for the Middle Way* says:

When anything is analyzed
It is without unity.
That which does not have unity
Also is without plurality.[12]

And the commentary following that says:

> For a plurality has the character of a composite of unities. If a unity does not exist, [plurality] also does not exist, just as if trees and so forth do not exist, forests and so forth do not exist.[13]

The Proof of Pervasion

In general, in order to ascertain the existence of the sign in the similar class *(sapakṣa, mthun phyogs)* and the non-existence [of the sign] in the dissimilar class *(vipakṣa, mi mthun phyogs)*, three valid cognizers *(pramāṇa, tshad ma)* are necessary:

1 a valid cognizer that ascertains the instance *(lakṣya, mtshan gzhi)* of the sign [in this proof],
2 a valid cognizer that refutes [that there is] a common locus of the sign and the object of negation *(pratiṣedhya, dgag bya)* and
3 a valid cognizer that ascertains that the predicate of the probandum *(sādhyadharma, bsgrub bya'i chos)* and the object of negation are a dichotomy.

With respect to the first, the valid cognizer that ascertains the lack of a truly existent unity or plurality has already been explained here. With respect to the other two, regarding the valid cognizer which ascertains that true existence and non-true existence are a dichotomy, since it is ascertained that existence and non-existence are a dichotomy such that by the exclusion of one the other is included, one eliminates the superimposition that a third category might occur with respect to true existence and non-true existence whereby, through merely turning one's mind [to them], one can ascertain that [true existence and non-true existence] are a dichotomy.

Objection: Since true existence lacks being a truly existent unity or plurality, does the sign not occur in the dissimilar class?

Answer: That alone does not constitute the occurrence of the sign in the dissimilar class; in order for the sign to occur in the dissimilar class, a common locus that is both the object of negation and the sign must occur, and since a common locus that both truly exists and lacks being a truly existent unity or plurality does not occur, there is no fault.

Regarding the ascertainment with valid cognition that a common locus of those two does not occur, the valid cognizer which ascertains that one and many are a dichotomy such that if one is excluded the other is included eliminates superimpositions of a third category that is both one and many or neither [one nor many] with respect to mere existence. Having thereby also, with respect to true existence, eliminated superimpositions [that there is] a third category that is both a truly existence unity and plurality or neither [a truly existent unity nor plurality, one can ascertain that a common locus of the lack of being a truly existent unity or plurality and true existence does not occur merely by turning one's mind to it. This was stated by the omniscient Kay-drup.

Also, Śāntarakṣita's *Ornament for the Middle Way* says:

> Things which have an aspect
> Other than one or many
> Are not feasible because
> These two are mutually exlcusive.[14]

The commentary following that says at the point of proving the pervasion of this reason, "Since a nature of unity and a nature of plurality are characteristics that abide in mutual exclusivity [as a dichotomy], another category is eliminated."[15] Kamalaśīla's *Illumination of the Middle Way* says:

> Those which pervade all aspects are eliminators of another category, for example, particularities such as physical and non-physical. One and many are like that. Through eliminating the pervader [i.e., one and many], it is definite that the pervaded [true existence] is eliminated whereby there is no doubt that the reason [i.e., not being one or many] is eliminated from the discordant class [true existence] because another category does not occur.

Objection: Does the valid cognizer that ascertains the pervasion in the proof of the person as not truly existent by the sign of lacking being either a truly existent unity or plurality ascertain the pervasion of the emptiness of true existence with respect to all categories of instances of the lack of being a truly existent unity or plurality? If it does ascertain [it with respect to everything], then it follows that the inferential cognizer that comprehends the probandum in the proof of that does not newly eliminate superimpositions. If you say that it does not ascertain [that pervasion with respect to all phenomena], that is not correct because if the emptiness of the generality *(sāmānya, spyi)* is ascertained, the emptiness of the particularities *(viśeṣa, bye brag)* is necessarily ascertained.

Answer: Kay-drup-ma-way-nyi-ma says:

> The valid cognizer that comprehends that the permanent is empty of [being a] product does not ascertain the non-occurrence of [being a] product with respect to all categories of the instances of the permanent, but it does eliminate the superimpositions of conceiving [the permanent] as being [products such that] at a later time, through merely turning the mind to a specific permanent phenomenon, the ascertainment of its emptiness of [being a] product is induced without relying on another valid cognizer.
>
> Objection: Then, the valid cognizer that ascertains the forward pervasion *(anvayavyāpti, rjes khyab)* would have to be able to eliminate the superimpositions of apprehending that all categories of instances of products are not necessarily impermanent, in which case it would [absurdly] follow that when the forward pervasion is ascertained, superimpositions with respect to the probandum are necessarily eliminated.
>
> Answer: This is not similar because although there is pervasion by the generality, there is not necessarily pervasion by its particulars and when the generality is negated, the particulars are necessarily also negated.

It is asserted that here it is the same.

Gyel-tsap-rin-bo-chay says:

> Although one might allow that the valid cognizer that ascertains that whatever is a product is necessarily impermanent ascertains, in relation to product, sound's emptiness of being permanent, it does not ascertain the emptiness of being permanent in the context of taking sound as the substratum. Thus, there is no fault. The valid cognizer which ascertains that all categories of the instances of products are necessarily impermanent does not ascertain that whatever is sound's productness is necessarily imperma-

> nent; rather, the probandum must be established when, having turned the mind to sound's productness, the assemblage of impermanence in all categories of the instances of products becomes the object of a valid cognizer. Hence, one does not incur the fault of the [absurd] consequence that the valid cognizer which comprehends the modes proving that [sound is impermanent] establishes the probandum.

Both the former [Kay-drup's] and latter [Gyel-tsap's] assertions seem for the most part to agree in their position, and the *Great Table of Contents* [?] *(Sa bchad chen mo)* speaks similarly to the matter.

When the assertions of the two sons are arranged in accordance with the thought of the foremost Tsong-kha-pa, [the position is as follows]. The valid cognizer that ascertains the three modes in the proof of sound as impermanent neither implicity realizes that sound is impermanent nor does it remove the superimpositions of apprehending that sound is permanent. When the valid cognizer that ascertains the three modes is produced, it can generate an awareness the mode of apprehension of which explicitly contradicts the superimpositions that conceive sound to be permanent in dependence on its [the awareness'] force without the need for an intervening valid cognizer. Therefore, there is no fault that the probandum is established when the pervasion is ascertained. Also, between those [the valid cognizer ascertaining the three modes and the inferential consciousness realizing the probandum], there is no need to state another sign that produces the inferential cognizer.

This appears to be the fundamental thought of all three, the foremost omniscient father [Tsong-kha-pa] and his sons [Gyel-tsap and Kay-drup]. Also, I think that it also accords with the thought of the [Indian] texts and that the procedure is similar here in this context [of the reasoning of the lack of being one or many] as well.

Regarding this, it seems good that some later scholars have used the term "realization through the power of reasoning" which is neither explicit realization nor implicit realization, but it is not suitable for "realization" here to refer to realization by that valid cognizer [which ascertains the three modes] because when statements in Tsong-kha-pa's *Great Commentary to [Nāgārjuna's] Treatise on the Middle Way* and Kay-drup's *Thousand Doses* are compared it seems that they assert that the inferential cognizer which realizes that sound is impermanent is merely *capable* of being produced in dependence on the power of that valid cognizer without interruption by another awareness.

Now I will analyze whether this reason of the lack of being one or many proves a meaning *(artha, don)* or an expression *(vyavahāra, tha snyad)*. With regard to this, it is stated in Śāntarakṣita's *Ornament for the Middle Way* and Kamalaśīla's *Illumination of the Middle Way* that this sign is a sign that is a non-observation of a pervader *(vyāpaka-anupalabdhi, khyab byed ma dmigs pa)*, but it is also explained in several statements of the foremost Tsong-kha-pa and his sons that it is [a sign] that is a non-observation of a nature *(svabhāva-anupalabdhi, rang bzhin ma dmigs pa)*. Also, Kay-drup's *Thousand Doses* says, "It proves a mere expression. Therefore, whatever is a proof of a mere expression is not necessarily a sign that is a non-observation of a nature."

Some authors of textbooks on Dharmakīrti's *Commentary on [Dignāga's "Compendium on] Valid Cognition" (Pramāṇavarttika)* say that whatever is a reason which is a non-observation of a cause */* *(karāṇa-anupalabdhi, rgyu ma dmigs pa)* or non-observation of a pervader must be a sign proving both a meaning and an expression because the great *paṇḍita* Dharmottara says:

> With respect to [cases when] the perceivability of the effect or the pervaded is unsuitable, the non-observation of a cause and a pervader bring about understanding of the actual non-existence of fire and the expression of the actual non-existence of fire.

However, it is not certain that that is the meaning of the passage.

Thus, there are many presentations such as just what proofs of expressions that are effect, nature, and non-observation signs are and how mere expressions are proved, but because they would interfere with the topic at hand, I will not elaborate on them here.

Regarding what is relevant here, generally two modes of positing meaning and expression appear in the statements of scholars. In the first, meaning refers to the definition *(lakṣaṇa, mtshan nyid)* and expression refers to the definiendum *(lakṣya, mtshon bya)*, and in the second, meaning refers to the meaning-reverse *(*arthavyatireka, don ldog)* of the predicate of the probandum and expression refers to its three conventions. The three conventions are verbal, mental, and physical conventions. Regarding this, some scholars of our own [Ge-luk] sect assert that this reason [of the lack of being one or many] is a sign proving a meaning, but since the omniscient Kay-drup asserts that it is a sign proving a mere expression and the foremost Gyel-tsap says in his *Great Purification of Forgetfulness (brJed byang chen mo)* that it proves a mere expression, this is the actual thought of the foremost Tsong-kha-pa.

Jam-yang-lek-ba-chö-jor-wa *('Jam-dbyangs-legs-pa-chos-'byor-wa)* raises these qualms:

> One might think that the reason for their asserting that this is a sign proving a mere expression is that if something has the full meaning of being truly established, then it must be true as either one or many, whereby the lack of being truly one or many is a correct sign proving a mere expression because, having already proven the meaning of non-true existence — the lack of being truly one or many — one is only proving the mere expression, "not truly existence."
>
> However, this is not correct, for if sound fulfilled the meaning of permanence, it would have to be a non-product whereby product would [absurdly] become [a sign] proving a mere expression in the proof of sound as impermanent.
>
> Also, if [you think] that the awareness that comprehends the presence of the reason in the subject of that sign must be asserted as a reasoning consciousness analyzing the ultimate [because you say that it is a sign proving a mere expression], this is also incorrect because the mere non-establishment of the person as being truly the same as or different from the aggregates is not an ultimate truth.

There appear to be many cases of others' answering him. However, it seems that they have not clearly distinguished whether or not the mere way in which Jam-yang-lek-ba-chö-jor interprets the ideas of Kay-drup-rin-bo-chay constitutes the assertion of [his] opponent. [In other words, they mistakenly think that Jam-yang-lek-ba-chö-jor has accurately represented Kay-drup's ideas.]

That this sign is a proof of a mere designation is not only the thought of the foremost Tsong-kha-pa and his sons, it also is that of the master Śāntarakṣita because his autocommentary to the *Ornament for the Middle Way* says, "This reason does not have a thesis in the meaning class because of proving the subjective consciousness, terms, and expressions of the object being proved."[16] He thus clearly states that it proves a mere expression.

Regarding how [this reason] becomes [a reason] proving an expression, a person who has ascertained with valid cognition the lack of true unity and plurality in terms of the subject and who has ascertained with valid cognition that whatever truly exists is necessarily either truly one or many would not willfully create a superimposing awareness logically proving the meaning of true existence with respect to the subject, and while not forgetting those modes, there is no chance for the superimposition of some third category to be produced. However, in order to have an awareness that thinks about non-true existence in terms of the subject, or in order to actually use the term "non-true existence" [with respect to the subject], this [non-true existence] becomes ascertained as an object or mere expression in dependence on the functioning of the earlier mindfulness of the three modes in a situation of unmuddled awareness. For example, a small child sees a small ox and sees that it is a composite of hump and dewlap and that the expression "ox" is used for it, but later, when he sees a large ox, he is not able to use the mental convention thinking, "This is an ox" or [such] a verbal convention due to the fact of not having known it before. [However], at that time he ascertains that it is an ox through mindfulness of the three modes, such as "This is an ox because of being an entity that is a composite of a dewlap and so forth." That must be posited as a case of proving a mere expression.

This is also stated clearly by the great *paṇḍiṭa* Śāntarakṣita. His autocommentary to the *Ornament for the Middle Way* says:

> [The subject] has already been shown to lack a nature of being one or many through the aforementioned logic, which is like, for example, "This is an ox because of being an entity that is a collection of dewlap and so forth." However, [non-true existence] is established as an object of consciousness, terms, and expressions for those (1) who cannot conceive nor express the definite lack of inherent existence that pervades all things in reality because error — having been transmitted from one [lifetime] to another from beginningless cyclic existence and having thoroughly increased adherence to the true existence [of things] — is difficult to abandon since one has not become accustomed [to the truth] through proper mental application and (2) who, despite wishing to generate ascertainment [of the truth] in others as well, cannot use the expressions. It is like [proving that

> something] does not exist because of not being observed, whereas it has the character of being observable [if it were present].[17]

The master Dharmottara also sets forth the meaning of establishing a mere expression in this way, but I will not elaborate on it here. Thus, it should be known that the explanation of the assertion of the great abbot Śāntarakṣita by the foremost Tsong-kha-pa and his sons accords with the texts and has great meaning.

Kay-drup's *Thousand Doses* says:

> With respect to any phenomenon, without superimposing that it is either a truly existent unity or plurality, there is no way that a superimposition [of true existence] that would be the superimposition of a third category could be generated. Therefore, [the reasoning of the lack of being one or many] establishes a mere expression.

This means that, at that time, there is no chance that the person could generate the superimposing consciousness which thinks that although the person does not exist as truly the same as the aggregates and does not exist as truly different from the aggregates, there is such and such a type of true existence of the person. Also, something that can be shown to be a third type of true establishment cannot be found. At that time, the proof by that person of a verbal or mental expression of non-true existence in dependence on the modes of the sign within holding the person as the substratum [or subject] is the way in which that sign is a proof of an expression. That is what [Kay-drup] said; he did not say that since, in general, that [person] *has already realized* the meaning of non-true existence of the person, that sign proves a mere expression. Nor did he assert that the awareness which comprehends the presence of the reason in the subject with respect to that sign is an awareness which comprehends the non-true existence of the person. Nor did he assert that the mere non-establishment of the person as either truly one or many with respect to the aggregates is an ultimate truth.

If it is explained in this way, the qualms stated [earlier] by Jam-yang-lek-ba-chö-jor are removed, and the meaning of the text is also interpreted well. However, to say such things as, "It follows that the non-establishment of the person as truly one with the aggregates is the mode of being of the person because the non-establishment of a truly existent unity is the mode of being of unity," not only is not helpful in removing the qualms of that king of scholars; it is only a senseless answer.

The non-establishment of the person as truly one or many, and so forth, in the sight of a Superior's meditative equipoise is the mode of being of the person, but it need not be the case that, in general, the non-establishment of the person as truly one or many has to be the mode of being of the person, just as the non-existence of the aggregates and so forth in the sight of a Superior's meditative equipoise is the mode of being of the aggregates and so forth, but in general the non-existence of the aggregates and so forth does not have to be the mode of being of the aggregates.

Beginning from these [points] there are still a great many topics to discuss, but let us leave it here for now. Tsong-kha-pa's *Differentiation of the Interpretable and Definitive* says, "These are great paths of reasoning of the followers of the protector Nāgārjuna, and those who wish to extend their minds in reasoning should learn them." Therefore, knowing the essentials of these reasonings is very important, and if they are known well, even if only the reason of the lack of being one or many is cultivated, one will not be bereft of something on which to meditate. Therefore, even if those who claim to view their own mind as the natural face of a Truth Body *(dharmakāya, chos sku)* learn only this reasoning and straighten their bodies [in meditation], it would be good.

16 The Two Truths

The basis of division of the two truths, the divisions, the difference between real and unreal conventional truths, the sameness and difference of the two truths, and so forth are similar to what was explained in the context of the Sautrāntika-Svātantrika-Mādhyamikas.

With regard to the valid cognizers that ascertain the two truths, there are two [types of Yogācāra-Svātantrikas] in terms of the mode of assertion of aspects *(ākāra, rnam pa)*. Āryavimuktisena, the master Śāntarakṣita, the king of scholars Kamalaśīla, and so forth are Mādhyamikas who are like the True Aspectarians conventionally. Tsong-kha-pa's *Differentiation of the Interpretable and Definitive* says:

> This system asserts that the aspects of blue, yellow, and so forth are things. Since the assertions of Dharmakīrti are also laid out that way, they are Mādhyamikas who make assertions that accord with the True Aspectarians conventionally.

Furthermore, they make assertions in a way similar to the Non-Pluralist True Aspectarians.

The great scholar and adept Den-ba-dar-gyay *(bsTan-pa-dar-rgyas)*, Jam-yang-shay-ba, and so forth said that although the great master Haribhadra is a follower of Śāntarakṣita, he is similar to a False Aspectarian because he clearly explains a false aspect at points such as [this statement] in his *Clear Meaning Commentary (Sphuṭārthā)*:

> Those who definitely think "if apprehended objects do not exist, apprehenders do not exist" refute the character of an aspect of an apprehender that is mere awareness, and ascertain that this non-dual exalted wisdom alone is an entity that exists in reality.

Paṇḍita Sahajavajra explains in his *Commentary on the "Ten Stanzas on Suchness" (Tattvadaśakaṭika)* that the great master Kambalapāda *(La-ba-ba)* is a Mādhyamika who makes assertions that accord with the False Aspectarians conventionally, and the fact that the master Jetāri also is a False Aspectarian is known from his commentary to his *Sugata Treatise (Sugatamatavibhaṅgakārikā).*

There were many scholars and adepts who were followers of these masters, and they are for the most part similar in making an assertion of self-knowing awarenesses and in not asserting a basis-of-all that is a different entity from the six collections of consciousness. In general, in the Land of Superiors *(āryavarśa)* [India] a few *paṇḍitas* who claimed to be Mādhyamikas asserted both self-knowers and a basis-of-all *(ālaya, kun gzhi),* and there also were a couple who asserted meditative equipoise with appearance — holding that the explicit object of the non-conceptual exalted wisdom of meditative equipoise is a composite of emptiness and appearance. However, merely because of that, the Yogācāra-Svātantrika-Mādhyamika system does not come to assert that a Superior's non-contaminated exalted wisdom of meditative equipoise has illusion-like appearance, etc. Such Indian *paṇḍitas* are merely cases [of people] putting the faults of their own minds into the tenet systems without having arrived at the thought of the great charioteers; they do not state positions having ascertained the mode of their own tenet system. For example, it must be said that the many incorrect presentations made by those who claim to be Prāsaṅgika-Mādhyamikas in Tibet are faults of their minds and that theirs is not the Prāsaṅgika-Mādhyamika system. Therefore, Tsong-kha-pa's *Great Exposition of the Stages of the Path* says,

> Although in general a few Indian and Tibetan masters who claim to be Mādhyamikas asserted this, I will delineate the system of the great Mādhyamikas who follow the master Nāgārjuna. Who could explain the minor ones?

Thus, the foremost, omniscient one asserts that he will primarily delineate the thought of the indisputable great charioteers who validly commented upon the thought of the Conqueror. This appears to be a statement of his displeasure with merely amassing many enumerations, drawing together in one place the many systems of all those who are called "*paṇḍiṭa*" and all those who were said to have become "adepts" *(siddha, grub pa).*

Although a basis-of-all that is a different entity from the six collections of consciousness is not asserted, the indication of certain subtle factors with the term "basis-of-all" upon dividing the sixth — the mental consciousness — into parts was set forth even by some great Mādhyamikas. This appears frequently, particularly in texts of the Mantra category.

In dependence on these ways of delineating non-true existence and the ways of presenting conventionalities, there are many distinctions with regard to how they comment on the meaning of interpretable and definitive sutras. They assert that Mother Sutras and so forth are indicated as being sutras of definitive meaning through the teaching in the *Sutra Unravelling the Thought*, of [the Buddha's] thought [when he taught] the three types of non-entityness. Their system's presentation of the three natures, which is unlike the presentation of the three natures as posited by the Cittamātrins, is asserted to be the main meaning of those sutras. However, the Cittamātrins' system of categorizing the three natures is set forth as a meaning of the sutra in relation to the thought of those disciples who temporarily are unable to realize emptiness and must be led gradually.

Also, with respect to the middle wheel [sutras], those passages that explicitly or implicitly affix the qualification "ultimately" to the object of negation are asserted to be literal and definitive. In those [middle wheel] sutras, those which teach with [statements] such as "Form does not exist," without clearly affixing the qualification "ultimately" or "truly" are asserted to be interpretable and not suitable to be taken literally. These should be known in detail from Tsong-kha-pa's *Essence of the Good Explanations*, and I wish to explain them elsewhere as well.

17 The Paths and Fruitions

They assert that Hearers and Solitary Realizers differ in their abandonment [of obstructions] and realization [of selflessness]; Hearers abandon the afflictive obstructions *(kleśāvaraṇa, nyon sgrib)* and Solitary Realizers abandon the coarse obstructions to omniscience *(sthaulyajñeyāvarana, shes sgrib rags pa)* — the conception apprehending objects as entities other [than the perceiving consciousness]. The paths are respectively the path realizing the mere selflessness of the person and the path realizing, in addition to that, the suchness that is the emptiness of duality.

Earlier [scholars] asserted that the four levels of yoga treated in the chapter on peak application *(mūrdhaprayoga, rtse sbyor)* in Maitreya's *Ornament for Clear Realization* are to be related with four levels of faculties, but the opinion of the foremost Tsong-kha-pa and his sons is that it is not feasible that there is a level of person who has refuted [the view] that blue is a different entity from the consciousness perceiving blue but has not refuted [the view] that the consciousness perceiving blue is a different entity from blue. Therefore, the teaching of those [levels of yoga] as if they were stages refers to stages of explanation; they are not individual stages of vehicles.

Thus in this system, only three stages of vehicles based on the view are set forth: the small realizing the common selflessness, the middling realizing emptiness of subject and object as different substantial entities, and the great realizing that all phenomena are without true existence.

A person of sharp faculties *(tīkṣṇendriya, dbang po rnon po)* who has the Mahāyāna lineage in the beginning searches for suchness — reality — and having ascertained suchness well, engenders special compassion for other transmigrators *(gati, 'gro ba)* whose continua are completely disturbed by wrong views. Having created the heroic aspiration to highest enlightenment in order to accomplish the welfare of all transmigrators by himself alone, he learns the special deeds of method and wisdom. Śāntarakṣita's *Ornament for the Middle Way* says:

> Having first sought knowledge of reality
> They thoroughly ascertain the ultimate,
> And having engendered completely compassion
> For the world abiding in the darkness of wrong views,
> The wise, whose minds have spread toward enlightenment,
> Heroic in accomplishing the purposes of migrators,
> Learn thoroughly the discipline of the Subduer
> Adorned with awareness and compassion.[1]

A person of dull faculties *(mṛdvindriya, dbang po rtul po)* having the Mahāyāna lineage meditates again and again on the aspects of the four truths such as impermanence and suffering. When experience is well developed, he realizes that other sentient beings also travel in cyclic existence, which has a nature of suffering, and realizes dependent arising — that an effect which is a mere phenomenon arises from a cause which is a mere phenomenon. In dependence on this, he creates the aspiration to enlightenment induced by great compassion, and after that, from the time of learning the [Bodhisattva] deeds he makes effort at searching for knowledge of suchness. Thus, Śāntarakṣita's *Ornament for the Middle Way* says:

> The followers of pure faith
> Create the aspiration to complete enlightenment,
> Take up the Subduer's discipline,
> And then strive for knowledge of reality.[2]

Having developed the mind of enlightenment in that way, he strives at learning the six perfections. Consequently, and in dependence on many causal collections such as external conditions — a spiritual guide — and internal conditions — correct mental application, he generates the wisdom arisen from meditation that observes the suchness of all phenomena. At that time he attains the path of preparation.

Then from among the four similitudes with a portion of definite discrimination *(nirvedhabhāgīya, nges par 'byed pa'i cha)*, at the time of *heat (uṣman, drod)* and *peak (mūrdhan, rtse mo)*, the ability to abandon the conception of true existence with respect to objects increases. Then, at the time of creating *forbearance (kṣānti, bzod pa)*, the coarse potency of the innate manifest conception of true existence with respect to objects diminishes, and at the time of *supreme mundane quality (laukikāgradharma, chos mchog)*, the potency of the manifest conception of true existence with respect to subjects diminishes. Then, through the increase of the potency of the antidotes and the decrease of the vibrancy of the objects of abandonment, at the time of eventually developing the uninterrupted path of doctrinal forbearance with respect to [the first truth,] suffering on the Mahāyāna path of seeing, the seeds to be abandoned by the path of seeing — the actual objects damaged — cease, and when, through the imprint of that antidote, these come to have the quality of its being impossible for them to be produced, an analytical cessation *(pratisaṃkhyānirodha, so sor brtags 'gog)* is attained whereby a path of release is posited.

The explanation that the path of seeing is one moment is not the one moment that is the smallest unit of time but one session of meditative equipoise on emptiness. Also, one moment of clear realization *(abhisamaya, mngon rtogs)* of the truth is produced as the nature of the sixteen moments of forbearance *(kṣānti, bzod pa)* and knowledge *(jñāna, shes pa)*. That is in terms of meditative equipoise *(samāhita, mnyam gzhag)*; in general, the period up to entering direct meditative equipoise on emptiness for the purpose of actually destroying the seeds of the innate obstructions to omniscience *(sahajajñeyāvaraṇa, shes sgrib lhan skyes)* is included in the path of seeing.

During the path of seeing, the seeds of the one hundred twelve artificial afflictive obstructions *(parikalpitakleśāvaraṇa, nyon sgrib kun brtags)* included in the levels of the three realms [the Desire, Form, and Formless Realms] and the seeds of the one hundred eight artificial obstructions to omniscience *(parikalpitajñeyāvaraṇa, shes sgrib kun brtags)* are destroyed. The nine levels of the path of meditation *(bhāvanāmārga, sgom lam)* are said to abandon gradually the seeds of the sixteen afflictions to be abandoned on the path of meditation and the seeds of the one hundred eight obstructions to omniscience to be abandoned on the path of meditation. It is said that the vajra-like meditative stabilization *(vajropamasamādhi, rdo rje lta bu'i ting nge 'dzin)* at the end [of the continuum of being a sentient being] simultaneously abandons the subtle afflictive obstructions and the subtle obstructions to omniscience, and in the second moment the Truth Body *(dharmakāya, chos sku)* is actualized. These are presentations [of the path] for those definite in the Mahāyāna lineage.

Such a Truth Body is free from the level of predispositions *(vāsanā, bags chags)* of ignorance, non-contaminated actions that arise from elaborations of signs, a body of the nature of mind, and inconceivable thoroughly transforming transmigrations. Therefore, [the Buddha] has the perfection of purity, excellent self, bliss, and permanence.

Nevertheless, through the fulfillment of the power of his earlier highly developed great compassion [wishing] to establish all transmigrators in unsurpassed bliss, a Complete Enjoyment Body *(sambhogakāya, longs spyod rdzogs pa'i sku)* — a wish-granting jewel — which is an aggregation of subtle particles of uncontaminated wisdom *(anāsravajñāna, zag med ye shes)* having the utmost of all factors of method and wisdom, abides in the Highest Pure Land *(akaniṣṭha, 'og min)*, establishing the welfare of all transmigrators through Emanation Bodies *(nirmāṇakāya, sprul pa'i sku)* as long as there is cyclic existence. Śāntarakṣita's *Ornament for the Middle Way* says:

> The body which is an aggregation of subtle particles of the wisdom and compassion supreme in all ways, free from all the aggregations of the afflictive obstructions and the obstructions to omniscience, supreme in all ways, abides as long as there is cyclic existence.[3]

Some of the features of the paths and fruits that were not explained here can be known from the explanation in the chapter on the former Svātantrikas [pp. 339-342] and from what will be explained in the chapter on the Prāsaṅgikas. The presentation of the stages of the path of the system of these Svātantrikas that is set forth so extensively in the commentaries and explanatory commentaries to Maitreya's *Ornament for Clear Realization* accords with what is widely renowned in all quarters nowadays.

Glossary

English	*Sanskrit*	*Tibetan*
abiding	sthāna	gnas pa
absorption	samāpatti	snyoms 'jug
action	karma	las
Action Tantra	kriyātantra	bya rgyud
adept	siddha	grub pa
adventitious defilement	ākasmika-mala	glo bur gyi dri ma
affirming negative	paryudāsa-pratiṣedha	ma yin dgag
afflicted mind	kliṣṭamanas	nyon yid
affliction/ afflictive emotion	kleśa	nyon mongs
afflictive obstruction	kleśāvaraṇa	nyon sgrib
aging	jarā	rga ba
aggregate	skandha	phung po
aggregation	saṃghata	'dus pa
altruism	parahita	gzhan la phan pa
analytical cessation	pratisaṃkhyā-nirodha	so sor brtags 'gog
antidote	pratipakṣa	gnyen po
appearance	pratibhāsa	snang ba

English	*Sanskrit*	*Tibetan*
appearing object	*pratibhāsa-viṣaya	snang yul
apprehend	grahaṇa	'dzin pa
apprehended	grāhya	bzung ba
apprehended object	grāhya-viṣaya	bzung yul
apprehender	grāhaka	'dzin pa
arisen from hearing	śrutamayī	thos byung
arisen from meditation	bhāvanāmayī	sgom byung
arisen from thinking	cintāmayī	bsam byung
artificial	parikalpita	kun btags
ascertain/ascertainment	niścaya	nges pa
aspect	ākāra	rnam pa
aspirational mind of enlightenment	bodhipraṇidhicitta	smon sems
attachment	tṛṣṇa	sred pa
attribute	viśeṣa	khyad par
autonomous inference	svatantra-anumāna	rang rgyud rjes dpag
autonomous sign	svatantra-liṅga	rang rgyud kyi rtags
autonomous syllogism	svatantra-prayoga	rang rgyud kyi sbyor ba
basal subject		rang rten gyi chos can
base/basis	āśraya	rten
basis of affixing		'jug gzhi
basis of all	ālaya	kun gzhi
basis of debate		rtsod gzhi
basis of designation		gdags gzhi
bondage	bandha	'ching ba
Blissful Pure Land	sukhāvati	dbe ba can
Bodhisattva	bodhisattva	byang chub sems dpa'
body consciousness	kāya-vijñāna	lus kyi rnam par shes pa

English	*Sanskrit*	*Tibetan*
calm abiding	śamatha	zhi gnas
cause	hetu	rgyu
changeable factor	aniyata	gzhan 'gyur
Cittamātra	cittamātra	sems tsam
clairvoyance	abhijñā	mngon par shes pa
clear realization	abhisamaya	mngon rtogs
coarse selflessness		bdag med rags pa
common being	pṛthagjana	so so skye bo
commonly appearing subject		chos can mthun snang
compassion	karuṇā	snying rje
Complete Enjoyment Body	saṃbhogakāya	long spyod rdzogs pa'i sku
composite	saṃcita	bsags pa
compositional factor	saṃskāra	'du byed
compositional factor not associated with either mind or mental factors	citta-caitta-viprayukta-saṃskāra	sems sems byung dang ldan par ma yin pa'i 'du byed
conceptual consciousness/thought/thought consciousness	*kalpanā	rtog pa
conceptual subsequent cognizer	kalpanā-paricchinnajñāna	rtog pa brjad shes
concentration	dhyāna	bsam gtan
conception of self	ātmagraha	bdag tu 'dzin pa
condition	pratyaya	rkyen
conditionality	idaṃpratyayatā	rkyen 'di pa tsam nyid
conditional phenomenon	saṃskṛta-dharma	'dus byas kyi chos
Conqueror	jina	rgyal ba
consciousness	jñāna/vijñāna	shes pa/rnam shes
consequence	prasaṅga	thal 'gyur
constituent	dhātu	khams
consummate	pariniṣpanna	yongs grub

English	*Sanskrit*	*Tibetan*
contact	sparśa	reg pa
contaminated	sāsrava	zag bcas
contaminated action	sāsrava-karma	zag bcas kyi las
contamination	āsrava	zag pa
continuum	saṃtāna	rgyun
contradictory	virodha	'gal ba
contradictory consequence		'gal brjod thal 'gyur
contradictory in the sense of mutual exclusion	*anyonya-parihāravirodha	phan tshun spang 'gal
contradictory in the sense of not abiding together	*saha-anavastāvirodha	lhan cig mi gnas 'gal
contradictory object		'gal zla
contradictory reason	viruddha-hetu	'gal ba'i gtan tshigs
conventional existence	saṃvṛti-sat	kun rdzob tu yod pa
conventional mind of enlightenment	saṃvṛti-bodhicitta	kun rdzob byang chub kyi sems
conventional truth/ truth for a concealer	saṃvṛti-satya	kun rdzob bden pa
cooperative condition	sahakāri-pratyaya	lhan cig byed rkyen
correct proof	samyak-sādhana	sgrub byed yang dag
correct reason	samyak-nimitta	rgyu mtshan yang dag
correct reasoning	samyak-nyāya	rigs pa yang dag
correct sign	samyak-liṅga	rtags yang dag
correct view	samyak-dṛṣṭi	yang dag pa'i lta ba
counterpervasion	vyatireka-vyāpti	ldog khyab
cyclic existence	saṃsāra	'khor ba
definiendum	lakṣya	mtshon bya
definite discrimination	nirvedhabhāgīya	nges 'byed
definition	lakṣana	mtshan nyid

English	*Sanskrit*	*Tibetan*
definitive	nitārtha	nges don
dependence		ltos pa
dependent-arising	pratītyasamutpāda	rten 'byung
dependent phenomenon	paratantra	gzhan dbang
designation	vyavahāra	tha snyad
desire	rāga	'dod chags
Desire Realm	kāmadhātu	'dod khams
determined object	*adhyavasāya-viṣaya	zhen yul
determining factor	viniyata	yuls nges
direct cognition/ directly cognize		mngon sum du rtogs pa
direct perception/ direct perceiver	pratyakṣa	mngon sum
direct realization/ directly realize		mngon sum du rtogs pa
direct valid cognizer	pratyakṣa-pramāṇa	mngon sum tshad ma
discipline	vinaya	'dul ba
discrimination	samjñā	'du shes
disintegration	vināśa	'jig pa
dissimilar	vipakṣa	mi mthun phyogs
dissimilar example	vidṛṣtanta	mi mthun dpe
effect sign	kārya-hetu	'bras rtags
effort	vīrya	brtson 'grus
elaborations	prapañca	spros pa
element	bhūta	'byung ba
Emanation Body	nirmāṇakāya	sprul sku
empowering condition	adhipati-pratyaya	bdag rkyen
emptiness	śūnyatā	stong pa nyid
empty	śūnya	stong pa
Enjoyment Body	saṃbhogakāya	longs sku
enlightenment	bodhi	byang chub
entity	vastu	ngo bo
entityness	svabhāvatā	ngo bo nyid
entitynessless	niḥsvabhāvatā	ngo bo nyid med pa

English	*Sanskrit*	*Tibetan*
established/proven	siddha	grub pa
established base		gzhi grub
etymology		sgra bshad
exalted knower of all aspects/ omniscient consciousness	sarvākārajñāna	rnam mkhyen/rnam pa thams cad mkhyen pa
exalted knower of the modes	yathavajjñāna	ji lta ba gzigs pa'i ye shes
exalted knower of the varieties	yāvajjñāna	ji snyed gzigs pa'i ye shes
exalted wisdom	jñāna	ye shes
exalted wisdom of equipoise	samāhita-jñāna	mnyam bzhag ye shes
example	dṛṣṭānta	dpe
existence by way of its own character	svalakṣaṇa-siddhi	rang gi mtshan nyid kyis grub pa
existence by way of its own entityness	*svabhāvatā-siddhi	ngo bo nyid kyis grub pa
existence by way of its own mode of subsistence		rang gi sdod lugs gyi ngos nas grub pa
existence from the object's side	*svarūpya-siddhi	rang ngos nas grub pa
existence from the side of the basis of designation		gdags gzhi'i ngos nas grub pa
existence in the manner of coverings its basis of designation		gdags gzhi'i go sa gon pa'i tshul du yod pa
existence in the object designated	*prajñapti-viṣaya-siddha	btags yul gyi steng nas grub pa
existence in the basis of designation		gdags gzhi'i steng nas grub pa
existence through its own power	svairī-siddhi	rang dbang du grub pa
existent	sat	yod pa

English	*Sanskrit*	*Tibetan*
external object	bāhya-artha	phyi don
extreme	anta	mtha'
extreme of annihilation	uccedānta	chad mtha'
extreme of denial/ extreme of deprecation	apavādānta	skur 'debs kyi mtha'
extreme of existence	astyanta	yod mtha'
extreme of non-existence	nāstyanta	med mtha'
extreme of permanence	śaśvatānta	rtag mtha'
extreme of superimposition	āropānta	sgro 'dogs kyi mtha'
facsimiles of reasons	hetu-ābhāsa	gtan tshigs ltar snang
facsimiles of signs	*liṅga-ābhāsa	rtags ltar snang
faith	śraddhā	dad pa
False Aspectarian	alīkākāravādin	rnam rdzun pa
feeling	vedanā	tshor ba
Foe Destroyer	arhan	dgra bcom pa
Followers of Reasoning	*nyāya-anusārin	rigs pa'i rje su 'brangs pa
Followers of Scripture	*āgama-anusārin	lung gi rje su 'brang pa
forbearance	kṣānti	bzod pa
form	rūpa	gzugs
Form Body	rūpakāya	gzugs sku
form for the mental consciousness	dharmāyatana-rūpa	chos kyi skye mched pa'i gzugs
Form Realm	rūpadhātu	gzugs khams
form source	rūpāyatana	gzugs kyi skye mched
Formless Realm	arūpadhātu	gzugs med khams
forward pervasion	anvaya-vyāpti	rjes khyab
free from thought	kalpanā-apodha	rtog bral

English	*Sanskrit*	*Tibetan*
fruit	phala	'bras bu
generality	sāmānya	spyi
generally characterized phenomenon	sāmānya-lakṣaṇa	spyi mtshan
generic image/ meaning generality	arthasāmānya	don spyi
giving	dāna	sbyin pa
great compassion	mahākaruṇā	snying rje chen po
great element	mahābhūta	'byung ba chen po
ground	bhūmi	sa
harmony with enlightenment	bodhi-pakṣa	byang chub kyi phyogs
Hearer	śrāvaka	nyan thos
hearing	śruta	thos pa
heat	uṣmagata	drod
hidden phenomenon	parokṣa	lkog gyur
Highest Pure Land	akaniṣṭa	'og min
Highest Yoga Tantra	anuttara-yoga-tantra	bla med gyi rgyud
I	ahaṃ	nga
ignorance	avidyā	ma rig pa
imaginary	parikalpita	kun btags
imaginary phenomenon	parikalpita-dharma	kun btags pa'i chos
immediately preceding condition	samanantara-pratyaya	de ma thag rkyen
impermanent	anitya	mi rtag pa
impermanent thing	bhāva	dngos po
imputedly existent	prajñāptisat	btags yod
incontrovertible	avisaṃvadin	mi slu ba
indefinite reason	anaikāntika-hetu	ma nges pa'i gtan tshigs

English	*Sanskrit*	*Tibetan*
individual knowledge	pratyātmavedya	so so rang rig
inference/inferential cognizer	anumāna	rjes dpag
inferential valid cognizer	anumāna-pramāṇa	rjes dpag tshad ma
inherent existence	svabhāva-siddhi	rang bzhin gyis grub pa
innate	sahaja	lhan skyes
innate afflictions	sahaja-kleśa	nyon mongs lhan skyes
intelligence	buddhi/mati	blo gros
intention	cetanā	sems pa
interpretable	neyārtha	drang don
Īśvara	īśvara	dbang phyug
knower	saṃvedana	rig pa
knowledge	abhidharma	chos mngon pa
Land of Superiors	āryavarśa	'phags yul
latency	vāsanā	bag chags
liberation	vimokṣa/mokṣa	thar pa
lineage	gotra	rigs
love	maitri	byams pa
Mādhyamika	mādhyamika	dbu ma pa
manifest phenomenon	abhimukhī	mngon gyur
matter	kanthā	bem po
meaning/object	artha	don
meaning of the term	śabda-artha	sgra don
meditative absorption	samāpatti	snyoms 'jug
meditative equipoise	samāhita	mnyam bzhag
meditative stabilization	samādhi	ting nge 'dzin
mental and physical aggregates	skandha	phung po

English	*Sanskrit*	*Tibetan*
mental consciousness	manovijñāna	yid kyi rnam shes
mental direct perceiver	mānasa-pratyakṣa	yid kyi mngon sum
mental engagement	manaskāra	yid la byed pa
mental factor	caitta	sem byung
mere subject		chos can 'ba' zhig pa
merit	puṇya	bsod nams
method	upāya	thabs
migrator	gati	'gro ba
mind	citta	sems
mind-basis-of-all	ālaya-vijñāna	kun gzhi rnam shes
mind of enlightenment	bodhicitta	byang chub kyi sems
mindfulness	smṛti	dran pa
mistaken	bhrānti	'khrul pa
mode	rūpa	mtshul
mode of being		gnas lugs
moment	kṣaṇa	skad cig
mutual exclusion	*anyonya-parihāra	phan tshun spang 'gal
nature	prakṛti	rang bzhin
Nature Body	svabhāvikakāya	ngo bo nyid sku
negation/negative phenomenon	pratiṣedha	dgag pa
negative, affirming	paryudāsa-pratiṣedha	ma yin dgag
negative, non-affirming	prasajya-pratiṣedha	med dgag
Nihilist	ayata	rgyang 'phen pa
noble/superior	ārya	'phags pa
nominal existence		ming tsam du yod pa
non-affirming negative	prasajya-pratiṣedha	med dgag
non-analytical cessation	apratisaṃkhyā-nirodha	so sor brtags min gyi 'gog pa
non-associated	viprayukta-	ldan min 'du byed

English	*Sanskrit*	*Tibetan*
compositional factor	saṃskāra	
non-conceptual	nirvikalpaka	rtog med
non-conceptual wisdom	nirvikalpa-jñāna	rnam par mi rtog pa'i ye shes
non-entityness	niḥsvabhāvatā	ngo bo nyid med
non-established reason	asiddha-hetu	ma grub pa'i gtan tshigs
non-existent	asat	med pa
non-mistaken	abhrānta	ma 'khrul ba
non-observation of a cause	kāraṇa-anupalabdhi	rgyu ma dmigs pa
non-observation of a nature	svabhāva-anupalabdhi	rang bzhin ma dmigs ba
non-observation of a pervader	vyāpaka-anupalabdhi	khyab byed ma dmigs ba
non-observation of an effect	kārya-anupalabdhi	'bras bu ma dmigs pa
non-observation sign	anupalabdhi-liṅga	ma dmigs pa'i rtags
non-revelatory form	avijñāpti-rūpa	rnam par rig byed ma yin pa'i gzugs
non-thing	abhāva	dngos med
non-virtuous	akuśala	mi dge ba
object	viṣaya/artha	yul/don
object of apprehension	grāhya-viṣaya	bzung yul
object of comprehension	prameya	gzhal bya
object of engagement	*pravṛtti-viṣaya	'jug yul
object of expression	vākya	brjod bya
object of knowledge	jñeya	shes bya
object of negation	*pratiṣedhya	dgag bya
object of negation by reasoning	*yukti-pratiṣedhya	rigs pa'i dgag bya
object of negation by the path	*mārga-pratiṣedhya	lam gyi dgag bya
object of	ālambana	dmigs yul/dmigs pa

English	*Sanskrit*	*Tibetan*
observation/ observed object		
object of thought	*kalpanā-viṣaya	rtog yul
object pervaded	vyāpa	khyab bya
objective existence	*viṣaya-siddhi	yul gyi steng nas grub pa
observed-object-condition	ālambana-pratyaya	dmigs rkyen
obstructions to liberation/ afflictive obstructions	kleśāvaraṇa	nyon mong pa'i sgrib pa
obstructions to omniscience	jñeyāvaraṇa	shes bya'i sgrib pa
omnipresent factor	sarvatraga	kun 'gro
omniscience	sarvākārajñāna	rnam pa tham ced mkhyen pa
only imputed	prajñaptimātra	btags tsam
other-approved reason	paraprasiddha-liṅga	gzhan grags kyi rtags
other-approved syllogism	paraprasiddha-prayoga	gzhan grags kyi sbyor ba
own character	svalakṣaṇa	rang mtshan
own continuum/ autonomous	svatantra	rang rgyud
own power	svairī	rang dbang
pain/suffering	duḥkha	sdug bsngal
particularity	viśeṣa	bye brag
party	pakṣa	rgol ba
path	mārga	lam
path of accumulation	saṃbhāra-mārga	tshogs lam
path of meditation	bhāvāna-mārga	sgom lam
path of no more learning	aśaikṣa-mārga	mi slob lam
path of preparation	prayogā-mārga	sbyor lam
path of release	vimukti-mārga	rnam grol lam
path of seeing	darśana-mārga	mthong lam

English	*Sanskrit*	*Tibetan*
patience	kṣānti	bzod pa
peak	mūrdhan	rtse mo
Perfection Vehicle	pāramitāyāna	phar phyin kyi theg pa
Perfection	pāramitā	phar phyin
Performance Tantra	caryātantra	spyod rgyud
permanent phenomenon	nitya	rtag pa
person	pudgala	gang zag
personal deity	iṣṭadevatā	yid dam gyi lha
pervader	vyāpaka	khyab byed
pervasive suffering of conditioning	vyāptisaṃskāra-duḥkhatā	khyab pa 'du byed kyi sdug bsngal
pervasion	vyāpti	khyab pa
phenomenon	dharma	chos
phenomenon-source	dharmāyatana	chos kyi skye mched
pleasure	sukhā	bde ba
position	pakṣa	phyogs
potency	vāsanā/bāla	bag chags/nus pa
Prāsaṇgika	prāsaṇgika	thal 'gyur pa
predicate of the probandum	sādhyadharma	bsgrub bya'i chos
predisposition	vāsanā	bag chags
principal	pradhāna	gtso bo
produced	utpādya	bskyed bya
producer	utpatti	skyed byed
proof statement	sādhana-vākya	sgrub ngag
property of the subject	pakṣadharma	phyogs chos
Proponent of No Entityness	niḥsvabhāvavādin	ngo bo nyid med par smra ba
Proponent of True Existence		dngos smra ba
real conventional truth	tathya-saṃvṛti-satya	yang dag kun rdzob bden pa
real existence	*samyak-siddhi	yang dag par grub pa
reality	dharmatā	chos nyid

English	*Sanskrit*	*Tibetan*
realize	adigam	rtogs
reason	hetu	gtan tshigs
reasoning	yukti	rigs pa
referent object	*adhyavasāya-viṣaya	zhen yul
related object		'brel zla
relationship	saṃbandha	'brel ba
renown	prasiddha	grags pa
renowned to oneself	svaprasiddha	rang la grags pa
renowned to others	paraprasiddha	gzhan la grags pa
requiring interpretation	neyārtha	drang don
reverse	vyatireka	ldog pa
root affliction	mūlakleśa	rtsa nyon
same reverse	*eka-vyatireka	ldog pa gcig
Sāṃkhya	sāṃkhya	grangs can pa
Sautrāntika	sautrāntika	mdo sde pa
Sautrāntika-Svātantrika-Mādhyamika	sautrāntika-svātantrika-mādhyamika	mdo sde spyod pa'i dbu ma rang rgyud pa
scholar-adept	paṇḍiṭa-siddha	mkhas grub
second party	pūrva-pakṣa	phyi rgol
secondary affliction	upakleśa	nye nyon
seed	bīja	sa bon
self	ātman	bdag
self-approved inference	svaprasiddha-anumānu	rang grags rjes dpag
self-approved reason	svaprasiddha-liṅga	rang grags kyi rtags
self-knower	svasaṃvedana	rang rig
self-knowing direct perceiver	svasaṃvedana-pratyakṣa	rang rig mngon sum
self of persons	pudgalātman	gang zag gi bdag
self of phenomena	dharmātman	chos kyi bdag
self-sufficient		rang rkya ba
selflessness	nairātmya	bdag med
selflessness of persons	pudgala-nairātmya	gang sag gi bdag med

English	*Sanskrit*	*Tibetan*
selflessness of phenomena	dharma-nairātmya	chos kyi bdag med
sense consciousness	indriya-jñāna	dbang shes
sense direct perceiver	indriya-pratyakṣa	dbang po'i mngon sum
sense power	indriya	dbang po
sentient being	sattva	sems can
sign	liṅga	rtags
sign proving the expression		tha snyad sgrub kyi rtags
sign proving the meaning		don sgrub kyi rtags
sign which is a non-observation of a related object		'brel zla ma dmigs pa'i rtags
sign which is a non-observation of the suitable to appear		snang rung ma dmigs pa'i rtags
sign which is an observation of a contradictory object		'gal zla dmigs pa'i rtags
similar class	sapakṣa	mthun phyogs
similar example	*sadṛṣṭānta	mthun dpe
skillful means	upāya-kauśala	thab mkhas
Solitary Realizer	pratyekabuddha/svajina	rang sang rgyas/rang rgyal
sound	śabda	sgra
source	āyatana	skye mched
space	ākāśa	nam mkha'
special insight	vipaśyanā	lhag mthong
specifically characterized phenomenon	svalakṣaṇa	rang mtshan
sphere of reality	dharmadhātu	chos kyi dbyings
stabilization	samādhi	ting nge 'dzin
subject	dharmin	chos can

English	*Sanskrit*	*Tibetan*
subsequent attainment	pṛṣṭhalabdha	rjes thob
subsequent cognizer	*paricchinna-jñāna	bcad shes
substantial cause	upādāna	nyer len
substantial entity	dravya	rdzas
substantial existence	dravya-sat	rdzas su yod pa
substantially established	dravya-siddha	rdzas su grub pa
substantially existent	dravya-sat	rdzas su yod pa
suchness	tathatā	de bzhin nyid/de kho na nyid
suffering of change	vipariṇāmaduḥ-khatā	'gyur ba'i sdug bsngal
suffering of conditioning	saṃskāraduḥkhatā	'du byed kyi sdug bsngal
suffering of pain	duḥkhaduḥkhatā	sdug bsngal gyi sdug bsngal
Sugata	sugata	bde bar gshegs pa
Sugata essence	sugata-garbha	bde bar gshegs pa'i snying po
Sun Friend	ādityabandhu	nyi ma'i gnyen
superficial cause of error	*pratibhāśikī-bhrānti-hetu	phral gyi 'khrul rgyu
superimpositions	āropa	sgro 'dogs
Superior	ārya	'phags pa
supramundane	lokottara	'jig rten las 'das pa
Supramundane Victor	bhagavan	bcom ldan 'das
supreme mundane qualities	laukikāgraya-dharma	'jig rten pa'i chos kyi mchog
Svātantrika	svātantrika	rang rgyud pa
syllogism	prayoga	sbyor ba
synonym	ekārtha	don gcig
tangible object	sparṣṭavya	reg bya
Tathāgata	tathāgata	de bzhin gshegs pa
Tathagata essence	tathāgata-garbha	de bzhin gshegs pa'i

English	*Sanskrit*	*Tibetan*
		snying po
tenet/system of tenets	siddhānta/ siddhyanta	grub mtha'
term	śabda	sgra
thesis	pratijñā	dam bca'
thing/actuality	bhāva	dngos po
Three Bodies	trikāya	sku gsum
three modes	trirūpa	mtshul gsum
thought/thought consciousness	kalpanā	rtog pa
time	kāla	dus
treatise	śāstra	bstan bcos
True Aspectarian	satyākāravādin	rnam bden pa
true cessation	nirodha-satya	'gog bden
true establishment	satya-siddhi	bden par grub pa
true existence	satya-sat	bden par yod pa
truly established	satya-siddha	bden par grub pa
truly existent	satya-sat	bden par yod pa
truth	satya	bden pa
truth for a concealer	saṃvṛti-satya	kun rdzob bden pa
Truth Body	dharmakāya	chos sku
two truths	satyadvaya	bden pa gnyis
ultimate	paramārtha	don dam pa
ultimate existence	paramārtha-siddhi	don dam par grub pa
ultimate mind of enlightenment	paramārtha-bodhicitta	don dam byang chub kyi sems
ultimate truth	paramārtha-satya	don dam bden pa
ultimately established	paramārtha-siddha	don dam par grub pa
uncommon empowering condition	asādhārana-adhipatipratyaya	thun mong ma yin pa'i bdag rkyen
unconditioned phenomena	asaṃskṛta-dharma	'dus ma byas kyi chos
uncontaminated wisdom	anāsrava-jñāna	zag med ye shes

English	*Sanskrit*	*Tibetan*
uninterrupted path	ānantarya-mārga	bar ched med lam
unreal conventional truth	mithyā-saṃvṛti-satya	log pa'i kun rdzob bden pa
Vaibhāṣika	vaibhāṣika	bye brag smra ba
vajra-like meditative stabilization	vajropamasamādhi	rdo rje lta bu'i ting nge 'dzin
valid cognition/ valid cognizer	pramāṇa	tshad ma
valid establishment	pramāṇa-siddhi	tshad ma'i grub pa
validly established	pramāṇa-siddha	tshad ma'i grub pa
vehicle	yāna	theg pa
view	dṛṣṭi	lta ba
virtuous	kuśula	dge ba
visible form	rūpa	gzugs
wisdom	prajñā/jñāna	shes rab/ye shes
wisdom arisen from hearing	śrutamayī-prajñā	thos byung gi shes rab
wisdom arisen from meditation	bhāvanāmayi-prajñā	sgom byung gi shes rab
wisdom arisen from thinking	cintāmayī-prajñā	bsam byung gi shes rab
Wisdom Truth Body	jñānakāya	ye shes chos sku
wrong consciousness	viparyaya-jñāna	log shes
wrong view	mithyā-dṛṣṭi	log lta
Yoga Tantra	yogatantra	rnal 'byor rgyud
Yogācāra-Svātantrika-Mādhyamika	yogācāra-svātantrika-mādhyamika	rnal 'byor spyod pa'i dbu ma rang rgyud pa
yogic direct perceiver	yogi-pratyakṣa	rnal 'byor mngon sum

Bibliography of Works Cited

Sūtras and tantras are listed alphabetically by English title in the first section; Indian and Tibetan works are arranged alphabetically by author in the second; works in English and French are listed alphabetically by author in the third section.

The words *ārya*, *mahāyāna*, and *śrī* have been deleted from the Sanskrit and Tibetan titles, and many of the English titles have been abbreviated. The fact that the titles of Sanskrit and Tibetan texts have been translated into English does not suggest that the works themselves have been translated. A published translation is noted for works that have been translated.

For modern editions of Indian Mādhyamika texts and their Tibetan translations, see David Seyfort Ruegg, *The Literature of the Madhyamaka School of India* (Wiesbaden: Otto Harrassowitz, 1981)

Abbreviations

P: *Tibetan Tripiṭaka* (Tokyo-Kyoto: Tibetan Tripitaka Research Foundation, 1956)

Toh: *A Complete Catalogue of the Tohuku University Collection of Tibetan Works on Buddhism*, ed. Prof. Yensho Kanakura (Sendai, Japan, 1934 and 1953)

I. SUTRAS AND TANTRAS

Advice to Kātyāyana Sutra
Kātyāyanāvavādasūtra
Ka tya ya na yi bdams ngag gi mdo
Included in P 1035

Brief Scriptures on Discipline
Vinayakṣudravastu
'Dul ba phran tshegs kyi gzhi
P 1035

Chapter on the Supramundane
Lokottaraparivarta
'Jig rten las 'das pa'i le'u
[?]

Compendium of Doctrine Sutra
Dharmsaṃgītisūtra
Chos yang dag par sdud pa'i mdo
P 904

Descent into Laṅkā Sutra
Laṅkāvatārasūtra
Lang kar gsheg pa'i mdo
P 775
Translation by D. T. Suzuki, *The Lankavatara Sutra* (London: Routledge and Kegan Paul, 1932)

Diamond Cutter Sutra
Vajracchedikā
rDo rje gcod pa
P 739
Translation by Edward Conze, *Buddhist Wisdom Books* (New York: Harper and Row, 1972).

Garland Sutra
Buddhāvataṃsakanāmamahāvaipulyasūtra
Sangs rgyas phal po che zhes bya ba shin tu rgyas pa chen po'i mdo
P 761

Great Cloud Sutra
Mahāmeghasūtra
sPrin chen po'i mdo
P 898

Great Drum Sutra
Mahābherīhārakaparivartasūtra

rNga bo che chen po'i le'u'i mdo
P 888
Guhyasamāja Tantra
Sarvatathāgatakāyavākcittarahasyaguhyasamājanāmamahākalparāja
De bzhin gshegs pa tham cad kyi sku gsung thugs kyi gsang chen gsang ba 'dus pa zhes bya ba brtag pa'i rgyal po chen po
P 81; Sanskrit edition by S. Bagchi, Dharbanga India: Mithila Institute, 1965.
Heart of the Perfection of Wisdom Sutra
Bhagavatīprajñāpāramītahṛdayasūtra
bCom ldan 'das ma shes rab kyi pha rol tu phyin pa'i snying po'i mdo
P 160
Translation by Edward Conze in *Buddhist Wisdom Books* (New York: Harper and Row, 1972)
Kāśyapa Chapter Sutra
Kāśyapaparivartasūtra
'Od srung gi le'u'i mdo
P 760.43
Kindred Sayings III
Saṃyutta-nikāya III
London: Pali Text Society, Luzac and Company, 1960
Translation by F. L. Woodward, *The Book of Kindred Sayings III* (London: PTS, 1954)
King of Meditative Stabilizations Sutra
Samādhirājasūtra
Ting nge 'dzin rgyal po'i mdo
P 795
Partial translation by K. Regamey, *Three Chapters of the Samādhirājasūtra* (Warsaw, 1958)
Mañjuśrī Root Tantra
Mañjuśrīmūlatantra
'Jam dpal gyi rtsa ba'i rgyud
P 162
Meeting of Father and Son Sutra
Pitāputrasamāgamasūtra
Yab dang sras mjal ba'i mdo
P 760.16
Ornament Illuminating the Wisdom Entering the Sphere of All Buddhas

Sutra
Sarvabuddhaviṣayāvatārajñānālokālaṃkārasūtra
Sangs rgyas thams cad kyi yul la 'jug pa'i ye shes snang ba'i rgyan gyi mdo
P 768

Perfection of Wisdom in One Hundred Thousand Stanzas Sutra
Śatasahāsrikāprajñāpāramitāsūtra
Shes rab kyi pha rol tu phyin pa stong phrag brgya pa'i mdo
P 730

Perfection of Wisdom in Twenty-five Thousand Stanzas Sutra
Pañcaviṃśatisāhasrikāprajñapāramitāsūtra
Shes rab kyi pha rol tu phyin pa stong phrag nyi shu lnga pa
P 731
Translation by E. Conze, *The Large Sutra on Perfect Wisdom* (Berkeley: University of California Press, 1975)

Purposeful Statements
Udānavarga
Ched du brjod pa'i tshoms
P 39
Translation by W. Rockhill, *Udānavarga* (Amsterdam: Oriental Press, 1975)

Rice Seedling Sutra
Śalistambasūtra
Sā lu'i ljang pa'i mdo
P 876

Sūtra on the Heavily Adorned
Ghanavyūhasūtra
rGyan stug po bkod pa'i mdo
P 778

Sutra on the Ten Grounds
Daśabhūmikasūtra
mDo sde sa bcu pa
P 761.31
Translation by M. Honda in "An Annotated Translation of the 'Daśabhūmika'" in *Studies in Southeast and Central Asia*, ed. D. Sinor; Śatapiṭaka Series 74 (New Delhi, 1968), pp 115-276.

Sutra Unravelling the Thought
Saṃdhinirmocanasūtra
dGongs pa nges par 'grel pa'i mdo
P 774

Translation by É. Lamotte, *Saṃdinirmocana-sūtra* (Paris: Adrien Maisonneuve, 1935)

Teaching of Akṣayamati
Akṣayamatinirdeśasūtra
bLo gros mi zad pas bstan pa'i mdo
P 842

Treasury of Tathāgathas Sutra
Tathāgatakośasūtra
De bzhin gshegs pa'i mdzod kyi mdo
[?]

II OTHER SANSKRIT AND TIBETAN SOURCES

Abhayākāragupta
Moonbeams of Essentials
Marmakaumudi
gNad kyi zla 'od
[?]

Advayavajra (gNyis med rdo rje)/ Maitrīpāda, 11th century
Jewel Garland of Principles
Tattvaratnāvalī
De kho na nyid rin chen phreng ba
P 3085

Akutobhayā (Ga-las-'jigs-med)[1]
Akutobhayā's Commentary on (Nāgārjuna's) "Treatise on the Middle Way"
Mūlamadhyamakavṛtti-akutobhaya
dbU ma rtsa ba'i 'grel pa ga las 'jigs med
P 5229

Amarasiṃha ('Chi-med-seng-ge), 6th century
Amarasiṃha's Treasury
Amarakośa
'Chi med mdzod
P 5787

Āryadeva ('Phags-pa-lha)
Compendium on the Essence of Exalted Wisdom
Jñānasārasamuccaya
Ye shes snying po kun btus
P 5251

Establishment of the Reasoning and Logic Refuting Error
Skhalitapramathanayuktihetusiddhi

'Khrul pa bzlog pa'i rigs pa gtan tshigs grub pa
P 5247
Four Hundred/Treatise of Four Hundred Stanzas
Catuḥśatakaśāstrakārikā
bsTan bcos bzhi brgya pa zhes bya ba'i tshig le'ur byas pa
P 5246
Length of a Forearm
Hastavālaprakaraṇakārikā
Rab tu byed pa lag pa'i tshad kyi tshig le'ur byas pa
P 5248
Āryavimuktisena ('Phags-pa-grol-sde)
Illumination of the Perfection of Wisdom in Twenty-Five Thousand Stanzas
Pañcavimśatisāhasrikāprajñapāramitopadeśaśāstrābhisamayālaṃkāravṛtti
Shes rab kyi pha rol tu phyin pa stong phrag nyi shu lnga pa'i man ngag gi bstan bcos mngon par rtogs pa'i rgyan gyi 'grel pa
P 5185
Asaṅga (Thogs-med), 4th century
Compendium of Knowledge
Abhidharmasamuccaya
mNgon pa kun btus
P 5550
Translation by W. Rahula, *Le Compendium de la Super-Doctrine Philosophie* (Paris: École Française d' Extrême Orient, 1971)
Atīśa, c. 982-1054
Commentary on the Difficult Points of Lamp for the Path to Enlightenment
Bodhimārgapradīpapañjikā
Byang chub lam gyi sgron ma'i dka' 'grel
P 5344
Translation by R. Sherburne, *A Lamp for the Path and Commentary* (London: Allen and Unwin, 1983)
Introduction to the Two Truths
Satyadvayāvatāra
bDen pa nyis la 'jug pa
P 5380
Translation by C. Lindtner in "Atisa's Introduction to the Two Truths, and Its Sources." *Journal of Indian Philosophy*, Vol.

9 (1981), pp. 161-214.

Avalokitavrata (sPyan-ras-gzigs-brtul-zhugs), 8th century

Commentary on (Bhāvaviveka's) "Lamp for (Nāgārjuna's) 'Wisdom'"

Prajñāpradīpaṭīkā

Shes rab sgron ma'i rgya cher 'grel pa

P 5259

Ba-so Cho-gyi-gyel-tsen (Ba-so Chos-kyi-rgyal-mtshan). See Jam-yang-shay-ba, et al.

Bel-den Drak-ba (dPal-ldan-grags-pa)

Beautiful Ornament of Faith, A Good Explanation

Legs bshad dad pa'i mdzes rgyan

Mundgod, India: Drepung Loseling Printing Press, 1979

Bhāvaviveka (Legs-ldan-'byed), c. 500-570

Blaze of Reasoning, Commentary on the "Heart of the Middle Way"

Madhyamakahṛdayavṛttitarkajvālā

dbU ma'i snying po'i 'grel pa rtog ge 'bar ba

P 5256

Partial translation of Chapter III by S. Iida, in *Reason and Emptiness* (Tokyo: Hokuseido, 1980)

Heart of the Middle Way

Madhyamakahṛdayakārikā

dbU ma'i snying po'i tshig le'ur byas pa

P 5255

See Iida (above) for list of translated chapters.

Lamp for (Nāgārjuna's) "Wisdom," Commentary on the "Treatise on the Middle Way"

Prajñāpradīpamūlamadhyamakavṛtti

dbU ma rtsa ba'i 'grel pa shes rab sgron ma

P 5253

Translation of Chapter I by Y. Kajiyama in *Wiener Zeitschrift fur die Kunde Sud und Ostasiens*, Vol 7, 1965

Bhavaviveka the Lesser (Legs-ldan-chung-ba)

Precious Lamp for the Middle Way

Madhyamakaratnapradīpa

dbU ma rin po che'i sgron ma

P 5254

Buddhapālita (Sangs-rgyas-bskyangs), c. 500

Buddhapālita's Commentary on (Nāgārjuna's) "Treatise on the Middle Way"

Buddhapālitamūlamadhyamakavṛtti
dbU ma rtsa ba'i 'grel pa buddha pa li ta
P 5242
Candrakīrti (Zla-ba-grags-pa), c. 600-650
Brilliant Lamp Commentary
Pradīpoddyotana
'Grel pa sgron gsal
p 2650
Clear Words, Commentary on (Nagarjuna's) "Treatise on the Middle Way"
Mūlamadhyamakavṛttiprasannapadā
dbU ma rtsa ba'i 'grel pa tshig gsal ba
P 5260
Sanskrit edition: *Mūlamadhyamakākārikas (Mādhyamikasūtras) de Nāgārjuna avec la Prasannapadā Commentaire de Candrakīrti*. Publiée par Louis de la Vallée Poussin (Osnabrück: Biblio Verlag, 1970). Partial translation by J. May, *Candrakīrti Prasannapadā Madhyamakavṛtti* (Paris: Adrien-Maisonneuve, 1959); also J. W. de Jong, *Cing Chapitres de la Prasannapadā* (Paris: Paul Geuthner, 1949); also M. Sprung, *Lucid Exposition of the Middle Way* (London: Routledge, 1979)
Commentary on (Āryadeva's) "Four Hundred Stanzas on the Yogic Deeds of the Bodhisattvas"
Bodhisattvayogacaryācatuḥśatakaṭīkā
Byang chub sems dpa'i rnal 'byor spyod pa bzhi bryga pa'i rgya cher 'grel pa
P 5266
Commentary on (Nagarjuna's) "Sixty Stanzas of Reasoning"
Yukitṣaṣtikavṛtti
Rigs pa drug cu pa'i 'grel pa
P 5265
Commentary on the "Supplement to the Middle Way"
Madhyamakāvatārabhāṣya
dbU ma la 'jug pa'i bsad pa
P 5263
Partial translation by L. de la Vallée Poussin, Museon 8 (1907) pp 249-317; 11 (1910) pp 271-358; and 12 (1911) pp 235-328.
Supplement to the Middle Way
Madhyamakāvatāra

dbU ma la 'jug pa
P 5261; P 5262
Also: *Madhyamakāvatāra par Candrakirti*. Publiée par Louis de la Vallée Poussin
(Osnabrück: Biblio Verlag, 1970)
Partial translation by J. Hopkins in *Compassion in Tibetan Buddhism* (Valois, NY: Snow Lion, 1980)

Da-di-ge-shay Rin-chen-don-drup (Bra-sti-dge-bshes Rin-chen-don-grub). See Jam-yang-shay-ba, et al.

Dak-tsang (sTag-tsang-lo-tsa-ba Shes-rab-rin-chen), b. 1405
Ocean of Good Explanations, Explanation of "Freedom from Extremes Through Understanding All Tenets"
Grub mtha' kun shes nas mtha' bral grub pa zhes bya ba'i bstan bcos rnam par bshad pa legs bshad kyi rgya mtsho
Thim-phu: Kun-gzang-stobs-rgyal, 1976

De-druk-ken-chen Nga-wang-rap-den (sDe-drug-mkhan-chen Ngag-dbang-rab-brtan). See Jam-yang-shay-ba, et al.

Den-dar-hla-ram-ba (bsTan-dar-lha-ram-pa), b. 1759
Presentation of the Lack of Being One or Many
gCig du bral gyi rnam gzhag legs bshad rgya mtsho las btus pa'i 'khrul spong bdud rtsi'i gzegs ma
Collected gzung 'bum of Bstan-dar Lha-ram of A-lag-sha
Vol. 1
New Delhi: Lama Guru Deva, 1971

Dharmakīrti (Chos-kyi-grags-pa), 7th century
Commentary on (Dignāga's) "Compendium on Valid Cognition"
Pramāṇavarttikakārikā
Tshad ma rnam 'grel gyi tshig le'ur byas pa
P 5709

Dignāga (Phyogs-glang), c. 480-540
Analysis of the Object of Observation
Ālambanaparīkṣa
dMigs pa brtag pa
P 5703
Compendium on Valid Cognition
Pramāṇasamuccaya
Tshad ma kun las btus pa
P 5700
Partial translation by M. Hattori, *Dignāga, on Perception* (Cambridge: Harvard, 1968)

Ga-wa-jam-ba (dGa'-ba'-byams-pa)
Commentary on (Tsong-kha-pa's) "Praise of Dependent Arising," A Garland of White Light
rTen 'brel bstod pa'i dikka 'od kar 'phreng ba
no place, no date
Gen-dun-den-dzin-gya-tso (dGe-'dun-bstan-'dzin-rgya-tsho). See Sha-mar Gen-dun-den-zin-gya-tso.
Gen-dun-drup (dGe-'dun-grub, Dalai Lama I), 1391-1475
Ship Entering the Ocean of Tenets
Grub mtha' rgya mtshor 'jug pa'i gru rdzings
[?]
Gon-chok-jik-may-wang-bo (dKon-mchog-'jigs-med-dbang-po), 1728-1791
Precious Garland of Tenets/Presentation of Tenets, A Precious Garland
Grub pa'i mtha'i rnam par bzhag pa rin po che'i phreng ba
Dharmsala, India: Shes rig par khang, 1969
Translation by Geshe Sopa and J. Hopkins, *Practice and Theory of Tibetan Buddhism* (New York: Grove Press, 1976)
Presentation of the Grounds and Paths, Beautiful Ornament of the Three Vehicles
Sa lam gyi rnam bzhag theg gsum mdzes rgyan
Buxadour: Gomang College, 1965
Also: The Collected Works of dkon-mchog-'jigs-med-bang-po, Vol.7
New Delhi: Ngawang Gelek Demo, 1972
Guṇaprabha (Yon-tan-'od)
Discourse on Discipline
Vinayasūtra
'Dul ba'i mdo
P 5619
Gyel-tsap (rGyal-tshab), 1364-1432
Great Purification of Forgetfulness Regarding Valid Cognition
Tshad ma'i brjed byang chen mo
Toh. 5438
Heart Ornament, An Explanation of the Root Text and Commentary of (Maitreya's) "Ornament for Clear Realization"
mNgon rtogs pa'i rgyan gyi rtsa ba 'grel pa dang bcas pa'i rnam bshad snying po'i rgyan
Toh. 5433

Illumination of the Meaning of the Essence of (Nāgārjuna's) "Precious Garland"
dbU ma rin chen 'phreng ba'i snying po'i don gsal par byed pa
Toh. 5427
Purification of Forgetfulness of (Śāntarakṣita's) "Ornament for the Middle Way"
dbU ma rgyan gyi brjed byang
Sarnath, India: Pleasure of Elegant Sayings Press, 1976
Haribhadra (Seng-ge-bzang-po), late 8th century
Clear Meaning Commentary
Abhisamayālaṃkāranāmaprajñapāramitopadeśaśastravṛtti
Shes rab kyi pha rol tu phyin pa'i man ngag gi bstan bcos mngon par rtogs pa'i rgyan ces bya ba'i grel pa
P 5191
Commentary for Easy Understanding of the Condensed (Perfection of Wisdom) Sutra
Sañcayagāthāpañjikāsubodhinī
sDud pa tshigs su bcad pa dka' 'grel rtogs sla
P 5196
Illumination of (Maitreya's) "Ornament for Clear Realization," Explanation of the Perfection of Wisdom in Eight Thousand Stanzas
Aṣṭasāharikāprajñāpāramitāvyākyānābhisamayālaṃkārāloka
Shes rab kyi pha rol tu phyin pa brgyad stong pa'i bshad pa mngon par rtogs pa'i rgyan gyi snang ba
P 5192
Jam-bel-sam-pel, Ge-shay ('Jam-dpal-bsam-phel, dGe-gshes), d. 1975
Presentation of Awareness and Knowledge, Composite of All the Important Points, Opener of the Eye of New Intelligence
Blo rig gi rnam bzhag nyer mkho kun 'dus blo gsar mig 'byed
Modern blockprint, n.p., n.d.
Translation by E. Napper in Lati Rinbochay, *Mind in Tibetan Buddhism* (Valois, NY: Snow Lion, 1980)
Jam-yang-chok-hla-ö-ser ('Jam-dbyangs-phyogs-hla-od-zer), 15th century
Collected Topics of Ra-dö
Rva stod bsdus grva
Dharamsala, India: Damchoe Sangpo, Library of Tibetan Works and Archives (Printed at Jayyed Press, Ballimaran, Delhi), 1980

Jam-yang-shay-ba ('Jam-dbyangs-bzhad-pa), 1648-1721
Analysis of the First Chapter (of Maitreya's "Ornament for Clear Realization")
sKabs dang po'i mtha' dpyod
Sarnath, India: Mongolian Lama Guru Deva, 1965
Analysis of the Third Chapter (of Maitreya's "Ornament for Clear Realization")
sKabs gsum pa'i mtha' dpyod
Sarnath, India: Mongolian Lama Guru Deva, 1965
Great Exposition of Tenets/Explanation of "Tenets," Sun of the Land of Samantabhadra Brilliantly Illuminating All of Our Own and Others' Tenets and the Meaning of the Profound (Emptiness), Ocean of Scripture and Reasoning Fulfilling All Hopes of All Beings
Grub mtha'i rnam bshad rang gzhan grub mtha' kun dang zab don mchog tu gsal ba kun bzang zhing gi nyi ma lung rigs rgya mtsho skye dgu'i re ba kun skong
Musoorie: Dalama, 1962
Great Exposition of the Middle Way/Conclusions about (Candrakīrti's) "Supplement to the Middle Way," Treasury of Scripture and Reasoning, Thoroughly Illuminating the Profound Meaning (of Emptiness), Entrance for the Fortunate
dbU ma 'jug pa'i mtha' dpyod lung rigs gter mdzod zab don kun gsal skal bzang 'jug ngogs
Buxaduor: Gomang, 1967
Jam-yang-shay-ba, et al.
Jam-yang-shay-ba, Ba-so Cho-gyi-gyel-tsen (Ba-so Chos-kyi rgyal-mtshan), De-druk-ken-chen Nga-wang-rap-den (sDe-drug-mkhan-chen Ngag-dbang-rab-brtan), and Da-di-ge-shay Rin-chen-don-drup (Bra-sti-dge-bshes Rin-chen-don-grub)
Four Interwoven Annotations to (Tsong-kha-pa's) "Great Exposition of the Stages of the Path"
Lam rim mchan bzhi sbrags ma
New Delhi: Chophel Lekden, 1972
Jang-gya (lCang-skya), 1717-1786
Presentation of Tenets/Clear Exposition of the Presentations of Tenets, Beautiful Ornament for the Meru of the Subduer's Teaching
Grub pa'i mtha'i rnam par bshag pa gsal bar bshad pa thub bstan lhun po'i mdzes rgyan
Sarnath, India: Pleasure of Elegant Sayings Press, 1970

Jay-dzun-ba (rJe-btsun-pa), 1469-1546
Good Explanation of the General Meaning, Clarifying the Difficult Points of (Tsong-kha-pa's) "Illumination of the Thought, Explanation of the 'Supplement to the Middle Way,'" A Necklace for the Fortunate
bsTan bcos dbu ma la 'jug pa'i rnam bshad dgongs pa rab bsal gyi dka' gnad gsəl bar byed pa'i spyi don legs bshad skal bzang mgul rgyan
Modern blockprint: no place, no date

Jetāri (dGra-las-rgyal-ba)
Sugata Treatise
Sugatamatavibhaṅgakārikā
bDer gzhegs gzhung gi rab byed
P 5296

Jñānagarbha (Ye-shes-snying-po), early 8th century
Commentary on the Differentiation of the Two Truths
Satyadvayavibhaṅgavṛtti
bDen pa gnyis rnam par 'byed pa'i 'grel pa
[Not in P] Toh. 3882
Differentiation of the Two Truths
Satyadvayavibhaṇgakārikā
bDen gnyis rnam 'byed
[Not in P] Toh. 3881

Jñānamitra (Ye-shes-bshes-gnyen)
Explanation of the "Heart of the Perfection of Wisdom"
Prajñāpāramitāhṛdayavyākhya
Shes rab kyi pha rol tu phyin pa'i snying po'i rnam par bshad pa
P 5218

Jñānaśrībhadra (Ye-shes-dpal-bzang-po)
Commentary on the "Descent into Laṅkā"
Laṅkāvatāravṛtti
Langkar gshegs pa'i 'grel pa
P 5519

Jñānavajra (Ye-shes-rdo-rje)
Commentary on the "Descent into Laṅkā," Ornament of the Heart of the Tathāgata
Laṅkāvatāranāmamahāyānasūtravṛttitathāgatahṛdayālaṃkāra
Langkar gshegs pa zhes bya ba theg pa chen po'i mdo'i 'grel pa de bzhin gshegs pa'i snying po'i rgyan
P 5520

Kamalaśīla, c. 740-795
Commentary on the Difficult Points of (Śāntarakṣita's) "Compendium of Principles"
Tattvasaṃgrahapañjikā
De kho na nyid bsdus pa'i dka' 'grel
P 5765
Translation by G. Jha, *The Tattvasaṃgraha of Śāntarakṣita with the Commentary of Kamalaśīla*, Gaekwad's Oriental Series, Vol. lxxx-lxxxiii (Baroda: 1937-1939)
Commentary on the Difficult Points of (Śāntarakṣita's) "Ornament for the Middle Way"
Madhyamakālaṃkārapañjikā
dbU ma rgyan gyi dka' 'grel
P 5286
Illumination of the Middle Way
Madhyamakāloka
dbU ma snang ba
P 5287
Stages of Meditation
Bhāvanākrama
sGom pa'i rim pa
P 5310-12
Kay-drup (mKhas-grub), 1386-1438
Thousand Doses/Opening the Eye of the Fortunate, Treatise Brilliantly Clarifying the Profound Emptiness
sTong thun chen mo/Zab mo stong pa nyid rab tu gsal bar byed pa'i bstan bcos skal bzang mig 'byed
Toh. 5459
Long-chen-rap-jam (kLong-chen-rab-'byams), 1308-1363
Treasury of Tenets, Illuminating the Meaning of All Vehicles
Theg pa mtha' dag gi don gsal bar byed pa grub pa'i mtha' rin po che'i mdzod
Gangtok: Dodrup Chen Rinpoche, 1969
Lo-sang-gön-chok (bLo-bzang-dkon-mchog)
Word Commentary on the Root Text of (Jam-yang-shay-ba's) "Tenets," A Crystal Mirror
Grub mtha' rtsa ba'i tshig tik shel dkar me long
In *Three Commentaries on the Grub mtha' rtsa ba gdoṅ lṅa'i sgra dbyaṅs of 'Jam-dbyaṅs-bzad-pa'i-rdo-rje nga-dbaṅ-brtson-'grus*
Delhi: Chophel Lekden, 1978

Mahāvyutpatti
Bye brag rtogs byed chen po
ed. Ryozaburo Sakaki
Tokyo: Suzuki Research Foundation, 1962
Maitreya (Byams-pa)
Ornament for Clear Realization
Abhisamayālaṃkāra
mNgon par rtogs pa'i rgyan
P 5184
Translation by E. Conze, *Abhisamayālaṃkāra*, Serie Orientale Roma VI (Rome: Is.M.E.O., July 1954)
Ornament for the Mahāyāna Sutras
Mahāyānasūtrālaṃkārakārikā
Theg pa chen po'i mdo sde'i rgyan gyi tshig le'ur byas pa
P 5521
Maitrīpāda
Ten Stanzas on Suchness
Tattvadaśaka
De kho na nyid bcu pa
P 3080
Mi-pam-gya-tso (Mi-pham-rgya-mtsho), 1846-1912
Explanation of (Śāntarakṣita's) "Ornament for the Middle Way," Sacred Word of the Smiling Lama Mañjuśrī
dbU ma rgyan gyi rnam bshad 'jam dbyangs bla ma dgyes pa'i zhal lung
In *Collected Works of Jam-mgon 'Ju Mi-pham rgya-mtsho,*
Vol. 12
Gangtok, 1971
Nāgabodhi (kLu-byang-chub)
Ordered Stages of the Means of Achieving Guhyasamāja
Samājasādhanavyavasthāli
'Dus pa'i sgrub pa'i thabs rnam par gzhag pa'i rim pa
P 2764
Nāgārjuna (kLu-sgrub)
Commentary on the "Refutation of Objections"
Vigrahavyavārtinīvṛtti
rTsod pa bzlog pa'i 'grel pa
P 5232
Commentary on "Seventy Stanzas on Emptiness"
Śūnyatāsaptativṛtti

sTong pa nyid bdun cu pa'i 'grel pa
P 5231

Commentary on the "Treatise Called 'The Finely Woven'"
Vaidulyasūtranāmavṛtti
Zhib mo rnam par 'thag pa'i 'grel pa
[?]

Compendium of Sutra
Sūtrasamuccaya
mDo kun las bdus pa
P 5330

Drop for Supporting the People
Nītiśāstrajanapoṣaṇabindhu
Lugs kyi bstan bcos skye bo gso ba'i thigs
P 5822

Essay on the Mind of Enlightenment
Bodhicittavivaraṇa
Byang chub sems kyi 'grel pa
P 2665; P 2666
Translation by C. Lindtner in *Nagarjuniana* (Copenhagen: Akademisk Forlag, 1982)

Five Stages
Pañcakrama
Rim pa lnga pa
P 2667

Friendly Letter
Suhṛllekha
bShes pa'i spring yig
P 5682
Translation by Jamspal, et. al., *Nāgārjuna's Letter to King Gautamīputra* (Delhi: Motilal, 1978)

Hundred Applications
Yogaśataka
sByor pa brgya
P 5795

Hundred Wisdoms
Prajñāśataka
Shes rab brgya
p 5414

Praise of the Inconceivable
Acintyastava

bSam gyis mi khyab par bstod pa
P 2019
Translation by C. Lindtner in *Nāgārjuniana* (Copenhagen: Akademisk Forlag, 1982)
Praise of the Sphere of Reality
Dharmadhātustotra
Chos kyi dbyings su bstod pa
P 2010
Praise of the Supramundane
Lokātītastava
'Jig rten las 'das par bstod pa
P 2012
Translation by C. Lindtner in *Nāgārjuniana* (Copenhagen: Akademish Forlag, 1982)
Precious Garland of Advice for the King
Rājaparikathāratnāvalī
rGyal po la gtam bya ba rin po che'i phreng ba
P 5658
Translation by J. Hopkins and Lati Rimpoche in *The Precious Garland and the Song of the Four Mindfulnesses* (London: Allen and Unwin, 1975)
Refutation of Objections
Vigrahavyāvartanīkārikā
rTsod pa bzlog pa'i tshig le'ur byas pa
P 5228
Translation by K. Bhattacharya, *The Dialectical Method of Nāgārjuna* (Delhi: Motilal, 1978)
Seventy Stanzas on Emptiness
Śūnyatāsaptatikārikā
sTong pa nyid bdun cu pa'i tshig le'ur byas pa
P 5227
Translation by C. Lindtner in *Nāgārjuniana* (Copenhagen: Akademisk Forlag, 1982)
Sixty Stanzas of Reasoning
Yuktiṣaṣṭikakārikā
Rigs pa drug cu pa'i tshig le'ur byas pa
P 5225
Translation by C. Lindtner in *Nāgārjuniana* (Copenhagen: Akademisk Forlag, 1982)
Treatise called "The Finely Woven"

Vaidalyasūtranāma
Zhib mo rnam par 'thag pa zhes bya ba'i mdo
P 5226
Treatise on the Middle Way/Fundamental Treatise on the Middle Way Called "Wisdom"
Madhyamakaśāstra/Prajñānāmamūlamadhyamakakārikā
dbU ma rtsa ba'i tshig le'ur byas pa shes rab ces bya ba
P 5224
Translation by F. J. Streng in *Emptiness: A Study in Religious Meaning* (Nashville and New York: Abingdon Press, 1967); etc.

Nga-wang-bel-den (Ngag-dbang-dpal-ldan) b. 1797
Annotations for (Jam-yang-shay-ba's) "Great Exposition of Tenets," Freeing the Knots of the Difficult Points, Precious Jewel of Clear Thought
Grub mtha' chen mo'i mchan 'grel dka' gnad mdud grol blo gsal gces nor
Sarnath, India: Pleasure of Elegant Sayings Press, 1964
Explanation of the Conventional and the Ultimate in the Four Systems of Tenets
Grub mtha' bzhi'i lugs kyi kun rdzob dang don dam pa'i don rnam par bshad pa legs bshad dpyid kyi dpal mo'i glu dbyangs
New Delhi: Guru Deva, 1972

Nga-wang-dra-shi (Ngag-dbang-bkra-shis), 1648-1721
The Collected Topics by a Spiritual Son of Jam-yang-shay-ba
Sras bsdus grva
n.p., n.d.

Nyen-don-bel-jor-hlun-drup (gNyen-ston-dpal-'byor lhun-grub)
Commentary on the Difficult Points of (Tsong-kha-pa's) "Essence of the Good Explanations," A Lamp for the Teaching
Legs bshad snying po'i bka' 'grel bstan pa'i sgron me
Modern blockprint: no place, no date

Pa-bong-ka (Pha-bong-kha), 1878-1941
Lecturers on the Stages of the Path, compiled by Trijang Rinpochay
Lam rim zin bris/rNam grol lag bcangs su gtog pa'i man ngag zab mo tshang la ma nor ba mtshungs med chos kyi rgyal po'i thugs bcud byang chub lam gyi rim pa'i nyams khrid kyi zin bris gsung rab kun gyi bcud bsdus gdams ngag bdud rtsi'i snying po

Mundgod, India: Gan-den Shar-dzay, n.d.
Pan-chen So-nam-drak-ba (Pan-chen bSod-nams-grags-pa), 1478-1554
General Meaning of (Maitreya's) "Ornament for Clear Realization"
Phar phyin spyi don/Shes rab kyi pha rol tu phyin pa'i man ngag gi bstan bcos mngon par rtogs pa'i rgyan 'grel pa dang bcas pa'i rnam bshad snying po rgyan gyi don legs par bshad pa yum don gsal ba'i sgron me
Buxadour, India: Nang bstan shes rig 'dzin skyong slob gnyer khang, 1963
Parahitabhadra (gZhan-la-phan-pa-bzang-po)
Commentary on (Nāgārjuna's) "Seventy Stanzas on Emptiness"
Śūnyatāsaptativivṛttiṭīkā
sTong pa nyid bdun cu pa'i 'grel pa
P 5269
Pur-bu-jok (Phur-bu-lcog Byams-pa rgya-mtsho), 1825-1901
Explanation of the Lesser Path of Reasoning in *Magical Key to the Path of Reasoning, Presentation of the Collected Topics Revealing the Meaning of the Treaties on Valid Cognition*
Rigs lam chung ngu'i rnam bshad pa *in* Tshad ma'i gzhung don 'byed pa'i bsdus grva'i rnam bzhag rigs lam 'phrul gyi sde mig
Buxa, India: n.p., 1965
Explanation of the Presentation of Objects and Object Possessors as well as Awareness and Knowledge in *Magical Key to the Path of Reasoning, Presentation of the Collected Topics Revealing the Meaning of the Treatises on Valid Cognition*
Yul yul can dang blo rig gi rnam par bshad pa *in* Tshad ma'i gzhung don 'byed pa'i bsdus grva'i rnam bzhag rigs lam 'phrul gyi sde mig
Buxa, India: n.p., 1965
The Topic of Signs and Reasonings from "Great Path of Reasoning" in *The Magic Key to the Path of Reasoning, Presentation of the Collected Topics Revealing the Meaning of the Texts on Valid Cognition*
Tshad ma'i gzhung don 'byed ba'i bsdus grva'i rnam gzhag gyi lde mig
Buxa, India: n.d., 1965
Ratnākaraśānti (Shanti-pa/Rin-chen-'byung-gnas-zhi-ba) c. 1000
Presentation of the Three Vehicles

Triyānavyavasthāna
Theg pa gsum rnam par bzhag pa
P 4535

Sahajavajra (lHan-skyes-rdo-rje)
Commentary on (Maitrīpāda's) "Ten Stanzas on Suchness"
Tattvadaśakaṭīkā
De kho na nyid bcu pa'i rgya cher 'grel pa
P 3099

Śāntarakṣita (Zhi-ba-'tsho), 8th century
Commentary on the "Ornament to the Middle Way"
Madhyamakālaṃkāravṛtti
dbU ma'i rgyan gyi 'grel pa
P 5285
Compendium of Principles
Tattvasaṃgrahakārikā
De kho na nyid bsdus pa'i tshig le'ur byas pa
P 5764
Translation by G. Jha, *The Tattvasaṃgraha of Śāntarakṣita with the Commentary of Kamalaśīla*, Gaekwad's Oriental Series Vol. lxxx and lxxxiii (Baroda: 1937-1939)
Ornament to the Middle Way
Madhyamakālaṃkāra
dbU ma'i rgyan gyi tshig le'ur byas pa
P 5284

"Śāntarakṣita"[2]
Commentary on (Jñānagarbha's) "Differentiation of the Two Truths"
Satyadvayavibhaṅgaṭīkā
bDen pa gnyis rnam par 'byed pa'i 'grel ba
P 5283

Śāntideva (Zhi-ba-lha) c. 700
Compendium of Instructions
Sikṣāsamuccayakārikā
bsLab pa kun las btus pa'i tshig le'ur byas pa
P 5336; Sanskrit edition by Cecil Bendall, *Çkshāsamuccaya*, Indo-Iranian Reprints 1 (The Hague: Mouton and Co., 1957)
Engaging in the Bodhisattva Deeds
Bodhi[sattva]caryāvatāra
Byang chub sems dpa'i spyod pa la 'jug pa
P 5272; Sanskrit edition by P. L. Vaidya (Dharbanga: Mithila Institute, 1960).

Translation from the Tibetan by Stephen Batchelor, *A Guide to the Bodhisattva's Way of Life* (Dharmsala: LTWA, 1979)

Sha-mar Gen-dun-den-zin-gya-tso (Zhwa-dmar dGe-'dun-bstan-'dzin-rgya mtsho), 1852-1910

Lamp Illuminating the Profound Thought, Set Forth to Purify Forgetfulness of the Difficult Points of (*Tsong-kha-pa's*) *"Great Exposition of Special Insight"*

lHag mthong chen mo'i dka' gnad rnams brjed byang du bkod pa dgongs zab snang ba'i sgron me

Delhi: Mongolian Lama Guru Deva, 1972

Śūra (dPa'-bo)

Cultivation of the Ultimate Mind of Enlightenment/Essay on the Stages of Cultivating the Ultimate Mind of Enlightenment

Paramārthabodhicittabhāvanākramavarṇasaṃgraha

Don dam pa byang chub kyi sems bsgom pa'i rim pa yi ger bris pa

P 5431

Tsong-kha-pa, 1357-1419

Explanation of the Eight Great Difficult Points in (*Nāgārjuna's*) *"Treatise on the Middle Way"*

rTsa ba shes rab kyi dka' gnas chen po brgyad kyi bshad pa

Sarnath, India: Pleasure of Elegant Sayings Press, 1970

Essence of the Good Explanations, Treatise Discriminating the Interpretable and the Definitive

Drang ba dang nges pa'i don rnam par phye ba'i bstan bcos legs bshad snying po

P 6142

Also: Sarnath, India: Pleasure of Elegant Sayings Press, 1973

Translation by R. Thurman, *Tsong-kha-pa's Speech of Gold in the "Essence of True Eloquence"* (Princeton: Princeton University Press, 1984)

Golden Rosary of Eloquence/Extensive Explanation of (*Maitreya's*) *"Treatise of Quintessential Instructions on the Perfection of Wisdom, Ornament for Clear Realization," As Well As Its Commentaries*

Legs bshad gser gyi phreng ba/Shes rab kyi pha rol tu phyin pa'i man ngag gi bstan bcos mngon par rtogs pa'i rgyan 'grel pa dang bcas pa'i rgya cher bshad pa

P 6150

Also: Sarnath, India: Pleasure of Elegant Sayings Press, 1970

Great Exposition of Special Insight
lHag mthong chen mo
In *Tsong-kha-pa's Statements on the Mādhyamika View*, Vol. 1
rJe tsong kha pa'i gsung dbu ma'i lta ba'i skor
Sarnath, India: Pleasure of Elegant Sayings Press, 1975
Translation by A. Wayman, *Calming the Mind and Discerning the Real* (New York: Columbia, 1978)
Great Exposition of the Stages of the Path
Lam rim chen mo
P 6001
Also: Dharmsala, India: Shes rig par khang, 1964
Illumination of the Thought, Extensive Explanation of (*Candrakīrti's*) *"Supplement to the Middle Way"*
dbU ma la 'jug pa'i rgya cher bshad pa dgongs pa rab gsal
P 6143
Also: Sarnath, India: Pleasure of Elegant Sayings Press, 1973
Partial translation by J. Hopkins in *Compassion in Tibetan Buddhism* (Valois, NY: Snow Lion, 1980)
Middling Exposition of the Stages of the Path
Lam rim 'bring
P 6002
Also: Dharmsala: Shes rig par khang, 1968
Partial translation by R. Thurman in *Life and Teachings of Tsong-Khapa* (Dharmsala: LTWA, 1982)
Notes on (*Śāntarakṣita's*) *"Ornament for the Middle Way"*
dbU ma rgyan gyi zin bris
P 6141
Also: Sarnath, India: Pleasure of Elegant Sayings Press, 1976
Ocean of Reasoning, Explanation of (*Nāgārjuna's*) *"Treatise on the Middle Way"*
dbU ma rtsa ba'i tshig le'ur byas pa shes rab ces bya ba'i rnam bshad rigs pa'i rgya mtsho
P 6153
Also: Sarnath, India: Pleasure of Elegant Sayings Press, 1973
Translation of Chapter II by J. Hopkins, "Ocean of Reasoning" (Dharmsala: LTWA, 1977)
Praise of Dependent Arising/Praise of the Supramundane and Victorious Buddha for his Teaching the Profound Dependent Arising, Essence of Good Explanations
Sangs rgyas bcom ldan 'das la zab mo rten cing 'brel bar 'byung

ba gsung ba'i sgo nas bstod pa legs par bshad pa'i snying po
P 6016
Vasubandhu (dbYig-gnyen), 4th century
Explanation of the "Treasury of Knowledge"
Abhidharmakośabhāṣya
Chos mngon pa'i mdzod kyi bshad pa
P 5591; Sanskrit edition by Swami Dwarikadas Shastri (Varanasi: Buddha Bharati, 1972)
Translation by L. de la Vallée Poussin, *L'Abhidharmakośa de Vasubandhu* (Paris: Geuthner, 1923-1931)
Reasonings for Explanation
Vyākhyāyukti
rNam bshad rigs pa
P 5562
Treasury of Knowledge
Abhidharmakośakārikā
Chos mngon pa'i mdzod kyi tshig le'ur byas pa
P 5590
For translation, see previous entry
Ye-shay-day (Ye-shes-sde), c. 800
Differences Between the Views
lTa ba'i khyad par
P 5847
Ye-shay-gyel-tsen (Ye-shes-rgyal-mtshan), 1713-1793
Clear Exposition of the Modes of Minds and Mental Factors, Necklace for Those of Clear Mind
Sems dang sems byung gi tshul gsal bar ston pa blo gsal mgul rgyan
The Collected Works of Tshe-mchog-glin-yongs-'dzin ye-ses-rgyal-mtshan, Vol. 16
New Delhi: Tibet House, 1974
Translation by H. Guenther and L. Kawamura, *Mind in Buddhist Psychology* (Emeryville: Dharma Press, 1975)

III. WORKS IN ENGLISH AND FRENCH

Aronson, Harvey B. "The Buddhist Path: A Translation of the Sixth Chapter of the First Dalai Lama's *Path of Liberation*." *The Tibet Journal*, Vol 5, 1980.
Atīśa. *A Lamp for the Path and Commentary*. Translated by Richard

Sherburne. London: Allen and Unwin, 1983.

Bhattacharya, K. *The Dialectical Method of Nāgārjuna*. Delhi: Motilal Banarsidass, 1978.

Broughton, Jeffrey. "Early Ch'an Schools in Tibet." In *Studies in Ch'an and Hua-Yen*, pp. 1-68. Edited by Robert M. Gimello and Peter N. Gregory. Honolulu: University of Hawaii Press, 1983.

Buddhaghosa. *The Path of Purification (Visuddhimagga)*. Translated by Bhikku Nyanamoli. 2nd edition. (Colombo, Ceylon: A. Semage, 1964).

Chandra, Lokesh. *Materials for a History of Tibetan Literature*. New Delhi: International Academy of Indian Culture, 1963.

Chang, Garma C. C., trans. *The Hundred Thousand Songs of Milarepa* Secaucus, New Jersey, University Books, 1962.

Conze, Edward. *Abhisamayālaṃkāra*. Serie Orientale Roma VI. Rome: Is. M.E.O., July 1954.

———. *Buddhist Thought in India*. Ann Arbor: University of Michigan Press, 1973.

———. *Buddhist Wisdom Books*. New York: Harper and Row, 1972.

———. *The Large Sutra on Perfect Wisdom*. Berkeley: University of California Press, 1975.

Dasgupta, Surendranath. *A History of Indian Philosophy*, Vol 1. Delhi: Motilal Banarsidass, 1975.

de Jong, Jan W. *Cing Chapitres de la Prasannapadā*. Paris: Geuthner, 1949.

———. "The Problem of the Absolute in the Madhyamaka School." In *Buddhist Studies by J.W. de Jong*, pp. 53-58. Edited by Gregory Schopen. Berkeley: Asian Humanities Press, 1979.

della Santina, Peter. *Mādhyamika Schools in India*. Delhi: Motilal Banarsidass, forthcoming.

Demiéville, Paul. *Le Concile de Lhasa*. Paris: Impr. Nationale de France, 1952.

Drake, Durant. *Essays in Critical Realism*. New York: Peter Smith, 1941.

Eckel, M. David. "A Question of Nihilism: Bhāvaviveka's Response to the Fundamental Problems of Mādhyamika Philosophy." Ph.D. dissertation, Harvard University, 1980.

———. *Jñānagarbha's Commentary on the Distinction Between the Two Truths*. Albany: State University of New York Press, 1986.

Encyclopedia of Philosophy. S.v. "Phenomenalism," by R. J. Hirst.

———. S.v. "Realism," by R.J. Hirst.

______. S.v. "Skepticism," by Richard H. Popkin.

Encyclopedia of Religion and Ethics. S.v. "Madhyamaka, Madhyamikas," by Louis de la Vallée Poussin.

______. *S.v. "Nihilism (Buddhist)," by Louis de la Vallée Poussin.*

Gomez, Luis O., *"Indian Materials on the Doctrine of Sudden Enlightenment."* In *Early Ch'an in China and Tibet*, pp. 393-434. Edited by Lewis Lancaster and Whalen Lai. Berkeley: Berkeley Buddhist Studies Series, 1983.

______. "The Direct and Gradual Approaches of Zen Master Mahāyāna: Fragments of the Teachings of Mo-ho-yen." In *Studies in Ch'an and Hua Yen*, pp.69-167. Edited by Robert M. Gimello and Peter N. Gregory. Honolulu: University of Hawaii Press, 1983.

Guenther, Herbert V. *Buddhist Philosophy in Theory and Practice.* Baltimore: Penguin Books, 1972.

Guenther, Herbert V. and Kawamura, Leslie S. *Mind in Buddhist Psychology.* Emeryville, California: Dharma Press, 1975.

Hattori, Masaaki. *Dignāga, On Perception.* Cambridge: Harvard University Press, 1968.

Heidegger, Martin. *Poetry, Language, Thought.* New York: Harper and Row, 1971.

Honda, M. 'An Annotated Translation of the "Daśabhūmika."' In *Studies in Southeast and Central Asia*, pp. 115-276. Edited by D. Sinor. Satapitaka Series 74. Delhi: 1968.

Hopkins, Jeffrey. Translator. *Compassion in Tibetan Buddhism.* Ithaca, New York: Snow Lion Publications 1980.

______. *Meditation on Emptiness.* London: Wisdom Publications, 1983.

Houston, G.W. *Sources for the History of the bSam yas Debate.* Sankt Augustion: VGH-Wissenschaftsverlag, 1980.

Ichigo, Masamichi. "A Synopsis of the Madhyamakālaṃkāra of Śāntarakṣita." *Journal of Indian and Buddhist Studies*, Vol 20, 1972.

Iida, Shotaro. "The Nature of Saṃvṛti and the Relationship to Paramārtha to It in Svātantrika Mādhyamika." In *The Problem of the Two Truths in Buddhism and Vedānta*, pp. 64-77. Edited by Mervyn Sprung. Dordrecht, Holland: D. Reidel Publishing, 1973.

______. *Reason and Emptiness: A Study of Logic and Mysticism.* Tokyo: Hokuseido Press, 1980.

Iida, Shotaro and Hirabayashi, Jay. "Another Look at the Mādhyamika vs. Yogācāra Controversy Concerning Existence and Non-existence." In *Prajñāpāramitā and Related Systems: Studies in Honor of Edward Conze*, pp. 341-360. Edited by Lewis Lancaster. Berkeley: Berkeley Buddhist Studies Series, 1977.

Jackson, Roger. "Sa skya paṇḍita's Account of the Bsam yas Debate: History as Polemic." *Journal of the International Association of Buddhist Studies*. Vol 20, No 1, 1982.

Jamspal, Lozang, Chophel, Ngawang Samten, della Santina, Peter. *Nāgārjuna's Letter to King Gautamīputra*. Delhi: Motilal Banarsidass, 1978.

Jha, Ganganatha. Trans. *The Tattvasangraha of Śāntarakṣita with the Commentary of Kamalaśīla*. Baroda, India: Oriental Institute, 1937.

Kajiyama, Yuichi. Trans. "Bhāvaviveka's *Prajñāpradīpa* (1 Kapitel)." *Wiener Zeitschrift fur die kunde Sud-und Ostasiens*, Vol 7, 1965.

———. "Introduction to the Logic of Svātantrika-Mādhyamika." *Nava-Nalanda Mahāvihāra Research Publication*, Vol 1, 1957.

———. "Later Madhyamikas on Epistemology and Meditation." In *Mahāyāna Buddhist Meditation: Theory and Practice*, pp. 114-143. Edited by Minoru Kiyota. Honolulu: University of Hawaii Press, 1978.

Keith, Arthur Berriedale. *Buddhist Philosophy in India and Ceylon*. New Delhi: Oriental Books Reprint Company, 1979.

Klein, Anne C. "Mind and Liberation: The Sautrāntika Tenet System in Tibet." Ph.D. Dissertation, University of Virginia, 1981.

la Vallée Poussin, Louis de. *L'Abhidharmakośa de Vasubandhu*. Bruxelles: Institut Belge des Hautes Études Chinoises, 1971.

———. "Le Joyau dans la main." *Melanges Chonois et Bouddhiques*, Vol 2, 1932.

———. Madhyamakāvatāra. *Museon* 8 (1907), pp. 249-317; 11 (1910), pp. 271-358; 12 (1911), pp. 235-328.

Lamotte, Étienne. *Le Traite de la Grande Vertu de Sagesse de Nāgārjuna*, Tome 1. Louvain: Institut Orientaliste, 1966.

———. *Saṃdhinirmocana-sūtra*. Paris: Adrien Maisonneuve, 1935.

Lati Rinbochay. *Mind in Tibetan Buddhism*. Translated by Elizabeth Napper. Ithaca, New York: Snow Lion Publications, 1980.

Lessing, Ferdinand and Wayman, Alex. *Mkhas grub rje's Fun-*

damentals of the Buddhist Tantras. The Hague: Mouton, 1968.

Lindtner, Christian. "Atīśa's Introduction to the Two Truths, and Its Sources." *Journal of Indian Philosophy*, Vol 9 (1981), pp. 161-214.

———. *Nāgārjuniana: Studies in the Writings and Philosophy of Nāgārjuna*. Copenhagen: Akademisk Forlag, 1982.

Lipman, Kennard. "A Study of Śāntarakṣita's *Madhyamakālaṃkāra*." Ph.D. dissertation, University of Saskatchewan, 1979.

May, Jacques. *Prasannapadā Madhyamakavṛtti, douze chapitres traduits du sanscrit et du tibetain*. Paris: Adrien Maisonneuve, 1959.

Mullin, Glenn and Tsonawa, Lozang N. *Four Songs to Je Rinpoche*. Dharmsala, India: LTWA, 1978.

Murti, T.R.V. "Saṃvṛtti and Paramārtha in Mādhyamika and Vedānta." In *The Problem of the Two Truths in Buddhism and Vedānta*, pp. 9-26. Edited by Mervyn Sprung. Dordrecht, Holland: D. Reidel Publishing, 1973.

———. *The Central Philosophy of Buddhism*. London: Allen and Unwin, 1980.

Nāgārjuna and the Seventh Dalai Lama. *The Precious Garland and the Song of the Four Mindfulnesses*. Translated by Jeffrey Hopkins and Lati Rimpoche. New York: Harper and Row, 1975.

Ngawang Dhargyey. *The Tibetan Tradition of Mental Development*. Dharmsala: LTWA, 1978.

Obermiller, E. *History of Buddhism by Bu-ston*. Heidelberg: Heft, 1932.

Otto, Rudolf. *The Idea of the Holy*. London: Oxford University Press, 1976.

Pike, Kenneth L. *Language in Relation to a Unified Theory of the Structure of Human Behavior*. The Hague: Mouton and Co., 1967.

Rahula, Walpola. *Le Compendium de la Super-Doctrine Philosophie*. Paris: École Française d'Extrême-Orient, 1971.

Ramanan, K. Venkata. *Nāgārjuna's Philosophy as Presented in the Mahā-ā-Prajñāpāramitā-Śāstra*. Delhi: Motilal Banarsidass, 1978.

Rockhill, W.W. *Udānavarga*. Amsterdam: Oriental Press, 1975.

Roerich, George N. *The Blue Annals*. Delhi: Motilal Banarsidass, 1976.

Rogers, Katherine. "Tibetan Logic; A Translation with Commentary of Pur-bu-jok's 'The Topic of Signs and Reasonings from the "Great Path of Reasoning"' in the *Magic Key to the Path of Reasoning, Explanation of the Collected Topics Revealing the Mean-*

ing of the Texts on Valid Cognition. M.A. thesis, University of Virginia, 1980.

Ruegg, David Seyfort. "On the Reception and Early History of the dBu-ma (Madhyamaka) in Tibet." In *Tibetan Studies in Honour of Hugh Richardson*, pp. 277-279. Edited by Michael Aris and Aung San Suu Kyi. Warminster, England: Aris and Phillips Ltd., 1980.

———. *The Literature of the Madhyamaka School of Philosophy in India*. Wiesbaden: Otto Harrassowitz, 1981.

———. *The Study of Indian and Tibetan Thought: Some Problems and Perspectives*. Leiden: E.J. Brill, 1967.

Sastri, N. Aiyaswami. "Bhāvaviveka and his Method of Exposition." *Proceedings of the All-India Oriental Conference*, Vol 10, 1941.

———. "Karatalaratna." *Viśva-Bhārati Annals*, Vol 2, 1949.

Shakabpa, Tsepon W. D. *Tibet: A Political History*. New Haven: Yale University Press, 1967.

Shāntideva. *A Guide to the Bodhisattva's Way of Life*. Translated by Stephen Batchelor. Dharmsala: LTWA, 1979.

Smith, E. Gene. "The Biography of Lcang-skya Rol-pa'i-rdo-rje," *Collected Works of Thu'u-bkwan Blo-bzang-chos-kyi-nyi-ma*, Vol. 1. New Delhi: Ngawang Gelek Demo, 1969.

Sopa, Geshe Lhundup and Hopkins, Jeffrey. *Practice and Theory of Tibetan Buddhism*. New York: Grove Press, 1976.

Sprung, Mervyn. *Lucid Exposition of the Middle Way*. Boulder: Prajna Press, 1979.

Stcherbatsky, Theodore. *The Conception of Buddhist Nirvana*. Delhi: Motilal Banarsidass, 1977.

Steinkellner, Ernst and Tauscher, Helmut, ed. *Contributions of Tibetan and Buddhist Religion and Philosophy: Proceedings of the Csoma de Körös Symposium Held at Velm-Vienna, Austria, 13-19 September 1981*, Vol. 1. Vienna: Arbeitskreis für Tibetische und Buddhistische Studien Universität Wien, 1983.

Streng, Frederick, J. *Emptiness: A Study in Religious Meaning*. Nashville: Abingdon Press, 1967.

———. *Understanding Religious Life*. Encino, California: Dickenson Publishing Co., 1976.

Suzuki, Daisetz Teitaro. *The Lankavatara Sutra*. London: Routledge and Kegan Paul, 1932.

Tāranātha. *Tāranātha's History of Buddhism in India*. Translated by Lama Chimpa and Alaka Chattopadhyaya. Simla: Indian Institute of Advanced Study, 1970.

Thurman, Robert A.F. *Life and Teachings of Tsong Khapa*. Dharmsala: LTWA, 1982.

———. "Philosophical Nonegocentrism in Wittgenstein and Candrakīrti in their Treatment of the Private Language Problem." *Philosophy East and West*, Vol 30, 1980.

———. *Tsong Khapa's Speech of Gold in the "Essence of True Eloquence"*. Princeton: Princeton University Press, 1984.

Tsong-ka-pa. *Chapter Two of Ocean of Reasoning*. Translated by Jeffrey Hopkins. Dharmsala: LTWA, 1974.

———. *Tantra in Tibet*. Edited and translated by Jeffrey Hopkins. London: Allen and Unwin, 1977.

Tucci, Giuseppe. *Minor Buddhist Texts, Part II: First Bhāvanākrama of Kamalaśīla*. Serie Orientale Roma, IX.2. Rome: Is.M.E.O., 1958).

Vogel, Claus. *Indian Lexicography*. Wiesbaden: Otto Harrassowitz, 1979.

Warder, A.K. *Indian Buddhism*. 2d revised edition. Delhi: Motilal Banarsidass, 1980.

Wayman, Alex. *Calming the Mind and Discerning the Real*. New York: Columbia University Press, 1978.

Williams, Paul. "A Note on Some Aspects of Mi skyod rdo rje's Critique of dGe lugs pa Madhyamaka." *Journal of Indian Philosophy*, Vol 11 (1983), pp. 125-145.

Wittgenstein, Ludwig. *Tractatus Logico-Philosophicus*. Translated by D.F. Pears and B.F. McGuinness. London: Routledge and Kegan Paul, 1961.

Woodward, F.L., trans. *The Book of Kindred Savings III*. London: Pali Text Society, Luzac and Company, 1954.

Wylie, Turrell. "A Standard System of Tibetan Transcription." *Harvard Journal of Asian Studies*, Vol 22, 1959.

Notes

Abbreviations

(For the full entries of the Tibetan texts see the Bibliography.)

Annotations: Nga-wang-bel-den's *Annotations for (Jam-yang-shay-ba's) "Great Exposition of Tenets"*
Bel-den: Geshe Bel-den Drak-ba's *Beautiful Ornament of Faith, A Good Explanation*
Four: Four Interwoven Annotations to (Tsong-kha-pa's) "Great Exposition of the Stages of the Path" by Jam-yang-shay-ba, et al.
Den-dar: Den-dar-hla-ram-ba's *Presentation of the Lack of Being One or Many*
Essence: Tsong-kha-pa's *Essence of the Good Explanations*
Essence Comm: Nyen-don-bel-jor-hlun-drup's *Commentary on the Difficult Points of (Tsong-kha-pa's) "Essence of the Good Explanations," A Lamp for the Teaching*
Insight: Tsong-kha-pa's *Great Exposition of Special Insight*
Jam-yang-shay-ba: Jam-yang-shay-ba's *Great Exposition of Tenets*
Jang-gya: Jang-gya's *Presentation of Tenets*
P: *Tibetan Tripiṭaka* (Tokyo-Kyoto: Tibetan Tripiṭaka Research Foundation, 1956)
Two Truths: Nga-wang-bel-den's *Explanation of the Meaning of "Conventional" and "Ultimate" in the Four Tenet Systems*

NOTES TO THE TECHNICAL NOTE

1. Turrell Wylie, "A Standard System of Tibetan Transcription," *Harvard Journal of Asian Studies* 22 (1959), pp. 261-7.

2. See Jeffrey Hopkins, *Meditation on Emptiness* (London: Wisdom Publications, 1983), pp. 19-21

NOTES TO THE INTRODUCTION

1. Kensur Yeshe Thupten, oral commentary.

2. See *Mkhas grub rje's Fundamentals of the Buddhist Tantras*, trans. Ferdinand D. Lessing and Alex Wayman (The Hague: Mouton, 1968), pp. 86-89. For a discussion of the various commentaries to the *Treatise on the Middle Way*, see David Seyfort Ruegg, *The Literature of the Madhyamaka School of Philosophy in India* (Wiesbaden: Otto Harrassowitz, 1981) pp. 47-49.

3. This discussion of what constitutes the founding of a school is presented in Jang-gya, p. 288.15-20. Jang-gya also concludes that Devaśarman was a Svātantrika because Bhāvaviveka quotes his commentary to Nāgārjuna's *Treatise* approvingly.

4. Tsepon W.D. Shakabpa, *Tibet: A Political History* (New Haven: Yale University Press, 1967), p. 37, note 33.

5. For studies of the Council and its antecedents, see Paul Demiéville, *Le concile de Lhasa* (Bibliothèque de l'Institut des Hautes Études Chinoises, Vol. VII-Paris: Presses Universitaires de France, 1952); Giuseppe Tucci, ed., *First Bhāvanākrama of Kamalaśīla: Sanskrit and Tibetan Texts with Introduction and English Summary*, Minor Buddhist Texts, Part II: Serie Orientale Roma IX.2 (Rome: Is. M.E.O., 1958); G.W. Houston, *Sources for a History of the bSam yas Debate* (Sankt Augustin: VGH-Wissenschaftsverlag, 1980); Luis O. Gomez, "Indian Materials on the Doctrine of Sudden Enlightenment" in Whalen Lai and Lewis R. Lancaster, ed., *Early Ch'an in China and Tibet* (Berkeley: Berkeley Buddhist Studies Series, 1983), pp. 393-434; Luis O. Gomez, "The Direct and Gradual Approaches of the Zen Master Mahayana: Fragments of the Teachings of Mo-ho-yen" in Robert M. Gimello and Peter N. Gregory, ed., *Studies in Ch'an and Hua-yen* (Honolulu: University of Hawaii Press, 1983), pp. 69-167; and Jeffrey Broughton, "Early Ch'an Schools in Tibet" in Gimello and Gregory, ed., *Studies in Ch'an and Hua-yen* (Honolulu: University of Hawaii Press, 1983), pp. 1-68. Luis Gomez is currently completing a major study of the Council of Lhasa that will

include translations of all three *Bhāvanākrama*.

6. Frederick J. Streng, *Understanding Religious Life*, 2d ed. (Encino, California: Dickenson Publishing Company, 1976), p. 7.

7. Rudolf Otto, *The Idea of the Holy*, trans. John W. Harvey (London: Oxford University Press, 1976), p. 141.

8. *Ibid.*, p. 4

9. Much of Bhāvaviveka's argument is paraphrased by Jang-gya, pp. 328.3-342.12.

10. *Blaze of Reasoning* cited and explained by Jang-gya, pp. 340.16-341.8

11. This is Tsong-kha-pa's opinion (see *Essence*, p. 115.6-8) and seems to be supported by a reading of Bhāvaviveka's diatribes against the Yogācārins in both the *Blaze of Reasoning* and the *Lamp for (Nāgārjuna's) "Wisdom"*.

12. P 5284, Vol. 101 2.3.4. Cited by Jang-gya, p.368.8-10.

13. This gloss of Śāntarakṣita's stanza is provided by Jang-gya, pp. 368.18-369.1.

14. See Jam-yang-shay-ba, ca 10a.7-10b.3

15. Edward Conze, *Buddhist Thought in India* (Ann Arbor: University of Michigan Press, 1973) pp. 238-9.

16. D. Seyfort Ruegg, *The Study of Indian and Tibetan Thought: Some Problems and Perspectives* (Leiden: E.J. Brill, 1967), p. 15.

17. On the question of whether Jñānagarbha was a Sautrāntika-Svātantrika or a Yogācāra-Svātantrika, see chapter 2, note 16.

18. Ganganatha Jha, trans., *The Tattvasaṃgraha of Śāntarakṣita with the Commentary of Kamalaśīla* (Baroda, India: Oriental Institute, 1937).

19. See Jang-gya, p. 283.9-11.

20. A. K. Warder, *Indian Buddhism*, 2d rev. ed. (Delhi: Motilal Banarsidass, 1980), p. 480.

21. Theodore Stcherbatsky, *The Conception of Buddhist Nirvana*, 2d. rev. ed. (Delhi: Motilal Banarsidass, 1977), pp. 91-127.

22. Yuichi Kajiyama, "Bhāvaviveka's *Prajñāpradīpa* (l Kapitel)," *Wiener Zeitschrift fur die Kunde Sud-und Ostasiens* 7 (1963), pp. 37-62; 8 (1964), pp. 100-130. See also his "Introduction to the Logic of Svātantrika-Mādhyamika Philosophy," *Nava-Nalanda Mahavihara Research Publication*, 1 (1957), pp. 291-331.

23. Jeffrey Hopkins, *Meditation on Emptiness* (London: Wisdom Publications, 1983), pp. 441-530

24. See the Prāsaṅgika section of Robert A.F. Thurman, trans.,

Tsong Khapa's Speech of Gold in the "Essence of True Eloquence" (Princeton: Princeton University Press, 1984). See also Robert A.F. Thurman, "Philosophical Nonegocentrism in Wittgenstein and Candrakīrti in their Treatment of the Private Language Problem, *Philosophy East and West*, 30, 1980.

25. Louis de la Vallée Poussin, "Le Joyau dans la main," *Melanges Chinois et Bouddhiques* 2 (1932), pp. 68-138.

26. N. Aiyaswami Sastri, "Karatalaratna," *Viśva-Bhārati Annals*, 2, (Shantineketan, 1949), pp. 33-99. For a summary of the contents of the *Jewel in Hand*, see, by the same author, "Bhāvaviveka and his Method of Exposition," *Proceedings of the All-India Oriental Conference* 10 (1941), pp. 285-295.

27. N. Aiyaswami Sastri, "Madhyamakārthasaṃgraha of Bhavya," *Journal of Oriental Research*, Madras 5 (1931), pp. 41-49. It is noteworthy that neither the *Jewel in Hand* nor the *Condensed Meaning of the Middle Way* is mentioned by Tsong-kha-pa, Jam-yang-shay-ba, or Jang-gya. The former is not preserved in Tibetan, so they may not have been aware of its existence. The latter contains little that it not dealt with in more detail in Bhāvaviveka's longer works.

28. A relatively recent survey of modern scholarship on the *Essence of the Middle Way* and the *Blaze of Reasoning* can be found in Shotoro Iida, *Reason and Emptiness: A Study of Logic and Mysticism* (Tokyo: Hukuseido Press, 1980), pp. 12-16. Included in that study is Iida's translation of most of the third chapter of the two texts, the chapter on the "Search for Knowledge of Reality" (*tattvajñānaiṣāna*), which presents Bhāvaviveka's own view. Iida has also written two articles that discuss, in part, the third and fifth chapters of the *Blaze of Reasoning*. See Shotaro Iida, "The Nature of Samvṛti and the Relationship of Paramārtha to It in Svātantrika-Mādhyamika," in *The Problem of the Two Truths in Buddhism and Vedānta*, ed. Mervyn Sprung (Dordrecht, Holland: D. Reidel Publishing, 1973), pp. 64-77. Chapter Five of the *Blaze of Reasoning*, the chapter on Yogācāra, is discussed in Jay Hirabayashi and Shotaro Iida, "Another Look at the Mādhyamika vs. Yogācāra Controversy Concerning Existence and Non-existence," in *Prajñāpāramitā and Related Systems: Studies in Honor of Edward Conze*, ed. Lewis Lancaster (Berkeley: Berkeley Buddhist Studies Series, 1977), pp. 341-60. The important fourth chapter of the *Essence of the Middle Way* and the *Blaze of Reasoning*, the "Introduction to the Ascertainment of the

Reality of Hearers" (*śrāvakatattvaniścayāvatāra*), has been edited and translated by V.V. Gokhale and Robert A.F. Thurman, but, unfortunately, has not been published. It is scheduled to appear in *The Madhyamakahṛdaya of Bhāvaviveka*, edited by J. Takasaki, to be published by Tokyo University Press.

29. Iida includes a translation of the Svātantrika chapter of the *Precious Garland of Tenets* in his *Reason and Emptiness*, pp. 27-48. In 1971 the same text was translated as part of Herbert Guenther's *Buddhist Philosophy in Theory and Practice* (Baltimore: Penguin Books, 1972), pp. 130-6. In 1976 it appeared for the third time in a more readable translation as part of Sopa and Hopkins' *Practice and Theory of Tibetan Buddhism* (New York: Grove Press, 1976), pp. 122-32.

30. Mention should also be made of several doctoral dissertations and works in progress that contribute to our understanding of Svātantrika. In 1978, Peter della Santina completed a study of the difference between Svātantrika and Prāsaṇgika as understood by the Sa-gya order of Tibet. This doctoral dissertation for Delhi University is slated for publication by Motilal Banarsidass as *Mādhyamika School in India*. Kennard Lipman's "A Study of 'Śāntarakṣita's *Madhyamakālaṃkāra* (Ph.D. dissertation, University of Saskatchewan, 1979) is the first full-length study of the *Ornament for the Middle Way*. It considers several of the important issues raised by the text and includes a translation of Śāntarakṣita's root text as well as excerpts from the nineteenth century Nying-ma scholar Mi-pam's (*Mi-pham-rgya-mtsho*, 1846-1912) important commentary entitled, *Explanation of (Śāntarakṣita's) "Ornament for the Middle Way," Sacred Word of the Smiling Lama Mañjuśrī* (*dbU ma rgyan gyi rnam bshad 'jam dbyangs bla ma dgyes pa'i zhal lung*) (*Collected Works of Jam-mgon 'Ju Mi-pham rgya-mtsho*, Vol. 12, Gangtok, 1971). Masamichi Ichigo's edition and translation of the *kārikās* of the *Ornament for the Middle Way* are forthcoming from Kyoto University. Malcolm Eckel's 1980 dissertation from Harvard, "A Question of Nihilism: Bhāvaviveka's Response to the Fundamental Problems of Mādhyamika Philosophy," includes an annotated translation of the eighteenth, twenty-fourth, and twenty-fifth chapters of Bhāvaviveka's *Lamp for (Nāgārjuna's) "Wisdom"*. Eckel has completed a translation and analysis of the root text and autocommentary of Jñānagarbha's *Differentiation of the Two Truths* (*Satyadvayavibhaṅga*), forthcoming from the State University of New York Press.

31. For a discussion of several Indian and Tibetan versions of this reasoning, see T. Tillemans' article, "The 'Neither One Nor Many Argument' for *Śūnyatā* and its Tibetan Interpretations," in Ernst Steinkellner and Helmut Tauscher, ed., *Contributions on Tibetan and Buddhist Religion and Philosophy, Proceedings of the Csoma de Kőrös Symposium held at Velm-Vienna, Austria, 13-19 September 1981*, Vol. 2 (Vienna: Arbeitskreis für Tibetische und Buddhistische Studien Universität Wien, 1983), pp. 305-320).

32. *Essence*, p. 139.

33. D. Seyfort Ruegg, "On the Reception and Early History of the dBu-ma (Madhyamaka) in Tibet" in Michael Aris and Aung San Suu Kyi, ed., *Tibetan Studies in Honour of Hugh Richardson* (Warminster, England: Aris and Phillips Ltd., 1980) p. 279.

34. Kenneth L. Pike, *Language in Relation to a Unified Theory of the Structure of Human Behavior*, 2d rev. ed. (The Hague: Mouton and Co., 1967).

35. Pike, p. 37.

36. Pike, p. 38.

37. Ruegg, "On the Reception and Early History of the dBu-ma (Madhyamaka) in Tibet," p. 279.

38. This is most evident in late Indian Buddhist works such as Ratnākaraśānti's *Presentation of the Three Vehicles* (*Triyānavyavasthāna*) and Advayavajra's *Jewel Garland of Principles* (*Tattvaratnāvalī*).

39. For a discussion, edition, and translation of this work see Christian Lindtner, "Atīśa's Introduction to the Two Truths, and Its Sources," *Journal of Indian Philosophy*, 9 (1981), pp. 161-214.

40. In one case he was praised and criticized by the same person. The eighth Karmapa, Mi-gyö-dor-jay (*Mi-bskyod-rdo-rje*, 1507-1554) composed a song of praise entitled *Praise of the Peerless Tsong-kha-pa* (*mNyam med tsong-kha-pa'i bstod pa*), translated by Glenn H. Mullin and Lozang N. Tsonawa in *Four Songs to Je Rinpoche* (Dharmsala, India: Library of Tibetan Works and Archives, 1978), pp. 37-40. The eighth Karmapa also stridently criticizes Tsong-kha-pa's for being innovative in his interpretation of Candrakīrti. For an excellent discussion of his argument see Paul Williams, "A Note on Some Aspects of Mi bskyod rdo rje's Critique of dGe lugs pa Madhyamaka," *Journal of Indian Philosophy* 11 (1983), pp. 125-145.

41. David Seyfort Ruegg, *The Literature of the Madhyamaka School of Philosophy in India* (Wiesbaden: Otto Harrassowitz, 1981), p. VIII.

CHAPTER ONE: THE MIDDLE WAY

1. *Annotations,* dbu 53a.7.
2. Jang-gya, pp. 305.19-306.2.
3. Jang-gya, p. 309.5-6.
4. *Annotations,* dbu 2a. 4.
5. *Ibid.* This statement requires qualification in the context of Svātantrika-Mādhyamika because Bhāvaviveka asserts that one can be liberated from cyclic existence merely by realizing the selflessness of persons (*pudgalanairātmya*) without abandoning the conception of true existence. The conflicting positions of the Svātantrikas and Prāsaṅgikas on this point are discussed at length in Chapter Three.
6. Jang-gya, p. 306.2-3.
7. Tsong-kha-pa, *Great Commentary on (Nāgārjuna's) "Fundamental (Treatise on the Middle Way Called) Wisdom," An Ocean of Reasoning (rTsa she ḍig chen rigs pa'i ryga mtsho)* (Sarnath, India: Pleasure of Elegant Sayings Printing Press, 1973), p. 15. In future citations, this text will be referred to as *Ocean of Reasoning.*
8. Kensur Yeshe Thupten, oral commentary.
9. Jang-gya, p. 309.6-7
10. Kensur Yeshe Thupten, oral commentary.
11. *Insight,* p. 29.
12. *Ibid.*
13. Jang-gya, p. 306.14-15.
14. *Annotations,* dbu 2b.2-3.
15. Geshe Bel-den Drak-ba, oral commentary.
16. Jang-gya, 307.4-6.
17. Kensur Yeshe Thupten, oral commentary.
18. Hopkins, *Meditation on Emptiness,* p. 162.
19. P 5224, Vol. 95 2.2.4-3.1-2.
20. P 5225, Vol. 95 11.2.3-4.
21. *Essence,* p. 101.
22. *Ibid.*
23. *Ibid.*
24. P 2019, Vol. 46 37.4.4-5.
25. *Essence,* p. 101.
26. P 5682, Vol. 129 237.5.7
27. Jang-gya, p. 306.6-10
28. Kensur Yeshe Thupten, oral commentary. Also see Jang-gya, p. 306.10-13.
29. Jang-gya, pp. 311.17-312.8.

30. Kensur Yeshe Thupten, oral commentary.
31. *Ibid.*
32. Sopa and Hopkins, *Practice and Theory of Tibetan Buddhism*, p. 72.
33. *Ibid.*, p. 93. This interpretation of Sautrāntika appears to be unique to Ge-luk. For an analysis of their interpretation, see Anne Klein, *Mind and Liberation.*
34. Jang-gya, pp. 306.20-307.1.
35. *Insight*, p. 44.
36. Kensur Yeshe Thupten, oral commentary.
37. *Ibid.*
38. P 5658, Vol. 129, stanzas 394-97.
39. Kensur Yeshe Thupten, oral commentary.
40. *Essence*, pp. 98-9.
41. *Annotations*, dbu lb.2-3.
42. *Ibid.*, lb.2-5.
43. *Essence*, p. 99.
44. Kensur Yeshe Thupten, oral commentary.
45. *Essence*, pp. 99-100.
46. P 5228, Vol. 95, stanza 29.
47. P 5225, Vol. 95, stanza 50.
48. P 5246, Vol. 95, chapter XVI, 25.
49. T. R. V. Murti, *The Central Philosophy of Buddhism* (London: Allen and Unwin, 1980), p. 131.
50. Conze, *Buddhist Thought in India*, p. 241.
51. Surendranath Dasgupta, *A History of Indian Philosophy*, Vol. 1 (Delhi: Motilal Banarsidass, 1975), p. 140.
52. *Encyclopedia of Religion and Ethics*, s.v. "Nihilism (Buddhist)," by Louis de la Vallée Poussin. In fairness to Poussin, it must be noted that later in the same article he qualifies this statement, concluding that the Buddhists are not nihilists.
53. A. Berriedale Keith, *Buddhist Philosophy in India and Ceylon*, 2d ed. (New Delhi: Oriental Books Reprint Corporation, 1979), p. 239.
54. *Ibid.*, pp. 240-1.
55. *Insight*, pp. 135-6.
56. *Insight*, p. 138 and *Four*, p. 508.
57. *Insight*, p. 138 and *Four*, p. 509.
58. *Insight*, p. 138.
59. *Ibid.*, p. 137.

60. *Ibid.*, p. 138.

61. I translate *bhagavan* as "Supramundane Victor" following an etymology provided by Jñānamitra in his *Explanation of the Heart of the Perfection of Wisdom* (*Shes rab kyi pha rol tu phyin pa'i snying po'i rnam par bshad pa*, P 5218, Vol 94 285.2.6-8), "With respect to that, regarding *bhāga*, [it means] the destruction (*bhaṅga*) of demons. Demons, such as the demon of the aggregates, are not found when sought with this meaning of the perfection of wisdom and no demons abide [there], so it destroys. *Bhāga* [also means] endowed with the six fortunes, that is, since all the qualities of knowledge arise from the blessings of the perfection of wisdom, it is endowed. *Vat* [means] the non-abiding nirvana. Since all minds, intellects, and consciousnesses are overturned by this meaning of the perfection of wisdom, that is, since it is free from all predispositions, it is supramundane. (*de la bcom ldan zhes bya ba ni bdud bcom pa ste phung po'i bdud la sogs pa shes rab kyi pha rol tu phyin pa'i don 'dis bdud btsal du mi rnyed cing bdud thams cad mi gnas pa'i phyir bcom pa'o/ldan zhes bya ba ni legs pa drug dang ldan pa ste mkhyen pa'i yon tan thams cad kyang shes rab kyi pha rol tu phyin pa'i byin gyis brlabs las byung ba na ldan pa'o/'das zhes bya ba ni mi gnas pa'i mya ngan las 'das ba'o/shes rab kyi pha rol tu phyin pa'i don gyis sems dang yid dang rnam par shes pa tham cad bzlog ste bag chags thams cad dang bral bas na 'das zhes bya'o*).

Compare this to the etymologies provided in the *Ta chih tu lun*. See Lamotte, *Le Traite de la Grande Vertu de Sagesse*, Tome 1 (Louvain: Institut Orientaliste, 1949), pp. 115-126, especially, 115-117, which says, in part, "En outre *bhāga* signifie briser (*bhaṅga*) et *vat* marque le pouvoir. L'homme qui peut briser le desir (*rāga*), la haine (*dveṣa*) et la sotisse (*moha*) est nomme Bhagavat."

Jñānamitra's etymology should also be appraised in light of those provided by Buddhaghosa in the *Visuddhimagga* (VII.53-67). See Nyanamoli's translation, *The Path of Purification* (Colombo, Ceylon: A. Semage, 1964), pp. 224-230. Note especially the statement on page 226:

> Bhāgyavā bhaggavā yutto bhagehi ca vibhattavā.
> Bhattavā vanta-gamano bhavesu: bhagavā tato.

and Buddhaghosa's commentary, pp. 226-229.

62. *Insight*, p. 39.

63. *Ibid.*, p. 41.

64. Kensur Yeshe Thupten, oral commentary.

65. Conze, *Buddhist Thought in India*, p. 239.

66. P 5228, Vol. 95, stanza 28.

67. P 5225, Vol. 95, stanza 45.

68. P 2012, Vol. 46, stanza 8.

69. I follow Hopkins' translation of *avatāra* as "supplement". See *Meditation on Emptiness*, note 545, pp 867-871.

70. *Insight*, p. 144.

71. For a penetrating analysis of the question of whether Mādhyamikas have theses, see D. Seyfort Ruegg, "On the Thesis and Assertion in the Madhyamaka/dBu ma" in Steinkellner and Tauscher, ed., *Contributions on Tibetan and Buddhist Philosophy and Religion*, Vol. 2 (Vienna: Arbeitskreis für Tibetische und Buddhistische Studien Universität Wien, 1983), pp. 205-240.

CHAPTER TWO: SVĀTANTRIKA AND PRĀSAṄGIKA

1. The Five Collections of Reasoning are the *Refutation of Objections* (*Vigrahavyāvartanī*), the *Seventy Stanzas on Emptiness* (*Śūnyatāsaptati*), the *Sixty Stanzas of Reasoning* (*Yuktiṣaṣṭikā*), the *Treatise Called the "Finely Woven"* (*Vaidalyasūtranāma*), and the *Fundamental Treatise on the Middle Way, Called "Wisdom"* (*Prajñānāmamūlamadhyamakakārikā*). I will not provide here a complete bibliography on materials on the life and works of Nāgārjuna. For two Tibetan traditional biographies, see *Bu-ston's History of Buddhism*, trans., E. Obermiller, 2 pts. (Heidelberg: Heft, 1932), Part 2, pp. 122-130 and Tāranātha, *History of Buddhism in India*, trans., Lama Chimpa and Alaka Chattopadhyaya (Simla, India: Indian Institute of Advanced Study, 1970), pp. 106-119. Excellent treatments of the works of Nāgārjuna are to be found in David Seyfort Ruegg, *The Literature of the Madhyamaka School of Philosophy in India* (Wiesbaden: Otto Harrassowitz, 1981), pp. 4-47 and in Christian Lindtner, *Nāgārjuniana: Studies in the Writings and Philosophy of Nāgārjuna* (Copenhagen: Akademisk Forlag, 1982).

2. *Insight*, p. 15.

3. *Ibid.*

4. In *Four*, p. 171, Jam-yang-shay-ba disputes Ye-shay-day's contention that it is unclear whether Nāgārjuna asserted that external objects exist, citing the passage from the *Precious Garland* that says:

> To some [he teaches doctrines] based on non-duality.
> To some, the profound, frightening to the fearful,

> Having an essence of emptiness and compassion
> The means of achieving highest enlightenment.

According to Tsong-kha-pa, the first line identifies the doctrines taught to those of the Mahāyāna lineage who are temporarily incapable of understanding the Mādhyamika view and therefore are taught the emptiness of duality of subject and object (see *Essence*, p. 99). Since the stanza goes on to describe a more profound view, Jam-yang-shay-ba concludes that the non-existence of external objects is not the final mode of being and, hence, Nāgārjuna clearly does not reject the existence of external objects.

It is necessary, however, to consider other statements by Nāgārjuna before concluding unequivocally that he holds the position that external objects exist and rejects the mind-only view. He says in his *Sixty Stanzas of Reasoning* (34):

> Those [things] explained as the great elements and so forth
> Are completely included within consciousness.
>
> (*mahābhūtādi vijñāne proktaṃ samavarudhyate*)

We find in the *Essay on the Mind of Enlightenment* (*Bodhicittavivaraṇa*, 26-56) the most complete refutation of the Yogācāra view, with specific references to the *ālayavijñāna*, and the three natures. At stanza 27, the text says:

> The Subduer's teaching that
> "All of this is mind only"
> Is for the sake of removing the fear of the childish;
> It is not [a statement] of reality.
>
> *cittamātram idaṃ sarvam iti yā deśanā muneḥ*
> *uttrāsaparihārārthaṃ bālānāṃ sa nā tattvataḥ*

For an edition and translation of the *Bodhicittavivaraṇa*, see Lindtner, *Nagarjuniana* pp. 180-217. Whether the Nāgārjuna of the Five Collections of Reasoning is the author of the *Essay on the Mind of Enlightenment* is subject to debate. Lindtner feels that the work is that of the founder of Mādhyamika (see p. 180-181). Ruegg disagrees, ascribing the work to Nāgārjuna II (see Ruegg, *The Literature of the Madhyamaka School of Philosophy in India*, p. 104.

5. *Insight*, p. 16.
6. In *Four*, p. 172, Nga-wang-rap-den (*sDe-drug mKhan-chen*

Ngag-dbang-rab-brtan) argues that Ye-shay-day's chronology is inaccurate, noting that prior to Bhāvaviveka there was Śūra, who was a Mādhyamika who asserted the existence of external objects and prior to Śantarakṣita there was Āryavimutisena, who was a Mādhyamika who asserted that external objects do not exist. For a modern study of the chronology of the Mādhyamika school in India, see D. Seyfort Ruegg, "Toward a Chronology of the Madhyamaka School" in L.A. Hercus, et al., ed., *Indological and Buddhist Studies: Volume in Honour of Professor J.W. de Jong on his Sixtieth Birthday* (Canberra: Faculty of Asian Studies, 1982), pp. 505-530.

7. *Four*, p. 172.

8. *Insight*, p. 17.

9. George N. Roerich, trans., *The Blue Annals* (Delhi: Motilal Banarsidass, 1976), p. 342.

10. *Mūlamadhyamakakārikās de Nāgārjuna avec la Prasannapadā Commentaire de Candrakīrti* ed. Louis de la Vallée Poussin, Bibliotheca Buddhica IV (Osnabrück: Biblio Verlag, 1970), p. 655.

11. *Essence*, p. 139.

12. I use the term "entityness" to translate the Tibetan term *ngo bo nyid*, which is used to translate the Sanskrit *rūpatva* and *svabhāva*. "Entityness" is chosen here to suggest something that it is capable of independent existence, something similar to substance, as described by Wittgenstein in the *Tractatus Logico-Philosophicus* 2.024, "Substance is what subsists independently of what is the case." (Pear and McGuiness translation). It would be the Mādhyamika position that phenomena have entities, that is, that they exist, but that entityness, some kind of substantial property or absolute object, is a falsity hypostasized by ignorance. Entityness seems akin to what Heidegger calls "the thingness of the thing" in his essay, "The Origin of the Work of Art". He writes:

> This block of granite, for example, is a mere thing. It is hard, heavy, extended, bulky, shapeless, rough, colored, partly dull, partly shiny. We can take note of all these features in the stone. Thus we acknowledge its characteristics. But still, the traits signify something proper to the stone itself. They are the properties. The thing has them. The thing? What are we thinking of when we now have the thing in mind? Obviously a thing is not merely an aggregate of traits, nor an accumulation of properties by which that

> aggregate arises. A thing, as everyone thinks he knows, is that around which the properties have assembled. We speak in this connection of the core of things. The Greeks are supposed to have called it *to hupokeimenon*. For them, this core of the thing is something lying at the ground of the thing, something always already there. The characteristics, however, are called *ta sumbebekota*, that which has always turned up already along with the given core and occurs along with it.

See Martin Heidegger, *Poetry, Language, Thought* (New York: Harper and Row, 1971) pp. 22-23.

13. Jang-gya, 313.1-5.

14. *Essence*, p. 139.

15. *Ibid*, p. 140.

16. Warder places Avalokitavrata, Śāntarakṣita, and Kamalaśīla in the eighth century (see his *Indian Buddhism*, p. 479). Ruegg places Jñānagarbha in the eighth century as well (see his *The Literature of the Madhyamaka School of Philosophy in India*, p. 69). There is some controversy in the Tibetan tradition regarding the doctrinal affiliation of Jñānagarbha. He is generally considered to be have been a student of Śrīgupta, a Yogācāra-Mādhyamika. The historian Sum-ba-ken-bo (*Sum-pa-mkhan-po*) states that Jñānagarbha was a teacher of Śāntarakṣita, the founder of Yogācāra-Svātantrika-Mādhyamika (see Ruegg, p. 69, n. 225). Based presumably on the fact that Jñānagarbha was both the student and the teacher of masters with strong affinities for Yogācāra, Bu-ston identifies him as a Yogācāra-Svātantrika (see Obermiller, p. 135). The historian Tāranātha says that Jñānagarbha, "became famous as a great Mādhyamika follower of the view of Bhavya" [Bhāvaviveka] (see Chimpa and Chattopadhyaya, trans., p. 253). The Ge-luk position is that Jñānagarbha is a Sautrāntika-Svātantrika and a follower of Bhāvaviveka. In the famous Ge-luk synoposis of tenets, the *Precious Garland of Tenets* (*Grub mtha' rin chen phreng ba*) by Gön-chok-jik-may-wang-bo (*dKon-mchog-'jigs-me-dbang-po*) a Yogācāra-Svātantrika-Mādhyamika is defined as a Mādhyamika who does not assert the existence of external objects and who asserts the existence of self-knowers (*svasaṃvedana, rang rig*). A Sautrāntika-Svātantrika-Mādhyamika is defined as a Mādhyamika who does not assert the existence of self-knowers and who asserts that external objects exist

by way of their own character (see the Drepung Loseling Printing Press edition of 1980, p. 55. This edition is free of the many typographical errors and omissions that marred the 1969 Shes rig par khang edition.). According to these two definitions, Jñānagarbha seems to be a Sautrāntika-Svātantrika because in his most important work, the *Differentiation of the Two Truths* (*Satyadvayavibhaṅga*), he refutes an opponent who claims that there is such a thing as a self-knower (see *Satyadvayavibhaṅgavṛtti*, Toh. 3882, folio 4b2ff.) and he also does not deny the existence of external objects.

On the other hand, he displays a more accommodating view of the doctrine of mind-only than Bhāvaviveka does. Jñānagarbha writes, "The Supramundane Victor himself, the knower of actions and their effects, whose body is the nature of compassion, sees transmigrators bound by the chains of misconception in the prison of cyclic existence and completely destroys the conception of true existence by gradually setting forth the aggregates, constituents, sources, mind-only, and the selflessness of phenomena." (Toh. 3883, folio 13a3-4.) This is consonant with Śāntarakṣita's statement in the *Ornament for the Middle Way* that one comes to understand the non-existence of external objects through the teaching of mind-only and then comes to know that all phenomena, including the mind, are selfless through the Mādhyamika teaching. (P 5284, Vol. 101 2.3.4) Furthermore, Śāntarakṣita wrote a commentary (*ṭīkā*) to the *Differentiation of the Two Truths*, in which he disputes neither the refutation of self-knowers nor the existence of external objects. The Ge-luk position is that this commentary is not the work of the same Śāntarakṣita who wrote the *Ornament for the Middle Way*. They point to the fact that Kamalaśīla, in his commentary on the *Compendium of Principles* (*Tattvasaṃgraha*), makes a disparaging remark about the author of the commentary to Jñānagarbha's *Differentiation of the Two Truths* and that Kamalaśīla would not make such a remark about his own teacher, especially in a commentary on his teacher's work. They also point to Jñanagarbha's statement that direct perception and what is renowned in the world refute the assertion that objects and subjects do not exist as they appear. The commentator notes that it is correct to let this position stand. The Ge-luk-bas argue that Śāntarakṣita would never make such a statement because he asserted that objects falsely appear to be separate from a perceiving consciousness. (Nga-wang-bel-den summarizes Tsong-kha-pa's argument on this question in *Annotations*, dbu 42a.1-3.)

There is much more to be pursued beyond what I have indicated here. At any rate, if Śāntarakṣita was indeed the student of Jñānagarbha, it may have been the case that he composed his commentary to the *Differentiation of the Two Truths* early in his life (according to the Tibetan histories, he lived for 999 years!), with the positions set forth in the *Ornament for the Middle Way* representing a later and more mature view. Whether or not Śāntarakṣita composed the commentary, it seems safe to say that in spite of how he might be classified by the Tibetan historians and doxographers, Jñānagarbha thought of himself as neither a Yogācāra-Svātantrika nor as a Sautrāntika-Svātantrika, but as simply a Mādhyamika. The difficulties encountered in attempting to assign him a place in one of the two branches of Svātantrika suggest again that the philosophical climate of late Indian Buddhism was substantially more fluid (especially during the monsoon) than the Tibetan studies imply.

17. *Mūlamadhyamakakārikās de Nāgārjuna avec la Prasannapadā Commentaire de Candrakīrti*, p. 627.

18. *Encyclopedia of Religion and Ethics*, s.v. "Madhyamaka, Mādhyamikas," by Louis de la Vallée Poussin.

19. Conze, *Buddhist Thought in India*, pp. 238-239.

20. K. Venkata Ramanan, *Nāgārjuna's Philosophy as Presented in the Mahā-Prajñāpāramitā-Śāstra* (Delhi: Motilala Banarsidass, 1978), p. 341.

21. Jang-gya, p. 325.15-20.

22. Claus Vogel, *Indian Lexicography* (Wiesbaden: Otto Harrassowitz, 1979), p. 311.

23. Jang-gya, p. 325.10.

24. *Mahāvyutpatti*, 2 Vol. ed. by Ryozaburo Sakaki, 2d ed. (Tokyo, 1962), Vol. 1, p. 482 and Vol. 2, p. 163.

25. Jam-yang-shay-ba, ca 61a.5-6.

26. P 5709, Vol. 130 88.3.4.

27. Lati Rinbochay, oral commentary.

28. See Anne C. Klein, "Mind and Liberation: the Sautrāntika Tenet System in Tibet" (Ph.D. dissertation, University of Virginia, 1981), pp. 304-323.

29. Lati Rinbochay, oral commentary.

30. Geshe Jam-bel-sam-pel (*dGe-gshes 'Jam-dpal-bsam-phel*), *Presentation of Awareness and Knowledge, Composite of All the Important Points, Opener of the Eye of New Awareness* (*Blo rig gi rnam bzhag nyer mkho kun 'dus blo gsar mig 'byed*) (Modern blockprint, no place

given, no date given), 2a.2-3.

31. *Ibid.*

32. Lati Rinbochay, *Mind in Tibetan Buddhism,* trans., ed., with an Introduction by Elizabeth Napper (Ithaca, New York: Snow Lion Publications, 1980), p. 76.

33. Pur-bu-jok, *The Topic of Signs and Reasonings from the "Great Path of Reasoning"* in *The Magic Key to the Path of Reasoning, Presentation of the Collected Topics Revealing the Meaning of the Texts on Valid Cognition* (*Tshad ma'i gzhung don 'byed ba'i bsdus grva'i rnam par bshad pa rigs lam 'phrul gyi lde mig las rigs lam che ba rtags rigs kyi skor*) (Buxa, India: n.p., 1965), 5a.7-5b.1.

34. Katherine Rogers, "Tibetan Logic: A Translation, with Commentary, of Pur-bu-jok Jam-ba-gya-tso's *The Topic of Signs and Reasonings from the "Great Path of Reasoning"* (M.A. thesis, University of Virginia, 1980), pp. 53-54, 193, note 2.

35. Pur-bu-jok, *The Topic of Signs and Reasonings,* 5b2.2-3.

36. Pur-bu-jok, *Explanation of the Lesser Path of Reasoning* in *Magical Key to the Path of Reasoning, Presentation of the Collected Topics Revealing the Meaning of the Treatises on Valid Cognition* (*Tshad ma'i gzhung don 'byed pa'i bsdus grva'i rnam bzhag rigs lam 'phrul gyi lde mig ces bya ba las rigs lam chung ngu'i rnam bshad*) (Buxa, India: n.p., 1965), 5b.6.

37. Pur-bu-jok, *The Topic of Signs and Reasonings,* 5b.3-4.

38. For a discussion of the three modes, see Rogers, pp. 4-7, 62-75.

39. Hopkins, *Meditation on Emptiness,* p. 449.

40. Jam-yang-chok-hla-ö-ser (*'Jam-dbyangs-phyogs-lha-od-zer*), *Collected Topics of Ra-dö* (*Rva stod bsdus grva*) (Delhi: Jayyed Press, 1980), 154b.5-6.

41. *Ibid.*

42. Murti, *The Central Philosophy of Buddhism,* p. 131.

43. Anne Klein, "Mind and Liberation: The Sautrāntika Tenet System in Tibet," pp. 206-209.

44. Jam-yang-chok-hla-ö-ser, *The Collected Topics of Ra-dö,* 155a.1-3.

45. For an extensive treatment of the controversy between Bhāvaviveka and Candrakīrti on this point, see Jeffrey Hopkins, *Meditation on Emptiness,* pp. 441-530.

46. Jang-gya, p. 407.

47. *Insight,* p. 60.

48. *Ibid.*
49. *Ibid.*, pp. 60-61.
50. *Ibid.*, p. 62.
51. Lati Rinpochay, *Mind in Tibetan Buddhism*, p. 52.
52. *Insight*, p. 62.
53. Den-dar, 428.3-4.
54. *Essence*, p. 110.
55. *Annotations*, dbu 55a.8.
56. Jam-yang-shay-ba, ca 63b.4.
57. *Insight*, p. 64.
58. *Ibid.*
59. *Ibid.*
60. Jam-yang-shay-ba, ca 63b.6.
61. *Ibid.*, ca 64b.1-65a.3.
62. *Four*, 323.
63. *Ibid.*
64. *Ibid.*
65. *Ibid.*, 323-326.
66. Jang-gya, p. 326.11-13.
67. Jam-yang-shay-ba, ca 61b.7-62a.1.
68. *Insight*, p. 68.
69. Jang-gya, p. 364.5-8.
70. *Ibid.*, p. 364.9-10.
71. *Ibid.*, p. 325.12-15.
72. Jam-yang-shay-ba, ca 61a.7-8.
73. *Ibid.*, ca 62a.4 and Toh. 3882 4a.3, 5b.6.
74. *Annotations*, dbu 27b. 3-4.
75. *Ibid.*, dbu 27b.5.
76. *Four*, 535.
77. For a detailed discussion of the question of commonly appearing subjects, especially in the context of Candrakīrti's critique of Bhāvaviveka, see Jeffrey Hopkins, *Meditation on Emptiness*, pp. 505-526.
78. *Annotations*, dbu 27b.5-28a.1.
79. Den-dar, 448.4.
80. Jam-yang-shay-ba, ca 80a.5-6 and Toh. 3881, folio 2a.5.
81. Jam-yang-shay-ba, ca 80a.5-6 and Toh. 3881, folio 2b.4.
82. *Annotations*, dbu 49b.2-4.
83. *Ibid.*, dbu 41b.4.
84. Kensur Yeshe Thupten, oral commentary.

85. *Four*, 537-538.

86. P 5228, Vol. 95, stanza 30.

87. *Four*, 478.

88. *Insight*, p. 136.

89. *Annotations*, dbu 28a.1-2.

90. Jang-gya, 480.2-8.

91. The preceding three paragraphs are based on Jang-gya, pp. 478.5-481.1

92. *Insight*, p. 125.

93. *Ibid.*, p. 148.

94. Sha-mar Gen-dun-den-dzin-gya-tso (*Zhwa-dmar-dGe-'dun-bstan-'dzin-rgya-mtsho*), *Lamp Illuminating the Profound Thought Set Forth to Purify Forgetfulness of the Difficult Points of* (*Tsong-kha-pa's*) *"Great Exposition of Special Insight"* (*lHag mthong chen mo'i dka' gnad rnams brjed byang du bkod pa dgongs zab snang ba'i sgron me*), (New Delhi: Mongolian Lama Guru Deva, 1972), 17a.3-4. His argument that they fall to both extremes is based on a statement by Tsong-kha-pa that the conception that the absence which is the refutation of the object of negation really exists is a conception of an extreme of non-existence and that the conception that phenomena exist by way of their own character is a conception of an extreme of permanence. See Tsong-kha-pa, *Ocean of Reasoning*, p. 15.

95. Den-dar, 428.4-6.

96. Jang-gya, p. 312.8-17.

97. *Ibid.*, 312.18-20.

98. *Annotations*, dbu 53a.7-53b.2.

CHAPTER THREE: THE ROOT OF CYCLIC EXISTENCE

1. For a discussion of the etymology of *śrāvaka* and its translation as "*Hearer*", see Hopkins, *Meditation on Emptiness*, p. 840-845.

2. See Hopkins, *Meditation or Emptiness*, p. 845.

3. *Arhan* is translated as "Foe Destroyer" following the Tibetan *dgra bcom pa* which is based on the Sanskrit etymology of *arhan* as *ari han*. A Foe Destroyer is a person who has destroyed the foe of ignorance and achieved liberation. See also Hopkins, *Meditation on Emptiness*, pp 871-873.

4. *Saṃyutta Nikāya III*, ed. by M. Leon Feer (London: Pali Text Society, Luzac and Company, 1960), pp. 141-2. Available in English as *The Book of Kindred Sayings III*, trans. F. L. Woodward, Pali Text Society 13 (London: Luzac and Company, 1954), pp. 120-1.

5. The Buddha is called the Sun-Friend (*ādityabandhu*) (literally, he who has the sun as his friend) because the sun nurtured a drop of semen which had fallen from a dying ancestor of the Śākya lineage and caused it to grow into a man, thus allowing the Śākya clan to continue. See Roerich, *The Blue Annals*, pp. 7-8.

6. The following exegesis of the five similes is based on *Annotations*, dbu 31a.2-6 and Geshe Bel-den Drak-ba, oral commentary.

7. Sopa and Hopkins, *Practice and Theory of Tibetan Buddhism*, p. 72.

8. *Ibid.*

9. See Jang-gya, p. 388.3-14.

10. Lati Rinbochay, *Mind in Tibetan Buddhism*, p. 144.

11. Ye-shay-gyal-tsen (Ye-shes-rgyal-mtshan), *Clear Exposition of the Modes of Minds and Mental Factors, Necklace for Those of Clear Mind* (*Sems dang sems byung gi tshul gsal bar ston pa blo gsal mgul rgyan*) in *Collected Works of Tshe-mchog-gliṅ yoṅs-'dzin ye-ses-rgyal-mtshan* 16 (New Delhi: Tibet House, 1974), 14.5.

12. *Ibid.*, 16.1-2.

13. *Ibid.*, 15.3-6.

14. Sopa and Hopkins, *Practice and Theory of Tibetan Buddhism*, p. 60.

15. Geshe Ngawang Dhargyey, *Tibetan Tradition of Mental Development*, 3d ed. (Dharamasala, India: Library of Tibetan Works and Archives, 1978), p. 71.

16. Sopa and Hopkins, *Practice and Theory of Tibetan Buddhism*, p. 77.

17. *Annotations*, dngos 28b.4.

18. Pa-bong-ka (Pha-bong-kha), *Lectures on the Stages of the Path* (*Lam rim zin bris/rNam grol lag bcangs su gtod pa'i man ngag zab mo tshang la ma nor ba mtshungs med cho kyi rgyal po'i thugs bcud byang chub lam gyi rim pa'i nyams khrid kyi zin bris gsung rab kun gyi bcud bsdus gdams ngag bdud rtsi'i snying po*) compiled by Trijang Rinbochay (Mundgod, South India: Gan-den Shar-dzay, n.d.), 265b.5-266a.5. See also Harvey B. Aronson, "The Buddhist Path: A Translation of the Sixth Chapter of the First Dalai Lama's *Path of Liberation*," *Tibet Journal* 5 (August 1980): 29-51.

19. Tsong-kha-pa, *Great Exposition of the Stages to Enlightenment Composed by the Peerless Great Tsong-kha-pa* (*mNyam med Tsong kha pa chen pos mdzad pa'i byang chub lam rim che ba*) (Dharmsala, India: Tibetan Cultural Printing Press, n.d.), 148b.1-4.

20. *Ibid.*, 148a.4-6.
21. His Holiness the Dalai Lama, oral teaching.
22. Cited in Vasubandhu, *Treasury of Knowledge* (*Abhidharma-kosha*), chapter 6. See Swami Dwarikadas Shastri, ed., *Abhidharma-kośa and Bhāṣya of Acharya Vasubandhu with Sphutārthā Commentary of Ācārya Yaśomitra* Part III (Varanasi, India: Bauddha Bharati Series - 7, 1972), p. 877.
23. Tsong-kha-pa, *Great Exposition of the Stages of the Path*, 147b.5-148a.3.
24. Vasubandhu, *Treasury of Knowledge*, p. 881.
25. P 39 89.5.7.
26. Pa-bong-ka, 285a.5-285b.4.
27. Hopkins, *Meditation on Emptiness*, pp. 241-243.
28. Geshe Bel-den Drak-ba, oral commentary.
29. Lati Rinbochay, *Mind in Tibetan Buddhism*, pp. 144-5.
30. *L'Abhidharmakośa de Vasubandhu*, trans. Louis de la Vallée Poussin, 6 vol., (Brussels: Institut Belge Des Hautes Études Chinoiscs, 1971), 1: 40-1. Also, His Holiness the Dalai Lama, oral teaching.
31. Hopkins, *Meditation on Emptiness*, p. 268.
32. *Ibid.*, p. 270.
33. *Saṃyutta Nikāya*, pp. 141-2. For English translation, see *Book of Kindred Sayings III*, pp. 120-1.
34. Lati Rinbochay, *Mind in Tibetan Buddhism*, pp. 66-71.
35. Bel-den Drak-ba, p. 31.
36. *Ibid.*, p. 33.
37. *Ibid.*, p. 48.
38. Tsong-ka-pa, *Tantra in Tibet: The Great Exposition of Secret Mantra*, trans. and ed. Jeffrey Hopkins (London: George Allen and Unwin, 1977), p. 180.
39. P 5242, Vol. 95 91.3.6-91.4.1.
40. P 5253, Vol. 95 187.4.4-187.5.6.
41. The following discussion of the nine examples from this stanza from the *Diamond Cutter* is drawn from Jam-yang-shay-ba, ca 67b.1-8 and *Annotations*, dbu 31a.6-33a.2.
42. Geshe Bel-den Drak-ba, oral commentary.
43. Geshe Jam-bel Shen-pen, oral commentary.
44. P 5253, Vol. 95 187.4.4-187.5.6.
45. Geshe Bel-den Drak-ba, oral commentary.
46. *Ibid.*

47. P 5254, Vol. 95 91.3.7-91.4.1.
48. *Essence*, p. 151.
49. *Ibid.*
50. *Concerning Tenets and the Buddhist Sciences* (*Grub mtha' dang nang rig skor*), no author given (Dharamsala, India: Council for Tibetan Education, 1970), p. 79.
51. Bel-den Drak-ba, pp. 33-4.
52. *Essence Comm.*, ga 19a.2-4.
53. Bel-den Drak-ba, p. 48.
54. *Annotations*, dbu 25b.2. See *Saṃyutta Nikāya* I.135.
55. P 5626, Vol. 96 34.4.5-6.
56. *Ibid.* The statement is from the Sanskrit *Udānavarga* (XXIII. 14).
57. P 5626 Vol. 96 34.4.5-6. The statement is from the Sanskrit *Udānavarga* (XXI.1). See also *Dhammapada* (35).
58. *Essence*, p. 156.
59. *Annotations*, dbu 26a.1-4.
60. *Ibid.*, dbu 25b.8-26a.2.
61. *Ibid.*, dbu 26a.4-26b.1.
62. *Ibid.*, dbu 24b.6.
63. Jam-yang-shay-ba, ca 61b.6.
64. *Ibid.*, ca 61b.8.
65. *Madhyamakāvatāra par Candrakīrti*, ed. Louis de la Vallée Poussin (Osnabrück: Biblio Verlag, 1970), pp. 271-280.
66. *Annotations*, dbu 25a.8.
67. *Insight*, pp. 173-5.
68. Jam-yang-shay-ba, ca 62a.3-4.
69. His Holiness the Dalai Lama, oral teaching.
70. *Essence Comm.*, ga 25b.5-26a.2.
71. Preceding paragraphs from *Essence Comm.* ga 26b.3-27b.6.
72. Tsong-ka-pa, *Tantra in Tibet: The Great Exposition of Secret Mantra*, pp. 179-86 and His Holiness the Dalai Lama, oral teaching.
73. Sopa and Hopkins, *Practice and Theory of Tibetan Buddhism*, p. 141.
74. Tsong-kha-pa, *Explanation of the Eight Great Difficult Points of (Nāgārjuna's) "Fundamental (Treatise on the Middle Way Called) Wisdom"* (*rTsa ba shes rab kyi dka' gnas chen po brgyad kyi bshad pa*) (Sarnath, India: Pleasure of Elegant Sayings, 1970), p. 33.
75. Cited in Tsong-ka-pa, *Compassion in Tibetan Buddhism*, trans.

and ed. Jeffrey Hopkins (Ithaca, New York: Snow Lion Publications, 1980), p. 79.

76. Sopa and Hopkins, *Practice and Theory of Tibetan Buddhism*, p. 130 and His Holiness the Dalai Lama, oral teaching.

77. Kensur Yeshe Thupten, oral commentary.

78. *Essence*, p. 157.

79. *Essence Comm.*, ga 20a.7-20b.7.

80. *Essence*, p. 157.

81. *Essence Comm.*, 20b.7-21.a.2.

82. *Essence*, p. 151.

83. Jang-gya, p. 483.

84. Nāgārjuna and Kaysang Gyatso, *The Precious Garland and the Song of the Four Mindfulnesses*, trans. and ed. Jeffrey Hopkins and Lati Rimpoche (New York: Harper and Row, 1975), p. 22.

85. *Ibid.*, p. 484.

86. *Insight*, p. 20.

87. His Holiness the Dalai Lama, oral teaching.

88. Kensur Yeshe Thupten, oral commentary.

89. Nāgārjuna and Kaysang Gyatso, *The Precious Garland and the Song of the Four Mindfulnesses*, p. 75.

90. Tsong-kha-pa, *The Eight Great Difficult Points*, p. 28.

91. *Ibid.*, pp. 28-9.

92. Geshe Bel-den Drak-ba, oral commentary.

93. *Madhyamakāvatāra par Candrakīrti*, p. 264.

94. Jam-yang-shay-ba, ca 68a.4.

95. *Annotations*, dbu 33a.2-7.

96. *Ibid.*, dbu 33b.1-2.

97. Jam-yang-shay-ba, ca 68a.5-6.

98. *Essence Comm.*, ga 17a.3-4.

99. *Essence*, p. 153.

100. *Essence Comm.*, ga 18b.1-2.

101. Tsong-ka-pa, *Compassion in Tibetan Buddhism*, p. 171.

102. Tsong-kha-pa, *Illumination of the Thought of* (*Candrakīrti's "Supplement to the*) *Middle Way*" (*dbU ma dgongs pa rab gsal*) (Sarnath, India: Pleasure of Elegant Sayings Printing Press, 1973), pp. 65-73. For English translation, see Tsong-ka-pa, *Compassion in Tibetan Buddhism*, pp. 172-81.

103. Jay-dzun-ba (*rJe-btsun-pa*), *Good Explanation of the General Meaning, Clarifying the Difficult Points of* (*Tsong-kha-pa's*) *"Illumination of the Thought, Explanation of the 'Supplement to the Treatise on*

the Middle Way,' " *A Necklace for the Fortunate* (*bsTan bcos dbu ma la 'jug pa'i rnam bshad dgongs pa rab gsal gyi dka' gnad gsal bar byed pa'i spyi don legs bshad skal bzang mgul rgyan* (Modern blockprint: n.p., n.d.), 70a.1-2.

104. Nāgārjuna and Kaysang Gyatso, *The Precious Garland and the Song of the Four Mindfulnesses*, pp. 75-6.

105. *Madhyamakāvatāra par Candrakīrti*, p. 23.

106. *Essence Comm.*, ga 17b.3-18a.4.

107. See Lindtner, *Nagarjuniana*, p. 138.

108. Tsong-ka-pa, *Compassion in Tibetan Buddhism*, p. 174.

109. Jay-dzun-ba, 70b.1-3.

110. *Ibid.*, 70b.7-71a.1

111. *Ibid.*, 71a.3.

112. His Holiness the Dalai Lama, oral teaching.

CHAPTER FOUR: ULTIMATE EXISTENCE

1. P 5272, Vol. 99, chapter IX.140.
2. P 5255, Vol. 96 4.2.5-6.
3. P 5256, Vol. 96 27.3.1-4.
4. *Four*, 458.
5. Jam-yang-shay-ba, ca 71b.3-4.
6. P 5256, Vol. 96 27.5.6-7.
7. *Four*, 460.
8. J. W. de Jong, "The Problem of the Absolute in Madhyamaka," in *Buddhist Studies by J. W. de Jong*, de. Gregory Schopen (Berkeley: Asian Humanities Press, 1979), p. 57.
9. P 5256, Vol. 96 27.5.7-28.1.1.
10. *Four*, 460-1.
11. *Ibid.*, 461 and Jam-yang-shay-ba, ca 71b.8.
12. Sha-mar-gen-dun-den-dzin-gya-tso, 81a.1-4.
13. *Ibid.*, 80a.1-3 and *Annotations*, dbu 68b.7-69a.1.
14. *Annotations*, dbu 69a.1-3.
15. *Ibid.*, dbu 68a.3-4.
16. Sha-mar-gen-dun-den-dzin-gya-tso, 80b.1-3.
17. Murti, *The Central Philosophy of Buddhism*, p. 271.
18. *Ibid.*, p. 238.
19. Tsong-ka-pa, *Tantra in Tibet: The Great Exposition of Secret Mantra*, p. 70.
20. Jang-gya, 354.11-16.
21. Ken-sur Yeshe Thupten, oral commentary.

22. Jang-gya, pp. 343.19-344.13.
23. Kensur Yeshe Thupten, oral commentary.
24. Jang-gya, p. 344.6-9 and Kensur Yeshe Thupten, oral commentary.
25. Sha-mar-gen-dun-den-dzin-gya-tso, 82a.4-5.
26. Jam-yang-shay-ba, ca 72a.7-8.
27. *Annotations*, dbu 69a.6.
28. Jang-gya, p. 344.14-17 and Kensur Yeshe Thupten, oral commentary.
29. Den-dar, 430.4-5.
30. Jang-gya, pp. 371.20-372.10.
31. Jñānagarbha, *Differentiation of the Two Truths* (*Satyadvayavibhaṅgavṛtti*) (*bDen pa gnis rnam par 'byed pa'i 'grel pa*) Toh. 3882 (Tokyo: *sDe gde* Tibetan Tripiṭaka preserved at the Faculty of Letters, Univesity of Tokyo, 1978), Vol. 12, p. 2.3.3.
32. *Ibid.*, 3.2.7.
33. *Ibid.*, 3.2.6.
34. The exegesis of this passage is based on Jang-gya, 372.10-373.10 and *Annotations*, dbu 37a.4-38a.1.
35. The discussion of the magician's illusion is based on Den-dar, 433.5-435.6.
36. Jang-gya, p. 374.11-15.
37. *Ibid.*, p. 375.1-5.
38. Den-dar, 433.6-444.1.
39. *Annotations*, dbu 68a.5-6.
40. *Essence Comm.*, kha 37a.1-3.
41. *Insight*, p. 119.
42. *Ibid.*
43. *Ibid.*
44. *Four*, 457.
45. *Ibid.*
46. Kensur Yeshe Thupten, oral commentary.
47. Tsong-kha-pa, *Eight Great Difficult Points*, pp. 6-7.
48. Tsong-kha-pa, *Illumination of the Thought*, p. 211 ff. and His Holiness the Dalai Lama, oral teaching.
49. *Annotations*, dbu 70a.5-70b.2.
50. Sopa and Hopkins, *Practice and Theory of Tibetan Buddhism*, p. 67.
51. *Ibid.*, p. 75.
52. *Annotations*, stod 25a.3-25b.8.

53. Kensur Yeshe Thupten, oral commentary.
54. Anne Klein, "Mind and Liberatrion: The Sautrāntika Tenet System in Tibet," pp. 121-5.
55. *Ibid.*, pp. 129-30.
56. *Ibid.*, pp. 123, 127-8.
57. *Encyclopedia of Philosophy*, s.v. "Realism," by R.J. Hirst.
58. *Ibid.*
59. Sopa and Hopkins, *Practice and Theory of Tibetan Buddhism*, pp. 72-3.
60. Anne Klein, "Mind and Liberation: The Sautrāntika Tenet System in Tibet," p. 131.
61. *Encyclopedia of Philosophy*, s.v. "Realism," by R.J. Hirst.
62. *Encyclopedia of Philosophy*, s.v. "Phenomenalism," by R.J. Hirst.
63. Anne Klein, "Mind and Liberation: The Sautrāntika Tenet System in Tibet," p. 105.
64. Jang-gya, p. 370.2-4.
65. *Encyclopedia of Philosophy*, s.v. "Realism," by R.J. Hirst. See also Durant Drake, et al., *Essays in Critical Realism* (New York: Peter Smith, 1941), pp. 3-32.
66. *Encyclopedia of Philosophy*, s.v. "Skepticism," by Richard H. Popkin.
67. Den-dar, 425.3-4.
68. Hopkins, "*Meditation on Emptiness*," pp. 108-109.
69. Kensur Yeshe Thupten, oral commentary.

CHAPTER FIVE: THE REASONING CONSCIOUSNESS

1. P 5255, Vol 96 4.2.5-6.
2. P 5256, Vol. 96 27.4.3-5.
3. P 5256, Vol. 96 27.5.1-3.
4. Pur-bu-jok, *The Topic of Signs and Reasonings*, 7a. 4-6.
5. *Ibid.*, 7a.7-7b.3.
6. *Ibid.*, 8b.5-7.
7. *Ibid.*, 9a.6-9b.1.
8. *Ibid.*, 9b.1-2.
9. *Ibid.*, 10b.7-11a.7.
10. *Ibid.*, 11b.1-5.
11. *Ibid.*, 12a.7-12b.1.
12. *Ibid.*, 9a.6-9b.1.

13. P 5256, Vol. 96 27.3.5.
14. P 5256, Vol. 96 27.3.5-27.4.2.
15. Pur-bu-jok, *The Topic of Signs and Reasonings*, 9b.5-7.
16. *Annotations*, dbu 28.1.6-8.
17. P 5256, Vol. 96 28.1.6-8.
18. Pur-bu-jok, *The Lesser Path of Reasoning*, 5a.2-3.
19. P 5256, Vol. 96 28.2.5.
20. *Essence Comm.*, kha 22a.4-23b.6.
21. *Ibid.*, kha 23a.7-23b.4.
22. P 5256, Vol. 96 28.1.8-28.2.4.
23. P 5284, Vol. 101 1.1.8.
24. Jang-gya, p. 381.7-10.
25. Den-dar, 451.5-6.
26. Jang-gya, pp. 381.19-382.2
27. Den-dar, 452.4-453.2
28. Pur-bu-jok, *The Topic of Signs and Reasonings*, 18a.4-18b.1.
29. *Ibid.*, 19b.2-21a.6.
30. *Ibid.*, 21a.6-21b.4.
31. Jang-gya, p. 379.4-11.
32. Pur-bu-jok, *The Great Path of Reasoning*, 31b.1-2.
33. Nga-wang-dra-shi (*Ngag-dbang-bkra-shis*), *Collected Topics by a Spiritual Son of Jam-yang-shay-ba* (*Sras bsdus grva*), (no place, no date), p. 463.
34. Pur-bu-jok, *The Great Path of Reasoning*, 32b.1-3.
35. Lati Rinbochay, *Mind in Tibetan Buddhism*, p. 80.
36. Den-dar, 453.6-454.1.
37. *Ibid.*, 454.4.
38. *Ibid.*, 454.1-6.
39. *Ibid.*, 454.6-455.4.
40. Anne Klein, "Mind and Liberation: The Sautrāntika Tenet System in Tibet," pp. 164-5.
41. Tsong-kha-pa, *Notes on* (*Śāntarakṣita's*) *"Ornament for the Middle Way"* (*dbU ma rgyan gyi zin bris*) (Sarnath, India: Gelukpa Students' Welfare Committee, 1976), p. 45.
42. *Ibid.*, p. 46.
43. Lati Rinbochay, *Mind in Tibetan Buddhism*, p. 75.
44. Den-dar, 460.5-6.
45. *Ibid.*, 459.3-6.
46. Anne Klein, "Mind and Liberation: The Sautrāntika Tenet System in Tibet," p. 85.

47. *Ibid.*, p. 86.
48. Tsong-kha-pa, *Notes on* (*Śāntarakṣita's*) *"Ornament for the Middle Way,"* pp. 46-7.
49. Kensur Yeshe Thupten, oral commentary.
50. *Annotations*, dbu 49b.7-50a.3.
51. *Essence Comm.*, kha 39b.5-40a.2.
52. *Ibid.*, kha 40a.2-4.
53. Jam-yang-shay-ba (*'Jam-dbyangs-bshad-pa*), *Analysis of the First Chapter* (*of Maitreya's "Ornament for Clear Realization"*) (*sKabs dang po'i mtha' dpyod*) (Sarnath, India: Mongolian Lama Guru Deva, 1965), p. 83.
54. *Ibid.*
55. *Ibid.*, pp. 84-5.
56. Den-dar, 462.1.
57. *Ibid.*, 462.1-463.1.
58. Sopa and Hopkins, *Practice and Theory of Tibetan Buddhism*, p. 136.
59. Den-dar, 463.5-6.
60. P 5284, Vol. 101 1.1.8-1.2.1.
61. Den-dar, 464.2-5.
62. *Ibid.*, 464.5-465.3.
63. Jang-gya, p. 388.3-14.
64. See Masamichi Ichigo, "A Synopsis of the *Madhyamakālaṃkāra of Śāntarakṣita*," *Journal of Indian and Buddhist Studies* 20 (March 1972): 38-42. See also Yuichi Kajiyama, "Later Mādhyamikas on Epistemology and Meditation," in *Mahāyāna Buddhist Meditation: Theory and Practice*, ed. Minoru Kiyota (Honolulu: University of Hawaii Press, 1978), pp. 114-43.
65. P 5284, Vol. 101 2.1.2-3.
66. Jam-yang-shay-ba, *Analysis of the First Chapter of* (*Maitreya's "Ornament for Clear Realization"*), p. 86.
67. P 5285, Vol 101 7.4.7.
68. According to Jam-yang-shay-ba, *Analysis of the First Chapter*, p. 84, the valid cognizer ascertains the entity (*ngo bo*) of the sign. According to Jang-gya, p. 392.14, it ascertains the instance (*mtshan gzhi*) of the sign.
69. Jang-gya, p. 392.12-16.
70. Jam-yang-chok-hla-ö-ser, *Collected Topics of Ra-dö*, 46b.6-47a.1.
71. P 5284, Vol. 101 2.1.3.

72. Jam-yang-shay-ba, *Analysis of the First Chapter*, p. 82.
73. *Ibid.*
74. Jang-gya, p. 393.1-6.
75. *Ibid.*, 394.3-8.
76. *Ibid.*, 394.8-395.15.
77. Pur-bu-jok, *The Topic of Signs and Reasonings*, 11b.2-4.
78. *Ibid.*, 11a.5-7.
79. Den-dar, 468.5-469.3.
80. *Ibid.*, 469.5-470.4.
81. Pur-bu-jok, *The Topic of Signs and Reasonings*, 15a.7-16a.3.
82. Tsong-kha-pa, *Notes on (Śāntarakṣita's) "Ornament for the Middle Way,"* p. 35.
83. Pur-bu-jok, *The Topic of Signs and Reasonings*, 15b.5-6.
84. P 5285, Vol. 101 8.3.1-2.
85. Jang-gya, 397.15.

CHAPTER SIX: THE TWO TRUTHS

1. P 5224, Vol. 95, XXIV 8-9.
2. *Two Truths*, 48a.7
3. P 5272, Vol. 99, Chapter IX 1-2ab.
4. Jang-gya, p. 352.15.
5. Den-ma Lo-chö Rin-bo-chay, oral commentary.
6. *Two Truths*, 48b.2-7.
7. Pan-chen Sö-nam-drak-ba (*Pan-chen bSod-nams-grags-pa*), *General Meaning of (Maitreya's) "Ornament for Clear Realization"* (*Phar phyin spyi don*) (Buxadour: Nang bstan shes rig 'dzin skyong slob gnyer khang, 1963), 66b.2-5.
8. *Two Truths*, 49a.4-6.
9. *Ibid.*, 49a.2-4.
10. *Ibid.*, 48b.7-49a.1.
11. *Ibid.*, 60b.3-6.
12. Jang-gya, p. 353.11-12.
13. Sopa and Hopkins, *Practice and Theory of Tibetan Buddhism*, p. 124.
14. Lati Rinbochay, *Mind in Tibetan Buddhism*, p. 60.
15. *Ibid.*
16. Jang-gya, p. 356.9-10.
17. Kensur Yeshe Thupten, oral commentary.
18. *Two Truths*, 58a.2-3.
19. *Annotations*, dbu 38a.4-38b.3.

20. *Ibid.*
21. Jang-gya, p. 348.15-17.
22. Hopkins, *Meditation on Emptiness*, pp. 204-205.
23. *Madhyamakāvatāra par Candrakīrti*, pp. 301-304.
24. Jang-gya, p. 353.14-15.
25. *Ibid.*, p. 353.16-18.
26. *Two Truths*, 63a.1-5 and Kensur Yeshe Thupten, oral commentary.
27. *Two Truths*, 63a.5-63b.7.
28. *Ibid.*, 64b.6-65a.1.
29. See Chapter 2, note 16.
30. *Two Truths*, 65a.1.
31. *Ibid.*, 65a.1-2.
32. Den-dar, 448.4.
33. *Two Truths*, 65a.2-66b.2.
34. Jang-gya, p. 356.16-19.
35. Sopa and Hopkins, *Practice and Theory of Tibetan Buddhism*, p. 82.
36. Gön-chok-jik-may-wang-bo (*dKon-mchogs-'jigs-med-dbang-po*), *Presentation of the Grounds and Paths, Beautiful Ornament of the Three Vehicles* (*Sa lam gyi rnam bzhag theg gsum mdzes rgyan*) in *Collected Works of dkon-mchog-jigs-med-dbang-po* 7 (New Delhi: Ngawang Gelek Demo, 1972), 434.3-4.
37. *Ibid.*, 433.6.
38. *Ibid.*, 435.5.
39. Jam-yang-shay-ba, *Analaysis of the First Chapter*, p. 268.
40. *Ibid.*, pp. 268-9.
41. Jam-yang-shay-ba, *Analysis of the Third Chapter of* (*Maitreya's "Ornament for Clear Realization"*) (*sKabs gsum pa'i mtha' dpyod*) (Sarnath, India: Mongolian Lama Guru Deva, 1965), p. 21.
42. *Ibid.*, p. 22.
43. Jang-gya, p. 355.8-12.
44. Jam-yang-shay-ba, *Analysis of the Third Chapter*, p. 41.
45. Jang-gya, p. 355.14-18.
46. Lo-sang-gön-chok (*bLo-bzang-dkon-mchog*), *Word Commentary on the Root Text of* (*Jam-yang-shay-ba's*) *"Tenets," A Crystal Mirror* (*Grub mtha' rtsa ba'i tshig ṭik shel dkar me long*) (Delhi: Chopel Lekden, 1978), 100a.5-101a.3.
47. Gön-chok-jik-may-wang-bo, *Presentation of the Grounds and Path*, 446.3-7.

48. *Ibid.*, 446.7-447.1.
49. Kensur Yeshe Thupten, oral commentary.
50. Jang-gya, 358.17-359.3.
51. *Ibid.*, 372.3-5.
52. *Ibid.*
53. *Two Truths*, 62a.5.
54. The three etymologies are provided by Candrakīrti in his *Clear Words*, commenting on *MMK* XXIV.8. See P 5260, Vol. 98 76.2.5.
55. T. R. V. Murti, "Saṃvṛti and Paramārtha in Mādhyamika and Advaita Vedānta," in *The Problem of the Two Truths in Buddhism and Vedānta*, ed. Mervyn Sprung (Dordrecht, Holland: D. Reidel Publishing, 1973), p. 17.
56. Jang-gya, p. 353.11.
57. *Ibid.*, 359.17-18.
58. *Annotations*, dbu 41a.1-3.
59. Jang-gya, p. 359.13-15.
60. *Two Truths*, 69b.2-4.
61. See Anne Klein, "Mind and Liberation: The Sautrāntika Tenet System in Tibet," pp. 169-75.
62. *Two Truths*, 69a.5-7.
63. *Annotations*, dbu 41a.7-41b.2.
64. *Two Truths*, 70a.2-3.
65. *Annotations*, dbu 41a.3-4.
66. Jang-gya, p. 361.9-14.
67. *Annotations*, dbu 95b.2-3.
68. *Ibid.*, dbu 95a.7-96b.3.
69. *Two Truths*, 50a.3-6.
70. *Ibid.*, 50b.1-2.
71. *Ibid.*, 50b.3-4.
72. *Ibid.*, 50b.5-6.
73. *Ibid.*, 51a.1-2.
74. *Ibid.*, 51a.3-4.
75. *Ibid.*, 51a.5-6.
76. *Ibid.*, 51a.7-51b.1.
77. *Ibid.*, 50b.6-7, 51b.1-2.
78. The entire discussion of same entity and different reverses is based on Kensur Yeshe Thupten, oral commentary.

CHAPTER SEVEN: AN OVERVIEW OF THE SVĀTANTRIKA SYSTEM

1. The commentary to the Svāntrika chapter is found in *Annotations*, dbu 55a.6-58a.3.
2. The commentary to the Svātantrika chapter is found in Lo-sang-gön-chok, 94b.1-108b.1.
3. Lo-sang-gön-chok, 94b.3-95a.1.
4. *Ibid.*, 95a.2-4.
5. *Annotations*, dbu 55b.1-4, Lo-sang-gön-chok, 95b.1-96b.2.
6. *Annotations*, dbu 55b.6-8.
7. *Ibid.*, 55b.8-56a.3.
8. *Ibid.*, 56a.3.
9. *Ibid.*, 56a.3-5.
10. Lo-sang-gön-chok, 98b.2-3.
11. *Ibid.*, 98b.5-6.
12. *Annotations*, dbu 56a.6-8, Lo-sang-gön-chok, 99a.2-99b.1.
13. Lo-sang-gön-chok, 99b.3-5.
14. *Ibid.*, 99b.5-100a.5, 101b.2-5.
15. *Annotations*, dbu 56b.6-7.
16. Lo-sang-gön-chok, 102a.3-102b.5, *Annotations*, dbu 56b.7-57a.3.
17. Lo-sang-gön-chok, 103a.2-103b.3, Geshe Bel-den Drak-ba, oral commentary.
18. Geshe Bel-den Drak-ba, oral commentary.
19. *Essence*, p. 3.
20. Geshe Bel-den Drak-ba, oral commentary.
21. *Ibid.*
22. *Ibid.*
23. *Ibid.*
24. *Ibid.*
25. *Ibid.*
26. *Annotations*, dbu 57b.3-8; see Hopkins, *Meditation on Emptiness*," pp. 127-173.
27. *Annotations*, dbu 57b.8.

Notes to the Translation

INTRODUCTION TO THE TRANSLATION

1. This biographical sketch of Jang-gya is drawn from E. Gene Smith, "The Biography of Lcang-skya Rol-pa'i-rdo-rje," in the *Collected Works of Thu'u-bkwan Blo-bzang-chos-kyi-nyi-ma*, Vol. 1 (New Delhi: Ngawang Gelek Demo, 1969), pp. 2-12 and Lokesh Chandra, *Materials for a History of Tibetan Literature*, Vol. 1 (New Delhi: International Academy of Indian Culture, 1963), pp. 38-41.

2. For current scholarship on which of these works are considered to have written by the Nāgārjuna who is the author of the *Madhayamakaśāstra*, see Ruegg, *The Literature of the Madhyamaka School of Philosophy in India*, pp. 4-50 and Lindtner, *Nagarjuniana*. Notable by its absence from Jang-gya's list of Nāgārjuna's major works is the *Great Treatise on the Perfection of Wisdom* (*Ta chih tu lun*, **Mahāprajñāpāramitopadeśaśāstra*). That this text is not mentioned by Jang-gya, who had some acquaintance with Chinese Buddhist literature as Lama of the Seal under Emperor Ch'ien-lung, adds support to Lamotte's view that Nāgārjuna did not compose the text.

3. *Insight*, pp. 16-17.

4. For a study of the chronology of the designations of the divisions of the Mādhyamika school in Tibet, see K. Mimaki, "The *Blo gsal grub mtha'* and the Mādhyamika Classification in Tibetan *grub mtha'* Literature" in Steinkellner and Tauscher, ed., *Contributions on Tibetan and Buddhist Religion and Philosophy*, Vol. 2 (Vienna: Arbeitskreis für Tibetische und Buddhistische Studien Universität Wien, 1983) pp. 161-167.

5. See Jam-yang-shay-ba, ca 70al ff and Ruegg, *The Literature of the Madhyamaka School of Philosophy in India*, pp. 59-60.

6. The preceding discussion is drawn from *Annotations*, dbu 59b7-61a8.

7. For a more detailed treatment of the difference between Svātantrika and Prāsaṅgika on this point, see Robert A. F. Thurman, *Tsong Khapa's Speech of Gold in the "Essence of True Eloquence"* (Princeton: Princeton University Press, 1984) and my article, "The Hermeneutics of Suspicion in India Mahāyāna Buddhism" in Donald S. Lopez, Jr., ed., *Buddhist Hermeneutics* (Honolulu: University of Hawaii Press, forthcoming).

8. This is quoted by Jam-yang-shay-ba at ca 63a3. The Sanskrit is:

anye pracakṣate dhīrāḥ svanītāvabhimāninaḥ
tattvāmṛtāvatāro hi yogācāraḥ sudestaḥ

9. Translated from Louis de la Vallée Poussin, ed. *Madhyamakāvatāra par Candrakīrti*, Bibliotheca Buddhica IX (Osnabruck: Biblio Verlag, 1970), pp. 198-99. For a gloss, see *Annotations* dbu 43b8-44a5.

10. He says in his *Great Exposition of Tenets* ca 76a3, "*lang gshegs las rgyud smin rjes su phyi rol bden med la 'jug par bshad pa ltar zla bas dkral ba mthong nas zhi 'tsho sogs rnal 'byor spyod pa'i dbu ma la yang dbye na*"

11. For a further discussion of Nāgārjuna's position with regard to mind-only, see note 4 to chapter 2 of Part I.

12. Tsong-kha-pa and his followers align Śāntarakṣita with the position of the True Aspectarians based primarily on his refutation of the False Aspectarian position in stanzas 52-60 of the *Ornament for the Middle Way*. However, this does not seem to provide sufficient evidence to conclude that Śāntarakṣita held the True Aspectarian position. See Ruegg, *The Literature of the Madhyamaka School of Philosophy in India*, p. 92 and Yuichi Kajiyama, "Later Mādhyamikas on Epistemology and Meditation" in Minoru Kiyota, ed., *Mahāyāna Buddhist Meditation: Theory and Practice* (Honolulu: University of Hawaii Press, 1978), pp. 114-143.

CHAPTER ONE: THE LIFE AND WORKS OF NĀGĀRJUNA

1. P 775, Vol. 29 74.3.6-7. For another translation, see D. T. Suzuki, trans., *The Lankavatara Sutra* (London: Routledge and

Kegan Paul, 1932), p. 239.

2. P 775, Vol. 29 74.3.7-8. For another translation, see Suzuki, pp. 239-40.

3. According to *Tāranātha's History of Buddhism*, the text was 12,000 stanzas in length.

4. The biography of Nāgārjuna up to this point in a summary of Bu-dön's History. See Obermiller, *Bu-ston's History of Buddhism*, pp. 122-5.

5. According to Jeffrey Hopkins, Geshe Gedün Lodrö suggested that this text had been given the name of its author, Akutobhayā, as is the case with Buddhapālita's commentary on Nāgārjuna's *Treatise on the Middle Way*.

6. According to Warder, Parahita was a late Mādhyamika (c. 1000) who composed a subcommentary to Candrakīrti's *Śūnyatāsaptitivṛtti*. See Warder's India Buddhism, p. 510.

CHAPTER TWO: MĀDHYAMIKA SCHOOLS IN INDIA

1. The translation is uncertain.

2. According to L. T. Doboom Tulku, *sTong thun* should be translated as *Thousand Doses* because the text delineates many antidotes to ignorance.

3. *Essence*, p. 3.

4. The title of this text is usually abbreviated to *Heart Ornament, an Explanation (rNam bshad snying po'i rgyan)*.

5. *Essence*, p. 180.

6. *Ibid*., pp. 179-80.

7. Jam-yang-shay-ba, ca 9a.5.

8. In a passage not quoted by Jang-gya, Jam-yang-shay-ba goes on to say:

> Buddhapālita founded Prāsaṅgika but it is not clear whether or not he asserted autonomous [syllogisms]. Candrakīrti taught that Buddhapālita did not assert autonomous [syllogisms], proved the unsuitability of the use of autonomous [syllogism] by Mādhyamikas, overturned autonomous syllogisms, and damaged existence by way of own-character.

Thus, it appears, contrary to Jang-gya's opinion, that Jam-yang-shay-ba considered Buddhapālita to be the founder of Prāsaṅgika. See Jam-yang-shay-ba, ca 9a.5-7.

CHAPTER THREE: HISTORY OF MĀDHYAMIKA IN TIBET

1. For an English translation of Ye-shay-ö's famous letter decrying the degeneration of Buddhist practice in Tibet, see Samten G. Karmay, "The Ordinance of lHa Bla-ma Ye-shes-'od" in Michael Aris and Aung San Suu Kyi, ed., *Tibetan Studies in Honour of Hugh Richardson* (Warminster, England: Aris and Phillips Ltd., 1980), pp. 150-162.

2. *Introduction to the Two Truths*, *(Satyadvayāvatāra)* 14-16ab.

3. According to Kensur Yeshe Thupten, it is the opinion of Pan-chen Sö-nam-drak-ba that Dharmakīrti of Suvarṇadvīpa was a True Aspectarian *(satyākāravādin)* Cittamātrin.

4. P 3080, Vol. 68, 275.3.1.

5. Sahajavajra in his long commentary on this line in his *Tattvadaśakaṭīkā* does not seem to specify Candrakīrti but rather mentions Nāgārjuna, Āryadeva, and Candrakīrti, at P 3099, Vol. 68, 299.1.6.

6. This song appears in English translation in Garma C. C. Chang, trans., *The Hundred Thousand Songs of Milarepaa*, 2 vol. (Seacaucus, New Jersey: University Books, 1962), pp. 312-332.

7. Jang-gya refers to the *Sems tsam rgyan*, but no such work is attributed to Ratnākaraśānti in the Peking tripitaka. He presumably means the *Madhyamakālaṃkāravṛtti*, where Ratnākaraśānti does discuss four yogas or levels of yoga *(yogabhūmi)*. See Ruegg, *The Literature of the Madhyamaka School of Philosophy in India*, pp. 122-3.

8. For a brief treatment of the term One Pure Power *(dKar po chig thub)* and Sa-gya Paṇḍita's objections to it, see Roger Jackson, "Sa skya paṇḍita's Account of the bSam yas Debate: History as Polemmic," *Journal of the International Association of Buddhist Studies*, Vol. 5, No. 1 (1982), pp. 89-99.

9. See Ga-wa-jam-ba's *(dGa'-ba-byams-pa)*, *Commentary on (Tsong-kha-pa's) "Praise of Dependent Arising," A Garland of White Light (rTen 'brel stod pa'i dikka 'od dkar 'phreng ba)* (no place, no date), 28a.4.

CHAPTER FOUR: THE MIDDLE WAY

1. This statement forms part of Candrakīrti's commentary to Nāgārjuna's *Treatise on the Middle Way* XV.11. For the Sanskrit see Poussin's *Mūlamadhyamakakārikas (Mādhyamika-sūtras) de Nāgārjuna avec la Prasannapadā Commentaire de Candrakīrti*, pp. 274-5.

2. *Ibid.*, p. 275.

3. The son of Ulūka, also known as Aulūkya, is better known as Kaṇāda, the author of the *Vaiśeṣika Sūtras*. See Dasgupta, *A History of Indian Philosophy*, Vol. 1, p. 305.

4. See Gyel-tsap's *Illumination of the Meaning of the Essence of (Nāgārjuna's) "Precious Garland" (dbU ma rin chen 'phreng ba'i snying po'i don gsal par byed pa)* (no place, no date, modern block-print in possession of Geshe Gedün Lodrö), 17b.3.

5. *Precious Garland (Ratnāvalī)*, stanzas 61 and 62. Commented on by Gyel-tsap, 17b.1-18a.2.

6. For Candrakīrti's commentary, see P 5265. Vol. 98 181.3.1-181.5.3.

7. See Tsong-kha-pa's *Ocean of Reasoning* (Sarnath edition), pp. 15-16

8. *Precious Garland*, stanzas 394-6. For commentary, see *Essence*, pp. 98-99 and Gyel-tsap, 64a.2-6.

CHAPTER FIVE: SCRIPTURAL INTERPRETATION

1. P 842, Vol. 34, 64.3.6-64.4.1.

2. Louis de la Vallée Poussin, ed., *Mūlamadhyamakakārikās (Mādhyamikasūtras) de Nāgārjuna avec la Prasannapadā Commentaire de Candrakīrti*, Bibliotheca Buddhica IV (Osnabrück: Biblio Verlag, 1970), p. 42.6-8.

3. *Ibid.*, p. 42.9-11.

4. The Sanskrit is:

nītārthasūtrāntaviśeṣa jānati
yathopadiṣṭā sugatena śūnyatā
yāsmin punaḥ pudgala sattva pūruṣā
neyārthatām jānati sarvadharmān

Cited by Candrakīrti in the *Prasannapadā*. See Louis de la Vallée Poussin, ed., p. 44.2-5.

5. For Prajñāvarman's commentary, see P 5601, Vol. 119, 221.4.6ff.

6. P 5287, Vol. 101, 46.1.5-46.1.6.

7. P 5287, Vol. 101, 46.3.5-46.3.8.

CHAPTER SIX: THE PRACTICE OF THE PATH

1. A being of small capacity is a person who is primarily seeking high status in cyclic existence for himself alone. A being of middling

capacity is a person who is primarily seeking liberation from cyclic existence for himself alone through overcoming attachment to the marvels of cyclic existence.

2. The six perfections are giving *(dāna)*, ethics *(śīla)*, patience *(kṣānti)*, effort *(vīrya)*, concentration *(dhyāna)*, and wisdom *(prajñā)*.

3. The four ways of gathering students are giving gifts, speaking pleasantly, teaching others to fulfill their aims, and acting according to this teaching oneself. See Sopa and Hopkins, *Practice and Theory of Tibetan Buddhism*, p. 33.

4. Maitreya's *Ornament for Clear Realization (Abhisamayā-laṃ kāra)* IV.32.

5. For an explanation of leisure and fortune, see Sopa and Hopkins, *Practice and Theory of Tibetan Buddhism*, p. 33.

6. For an explanation of the sixteen aspects of the four truths, see Anne Klein, "Mind and Liberation: The Sautrāntika Tenet System in Tibet," pp. 551-7.

7. For a list of the thirty-seven harmonies, see Jeffrey Hopkins, *Meditation on Emptiness*, pp. 205-6.

CHAPTER SEVEN: SVĀTANTRIKA

1. *mDo sde spyod pa* is actually Sūtrāntācārin in Sanskrit, but is translated as "Sautrāntika" in order to indicate more easily this branch of Svātantrika's affinity with Sautrāntika.

2. P 5285, Vol. 101 13.1.4. The translation is based on Gyeltsap's *Purification of Forgetfulness of (Śāntarakṣita's) "Ornament for the Middle Way" (dbU ma rgyan gyi brjed byang)* (Sarnath, India: Pleasure of Elegant Sayings Press, 1976), pp. 97-98.

3. P 5285, Vol. 101 13.2.1.

CHAPTER EIGHT: REFUTATION OF CITTĀMATRA

1. P 5255, Vol. 96 11.2.8-11.3.2. Explained at P 5256, Vol. 96 91.3.2-8.

2. P 5255, Vol. 96 12.1.6-7. Explained at P 5256, Vol. 96, 97.3.1-5.

3. P 5255, Vol. 96 12.1.7. Explained at P 5256, Vol. 96, 97.3.5-97.4.2.

4. P 5255, Vol. 96 12.1.7.

5. P 5256, Vol. 96 97.4.2-4.

6. P 5255, Vol. 96 12.1.7-8.

7. P 5256, Vol. 96 97.4.7-8.
8. P 5255, Vol. 96 12.3.1.
9. P 5256, Vol. 96 99.3.1-7.
10. P 5255, Vol. 96 12.4.7-8. Explained at P 5256, Vol. 96, 102.1.8-102.2.3.
11. P 5255, Vol. 96 12.4.8-12.5.1.
12. P 5256, Vol. 96 102.2.6-102.3.2.
13. P 5255, Vol. 96 12.5.1-2.
14. P 5256, Vol. 96 102.3.8.
15. P 5256, Vol. 96 102.1.7.
16. P 5255, Vol. 96 11.3.4-5.
17. P 5256, Vol. 96 92.1.6-7.
18. P 5256, Vol. 96 92.1.8-92.2.1.
19. P 5255, Vol. 96 11.3.6.
20. P 5255, Vol. 96 11.3.6-8.
21. P 5256, Vol. 96 92.3.6.
22. P 5255, Vol. 96 11.4.7-11.5.1.
23. P 5255, Vol. 96 11.5.1-2. Explained at P 5256, Vol. 96, 94.4.8-94.5.2.
24. P 5255, Vol. 96 11.5.2-3. Explained at P 5256, Vol. 96, 94.5.2-95.1.5.
25. P 5256, Vol. 96 94.5.8-95.1.5.
26. P 5255, Vol. 96 11.5.4. Explained at P 5256, Vol. 96, 95.1.7-95.2.5.
27. P 5255, Vol. 96 11.3.8. Explained at P 5256, Vol. 96, 92.4.5-92.5.2.
28. P 5255, Vol. 96 11.3.8-11.4.1. Explained at P 5256, Vol. 96, 92.5.2-93.1.7.
29. P 5256, Vol. 96 93.1.1-4.
30. P 5255, Vol. 96 11.4.5-6. Explained at P 5256, Vol. 96, 94.2.2-4.
31. P 5256, Vol. 96 94.2.3-4.

CHAPTER NINE: THE MEANING OF ULTIMATE EXISTENCE

1. P 5256, Vol. 96 27.3.1-4.
2. P 5256, Vol. 96 27.5.7-28.1.1.
3. *Essence*, p. 132.
4. Jam-yang-shay-ba identifies the opponent as Je-drung Shay-rap-wang-bo *(rJe-drung Shes-rab-dbang-po)*. See Jam-yang-shay-ba,

Great Exposition of the Middle Way (dbU ma chen mo) (Buxaduor: Gomang, 1967), 207a.1.

5. Jam-yang-shay-ba, *Great Exposition of the Middle Way*, 206b.6-208a.1.

CHAPTER TEN: REFUTATION OF ULTIMATE EXISTENCE

1. The five great reasons are the diamond slivers, the refutation of production of the four extremes, the refutation of production of the four alternatives, the reasoning of dependent arising, and the reasoning of the lack of being one or many. For a discussion see Jeffrey Hopkins, *Meditation on Emptiness*, pp. 131-196.

2. P 5255, Vol. 96 4.2.5-6.

3. P 5256, Vol. 96 27.3.6.

CHAPTER ELEVEN: THE TWO TRUTHS

1. See Hopkins, *Meditation on Emptiness*, pp. 96-99.

CHAPTER THIRTEEN: THE INTEGRATION OF MIND-ONLY

1. P 5284, Vol. 101 2.3.4.

2. The phrase *mtshungs par ldan pa dang bcas pa'i* is omitted from translation.

3. P 5285, Vol. 101 13.2.4-5.

4. P 5285, Vol. 101 13.2.5-6.

5. Cited by Śāntarakṣita at P 5285, Vol 101 13.2.6-8.

6. Cited by Śāntarakṣita at P 5285, Vol 101 13.2.8-13.3.1.

7. Cited by Śāntarakṣita at P 5285, Vol 101 13.3.1-3. The Tibetan translation of the stanzas from the sutra cited by Jang-gya and Śāntarakṣita differs from that found in the Peking edition of the sutra (P 775, Vol. 29 75.5.3-4). The Peking edition reads:

sems tsam la ni gnas ni
phyi rol don la mi brtag go
yang dag dmigs la gnas nas ni
sems tsam las ni 'da' bar bya

sems tsam las ni 'das nas ni
snang ba med las 'da' bar bya
rnal 'byor snang pa med gnas na
theg pa chen po mi mthong ngo

Jñānavajra comments on these stanzas in his *Commentary to the "Descent into Laṅkā Sutra," Ornament of the Heart of the Tathāgata (Laṅkāvatāranāmamahāyānasūtravṛttitathāgatahṛdayalaṃkāra)* at P 5520, Vol. 107 315.3.6-315.4.1:

> The meaning of "[Through relying on] mind-only," etc. is that on the occasions of the heat *(uṣmān)* and peak *(mūrdhan)* [levels of the path of preparation], one abides in the conception of mind-only — the non-inherent existence of objects — and one does not imagine external objects. Eventually, on the occasion of the path of seeing, one abides in the correct observation that even apprehending minds do not have entityness ultimately, and one passes beyond the adherence to apprehending minds. Having passed beyond mind-only, one temporarily passes beyong abiding in non-apprehension — the exalted wisdom of meditative equipoise *(samāhita)* on the path of seeing, and so forth — and on the occasion of subsequent attainment *(pṛṣṭhalabdha)* completes the grounds *(bhūmi)* through training and so forth on the grounds.

8. P 5284, Vol. 101 2.3.5.

9. The five phenomena are signs *(mtshan ma)*, names *(ming)*, conceptions *(rnam rtog)*, suchness *(de bzhin nyid)*, and perfect exalted wisdom *(yang dag pa'i ye shes)*. See P 775, Vol. 29 66.2.6 ff.

10. P 5285, Vol. 101 13.4.2-3. The sutra source is P 775, Vol. 29 66.3.5-6.

11. P 5285, Vol. 101.

12. According to Obermiller, the *Eight Chapters* is a summary of the *Perfection of Wisdom in Twenty-Five Thousand Stanzas*. See his "The Doctrine of Prajñā-pāramitā as Exposed in the Abhisamayālaṃkāra of Maitreya," *Acta Orientalia*, Vol. 11, (1932): p. 9.

CHAPTER FOURTEEN: THE MEANING OF TRUE EXISTENCE

1. According to Kensur Ngawang Lekden, *rdzas* refers to a special salve that the magician places on the pebble or stick which, in conjunction with the mantra which is cast on the eyes of the audience, causes the pebble or stick to appear as a horse or elephant.

CHAPTER FIFTEEN: THE LACK OF BEING ONE OR MANY

1. P 5284, Vol. 101 1.1.8.

2. Translated with commentary in Anne Klein, "Mind and Liberation: The Sautrāntika Tenent System in Tibet," pp. 433-569.
3. *Pakṣadharma* is translated as "the property of the subject" because *pakṣa* refers to the subject in this case, not to the entire position. The name of the whole is used for a part.
4. P 5284, Vol. 101 1.1.8-1.2.1.
5. *Ibid.*, 1.2.1-1.2.2.
6. *Ibid.*, 1.2.2-1.2.4.
7. *Ibid.*, 1.2.5.
8. *Ibid.*, 1.2.5-6.
9. *Ibid.*, 1.2.6.
10. This stanza is omitted by Jang-gya and has been added from P 5284, Vol. 101 1.2.7.
11. P 5284, Vol. 101 1.2.6-8.
12. *Ibid.*, 2.1.2-3.
13. *Ibid.*, 7.4.7.
14. *Ibid.*, 2.1.3.
15. *Ibid.*, 8.2.8.
16. *Ibid.*, 8.3.1-2.
17. *Ibid.*, 8.3.2-5.

CHAPTER SEVENTEEN: THE PATHS AND FRUITS

1. P 5285, Vol. 101 15.1.8-15.2.1.
2. *Ibid.*, 15.2.1-2.
3. *Ibid.*, 14.4.4-5.

NOTES TO THE BIBLIOGRAPHY

1. See "Notes to the Translation," Chapter One, note 5.
2. See "Notes: Chapter Six," note 29.

Index

Technical terms are listed in the index under their English translation. For the Sanskrit and Tibetan of these terms, see the Glossary. Tibetan personal names are listed in phonetic form. For the transliterated form, see the Bibliography.

Abhidharmasamuccaya, see *Compendium of Knowledge*
Abhisamayālamkāra, see *Ornament for Clear Realization*
Ability to perform function, 50, 67, 95, 182, 207-208, 210, 222; *see also* Real and unreal conventionalities
Acintyastava, see *Praise of the Inconceivable*
Actual ultimate, 141, 198-199
Affirming negative, 163, 200; definition and example of, 172
Afflictive Obstructions, 17, 97-98, 104-106, 116-118, 128, 220, 223, 227; Prāsangika assertion concerning, 117-122, 132-133; Svātantrika antidote for, 118-120, 123-124, 132-133; *see also* Obstructions to liberation
Aggregates, 83-96
Akṣayamatinirddeśasūtra, see *Teaching of Akṣayamati*
Akutobhayā, 249
Analysis, see Reason
Analysis of the First Chapter of (Maitreya's) "Ornament for Clear Realization", 181
Analytical cessations, 180, 183
Annotations, 9, 81, 209
Appearance, existence in manner of, 74, 76, 182, 194, 196, 208, 210; *see also* Direct cognizer, sense; Inherent existence in Svātantrika; Objective mode of subsistence; and Sense perception
Appearance, false, in Prāsaṅgika, 16, 67, 72, 117, 118, 126, 145, 158-159, 211, 212
Artificial conceptions of self of persons, *see* Self of persons, artificial
Āryadeva, 49, 51, 55, 56, 58, 230, 250; citation of texts by 46, 47, 51, 277-278
Asaṅga, 13; citation of texts by, 85
Atīśa, 22, 55, 57, 256, 260-261 citation of texts by, 29, 261
Automomous syllogism, 14-15, 66, 75; significance of its use, 73-76; unsuitable for Prāsaṅgikas, 78-80;